Python® for Data Science

FOR

DUMMIES®

A Wiley Brand

by Luca Massaron
and John Paul Mueller

Python® for Data Science For Dummies®

Published by: **John Wiley & Sons, Inc.,** 111 River Street, Hoboken, NJ 07030-5774, www.wiley.com

Copyright © 2015 by John Wiley & Sons, Inc., Hoboken, New Jersey

Media and software compilation copyright © 2015 by John Wiley & Sons, Inc. All rights reserved.

Published simultaneously in Canada

For general information on our other products and services, please contact our Customer Care Department within the U.S. at 877-762-2974, outside the U.S. at 317-572-3993, or fax 317-572-4002. For technical support, please visit www.wiley.com/techsupport.

Wiley publishes in a variety of print and electronic formats and by print-on-demand. Some material included with standard print versions of this book may not be included in e-books or in print-on-demand. If this book refers to media such as a CD or DVD that is not included in the version you purchased, you may download this material at http://booksupport.wiley.com. For more information about Wiley products, visit www.wiley.com.

Library of Congress Control Number: 2013956848

ISBN: 978-1-118-84418-2

ISBN 978-1-118-84398-7 (ebk); ISBN ePDF 978-1-118-84414-4 (ebk)

Manufactured in the United States of America

10 9 8 7 6 5 4 3 2 1

Table of Contents

Introduction

You rely on data science absolutely every day to perform an amazing
array of tasks or to obtain services from someone else. In fact, you've
probably used data science in ways that you never expected. For example,
when you used your favorite search engine this morning to look for something, it made suggestions on alternative search terms. Those terms are
supplied by data science. When you went to the doctor last week and
discovered the lump you found wasn't cancer, it's likely the doctor made his
prognosis with the help of data science. In fact, you might work with data
science every day and not even know it. *Python for Data Science For Dummies*
not only gets you started using data science to perform a wealth of practical
tasks but also helps you realize just how many places data science is used.
By knowing how to answer data science problems and where to employ data
science, you gain a significant advantage over everyone else, increasing your
chances at promotion or that new job you really want.

About This Book

The main purpose of *Python for Data Science For Dummies* is to take the scare
factor out of data science by showing you that data science is not only really
interesting but also quite doable using Python. You might assume that you
need to be a computer science genius to perform the complex tasks normally
associated with data science, but that's far from the truth. Python comes
with a host of useful libraries that do all the heavy lifting for you in the background. You don't even realize how much is going on, and you don't need to
care. All you really need to know is that you want to perform specific tasks
and that Python makes these tasks quite accessible.

Part of the emphasis of this book is on using the right tools. You start with
Anaconda, a product that includes IPython and IPython Notebook — two
tools that take the sting out of working with Python. You experiment with
IPython in a fully interactive environment. The code you place in IPython
Notebook is presentation quality, and you can mix a number of presentation
elements right there in your document. It's not really like using a development environment at all.

You also discover some interesting techniques in this book. For example,
you can create plots of all your data science experiments using MatPlotLib,
for which this book provides you with all the details. This book also spends

considerable time showing you just what is available and how you can use it to perform some really interesting calculations. Many people would like to know how to perform handwriting recognition — and if you're one of them, you can use this book to get a leg up on the process.

Of course, you might still be worried about the whole programming environment issue, and this book doesn't leave you in the dark there, either. At the beginning, you find complete installation instructions for Anaconda and a quick primer (with references) to the basic Python programming you need to perform. The emphasis is on getting you up and running as quickly as possible, and to make examples straightforward and simple so that the code doesn't become a stumbling block to learning.

To make absorbing the concepts even easier, this book uses the following conventions:

- ✔ Text that you're meant to type just as it appears in the book is in **bold**. The exception is when you're working through a step list: Because each step is bold, the text to type is not bold.

- ✔ When you see words in *italics* as part of a typing sequence, you need to replace that value with something that works for you. For example, if you see "Type *Your Name* and press Enter," you need to replace *Your Name* with your actual name.

- ✔ Web addresses and programming code appear in `monofont`. If you're reading a digital version of this book on a device connected to the Internet, note that you can click the web address to visit that website, like this: `http://www.dummies.com`.

- ✔ When you need to type command sequences, you see them separated by a special arrow, like this: File⇨New File. In this case, you go to the File menu first and then select the New File entry on that menu. The result is that you see a new file created.

Foolish Assumptions

You might find it difficult to believe that we've assumed anything about you — after all, we haven't even met you yet! Although most assumptions are indeed foolish, we made these assumptions to provide a starting point for the book.

It's important that you're familiar with the platform you want to use because the book doesn't provide any guidance in this regard. (Chapter 3 does provide Anaconda installation instructions.) To provide you with maximum information about Python concerning how it applies to data science, this book doesn't discuss any platform-specific issues. You really do need to know how to install applications, use applications, and generally work with your chosen platform before you begin working with this book.

This book isn't a math primer. Yes, you see lots of examples of complex math, but the emphasis is on helping you use Python and data science to perform analysis tasks rather than learn math theory. Chapters 1 and 2 provide you with a better understanding of precisely what you need to know in order to use this book successfully.

This book also assumes that you can access items on the Internet. Sprinkled throughout are numerous references to online material that will enhance your learning experience. However, these added sources are useful only if you actually find and use them.

Icons Used in This Book

As you read this book, you see icons in the margins that indicate material of interest (or not, as the case may be).This section briefly describes each icon in this book.

Tips are nice because they help you save time or perform some task without a lot of extra work. The tips in this book are time-saving techniques or pointers to resources that you should try in order to get the maximum benefit from Python or in performing data science–related tasks.

We don't want to sound like angry parents or some kind of maniacs, but you should avoid doing anything that's marked with a Warning icon. Otherwise, you might find that your application fails to work as expected, you get incorrect answers from seemingly bulletproof equations, or (in the worst-case scenario) you lose data.

Whenever you see this icon, think advanced tip or technique. You might find these tidbits of useful information just too boring for words, or they could contain the solution you need to get a program running. Skip these bits of information whenever you like.

If you don't get anything else out of a particular chapter or section, remember the material marked by this icon. This text usually contains an essential process or a bit of information that you must know to work with Python or to perform data science–related tasks successfully.

Beyond the Book

This book isn't the end of your Python or data science experience — it's really just the beginning. We provide online content to make this book more flexible and better able to meet your needs. That way, as we receive email from you, we can address questions and tell you how updates to either Python or its associated add-ons affect book content. In fact, you gain access to all these cool additions:

- ✔ **Cheat sheet:** You remember using crib notes in school to make a better mark on a test, don't you? You do? Well, a cheat sheet is sort of like that. It provides you with some special notes about tasks that you can do with Python, IPython, IPython Notebook, and data science that not every other person knows. You can find the cheat sheet for this book at http://www.dummies.com/cheatsheet/pythonfordatascience. It contains really neat information such as the most common programming mistakes that cause people woe when using Python.

- ✔ **Dummies.com online articles:** A lot of readers were skipping past the parts pages in *For Dummies* books, so the publisher decided to remedy that. You now have a really good reason to read the parts pages — online content. Every parts page has an article associated with it that provides additional interesting information that wouldn't fit in the book. You can find the articles for this book at http://www.dummies.com/extras/pythonfordatascience.

- ✔ **Updates:** Sometimes changes happen. For example, we might not have seen an upcoming change when we looked into our crystal ball during the writing of this book. In the past, this possibility simply meant that the book became outdated and less useful, but you can now find updates to the book at http://www.dummies.com/extras/pythonfordatascience.

  In addition to these updates, check out the blog posts with answers to reader questions and demonstrations of useful book-related techniques at http://blog.johnmuellerbooks.com/.

- ✔ **Companion files:** Hey! Who really wants to type all the code in the book and reconstruct all those plots manually? Most readers would prefer to spend their time actually working with Python, performing data science tasks, and seeing the interesting things they can do, rather than typing. Fortunately for you, the examples used in the book are available for download, so all you need to do is read the book to learn Python for data science usage techniques. You can find these files at http://www.dummies.com/extras/matlab.

Where to Go from Here

It's time to start your Python for data science adventure! If you're completely new to Python and its use for data science tasks, you should start with Chapter 1 and progress through the book at a pace that allows you to absorb as much of the material as possible.

If you're a novice who's in an absolute rush to get going with Python for data science as quickly as possible, you can skip to Chapter 3 with the understanding that you may find some topics a bit confusing later. Skipping to Chapter 4 is possible if you already have Anaconda (the programming product used in the book) installed, but be sure to at least skim Chapter 3 so that you know what assumptions we made when writing this book. Make sure to install Anaconda with Python version 2.7.9 installed to obtain the best results from the book's source code.

Readers who have some exposure to Python and have Anaconda installed can save reading time by moving directly to Chapter 5. You can always go back to earlier chapters as necessary when you have questions. However, it's important that you understand how each technique works before moving to the next one. Every technique, coding example, and procedure has important lessons for you, and you could miss vital content if you start skipping too much information.

Part I

Getting Started with Python for Data Science

In this part . . .

✔ Discovering why being a data scientist is so cool

✔ Defining how Python makes data science easier

✔ Specifying the process normally used for data science tasks

✔ Installing Python so that it works well for data science tasks

✔ Getting up to speed on Python essentials

Chapter 1

Discovering the Match between Data Science and Python

Data science may seem like one of those technologies that you'd never use, but you'd be wrong. Yes, data science involves the use of advanced math techniques, statistics, and big data. However, data science also involves helping you make smart decisions, creating suggestions for options based on previous choices, and making robots see objects. In fact, people use data science in so many different ways that you literally can't look anywhere or do anything without feeling the effects of data science on your life. In short, data science is the person behind the partition in the experience of the wonderment of technology. Without data science, much of what you accept as typical and expected today wouldn't even be possible. This is the reason that being a data scientist is the sexiest job of the twenty-first century.

To make data science doable by someone who's less than a math genius, you need tools. You could use any of a number of tools to perform data science tasks, but Python is uniquely suited to making it easier to work with data science. For one thing, Python provides an incredible number of math-related libraries that help you perform tasks with a less-than-perfect understanding of precisely what is going on. However, Python goes further by supporting multiple coding styles and doing other things to make your job easier. Therefore, yes, you could use other languages to write data science applications, but Python reduces your workload, so it's a natural choice for those who really don't want to work hard, but rather to work smart.

This chapter gets you started with Python. Even though this book isn't designed to provide you with a complete Python tutorial, exploring some basic Python issues will reduce the time needed for you to get up to speed. (If you do need a good starting tutorial, please get my *Beginning Programming with Python For Dummies*, published by John Wiley & Sons, Inc.) You'll find that the book provides pointers to tutorials and other aids as needed to fill in any gaps that you may have in your Python education.

Choosing a data science language

There are many different programming languages in the world — and most were designed to perform tasks in a certain way or even make it easier for a particular profession's work to be done with greater ease. Choosing the correct tool makes your life easier. It's akin to using a hammer to drive a screw rather than a screwdriver. Yes, the hammer works, but the screwdriver is much easier to use and definitely does a better job. Data scientists usually use only a few languages because they make working with data easier. With this in mind, here are the four top languages for data science work in order of preference (used by 91 percent of the data scientists out there):

✔ **Python (general purpose):** Many data scientists prefer to use Python because it provides a wealth of libraries, such as NumPy, SciPy, MatPlotLib, pandas, and Scikit-learn, to make data science tasks significantly easier. Python is also a precise language that makes it easy to use multi-processing on large datasets — reducing the time required to analyze them. The data science community has also stepped up with specialized IDEs, such as Anaconda, that implement the IPython Notebook concept, which makes working with data science calculations significantly easier (Chapter 3 demonstrates how to use IPython, so don't worry about

it in this chapter). Besides all of these things in Python's favor, it's also an excellent language for creating glue code with languages such as C/C++ and Fortran. The Python documentation actually shows how to create the required extensions. Most Python users rely on the language to see patterns, such as allowing a robot to see a group of pixels as an object. It also sees use for all sorts of scientific tasks.

✔ **R (special purpose statistical):** In many respects, Python and R share the same sorts of functionality but implement it in different ways. Depending on which source you view, Python and R have about the same number of proponents, and some people use Python and R interchangeably (or sometimes in tandem). Unlike Python, R provides its own environment, so you don't need a third-party product such as Anaconda. However, R doesn't appear to mix with other languages with the ease that Python provides.

✔ **SAS (business statistical analysis):** The Statistical Analysis System (SAS) language is popular because it makes data analysis, business intelligence, data management, and predictive analytics easy. The SAS Institute originally created SAS as a means to perform statistical analysis. In other words, this is a business-specific language — one used to make decisions rather than to perform handwriting analysis or to detect specific natural patterns.

✔ **SQL (database management):** The most important thing to remember about Structured Query Language (SQL) is that it focuses on data rather than tasks. Businesses can't operate without good data management — the data is the business. Large organizations use some sort of relational database, which is normally accessible with SQL, to store their data. Most Database Management System (DBMS) products rely on SQL as their main language, and DBMS usually has a large number of data analysis and other data science features built in. Because you're accessing the data natively, there is often a significant speed gain in performing data science tasks this way. Database Administrators (DBAs) generally use SQL to manage or manipulate the data rather than necessarily perform detailed analysis of it. However, the data scientist can also use SQL for various data science tasks and make the resulting scripts available to the DBAs for their needs.

Defining the Sexiest Job of the 21st Century

At one point, the world viewed anyone working with statistics as a sort of accountant or perhaps a mad scientist. Many people consider statistics and analysis of data boring. However, data science is one of those occupations in which the more you learn, the more you want to learn. Answering one question often spawns more questions that are even more interesting than the one you just answered. However, the thing that makes data science so sexy is that you see it everywhere and used in an almost infinite number of ways. The following sections provide you with more details on why data science is such an amazing field of study.

Considering the emergence of data science

Data science is a relatively new term. William S. Cleveland coined the term in 2001 as part of a paper entitled "Data Science: An Action Plan for Expanding the Technical Areas of the Field of Statistics." It wasn't until a year later that the International Council for Science actually recognized data science and created a committee for it. Columbia University got into the act in 2003 by beginning publication of the *Journal of Data Science*.

However, the mathematical basis behind data science is centuries old because data science is essentially a method of viewing and analyzing statistics and probability. The first essential use of statistics as a term comes in 1749, but statistics are certainly much older than that. People have used statistics to recognize patterns for thousands of years. For example, the historian Thucydides (in his History of the Peloponnesian War) describes how the Athenians calculated the height of the wall of Platea in fifth century BC by counting bricks in an unplastered section of the wall. Because the count needed to be accurate, the Athenians took the average of the count by several solders.

The process of quantifying and understanding statistics is relatively new, but the science itself is quite old. An early attempt to begin documenting the importance of statistics appears in the ninth century when Al-Kindi wrote *Manuscript on Deciphering Cryptographic Messages.* In this paper, Al-Kindi describes how to use a combination of statistics and frequency analysis to decipher encrypted messages. Even in the beginning, statistics saw use in practical application of science to tasks that seemed virtually impossible to complete. Data science continues this process, and to some people it might actually seem like magic.

Outlining the core competencies of a data scientist

Like most complex trades today, the data scientist requires knowledge of a broad range of skills in order to perform the required tasks. In fact, so many different skills are required that data scientists often work in teams. Someone who is good at gathering data might team up with an analyst and someone gifted in presenting information. It would be hard to find a single person with all the required skills. With this in mind, the following list describes areas in which a data scientist could excel (with more competencies being better):

- ✔ **Data capture:** It doesn't matter what sort of math skills you have if you can't obtain data to analyze in the first place. The act of capturing data begins by managing a data source using database management skills. However, raw data isn't particularly useful in many situations — you must also understand the data domain so that you can look at the data and begin formulating the sorts of questions to ask. Finally, you must have data-modeling skills so that you understand how the data is connected and whether the data is structured.

✔ **Analysis:** After you have data to work with and understand the complexities of that data, you can begin to perform an analysis on it. You perform some analysis using basic statistical tool skills, much like those that just about everyone learns in college. However, the use of specialized math tricks and algorithms can make patterns in the data more obvious or help you draw conclusions that you can't draw by reviewing the data alone.

✔ **Presentation:** Most people don't understand numbers well. They can't see the patterns that the data scientist sees. It's important to provide a graphical presentation of these patterns to help others visualize what the numbers mean and how to apply them in a meaningful way. More important, the presentation must tell a specific story so that the impact of the data isn't lost.

Linking data science and big data

Interestingly enough, the act of moving data around so that someone can perform analysis on it is a specialty called Extract, Transformation, and Loading (ETL). The ETL specialist uses programming languages such as Python to extract the data from a number of sources. Corporations tend not to keep data in one easily accessed location, so finding the data required to perform analysis takes time. After the ETL specialist finds the data, a programming language or other tool transforms it into a common format for analysis purposes. The loading process takes many forms, but this book relies on Python to perform the task. In a large, real-world operation, you might find yourself using tools such as Informatica, MS SSIS, or Teradata to perform the task.

Understanding the role of programming

A data scientist may need to know several programming languages in order to achieve specific goals. For example, you may need SQL knowledge to extract data from relational databases. Python can help you perform data loading, transformation, and analysis tasks. However, you might choose a product such as MATLAB (which has its own programming language) or PowerPoint (which relies on VBA) to present the information to others. (If you're interested to see how MATLAB compares to the use of Python, you can get my book, *MATLAB For Dummies*, published by John Wiley & Sons, Inc.) The immense datasets that data scientists rely on often require multiple levels of redundant processing to transform into useful processed data. Manually performing these tasks is time consuming and error prone, so programming presents the best method for achieving the goal of a coherent, usable data source.

Given the number of products that most data scientists use, it may not be possible to use just one programming language. Yes, Python can load data, transform it, analyze it, and even present it to the end user, but it works only when the language provides the required functionality. You may have to choose other languages to fill out your toolkit. The languages you choose depend on a number of criteria. Here are the things you should consider:

- ✔ How you intend to use data science in your code (you have a number of tasks to consider, such as data analysis, classification, and regression)
- ✔ Your familiarity with the language
- ✔ The need to interact with other languages
- ✔ The availability of tools to enhance the development environment
- ✔ The availability of APIs and libraries to make performing tasks easier

Creating the Data Science Pipeline

Data science is partly art and partly engineering. Recognizing patterns in data, considering what questions to ask, and determining which algorithms work best are all part of the art side of data science. However, to make the art part of data science realizable, the engineering part relies on a specific process to achieve specific goals. This process is the data science pipeline, which requires the data scientist to follow particular steps in the preparation, analysis, and presentation of the data. The following sections help you understand the data science pipeline better so that you can understand how the book employs it during the presentation of examples.

Preparing the data

The data that you access from various sources doesn't come in an easily packaged form, ready for analysis — quite the contrary. The raw data not only may vary substantially in format, but you may also need to transform it to make all the data sources cohesive and amenable to analysis. Transformation may require changing data types, the order in which data appears, and even the creation of data entries based on the information provided by existing entries.

Performing exploratory data analysis

The math behind data analysis relies on engineering principles in that the results are provable and consistent. However, data science provides access to a wealth of statistical methods and algorithms that help you discover patterns in the data. A single approach doesn't ordinarily do the trick. You typically use an iterative process to rework the data from a number of perspectives. The use of trial and error is part of the data science art.

Learning from data

As you iterate through various statistical analysis methods and apply algorithms to detect patterns, you begin learning from the data. The data might not tell the story that you originally thought it would, or it might have many stories to tell. Discovery is part of being a data scientist. In fact, it's the fun part of data science because you can't ever know in advance precisely what the data will reveal to you.

Of course, the imprecise nature of data and the finding of seemingly random patterns in it means keeping an open mind. If you have preconceived ideas of what the data contains, you won't find the information it actually does contain. You miss the discovery phase of the process, which translates into lost opportunities for both you and the people who depend on you.

Visualizing

Visualization means seeing the patterns in the data and then being able to react to those patterns. It also means being able to see when data is not part of the pattern. Think of yourself as a data sculptor — removing the data that lies outside the patterns (the outliers) so that others can see the masterpiece of information beneath. Yes, you can see the masterpiece, but until others can see it, too, it remains in your vision alone.

Obtaining insights and data products

The data scientist may seem to simply be looking for unique methods of viewing data. However, the process doesn't end until you have a clear understanding of what the data means. The insights you obtain from manipulating and analyzing the data help you to perform real-world tasks. For example, you can use the results of an analysis to make a business decision.

In some cases, the result of an analysis creates an automated response. For example, when a robot views a series of pixels obtained from a camera, the pixels that form an object have special meaning and the robot's programming may dictate some sort of interaction with that object. However, until the data scientist builds an application that can load, analyze, and visualize the pixels from the camera, the robot doesn't see anything at all.

Understanding Python's Role in Data Science

Given the right data sources, analysis requirements, and presentation needs, you can use Python for every part of the data science pipeline. In fact, that's precisely what you do in this book. Every example uses Python to help you understand another part of the data science equation. Of all the languages you could choose for performing data science tasks, Python is the most flexible and capable because it supports so many third-party libraries devoted to the task. The following sections help you better understand why Python is such a good choice for many (if not most) data science needs.

Considering the shifting profile of data scientists

Some people view the data scientist as an unapproachable nerd who performs miracles on data with math. The data scientist is the person behind the curtain in an Oz-like experience. However, this perspective is changing. In many respects, the world now views the data scientist as either an adjunct to a developer or as a new type of developer. The ascendance of applications of all sorts that can learn is the essence of this change. For an application to learn, it has to be able to manipulate large databases and discover new patterns in them. In addition, the application must be able to create new data based on the old data — making an informed prediction of sorts. The new kinds of applications affect people in ways that would have seemed like science fiction just a few years ago. Of course, the most noticeable of these applications define the behaviors of robots that will interact far more closely with people tomorrow than they do today.

From a business perspective, the necessity of fusing data science and application development is obvious: Businesses must perform various sorts of analysis on the huge databases it has collected — to make sense of the information and use it to predict the future. In truth, however, the far greater impact of the melding of these two branches of science — data science and application development — will be felt in terms of creating altogether new kinds of applications, some of which aren't even possibly to imagine with clarity today. For example, new applications could help students learn with greater precision by analyzing their learning trends and creating new instructional methods that work for that particular student. This combination of sciences might also solve a host of medical problems that seem impossible to solve today — not only in keeping disease at bay, but also by solving problems, such as how to create truly usable prosthetic devices that look and act like the real thing.

Working with a multipurpose, simple, and efficient language

Many different ways are available for accomplishing data science tasks. This book covers only one of the myriad methods at your disposal. However, Python represents one of the few single-stop solutions that you can use to solve complex data science problems. Instead of having to use a number of tools to perform a task, you can simply use a single language, Python, to get the job done. The Python difference is the large number scientific and math libraries created for it by third parties. Plugging in these libraries greatly extends Python and allows it to easily perform tasks that other languages could perform, but with great difficulty.

Python's libraries are its main selling point; however, Python offers more than reusable code. The most important thing to consider with Python is that it supports four different coding styles:

- **Functional:** Treats every statement as a mathematical equation and avoids any form of state or mutable data. The main advantage of this approach is having no side effects to consider. In addition, this coding style lends itself better than the others to parallel processing because there is no state to consider. Many developers prefer this coding style for recursion and for lambda calculus.

- **Imperative:** Performs computations as a direct change to program state. This style is especially useful when manipulating data structures and produces elegant, but simple, code.

- **Object-oriented:** Relies on data fields that are treated as objects and manipulated only through prescribed methods. Python doesn't fully support this coding form because it can't implement features such as data hiding. However, this is a useful coding style for complex applications because it supports encapsulation and polymorphism. This coding style also favors code reuse.

- **Procedural:** Treats tasks as step-by-step iterations where common tasks are placed in functions that are called as needed. This coding style favors iteration, sequencing, selection, and modularization.

Learning to Use Python Fast

It's time to try using Python to see the data science pipeline in action. The following sections provide a brief overview of the process you explore in detail in the rest of the book. You won't actually perform the tasks in the following sections. In fact, you don't install Python until Chapter 3, so for now, just follow along in the text. Don't worry about understanding every aspect of the process at this point. The purpose of these sections is to help you gain an understanding of the flow of using Python to perform data science tasks. Many of the details may seem difficult to understand at this point, but the rest of the book will help you understand them.

The examples in this book rely on a web-based application named IPython Notebook. The screenshots you see in this and other chapters reflect how IPython Notebook looks in Firefox on a Windows 7 system. The view you see will contain the same data, but the actual interface may differ a little depending on platform (such as using a notebook instead of a desktop system), operating system, and browser. Don't worry if you see some slight differences between your display and the screenshots in the book.

You don't have to type the source code for this chapter in by hand. In fact, it's a lot easier if you use the downloadable source (see the Introduction for details on downloading the source code). The source code for this chapter appears in the P4DS4D; 01; Quick Overview.ipynb source code file.

Loading data

Before you can do anything, you need to load some data. The book shows you all sorts of methods for performing this task. In this case, Figure 1-1 shows how to load a dataset called Boston that contains housing prices and other facts about houses in the Boston area. The code places the entire dataset in the boston variable and then places parts of that data in variables named X and y. Think of variables as you would storage boxes. The variables are important because they make it possible to work with the data.

Training a model

Now that you have some data to work with, you can do something with it. All sorts of algorithms are built into Python. Figure 1-2 shows a linear regression model. Again, don't worry precisely how this works; later chapters discuss linear regression in detail. The important thing to note in Figure 1-2 is that Python lets you perform the linear regression using just two statements and to place the result in a variable named hypothesis.

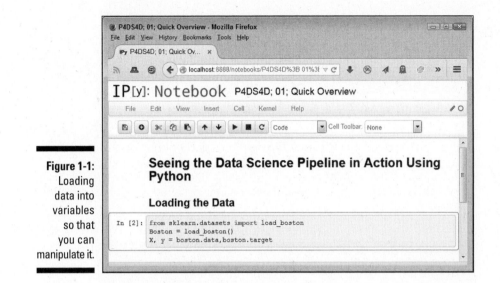

Figure 1-1:
Loading data into variables so that you can manipulate it.

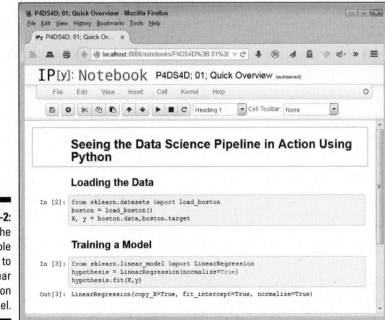

Figure 1-2:
Using the variable content to train a linear regression model.

Viewing a result

Performing any sort of analysis doesn't pay unless you obtain some benefit from it in the form of a result. This book shows all sorts of ways to view output, but Figure 1-3 starts with something simple. In this case, you see the coefficient output from the linear regression analysis.

One of the reasons that this book uses IPython Notebook is that the product helps you to create nicely formatted output as part of creating the application. Look again at Figure 1-3 and you see a report that you could simply print and offer to a colleague. The output isn't suitable for many people, but those experienced with Python and data science will find it quite usable and informative.

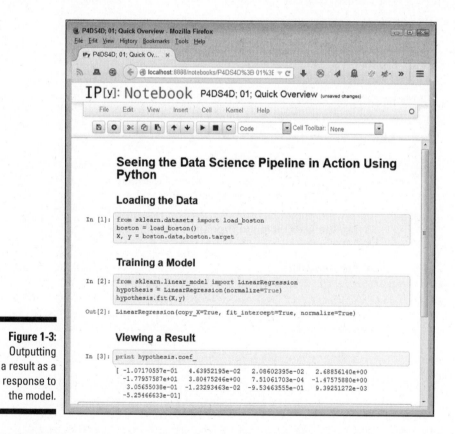

Figure 1-3:
Outputting
a result as a
response to
the model.

Within the screenshot:

Seeing the Data Science Pipeline in Action Using Python

Loading the Data

```
In [1]: from sklearn.datasets import load_boston
        boston = load_boston()
        X, y = boston.data,boston.target
```

Training a Model

```
In [2]: from sklearn.linear_model import LinearRegression
        hypothesis = LinearRegression(normalize=True)
        hypothesis.fit(X,y)

Out[2]: LinearRegression(copy_X=True, fit_intercept=True, normalize=True)
```

Viewing a Result

```
In [3]: print hypothesis.coef_

        [ -1.07170557e-01   4.63952195e-02   2.08602395e-02   2.68856140e+00
          -1.77957587e+01   3.80475246e+00   7.51061703e-04  -1.47575880e+00
           3.05655038e-01  -1.23293463e-02  -9.53463555e-01   9.39251272e-03
          -5.25466633e-01]
```

Chapter 2

Introducing Python's Capabilities and Wonders

In This Chapter

▶ Delving into why Python came about

▶ Getting a quick start with Python

▶ Using Python for rapid prototyping and experimentation

▶ Defining how Python provides speed of execution

▶ Defining the power of Python for the data scientist

▶ Exploring the Python and data science relationship

All computers run on just one language — machine code. However, unless you want to learn how to talk like a computer in 0s and 1s, machine code isn't particularly useful. You'd never want to try to define data science problems using machine code. It would take an entire lifetime (if not longer) just to define one problem. Higher-level languages make it possible to write a lot of code that humans can understand quite quickly. The tools used with these languages make it possible to translate the human-readable code into machine code that the machine understands. Therefore, the choice of languages depends on the human need, not the machine need. With this in mind, this chapter introduces you to the capabilities that Python provides that make it a practical choice for the data scientist. After all, you want to know why this book uses Python and not another language, such as Java or C++. These other languages are perfectly good choices for some tasks, but they're not as suited to meet data science needs.

The chapter begins with a short history of Python so that you know a little about why developers created Python in the first place. You also see some simple Python examples to get a taste for the language. As part of exploring Python in this chapter, you discover all sorts of interesting features that Python provides. Python gives you access to a host of libraries that are especially suited to meet the needs of the data scientist. In fact, you use a number of these libraries throughout the book as you work through the coding examples. Knowing about these libraries in advance will help you understand the programming examples and why the book shows how to perform tasks in a certain way.

Even though this chapter does show examples of working with Python, you don't really begin using Python in earnest until Chapter 4. This chapter provides you with an overview so that you can better understand what Python can do. Chapter 3 shows how to install the particular version of Python used for this book, and Chapter 4 gives you basic hands-on exercises on how to work with Python. In short, if you don't quite understand an example in this chapter, don't worry: You get plenty of additional information in later chapters.

Why Python?

Python is the vision of a single person, Guido van Rossum. You might be surprised to learn that Python has been around a long time — Guido started the language in December 1989 as a replacement for the ABC language. Not much information is available as to the precise goals for Python, but it does retain ABC's ability to create applications using less code. However, it far exceeds the ability of ABC to create applications of all types, and in contrast to ABC, boasts four programming styles. In short, Guido took ABC as a starting point, found it limited, and created a new language without those limitations. It's an example of creating a new language that really is better than its predecessor.

Using the right language for the job

Computer languages provide a means for humans to write down instructions in a systematic and understandable way. Computers don't actually understand computer languages — a computer relies on machine-code for instructions. The reason languages are so important is that humans don't characteristically understand machine language, so the conversion from something humans understand to something machines understand is essential. Python provides a specific set of features that make writing data science applications easier. As with any other language, it provides the right toolset for some situations and not for others. Use Python (or any other language) when it provides the functionality you need to accomplish a task. If you start finding the language getting in the way, it's time to choose a different language because in the end, the computer doesn't care which language you use. Computer languages are for people, not the other way around.

Python has gone through a number of iterations and currently has two development paths. The 2.*x* path is backward compatible with previous versions of Python, while the 3.*x* path isn't. The compatibility issue is one that figures into how data science uses Python because at least some of the libraries won't work with 3.*x*. In addition, some versions use different licensing because Guido was working at various companies during Python's development. You can see a listing of the versions and their respective licenses at `https://docs.python.org/3/license.html`. The Python Software Foundation (PSF) owns all current versions of Python, so unless you use an older version, you really don't need to worry about the licensing issue.

Grasping Python's core philosophy

Guido actually started Python as a skunkworks project. The core concept was to create Python as quickly as possible, yet create a language that is flexible, runs on any platform, and provides significant potential for extension. Python provides all these features and many more. Of course, there are always bumps in the road, such as figuring out just how much of the underlying system to expose. You can read more about the Python design philosophy at `http://python-history.blogspot.com/2009/01/pythons-design-philosophy.html`. The history of Python at `http://python-history.blogspot.com/2009/01/introduction-and-overview.html` also provides some useful information.

Discovering present and future development goals

The original development (or design) goals for Python don't quite match what has happened to the language since that time. Guido originally intended Python as a second language for developers who needed to create one-off code but who couldn't quite achieve their goals using a scripting language. The original target audience for Python was the C developer. You can read about these original goals in the interview at `http://www.artima.com/intv/pyscale.html`.

You can find a number of applications written in Python today, so the idea of using it solely for scripting didn't come to fruition. In fact, you can find listings of Python applications at `https://www.python.org/about/apps/` and `https://www.python.org/about/success/`.

Naturally, with all these success stories to go on, people are enthusiastic about adding to Python. You can find lists of Python Enhancement Proposals

(PEPs) at `http://legacy.python.org/dev/peps/`. These PEPs may or may not see the light of day, but they prove that Python is a living, growing language that will continue to provide features that developers truly need to create great applications of all types, not just those for data science.

Working with Python

This book doesn't provide you with a full Python tutorial. (However, you can get a great start with my book, *Beginning Programming with Python For Dummies,* published by John Wiley & Sons, Inc.) You do get a quick review of the language in Chapter 4. However, for now, it's helpful to get a brief overview of what Python looks like and how you interact with it, as in the following sections.

Getting a taste of the language

Python is designed to provide clear language statements but to do so in an incredibly small space. A single line of Python code may perform tasks that another language usually takes several lines to perform. For example, if you want to display something on-screen, you simply tell Python to print it, like this:

```
print "Hello There!"
```

This is an example of a 2.*x* print statement. The "Why Phython?" section of this chapter mentions that there are differences between the 2.*x* path and the 3.*x* path. If you use this line of code in 3.*x*, you get an error message:

```
File "<stdin>", line 1
   print "Hello There!"
                     ^
SyntaxError: invalid syntax
```

It turns out that the 3.*x* version of the same statement looks like this:

```
print("Hello There!")
```

The point is that you can simply tell Python to output text, an object, or anything else using a simple statement. You don't really need too much in the way of advanced programming skills. When you want to end your session, you simply type `quit()` and press Enter.

Understanding the need for indentation

Python relies on indentation to create various language features, such as conditional statements. One of the most common errors that developers encounter is not providing the proper indentation for code. You see this principle in action later in the book, but for now, always be sure to pay attention to indentation as you work through the book examples. For example, here is an `if` statement (a conditional that says that if something meets the condition, perform the code that follows) with proper indentation.

```
if 1 < 2:
    print("1 is less than 2")
```

The `print` statement must appear indented below the conditional statement. Otherwise, the condition won't work as expected, and you might see an error message, too.

Working at the command line or in the IDE

Anaconda is a product that makes using Python even easier. It comes with a number of utilities that help you work with Python in a variety of ways. The vast majority of this book relies on IPython Notebook, which is part of the Anaconda installation you create in Chapter 3. You saw this editor used in

Understanding the Anaconda package

The book approaches Anaconda as a product. In fact, you do install and interact with Anaconda as you would any other single product. However, Anaconda is actually a compilation of several open source applications. You can use these applications individually or in cooperation with each other to achieve specific coding goals. In most of the book, you use a single application, IPython Notebook, to accomplish tasks. However, you want to know about the other applications bundled in Anaconda to get the best use out of the product as a whole.

A large number of data scientists rely on the Anaconda product bundling, which is why this book uses it. However, you might find that some of the open source products come in a newer form when downloaded separately. For example, IPython actually comes in a newer form called Jupyter (`http://jupyter.org/`). Because of the differences in Jupyter and the fact that it hasn't been accepted by a large number of data scientists (because of file incompatibilities with IPython), you need to make the update to Jupyter carefully. Jupyter does work much the same as IPython, though, so you should be able to use it with the examples in this book with some modification if you choose.

Chapter 1 and you see it again later in the book. In fact, this book doesn't use any of the other Anaconda utilities much at all. However, they do exist, and sometimes they're helpful in playing with Python (as you do in Chapter 4). The following sections provide a brief overview of the other Anaconda utilities for creating Python code. You may want to experiment with them as you work through various coding techniques in the book.

Creating new sessions with Anaconda Command Prompt

Only one of the Anaconda utilities provides direct access to the command line, Anaconda Command Prompt. When you start this utility, you see a command prompt at which you can type commands. The main advantage of this utility is that you can start an Anaconda utility with any of the switches it provides to modify that utility's standard environment. Of course, you start all the utilities using the Python interpreter that you access using the `python.exe` command. (If you have both Python 3.4 and Python 2.7 installed on your system and open a regular command prompt or terminal window, you may see the Python 3.4 version start instead of the Python 2.7 version, so it's always best to open an Anaconda Command Prompt to ensure that you get the right version of Python.) So you could simply type **python** and press Enter to start a copy of the Python interpreter should you wish to do so. Figure 2-1 shows how the plain Python interpreter looks.

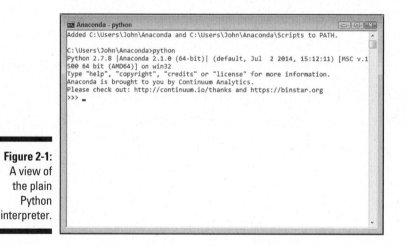

Figure 2-1:
A view of
the plain
Python
interpreter.

You quit the interpreter by typing **quit()** and pressing Enter. Once back at the command line, you can discover the list of `python.exe` command-line switches by typing **python -?** and pressing Enter. Figure 2-2 shows just some of the ways in which you can change the Python interpreter environment.

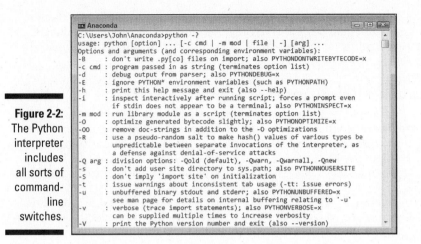

Figure 2-2:
The Python interpreter includes all sorts of command-line switches.

If you want, you can create a modified form of any of the utilities provided by Anaconda by starting the interpreter with the correct script. The scripts appear in the `Scripts` subdirectory. For example, type **python scripts/ipython-script.py** and press Enter to start the IPython environment without using the graphical command for your platform.

Entering the IPython environment

The Interactive Python (IPython) environment provides enhancements to the standard Python interpreter. The main purpose of the environment shown in Figure 2-3 is to help you use Python with less work. To see these enhancements, type **%quickref** and press Enter.

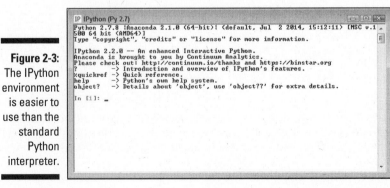

Figure 2-3:
The IPython environment is easier to use than the standard Python interpreter.

One of the more interesting additions to IPython is a fully functional clear screen (`cls`) command. You can't clear the screen easily when working in the Python interpreter, which means that things tend to get a bit messy after a while. It's also possible to perform tasks such as searching for variables using wildcard matches. Later in the book, you see how to use the magic functions to perform tasks such as capturing the amount of time it takes to perform a task for the purpose of optimization.

Entering IPython QTConsole environment

Trying to remember Python commands and functions is hard — and trying to remember the enhanced IPython additions is even harder. In fact, some people would say that the task is impossible (and perhaps they're right). This is where the IPython QTConsole comes into play. It adds a GUI on top of IPython that makes using the enhancements that IPython provides a lot easier, as shown in Figure 2-4. Of course, you give up a little screen real estate to get this feature, and some hardcore programmers don't like the idea of using a GUI, so you have to choose what sort of environment to work with when programming.

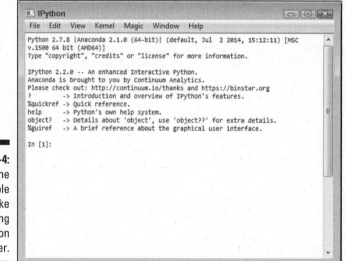

Figure 2-4:
Use the QTConsole to make working with IPython easier.

The enhanced commands appear in menus across the top of the window. All you need to do is choose the command you want to use. For example, to see the current application directory, choose Magic ⇨ OS Magics ⇨ %cd.

Editing scripts using Spyder

Spyder is a fully functional Integrated Development Environment (IDE). You use it to load scripts, edit them, run them, and perform debugging tasks. Figure 2-5 shows the default windowed environment.

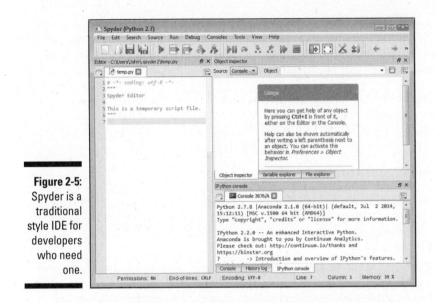

Figure 2-5:
Spyder is a
traditional
style IDE for
developers
who need
one.

The Spyder IDE is much like any other IDE that you might have used in the past. The left side contains an editor in which you type code. Any code you create is placed in a script file, and you must save the script before running it. The upper-right window contains various tabs for inspecting objects, exploring variables, and interacting with files. The lower-right window contains the Python console, a history log, and the IPython console. Across the top, you see menu options for performing all the tasks that you normally associate with working with an IDE.

Performing Rapid Prototyping and Experimentation

Python is all about creating applications quickly and then experimenting with them to see how things work. The act of creating an application design in code without necessarily filling in all the details is *prototyping*. Python uses less code than other languages to perform tasks, so prototyping goes faster. The fact that many of the actions you need to perform are already defined as part of libraries that you load into memory makes things go faster still.

Data science doesn't rely on static solutions. You may have to try multiple solutions to find the particular solution that works best. This is where experimentation comes into play. After you create a prototype, you use it to experiment with various algorithms to determine which algorithm works best in a particular situation. The algorithm you use varies depending on the answers you see and the data you use, so there are too many variables to consider for any sort of canned solution.

The prototyping and experimentation process occurs in several phases. As you go through the book, you discover that these phases have distinct uses and appear in a particular order. The following list shows the phases in the order in which you normally perform them.

1. **Building a data pipeline.** To work with the data, you must create a pipeline to it. It's possible to load some data into memory. However, after the dataset gets to a certain size, you need to start working with it on disk or by using other means to interact with it. The technique you use for gaining access to the data is important because it impacts how fast you get a result.

2. **Performing the required shaping.** The shape of the data — the way in which it appears and its characteristics (such a data type), is important in performing analysis. To perform an apples-to-apples comparison, like data has to be shaped the same. However, just shaping the data the same isn't enough. The shape has to be correct for the algorithms you employ to analyze it. Later chapters (starting with Chapter 6) help you understand the need to shape data in various ways.

3. **Analyzing the data.** When analyzing data, you seldom employ a single algorithm and call it good enough. You can't know which algorithm will produce the same results at the outset. To find the best result from your dataset, you experiment on it using several algorithms. This practice is emphasized in the later chapters of the book when you start performing serious data analysis.

4. **Presenting a result.** A picture is worth a thousand words, or so they say. However, you need the picture to say the correct words or your message gets lost. Using the MATLAB plotting functionality provided by the matplotlib library, you can create multiple presentations of the same data, each of which describes the data graphically in different ways. To ensure that your meaning really isn't lost, you must experiment with various presentation methods and determine which one works best.

Considering Speed of Execution

Computers are known for their prowess in crunching numbers. Even so, analysis takes considerable processing power. The datasets are so large that you can bog down even an incredibly powerful system. In general, the following factors control the speed of execution for your data science application:

✔ **Dataset size:** Data science relies on huge datasets in many cases. Yes, you can make a robot see objects using a modest dataset size, but when it comes to making business decisions, larger is better in most situations. The application type determines the size of your dataset in part, but dataset size also relies on the size of the source data. Underestimating the effect of dataset size is deadly in data science applications, especially those that need to operate in real time (such as self-driving cars).

✔ **Loading technique:** The method you use to load data for analysis is critical, and you should always use the fastest means at your disposal, even if it means upgrading your hardware to do so. Working with data in memory is always faster than working with data stored on disk. Accessing local data is always faster than accessing it across a network. Performing data science tasks that rely on Internet access through web services is probably the slowest method of all. Chapter 5 helps you understand loading techniques in more detail. You also see the effects of loading technique later in the book.

✔ **Coding style:** Some people will likely try to tell you that Python's programming paradigms make writing a slow application nearly impossible. They're wrong. Anyone can create a slow application using any language by employing coding techniques that don't make the best use of programming language functionality. To create fast data science applications, you must use best-of-method coding techniques. The techniques demonstrated in this book are a great starting point.

✔ **Machine capability:** Running data science applications on a memory-constrained system with a slower processor is impossible. The system you use needs to have the best hardware you can afford. Given that data science applications are both processor and disk bound, you can't really cut corners in any area and expect great results.

✔ **Analysis algorithm:** The algorithm you use determines the kind of result you obtain and controls execution speed. Many of the chapters in the latter parts of this book demonstrate multiple methods to achieve a goal using different algorithms. However, you must still experiment to find the best algorithm for your particular dataset.

A number of the chapters in this book emphasize performance, most notably speed and reliability, because both factors are critical to data science applications. Even though database applications tend to emphasize the need for speed and reliability to some extent, the combination of huge dataset access (disk-bound issues) and data analysis (processor-bound issues) in data science applications makes the need to make good choices even more critical.

Visualizing Power

Python makes it possible to explore the data science environment without resorting to using a debugger or debugging code, as would be needed in many other languages. The `print` statement (or function, depending on the version of Python you use) and `dir()` function let you examine any object interactively. In short, you can load something up and play with it for a while to see just how the developer put it together. Playing with the data, visualizing what it means to you personally, can often help you gain new insights and create new ideas. Judging by many online conversations, playing with the data is the part of data science that its practitioners find the most fun.

You can play with data using any of the tools found in Anaconda, but one of the best tools for the job is IPython because you don't really have to worry too much about the environment, and nothing you create is permanent. After all, you're playing with the data. Therefore, you can load a dataset to see just what it has to offer, as shown in Figure 2-6. Don't worry if this code looks foreign and hard to understand right now. Chapter 4 provides an overview that helps explain it. Just follow along with the concept of playing with data for now.

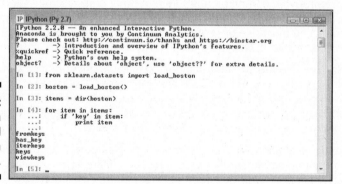

Figure 2-6:
Load a dataset and play with it a little.

In this case, you use Python code to discover all the key-related functions included with the dataset. You can use these functions to perform useful work with the dataset as part of building your application. For example, in Figure 2-7, you can see how the `keys()` function displays a list of keys you can use to access data.

When you have a list of keys you can use, you can access individual data items. For example, Figure 2-8 shows a list of all the feature names contained in the Boston dataset. Python really does make it possible to know quite a lot about a dataset before you have to work with it in depth.

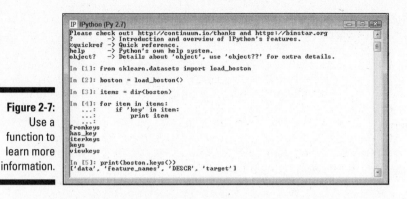

Figure 2-7: Use a function to learn more information.

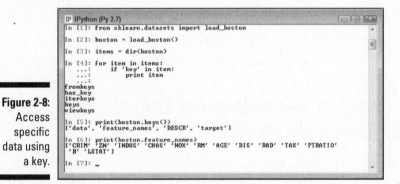

Figure 2-8: Access specific data using a key.

Using the Python Ecosystem for Data Science

You have already seen the need to load libraries in order to perform data science tasks in Python. The following sections provide an overview of the libraries you use for the data science examples in this book. Various book examples show the libraries at work.

Accessing scientific tools using SciPy

The SciPy stack (http://www.scipy.org/) contains a host of other libraries that you can also download separately. These libraries provide support for mathematics, science, and engineering. When you obtain SciPy, you get a set of libraries designed to work together to create applications of various sorts. These libraries are

- ✔ NumPy
- ✔ SciPy
- ✔ matplotlib
- ✔ IPython
- ✔ Sympy
- ✔ pandas

The SciPy library itself focuses on numerical routines, such as routines for numerical integration and optimization. SciPy is a general-purpose library that provides functionality for multiple problem domains. It also provides support for domain-specific libraries, such as Scikit-learn, Scikit-image, and statsmodels.

Performing fundamental scientific computing using NumPy

The NumPy library (`http://www.numpy.org/`) provides the means for performing n-dimensional array manipulation, which is critical for data science work. The Boston dataset used in the examples in Chapters 1 and 2 is an example of an n-dimensional array, and you couldn't easily access it without NumPy functions that include support for linear algebra, Fourier transform, and random-number generation (see the listing of functions at `http://docs.scipy.org/doc/numpy/reference/routines.html`).

Performing data analysis using pandas

The pandas library (`http://pandas.pydata.org/`) provides support for data structures and data analysis tools. The library is optimized to perform data science tasks especially fast and efficiently. The basic principle behind pandas is to provide data analysis and modeling support for Python that is similar to other languages, such as R.

Implementing machine learning using Scikit-learn

The Scikit-learn library (`http://scikit-learn.org/stable/`) is one of a number of Scikit libraries that build on the capabilities provided by NumPy and SciPy to allow Python developers to perform domain-specific tasks. In this case, the library focuses on data mining and data analysis. It provides access to the following sorts of functionality:

- ✔ Classification
- ✔ Regression
- ✔ Clustering
- ✔ Dimensionality reduction
- ✔ Model selection
- ✔ Preprocessing

A number of these functions appear as chapter headings in the book. As a result, you can assume that Scikit-learn is the most important library for the book (even though it relies on other libraries to perform its work).

Plotting the data using matplotlib

The matplotlib library (`http://matplotlib.org/`) provides you with a MATLAB-like interface for creating data presentations of the analysis you perform. The library is currently limited to 2D output, but it still provides you with the means to express graphically the data patterns you see in the data you analyze. Without this library, you couldn't create output that people outside the data science community could easily understand.

Parsing HTML documents using Beautiful Soup

The Beautiful Soup library (`http://www.crummy.com/software/BeautifulSoup/`) download is actually found at `https://pypi.python.org/pypi/beautifulsoup4/4.3.2`. This library provides the means for parsing HTML or XML data in a manner that Python understands. It allows you to work with tree-based data.

Besides providing a means for working with tree-based data, Beautiful Soup takes a lot of the work out of working with HTML documents. For example, it automatically converts the *encoding* (the manner in which characters are stored in a document) of HTML documents from UTF-8 to Unicode. A Python developer would normally need to worry about things like encoding, but with Beautiful Soup, you can focus on your code instead.

Chapter 3

Setting Up Python for Data Science

*B*efore you can do too much with Python or use it to solve data science problems, you need a workable installation. In addition, you need access to the datasets and code used for this book. Downloading the sample code and installing it on your system is the best way to get a good learning experience from the book. This chapter helps you get your system set up so that you can easily follow the examples in the remainder of the book.

Using the downloadable source doesn't prevent you from typing the examples on your own, following them using a debugger, expanding them, or working with the code in all sorts of ways. The downloadable source is there to help you get a good start with your data science and Python learning experience. After you see how the code works when it's correctly typed and configured, you can try to create the examples on your own. If you make a mistake, you can compare what you've typed with the downloadable source and discover precisely where the error exists. You can find the downloadable source for this chapter in the `P4DS4D; 03; Sample.ipynb` and `P4DS4D; 03; Dataset Load.ipynb` files. (The Introduction tells you where to download the source code for this book.)

Using Python 2.7.x for this book

There are currently two parallel Python developments. Most books rely on the newest version of a language for examples. However, there are actually two newest versions of Python that you can use as of this writing: 2.7.9 and 3.4.2. Python is unique in that some groups use one version and other groups use the other version. Because data scientists use the 2.7.x version of Python, for the most part, this book concentrates on that version. Using the 2.7.x version means that you're better able to work with other data scientists when you complete this book. If the book used the 3.4.x version instead, you might find it hard to understand examples that you see in real-world applications.

If you truly want to use the 3.4.x version with this book, you can do so, but you need to understand that the examples may not always work as written. For example, when using the Python 2.7 `print()` function, you don't absolutely need to include parenthesis. The Python 3.4 version of the same function raises an error unless you do use the parenthesis. Even though it seems like a minor difference, it's enough to cause confusion for some people

and you need to keep it in mind as you work through the examples.

Fortunately, you can find a number of online sites that document the version 2.7 and version 3.4 differences. One of the easiest sites to understand is nbviewer at `http://nbviewer.ipython.org/ github/rasbt/python_reference/ blob/master/tutorials/key_ differences_between_python_2_ and_3.ipynb`. Another good place to look is Spartan Ideas at `http://spartanideas. msu.edu/2014/06/01/ the-key-differences-between- python-2-7-x-and-python-3-x- with-examples/`. These sites will help you if you choose to use version 3.4 with this book. However, the book only supports version 2.7 and you use version 3.4 at your own risk. Make sure you keep an eye out for changes as data science evolves on the book's blog at `http://blog.johnmuellerbooks. com/category/technical/python- for-data-science-for-dummies/`. The blog will help you make any adjustments should they be needed to keep current.

Considering the Off-the-Shelf Cross-Platform Scientific Distributions

It's entirely possible to obtain a generic copy of Python and add all of the required data science libraries to it. The process can be difficult because you need to ensure that you have all the required libraries in the correct versions to ensure success. In addition, you need to perform the configuration required to ensure that the libraries are accessible when you need them. Fortunately, going through the required work is not necessary because a number of Python data science products are available for you to use. These products provide everything needed to get started with data science projects.

You can use any of the packages mentioned in the following sections to work with the examples in this book. However, the book's source code and downloadable source rely on Continuum Analytics Anaconda because this particular package works on every platform this book is designed to support: Linux, Mac OS X, and Windows. The book doesn't mention a specific package in the chapters that follow, but any screenshots reflect how things look when using Anaconda on Windows. You may need to tweak the code to use another package, and the screens will look different if you use Anaconda on some other platform.

Getting Continuum Analytics Anaconda

The basic Anaconda package is a free download that you obtain at `https://store.continuum.io/cshop/anaconda/`. Simply click Download Anaconda to obtain access to the free product. You do need to provide an email address in order to get a copy of Anaconda. After you provide your email address, you go to another page, where you can choose your platform and the installer for that platform. Anaconda supports the following platforms:

- ✔ Windows 32-bit and 64-bit (the installer may offer you only the 64-bit or 32-bit version, depending on which version of Windows it detects)
- ✔ Linux 32-bit and 64-bit
- ✔ Mac OS X 64-bit

The default download version installed Python 2.7, which is the version used in this book (see the "Using Python 2.7.*x* for this book" sidebar for details). You can also choose to install Python 3.4 by clicking the I Want Python 3.4 link. Both Windows and Mac OS X provide graphical installers. When using Linux, you rely on the `bash` utility.

It's possible to obtain Anaconda with older versions of Python. If you want to use an older version of Python, click the installer archive link about halfway down the page. You should use only an older version of Python when you have a pressing need to do so.

The Miniconda installer can potentially save time by limiting the number of features you install. However, trying to figure out precisely which packages you do need is an error-prone and time-consuming process. In general, you want to perform a full installation to ensure that you have everything needed for your projects. Even a full install doesn't require much time or effort to download and install on most systems.

The free product is all you need for this book. However, when you look on the site, you see that many other add-on products are available. These products can help you create robust applications. For example, when you add Accelerate to the mix, you obtain the ability to perform multicore and GPU-enabled operations. The use of these add-on products is outside the scope of this book, but the Anaconda site provides details on using them.

Getting Enthought Canopy Express

Enthought Canopy Express is a free product for producing both technical and scientific applications using Python. You can obtain it at `https://www.enthought.com/canopy-express/`. Click Download Free on the main page to see a listing of the versions that you can download. Only Canopy Express is free, the full Canopy product comes at a cost. However, you can use Canopy Express to work with the examples in this book. Canopy Express supports the following platforms:

✔ Windows 32-bit and 64-bit

✔ Linux 32-bit and 64-bit

✔ Mac OS X 32-bit and 64-bit

Choose the platform and version you want to download. When you click Download Canopy Express, you see an optional form for providing information about yourself. The download starts automatically, even if you don't provide personal information to the company.

One of the advantages of Canopy Express is that Enthought is heavily involved in providing support for both students and teachers. People also can take classes, including online classes, that teach the use of Canopy Express in various ways (see `https://training.enthought.com/courses`). Also offered is live classroom training specifically designed for the data scientist; read about this training at `https://www.enthought.com/services/training/data-science`.

Getting pythonxy

The pythonxy Integrated Development Environment (IDE) is a community project hosted on Google at `https://code.google.com/p/pythonxy/`. It's a Windows-only product, so you can't easily use it for cross-platform needs. (In fact, it supports only Windows Vista, Windows 7, and Windows 8.) However, it does come with a full set of libraries, and you can easily use it for this book, if desired.

Because pythonxy uses the GNU General Public License (GPL) v3 (see `http://www.gnu.org/licenses/gpl.html`), you have no add-ons, training, or other paid features to worry about. No one will come calling at your door hoping to sell you something. In addition, you have access to all the source code for pythonxy, so you can make modifications if desired.

Getting WinPython

The name tells you that WinPython is a Windows-only product that you can find at `http://winpython.sourceforge.net/`. This product is actually a takeoff of pythonxy and isn't meant to replace it. Quite the contrary: WinPython is simply a more flexible way to work with pythonxy. You can read about the motivation for creating WinPython at `http://sourceforge.net/p/winpython/wiki/Roadmap/`.

The bottom line for this product is that you gain flexibility at the cost of friendliness and a little platform integration. However, for developers who need to maintain multiple versions of an IDE, WinPython may make a significant difference. When using WinPython with this book, make sure to pay particular attention to configuration issues or you'll find that even the downloadable code has little chance of working.

Installing Anaconda on Windows

Anaconda comes with a graphical installation application for Windows, so getting a good install means using a wizard, much as you would for any other installation. Of course, you need a copy of the installation file before you begin, and you can find the required download information in the "Getting Continuum Analytics Anaconda" section of this chapter. The following procedure should work fine on any Windows system, whether you use the 32-bit or the 64-bit version of Anaconda.

1. **Locate the downloaded copy of Anaconda on your system.**

   The name of this file varies, but normally it appears as `Anaconda-2.1.0-Windows-x86.exe` for 32-bit systems and `Anaconda-2.1.0-Windows-x86_64.exe` for 64-bit systems. The version number is embedded as part of the filename. In this case, the filename refers to version 2.1.0, which is the version used for this book. If you use some other version, you may experience problems with the source code and need to make adjustments when working with it.

2. Double-click the installation file.

(You may see an Open File – Security Warning dialog box that asks whether you want to run this file. Click Run if you see this dialog box pop up.) You see an Anaconda 2.1.0 Setup dialog box similar to the one shown in Figure 3-1. The exact dialog box you see depends on which version of the Anaconda installation program you download. If you have a 64-bit operating system, it's always best to use the 64-bit version of Anaconda so that you obtain the best possible performance. This first dialog box tells you when you have the 64-bit version of the product.

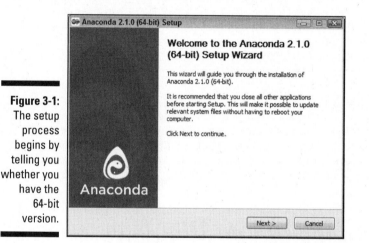

Figure 3-1: The setup process begins by telling you whether you have the 64-bit version.

3. Click Next.

The wizard displays a licensing agreement. Be sure to read through the licensing agreement so that you know the terms of usage.

4. Click I Agree if you agree to the licensing agreement.

You're asked what sort of installation type to perform, as shown in Figure 3-2. In most cases, you want to install the product just for yourself. The exception is if you have multiple people using your system and they all need access to Anaconda.

5. Choose one of the installation types and then click Next.

The wizard asks where to install Anaconda on disk, as shown in Figure 3-3. The book assumes that you use the default location. If you choose some other location, you may have to modify some procedures later in the book to work with your setup.

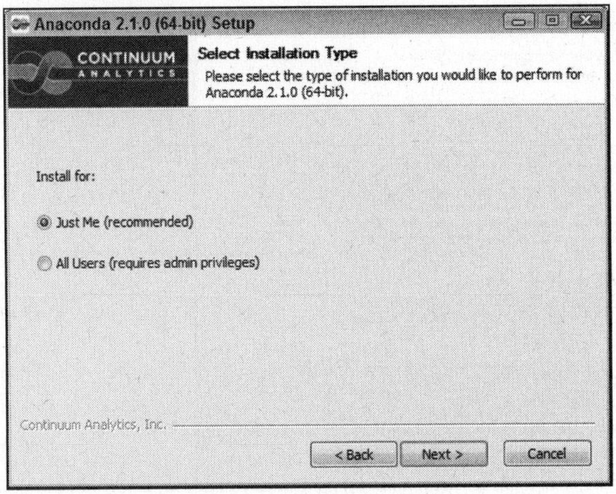

Figure 3-2:
Tell the wizard how to install Anaconda on your system.

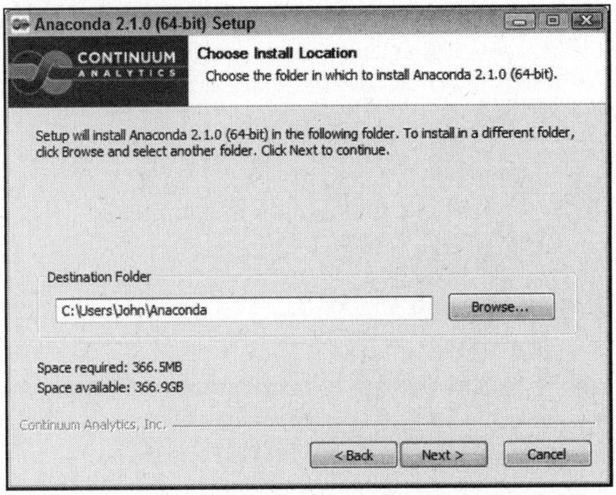

Figure 3-3:
Specify an installation location.

6. Choose an installation location (if necessary) and then click Next.

You see the Advanced Installation Options, shown in Figure 3-4. These options are selected by default and there isn't a good reason to change them in most cases. You might need to change them if Anaconda won't provide your default Python 2.7 (or Python 3.4) setup. However, the book assumes that you've set up Anaconda using the default options.

7. Change the advanced installation options (if necessary) and then click Install.

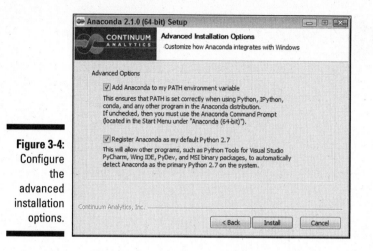

Figure 3-4:
Configure
the
advanced
installation
options.

You see an Installing dialog box with a progress bar. The installation process can take a few minutes, so get yourself a cup of coffee and read the comics for a while. When the installation process is over, you see a Next button enabled.

8. Click Next.

The wizard tells you that the installation is complete.

9. Click Finish.

You're ready to begin using Anaconda.

A word about the screenshots

As you work your way through the book, you'll use an IDE of your choice to open the Python and IPython Notebook files containing the book's source code. Every screenshot that contains IDE-specific information relies on Anaconda because Anaconda runs on all three platforms supported by the book. The use of Anaconda doesn't imply that it's the best IDE or that the authors are making any sort of recommendation for it — Anaconda simply works well as a demonstration product.

When you work with Anaconda, the name of the graphical (GUI) environment, IPython (Py 2.7) Notebook, is precisely the same across all three platforms, and you won't even see any significant difference in the presentation. The differences you do see are minor, and you should ignore them as you work through the book. With this in mind, the book does rely heavily on Windows 7 screenshots. When working on a Linux, Mac OS X, or other Windows version platform, you should expect to see some differences in presentation, but these differences shouldn't reduce your ability to work with the examples.

Installing Anaconda on Linux

You use the command line to install Anaconda on Linux — there is no graphical installation option. Before you can perform the install, you must download a copy of the Linux software from the Continuum Analytics site. You can find the required download information in the "Getting Continuum Analytics Anaconda" section of this chapter. The following procedure should work fine on any Linux system, whether you use the 32-bit or the 64-bit version of Anaconda.

1. **Open a copy of Terminal.**

   You see the Terminal window appear.

2. **Change directories to the downloaded copy of Anaconda on your system.**

   The name of this file varies, but normally it appears as `Anaconda-2.1.0-Linux-x86.sh` for 32-bit systems and `Anaconda-2.1.0-Linux-x86_64.sh` for 64-bit systems. The version number is embedded as part of the filename. In this case, the filename refers to version 2.1.0, which is the version used for this book. If you use some other version, you may experience problems with the source code and need to make adjustments when working with it.

3. **Type** bash Anaconda-2.1.0-Linux-x86 **(for the 32-bit version) or** Anaconda-2.1.0-Linux-x86_64.sh **(for the 64-bit version) and press Enter.**

   An installation wizard starts that asks you to accept the licensing terms for using Anaconda.

4. **Read the licensing agreement and accept the terms using the method required for your version of Linux.**

   The wizard asks you to provide an installation location for Anaconda. The book assumes that you use the default location of ~/anaconda. If you choose some other location, you may have to modify some procedures later in the book to work with your setup.

5. **Provide an installation location (if necessary) and press Enter (or click Next).**

   You see the application extraction process begin. After the extraction is complete, you see a completion message.

6. **Add the installation path to your** PATH **statement using the method required for your version of Linux.**

   You're ready to begin using Anaconda.

Installing Anaconda on Mac OS X

The Mac OS X installation comes only in one form: 64-bit. Before you can perform the install, you must download a copy of the Mac software from the Continuum Analytics site. You can find the required download information in the "Getting Continuum Analytics Anaconda" section of this chapter. The following steps help you install Anaconda 64-bit on a Mac system.

1. **Locate the downloaded copy of Anaconda on your system.**

   The name of this file varies, but normally it appears as Anaconda-2.1.0-MacOSX-x86_64.pkg. The version number is embedded as part of the filename. In this case, the filename refers to version 2.1.0, which is the version used for this book. If you use some other version, you may experience problems with the source code and need to make adjustments when working with it.

2. **Double-click the installation file.**

   You see an introduction dialog box.

3. **Click Continue.**

   The wizard asks whether you want to review the Read Me materials. You can read these materials later. For now, you can safely skip the information.

4. **Click Continue.**

   The wizard displays a licensing agreement. Be sure to read through the licensing agreement so that you know the terms of usage.

5. **Click I Agree if you agree to the licensing agreement.**

   The wizard asks you to provide a destination for the installation. The destination controls whether the installation is for an individual user or a group.

   You may see an error message stating that you can't install Anaconda on the system. The error message occurs because of a bug in the installer and has nothing to do with your system. To get rid of the error message, choose the Install Only for Me option. You can't install Anaconda for a group of users on a Mac system.

6. **Click Continue.**

   The installer displays a dialog box containing options for changing the installation type. Click Change Install Location if you want to modify where Anaconda is installed on your system (the book assumes that you use the default path of ~/anaconda). Click Customize if you want to modify how the installer works. For example, you can choose not to add

Anaconda to your PATH statement. However, the book assumes that you have chosen the default install options and there isn't a good reason to change them unless you have another copy of Python 2.7 installed somewhere else.

7. Click Install.

You see the installation begin. A progress bar tells you how the installation process is progressing. When the installation is complete, you see a completion dialog box.

8. Click Continue.

You're ready to begin using Anaconda.

Downloading the Datasets and Example Code

This book is about using Python to perform data science tasks. Of course, you could spend all your time creating the example code from scratch, debugging it, and only then discovering how it relates to data science, or you can take the easy way and download the prewritten code so that you can get right to work. Likewise, creating datasets large enough for data science purposes would take quite a while. Fortunately, you can access standardized, precreated data sets quite easily using features provided in some of the data science libraries. The following sections help you download and use the example code and datasets so that you can save time and get right to work with data science–specific tasks.

Using IPython Notebook

To make working with the relatively complex code in this book easier, you use IPython Notebook. This interface makes it easy to create Python notebook files that can contain any number of examples, each of which can run individually. The program runs in your browser, so which platform you use for development doesn't matter; as long as it has a browser, you should be OK.

Starting IPython Notebook

Most platforms provide an icon to access IPython (Py 2.7) Notebook (the version number may be different on your system). All you need to do is open this icon to access IPython Notebook. For example, on a Windows system, you choose Start ➪ All Programs ➪ Anaconda ➪ IPython (Py 2.7) Notebook. Figure 3-5 shows how the interface looks when viewed in a Firefox browser.

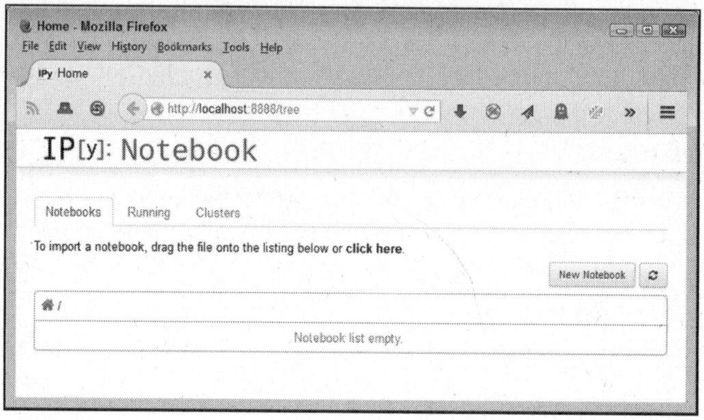

Figure 3-5:
IPython
Notebook
provides
an easy
method to
create data
science
examples.

The precise appearance on your system depends on the browser you use and the kind of platform you have installed.

If you have a platform that doesn't offer easy access through an icon, you can use these steps to access IPython Notebook:

1. **Open a Command Prompt or Terminal Window on your system.**

   You see the window open so that you can type commands.

2. **Change directories to the \Anaconda\Scripts directory on your machine.**

   Most systems let you use the CD command for this task.

3. **Type** ..\python ipython-script.py notebook **and press Enter.**

   The IPython Notebook page opens in your browser.

Stopping the IPython Notebook server

No matter how you start IPython Notebook (or just Notebook, as it appears in the remainder of the book), the system generally opens a command prompt or terminal window to host Notebook. This window contains a server that makes the application work. After you close the browser window when a session is complete, select the server window and press Ctrl+C or Ctrl+Break to stop the server.

Defining the code repository

The code you create and use in this book will reside in a repository on your hard drive. Think of a *repository* as a kind of filing cabinet where you put your code. Notebook opens a drawer, takes out the folder, and shows the code to you. You can modify it, run individual examples within the folder, add new examples, and simply interact with your code in a natural manner. The following sections get you started with Notebook so that you can see how this whole repository concept works.

Dealing with the MathJax error

You may find yourself staring at an odd error like the one shown in Figure 3-6 when you try to perform certain tasks, such as creating a new notebook. The book doesn't actually use the MathJax library, so you can simply dismiss the message box if you like.

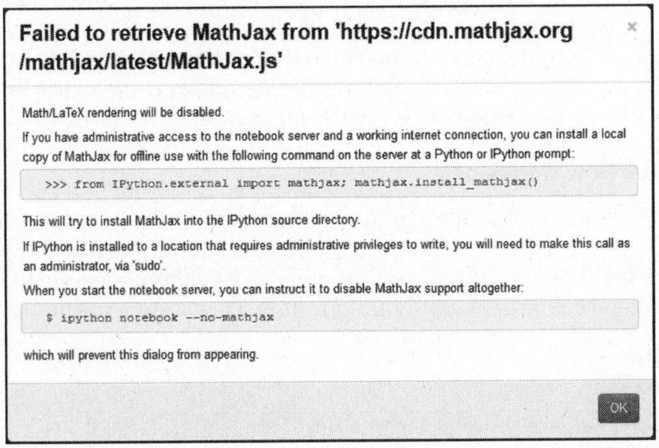

Figure 3-6: It's safe to ignore the MathJax error when working in this book.

Failed to retrieve MathJax from 'https://cdn.mathjax.org /mathjax/latest/MathJax.js'

Math/LaTeX rendering will be disabled.

If you have administrative access to the notebook server and a working internet connection, you can install a local copy of MathJax for offline use with the following command on the server at a Python or IPython prompt:

```
>>> from IPython.external import mathjax; mathjax.install_mathjax()
```

This will try to install MathJax into the IPython source directory.

If IPython is installed to a location that requires administrative privileges to write, you will need to make this call as an administrator, via 'sudo'.

When you start the notebook server, you can instruct it to disable MathJax support altogether:

```
$ ipython notebook --no-mathjax
```

which will prevent this dialog from appearing.

OK

However, you may eventually need the MathJax library, so the best approach is to fix the problem. The following steps help you install a local copy of the MathJax library so that you no longer see the error message.

1. **Open a Command Prompt or Terminal Window on your system.**

   The window opens so that you can type commands.

2. **Change directories to the \Anaconda directory on your machine.**

   Most systems let you use the CD command for this task.

3. **Type** python **and press Enter.**

   A new copy of Python starts.

4. **Type** from IPython.external import mathjax; mathjax.install_mathjax() **and press Enter.**

   Python tells you that it's extracting a copy of the mathjax library to a specific location on your system.

The extraction process can take a long time to complete. Get a cup of coffee, discuss the latest sports with a friend, or read a good book, but don't disturb the download process or you won't get a complete copy of the MathJax library. The result will be that Notebook could fail to work properly (if it works at all). After some period of time, the extraction process is complete and you return to the Python prompt.

5. Type quit() **and press Enter.**

The MathJax library is now ready for use. You must restart any Notebook servers before proceeding.

Creating a new notebook

Every new notebook is like a file folder. You can place individual examples within the file folder, just as you would sheets of paper into a physical file folder. Each example appears in a cell. You can put other sorts of things in the file folder, too, but you see how these things work as the book progresses. Use these steps to create a new notebook.

1. Click New Notebook.

You see a new tab open in the browser with the new notebook, as shown in Figure 3-7. Notice that the notebook contains a cell and that Notebook has highlighted the cell so that you can begin typing code in it. The title of the notebook is Untitled0 right now. That's not a particularly helpful title, so you need to change it.

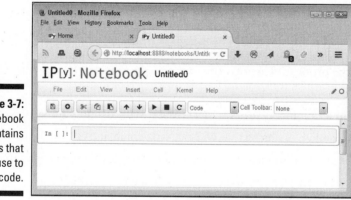

Figure 3-7:
A notebook contains cells that you use to hold code.

2. Click Untitled0 on the page.

Notebook asks whether you want to use as a new name, as shown in Figure 3-8.

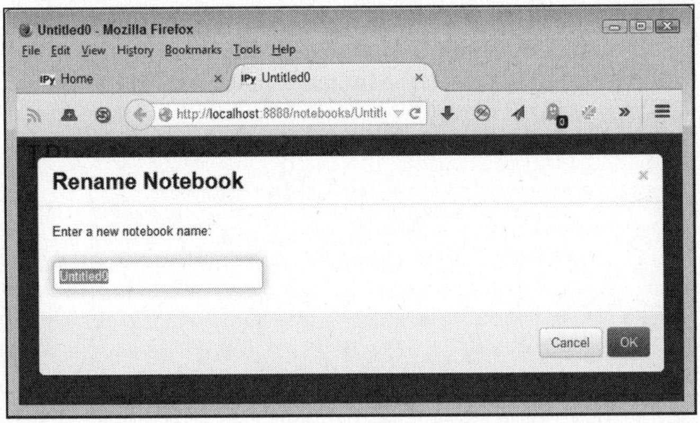

Figure 3-8:
Provide a
new name
for your
notebook.

3. Type P4DS4D; 03; Sample **and press Enter.**

The new name tells you that this is a file for Python for Data Science For Dummies, Chapter 3, Sample.ipynb. Using this naming convention will make it easy for you to differentiate these files from other files in your repository.

Of course, the Sample notebook doesn't contain anything just yet. Place the cursor in the cell, type **print 'Python is really cool!'**, and then click the Run button (the button with the right-pointing arrow on the toolbar). You see the output shown in Figure 3-9. The output is part of the same cell as the code. However, Notebook visually separates the output from the code so that you can tell them apart. Notebook automatically creates a new cell for you.

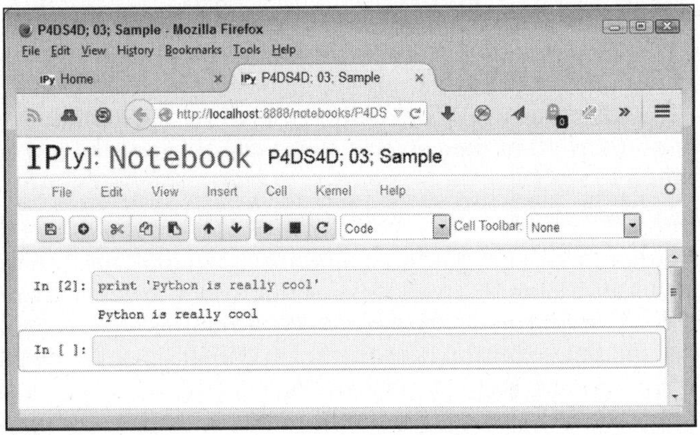

Figure 3-9:
Notebook
uses cells to
store your
code.

When you finish working with a notebook, it's important to shut it down. To close a notebook, choose File ➪ Close and Halt. You return to the Home page, where you can see the notebook you just created added to the list, as shown in Figure 3-10.

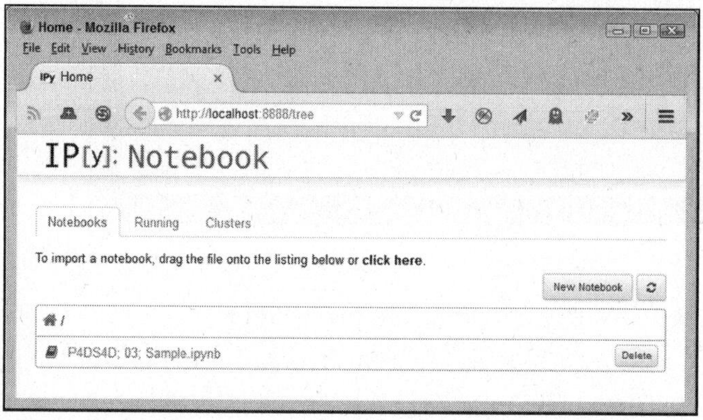

Figure 3-10: Any notebooks you create appear in the repository list.

Exporting a notebook

It isn't much fun to create notebooks and keep them all to yourself. At some point, you want to share them with other people. To perform this task, you must export your notebook from the repository to a file. You can then send the file to someone else who will import it into his or her repository.

The previous section shows how to create a notebook named P4DS4D; 03; Sample. You can open this notebook by clicking its entry in the repository list. File reopens so that you can see your code again. To export this code, choose File ➪ Download As ➪ IPython Notebook. What you see next depends on your browser, but you generally see some sort of dialog box for saving the notebook as a file. Use the same method for saving the IPython Notebook file as you use for any other file you save using your browser.

Removing a notebook

Sometimes notebooks get outdated or you simply don't need to work with them any longer. Rather than allow your repository to get clogged with files you don't need, you can remove these unwanted notebooks from the list. Notice the Delete button next to the P4DS4D; 03; Sample.ipynb entry in Figure 3-10. Use these steps to remove the file:

1. Click Delete.

You see a Delete notebook warning message like the one shown in Figure 3-11.

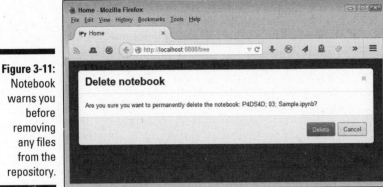

Figure 3-11:
Notebook
warns you
before
removing
any files
from the
repository.

2. **Click Delete.**

   Notebook removes the notebook file from the list. However, you won't actually see the change.

3. **Click Refresh Notebook List (the button with two arrows forming a circle in it).**

   You see the file removed from the list.

Importing a notebook

In order to use the source code from this book, you must import the downloaded files into your repository. The source code comes in an archive file that you extract to a location on your hard drive. The archive contains a list of .ipynb (IPython Notebook) files containing the source code for this book (see the Introduction for details on downloading the source code). The following steps tell how to import these files into your repository:

1. **Click the Click Here link on the Notebook Home page.**

   What you see depends on your browser. In most cases, you see some type of File Upload dialog box that provides access to the files on your hard drive.

2. **Navigate to the directory containing the files you want to import into Notebook.**

3. **Highlight one or more files to import and click the Open (or other, similar) button to begin the upload process.**

   You see the file added to an upload list, as shown in Figure 3-12. The file isn't part of the repository yet — you've simply selected it for upload.

4. **Click Upload.**

   Notebook places the file in the repository so that you can begin using it.

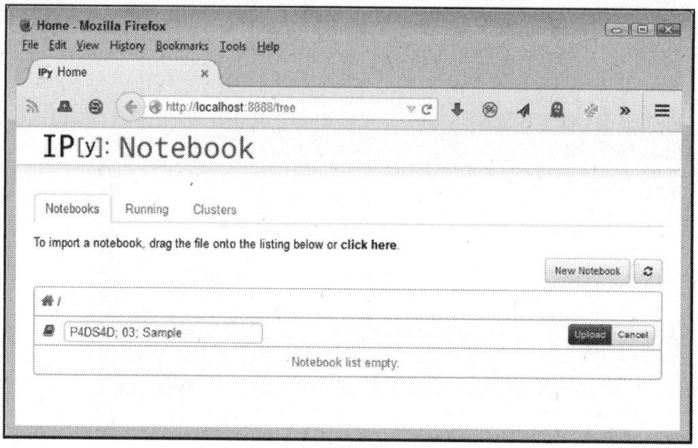

Figure 3-12:
The files
you want to
add to the
repository
appear as
part of an
upload list.

Understanding the datasets used in this book

This book uses a number of datasets, all of which appear in the Scikit-learn library. These datasets demonstrate various ways in which you can interact with data, and you use them in the examples to perform a variety of tasks. The following list provides a quick overview of the function used to import each of the datasets into your Python code:

- ✔ `load_boston()`: Regression analysis with the Boston house-prices dataset
- ✔ `load_iris()`: Classification with the iris dataset
- ✔ `load_diabetes()`: Regression with the diabetes dataset
- ✔ `load_digits([n_class])`: Classification with the digits dataset
- ✔ `fetch_20newsgroups(subset='train')`: Data from 20 newsgroups
- ✔ `fetch_olivetti_faces()`: Olivetti faces dataset from AT&T

The technique for loading each of these datasets is the same across examples. The following example shows how to load the Boston house-prices dataset. You can find the code in the P4DS4D; 03; Dataset Load.ipynb notebook.

```
from sklearn.datasets import load_boston
Boston = load_boston()
print Boston.data.shape
```

To see how the code works, click Run Cell. The output from the print call is
(506L, 13L). You can see the output shown in Figure 3-13.

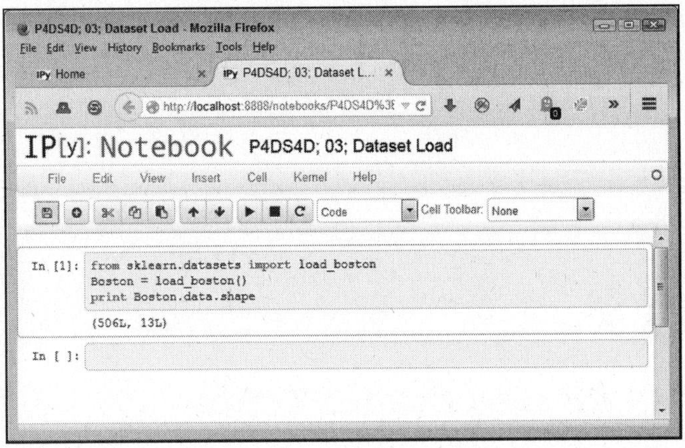

Figure 3-13:
The Boston
object
contains
the loaded
dataset.

Chapter 4

Reviewing Basic Python

Chapter 3 helped you create a Python installation that's specific to data science. However, you can use this installation to perform common Python tasks as well, and that's actually the best way to test your setup to know that it works as intended. If you already know Python, you might be able to skip this chapter and move on to the next chapter; however, it's probably best to skim the material as a minimum and test some of the examples, just to be sure you have a good installation.

The focus of this chapter is to provide you with a good overview of how Python works as a language. Of course, part of that focus is how you use Python to solve data science problems. However, you can't use this book to learn Python from scratch. To learn Python from scratch, you need a book such as my book *Beginning Programming with Python For Dummies* (published by John Wiley & Sons, Inc.) or a tutorial such as the one at `https://docs.python.org/2/tutorial/`. The chapter assumes that you've worked with other programming languages and have at least an idea of how Python works. This limitation aside, the chapter gives you a good reminder of how things work in Python, which is all that many people really need.

This book uses Python 2.7.*x*. The latest version of Python as of this writing is version 2.7.9. If you try to use this book with Python 3.4.2 (or above), you may need to modify the examples to compensate for the differences in that version. The "Using Python 2.7.*x* for this book" sidebar in Chapter 3 provides you with details about Python version differences. Going through the examples in this chapter will help you know what to expect with other examples in the book should you decide to use version 3.4.2 when solving data science problems.

Stylistic concerns with Python

Python developers designed Python to be easy to read and understand. For this reason, it comes with certain style conventions. You can see these conventions listed in Pep-8 (`https://www.python.org/dev/peps/pep-0008/`). If you want to exchange your code with someone else or use it in a public venue, you need to follow the conventions relatively closely. However, personal code or example code that you create need not follow the conventions precisely.

You must use the whitespace rules when writing your code because Python uses them to determine where code segments begin and end. In addition, Python has some odd rules that might seem randomly implemented, but they make the code easier to work with. For example, you can't mix tabs and spaces in the same document to create whitespace when working with Python 3 (Python 2 does allow mixing of tabs and spaces). The preference is to use spaces, and the Python editors on the market tend to use spaces by default.

Some stylistic concerns are more about preference than about making the code work.

For example, method names are supposed to use all lowercase letters and use underscores to separate words, such as `my_method`. However, you can use camel case when desired, such as `myMethod`, or even pascal case, such as `MyMethod`, and the code will compile just fine. If you want to make a method private, however, you must use a leading underscore for it, such as `_my_method`. Adding two underscores, such as `__my_method`, invokes Python's name mangling to make it harder (albeit not impossible) for someone to use the method. The point is that you don't have to be a slave to the stylistic rules as long as you're willing to live with the consequences of not following them completely.

Python does include magic words, such as `__init__`, `__import__`, and `__file__`. You don't ever create these names yourself, and you use only the existing magic words as defined by Python. A listing of these magic words appears at `http://www.rafekettler.com/magicmethods.html`. The guide tells you the most common uses for the magic words as well.

Working with Numbers and Logic

Data science involves working with data of various sorts, but much of the work involves numbers. In addition, you use logical values to make decisions about the data you use. For example, you might need to know whether two values are equal or whether one value is greater than another value. Python supports these number and logic value types:

✔ Any whole number is an *integer*. For example, the value 1 is a whole number, so it's an integer. On the other hand, 1.0 isn't a whole number; it has a decimal part to it, so it's not an integer. Integers are represented by the `int` data type. On most platforms, you can store numbers between −9,223,372,036,854,775,808 and 9,223,372,036,854,775,807 within an `int` (which is the maximum value that fits in a 64-bit variable).

✔ Any number that includes a decimal portion is a *floating point* value. For example, 1.0 has a decimal part, so it's a floating-point value. Many people get confused about whole numbers and floating-point numbers, but the difference is easy to remember. If you see a decimal in the number, it's a floating-point value. Python stores floating-point values in the `float` data type. The maximum value that a floating-point variable can contain is $\pm 1.7976931348623157 \times 10^{308}$ and the minimum value that a floating point variable can contain is $\pm 2.2250738585072014 \times 10^{-308}$ on most platforms.

✔ A *complex number* consists of a real number and an imaginary number that are paired together. Just in case you've completely forgotten about complex numbers, you can read about them at `http://www.mathsisfun.com/numbers/complex-numbers.html`. The imaginary part of a complex number always appears with a *j* after it. So, if you want to create a complex number with 3 as the real part and 4 as the imaginary part, you make an assignment like this: `myComplex = 3 + 4j`.

✔ Logical arguments require Boolean values, which are named after George Bool. When using a Boolean value in Python, you rely on the `bool` type. A variable of this type can contain only two values: `True` or `False`. You can assign a value by using the `True` or `False` keywords, or you can create an expression that defines a logical idea that equates to true or false. For example, you could say `myBool = 1 > 2`, which would equate to False because 1 is most definitely not greater than 2.

Now that you have the basics down, it's time to see the data types in action. The following paragraphs provide a quick overview of how you can work with both numeric and logical data in Python.

Performing variable assignments

When working with applications, you store information in *variables*. A variable is a kind of storage box. Whenever you want to work with the information, you access it using the variable. If you have new information you want to store, you put it in a variable. Changing information means accessing the variable first and then storing the new value in the variable. Just as you store things in boxes in the real world, so you store things in variables (a kind of storage box) when working with applications. To store data in a variable, you *assign* the data to it using any of a number of *assignment operators* (special symbols that tell how to store the data). Table 4-1 shows the assignment operators that Python supports.

Table 4-1	Python Assignment Operators	
Operator	*Description*	*Example*
=	Assigns the value found in the right operand to the left operand	MyVar = 2 results in MyVar containing 2
+=	Adds the value found in the right operand to the value found in the left operand and places the result in the left operand	MyVar += 2 results in MyVar containing 7
-=	Subtracts the value found in the right operand from the value found in the left operand and places the result in the left operand	MyVar -= 2 results in MyVar containing 3
*=	Multiplies the value found in the right operand by the value found in the left operand and places the result in the left operand	MyVar *= 2 results in MyVar containing 10
/=	Divides the value found in the left operand by the value found in the right operand and places the result in the left operand	MyVar /= 2 results in MyVar containing 2.5
%=	Divides the value found in the left operand by the value found in the right operand and places the remainder in the left operand	MyVar %= 2 results in MyVar containing 1
**=	Determines the exponential value found in the left operand when raised to the power of the value found in the right operand and places the result in the left operand	MyVar ** 2 results in MyVar containing 25
//=	Divides the value found in the left operand by the value found in the right operand and places the integer (whole number) result in the left operand	MyVar //= 2 results in MyVar containing 2

Doing arithmetic

Storing information in variables makes it easily accessible. However, in order to perform any useful work with the variable, you usually perform some type of arithmetic operation on it. Python supports the common arithmetic operators you use to perform tasks by hand. They appear in Table 4-2.

Table 4-2	**Python Arithmetic Operators**	
Operator	*Description*	*Example*
+	Adds two values together	5 + 2 = 7
-	Subtracts the right-hand operand from left operand	5 – 2 = 3
*	Multiplies the right-hand operand by the left operand	5 * 2 = 10
/	Divides the left-hand operand by the right operand	5 / 2 = 2.5
%	Divides the left-hand operand by the right operand and returns the remainder	5 % 2 = 1
**	Calculates the exponential value of the right operand by the left operand	5 ** 2 = 25
//	Performs integer division, in which the left operand is divided by the right operand and only the whole number is returned (also called floor division)	5 // 2 = 2

Sometimes you need to interact with just one variable. Python supports a number of *unary operators*, those that work with just one variable, as shown in Table 4-3.

Table 4-3	**Python Unary Operators**	
Operator	*Description*	*Example*
~	Inverts the bits in a number so that all of the 0 bits become 1 bits and vice versa.	~4 results in a value of –5
-	Negates the original value so that positive becomes negative and vice versa.	–(–4) results in 4 and –4 results in –4
+	Is provided purely for the sake of completeness. This operator returns the same value that you provide as input.	+4 results in a value of 4

Computers can perform other sorts of math tasks because of the way in which the processor works. It's important to remember that computers store data as a series of individual bits. Python makes it possible to access these individual bits using *bitwise operators,* as shown in Table 4-4.

Table 4-4	Python Bitwise Operators	
Operator	*Description*	*Example*
& (And)	Determines whether both individual bits within two operators are true and sets the resulting bit to true when they are.	0b1100 & 0b0110 = 0b0100
| (Or)	Determines whether either of the individual bits within two operators are true and sets the resulting bit to true when they are.	0b1100 | 0b0110 = 0b1110
^ (Exclusive or)	Determines whether just one of the individual bits within two operators is true and sets the resulting bit to true when one is. When both bits are true or both bits are false, the result is false.	0b1100 ^ 0b0110 = 0b1010
~ (One's complement)	Calculates the one's complement value of a number.	~0b1100 = –0b1101 ~0b0110 = –0b0111
<< (Left shift)	Shifts the bits in the left operand left by the value of the right operand. All new bits are set to 0 and all bits that flow off the end are lost.	0b00110011 << 2 = 0b11001100
>> (Right shift)	Shifts the bits in the left operand right by the value of the right operand. All new bits are set to 0 and all bits that flow off the end are lost.	0b00110011 >> 2 = 0b00001100

Comparing data using Boolean expressions

Using arithmetic to modify the content of variables is a kind of data manipulation. To determine the effect of data manipulation, a computer must compare the current state of the variable against its original state or the state of a known value. In some cases, detecting the status of one input against another is also necessary. All these operations check the relationship between two variables, so the resulting operators are relational operators, as shown in Table 4-5.

Sometimes a relational operator can't tell the whole story of the comparison of two values. For example, you might need to check a condition in which two

Table 4-5	Python Relational Operators	
Operator	*Description*	*Example*
==	Determines whether two values are equal. Notice that the relational operator uses two equals signs. A mistake many developers make is using just one equals sign, which results in one value being assigned to another.	1 == 2 is False
!=	Determines whether two values are not equal. Some older versions of Python allowed you to use the <> operator in place of the != operator. Using the <> operator results in an error in current versions of Python.	1 != 2 is True
>	Verifies that the left operand value is greater than the right operand value.	1 > 2 is False
<	Verifies that the left operand value is less than the right operand value.	1 < 2 is True
>=	Verifies that the left operand value is greater than or equal to the right operand value.	1 >= 2 is False
<=	Verifies that the left operand value is less than or equal to the right operand value.	1 <= 2 is True

separate comparisons are needed, such as `MyAge > 40` and `MyHeight < 74`. The need to add conditions to the comparison requires a logical operator of the sort shown in Table 4-6.

Table 4-6	Python Logical Operators	
Operator	*Description*	*Example*
and	Determines whether both operands are true.	True and True is True
		True and False is False
		False and True is False
		False and False is False

(continued)

Table 4-6 (continued)

Operator	Description	Example
or	Determines when one of two operands is true.	True or True is True
		True or False is True
		False or True is True
		False or False is False
not	Negates the truth value of a single operand. A true value becomes false and a false value becomes true.	not True is False
		not False is True

Computers provide order to comparisons by making some operators more significant than others. The ordering of operators is *operator precedence*. Table 4-7 shows the operator precedence of all the common Python operators, including a few you haven't seen as part of a discussion yet. When making comparisons, always consider operator precedence because otherwise, the assumptions you make about a comparison outcome will likely be wrong.

Table 4-7   **Python Operator Precedence**

Operator	Description
()	You use parentheses to group expressions and to override the default precedence so that you can force an operation of lower precedence (such as addition) to take precedence over an operation of higher precedence (such as multiplication).
**	Exponentiation raises the value of the left operand to the power of the right operand.
~ + -	Unary operators interact with a single variable or expression.
* / % //	Multiply, divide, modulo, and floor division.
+ -	Addition and subtraction.
>> <<	Right and left bitwise shift.
&	Bitwise AND.
^ |	Bitwise exclusive OR and standard OR.
<= < > >=	Comparison operators.

Operator	Description
== !=	Equality operators.
= %= /= //= -= += *= **=	Assignment operators.
is is not	Identity operators.
in not in	Membership operators.
not or and	Logical operators.

Creating and Using Strings

Of all the data types, strings are the most easily understood by humans and not understood at all by computers. A *string* is simply any grouping of characters you place within double quotation marks. For example, myString = "Python is a great language." assigns a string of characters to myString.

The computer doesn't see letters at all. Every letter you use is represented by a number in memory. For example, the letter *A* is actually the number 65. To see this for yourself, type **ord("A")** at the Python prompt and press Enter. You see 65 as output. It's possible to convert any single letter to its numeric equivalent using the ord() command.

Because the computer doesn't really understand strings, but strings are so useful in writing applications, you sometimes need to convert a string to a number. You can use the int() and float() commands to perform this conversion. For example, if you type **myInt = int("123")** and press Enter at the Python prompt, you create an int named myInt that contains the value 123.

You can convert numbers to a string as well by using the str() command. For example, if you type **myStr = str(1234.56)** and press Enter, you create a string containing the value "1234.56" and assign it to myStr. The point is that you can go back and forth between strings and numbers with great ease. Later chapters demonstrate how these conversions make many seemingly impossible tasks quite doable.

As with numbers, you can use some special operators with strings (and many objects). The *member operators* make it possible to determine when a string contains specific content. Table 4-8 shows these operators.

Table 4-8	Python Membership Operators	
Operator	*Description*	*Example*
in	Determines whether the value in the left operand appears in the sequence found in the right operand	"Hello" in "Hello Goodbye" is True
not in	Determines whether the value in the left operand is missing from the sequence found in the right operand	"Hello" not in "Hello Goodbye" is False

The discussion in this section also makes it obvious that you need to know the kind of data that variables contain. You use the *identity operators* to perform this task, as shown in Table 4-9.

Table 4-9	Python Identity Operators	
Operator	*Description*	*Example*
is	Evaluates to true when the type of the value or expression in the right operand points to the same type in the left operand	type(2) is int is True
is not	Evaluates to true when the type of the value or expression in the right operand points to a different type than the value or expression in the left operand	type(2) is not int is False

Interacting with Dates

Dates and times are items that most people work with quite a bit. Society bases almost everything on the date and time that a task needs to be or was completed. We make appointments and plan events for specific dates and times. Most of our day revolves around the clock. Because of the time-oriented nature of humans, it's a good idea to look at how Python deals with interacting with date and time (especially storing these values for later use). As with everything else, computers understand only numbers — date and time don't really exist.

To work with dates and times, you must issue a special import datetime command. Technically, this act is called *importing a module*. Don't worry how the command works right now — just use it whenever you want to do something with date and time.

Computers do have clocks inside them, but the clocks are for the humans using the computer. Yes, some software also depends on the clock, but again, the emphasis is on human needs rather than anything the computer might require. To get the current time, you can simply type **datetime.datetime. now()** and press Enter. You see the full date and time information as found on your computer's clock (see Figure 4-1).

Figure 4-1:
Get the
current
date and
time using
the now()
command.

```
IP IPython (Py 2.7)
Python 2.7.8 |Anaconda 2.1.0 (64-bit)! (default, Jul  2 2014, 15:12:11) [MSC v.1
500 64 bit (AMD64)]
Type "copyright", "credits" or "license" for more information.

IPython 2.2.0 -- An enhanced Interactive Python.
Anaconda is brought to you by Continuum Analytics.
Please check out: http://continuum.io/thanks and https://binstar.org
?         -> Introduction and overview of IPython's features.
%quickref -> Quick reference.
help      -> Python's own help system.
object?   -> Details about 'object', use 'object??' for extra details.

In [1]: import datetime

In [2]: datetime.datetime.now()
Out[2]: datetime.datetime(2015, 3, 16, 14, 45, 11, 764000)

In [3]: _
```

You may have noticed that the date and time are a little hard to read in the existing format. Say that you want to get just the current date, and in a readable format. To accomplish this task, you access just the date portion of the output and convert it into a string. Type **str(datetime.datetime.now().date())** and press Enter. Figure 4-2 shows that you now have something a little more usable.

Interestingly enough, Python also has a time() command, which you can use to obtain the current time. You can obtain separate values for each of the components that make up date and time using the day, month, year, hour, minute, second, and microsecond values. Later chapters help you understand how to use these various date and time features to make working with data science applications easier.

```
IP IPython (Py 2.7)                                               [-][□][×]
Python 2.7.8 |Anaconda 2.1.0 (64-bit)| (default, Jul 2 2014, 15:12:11) [MSC v.1
500 64 bit (AMD64)]
Type "copyright", "credits" or "license" for more information.

IPython 2.2.0 -- An enhanced Interactive Python.
Anaconda is brought to you by Continuum Analytics.
Please check out: http://continuum.io/thanks and https://binstar.org
?          -> Introduction and overview of IPython's features.
%quickref  -> Quick reference.
help       -> Python's own help system.
object?    -> Details about 'object', use 'object??' for extra details.

In [1]: import datetime

In [2]: datetime.datetime.now()
Out[2]: datetime.datetime(2015, 3, 16, 14, 45, 11, 764000)

In [3]: str(datetime.datetime.now().date())
Out[3]: '2015-03-16'

In [4]: _
```

Figure 4-2:
Make the
date and
time more
readable
using the
str()
command.

Creating and Using Functions

To manage information properly, you need to organize the tools used to perform the required tasks. Each line of code that you create performs a specific task, and you combine these lines of code to achieve a desired result. Sometimes you need to repeat the instructions with different data, and in some cases your code becomes so long that it's hard to keep track of what each part does. Functions serve as organization tools that keep your code neat and tidy. In addition, functions make it easy to reuse the instructions you've created as needed with different data. This section of the chapter tells you all about functions. More important, in this section you start creating your first serious applications in the same way that professional developers do.

Creating reusable functions

You go to your closet, take out pants and shirt, remove the labels, and put them on. At the end of the day, you take everything off and throw it in the trash. Hmmm . . . that really isn't what most people do. Most people take the clothes off, wash them, and then put them back into the closet for reuse. Functions are reusable, too. No one wants to keep repeating the same task; it becomes monotonous and boring. When you create a function, you define a package of code that you can use over and over to perform the same task. All you need to do is tell the computer to perform a specific task by telling it which function to use. The computer faithfully executes each instruction in the function absolutely every time you ask it to do so.

When you work with functions, the code that needs services from the function is named the *caller,* and it calls upon the function to perform tasks for it. Much of the information you see about functions refers to the caller. The caller must supply information to the function, and the function returns information to the caller.

At one time, computer programs didn't include the concept of code reusability. As a result, developers had to keep reinventing the same code. It didn't take long for someone to come up with the idea of functions, though, and the concept has evolved over the years until functions have become quite flexible. You can make functions do anything you want. Code reusability is a necessary part of applications to

- ✔ Reduce development time

- ✔ Reduce programmer error

- ✔ Increase application reliability

- ✔ Allow entire groups to benefit from the work of one programmer

- ✔ Make code easier to understand

- ✔ Improve application efficiency

In fact, functions do a whole list of things for applications in the form of reusability. As you work through the examples in this book, you see how reusability makes your life significantly easier. If not for reusability, you'd still be programming by plugging 0s and 1s into the computer by hand.

Creating a function doesn't require much work. To see how functions work, open a copy of IPython and type in the following code (pressing Enter at the end of each line):

```
def SayHello():
    print('Hello There!')
```

To end the function, you press Enter a second time after the last line. A function begins with the keyword `def` (for define). You provide a function name, parentheses that can contain function *arguments* (data used in the function), and a colon. The editor automatically indents the next line for you. Python relies on whitespace to define *code blocks* (statements that are associated with each other in a function).

You can now use the function. Simply type **SayHello()** and press Enter. The parentheses after the function name are important because they tell Python to execute the function, rather than tell you that you are accessing a function as an object (to determine what it is). Figure 4-3 shows the output from this function.

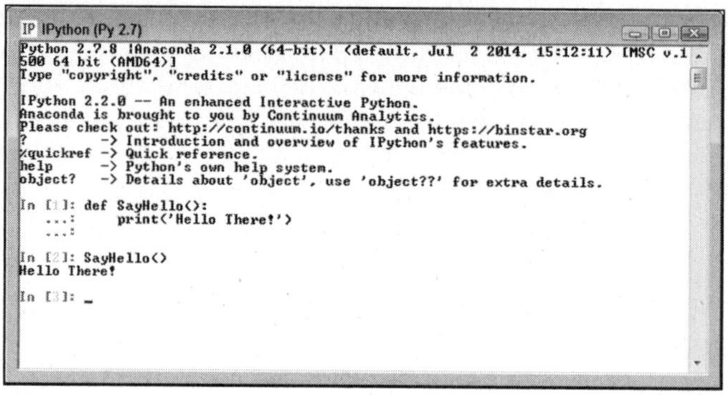

Figure 4-3:
Creating
and using
functions
is straight-
forward.

Calling functions in a variety of ways

Functions can accept arguments (additional bits of data) and return values. The ability to exchange data makes functions far more useful than they otherwise might be. The following sections describe how to call functions in a variety of ways to both send and receive data.

Sending required arguments

A function can require the caller to provide arguments to it. A required argument is a variable that must contain data for the function to work. Open a copy of IPython and type the following code:

```
def DoSum(Value1, Value2):
    return Value1 + Value2
```

You have a new function, DoSum(). This function requires that you provide two arguments to use it. At least, that's what you've heard so far. Type **DoSum()** and press Enter. You see an error message, as shown in Figure 4-4, telling you that DoSum requires two arguments.

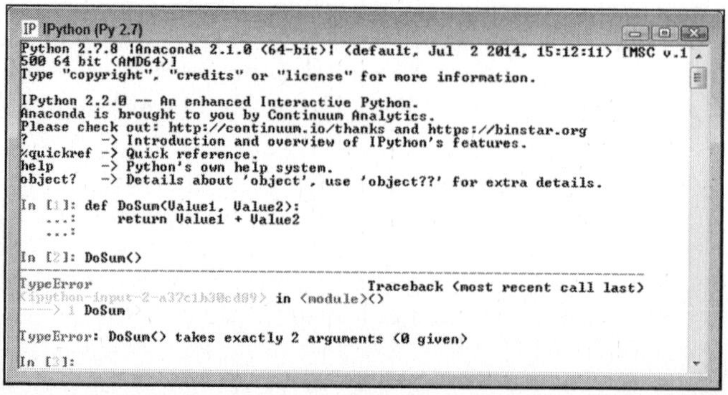

Figure 4-4:
You must
supply an
argument
or you get
an error
message.

Trying `DoSum()` with just one argument would result in another error message. In order to use `DoSum()` you must provide two argument. To see how this works, type **DoSum(1, 2)** and press Enter. You see the result in Figure 4-5.

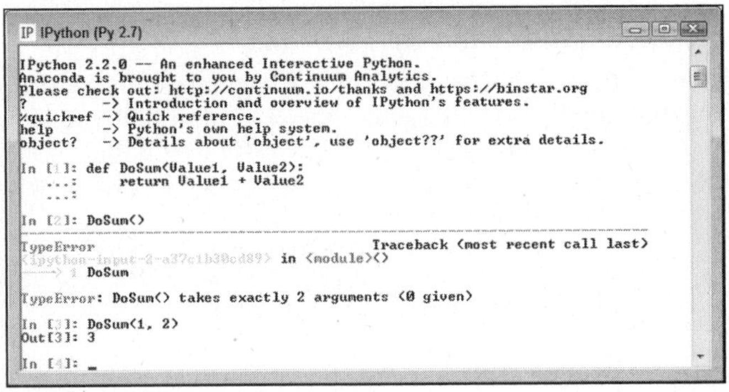

Figure 4-5:
Supplying two
arguments
provides the
expected
output.

Notice that `DoSum()` provides an output value of 3 when you supply 1 and 2 as inputs. The `return` statement provides the output value. Whenever you see `return` in a function, you know the function provides an output value.

Sending arguments by keyword

As your functions become more complex and the methods to use them do as well, you may want to provide a little more control over precisely how you call the function and provide arguments to it. Until now, you have *positional arguments*, which means that you have supplied values in the order in which they appear in the argument list for the function definition. However, Python also has a method for sending arguments by keyword. In this case, you supply the name of the argument followed by an equals sign (=) and the argument value. To see how this works, open a copy of IPython and type the following code:

```
def DisplaySum(Value1, Value2):
    print(str(Value1) + ' + ' + str(Value2) + ' = ' +
    str((Value1 + Value2)))
```

Notice that the `print()` function argument includes a list of items to print and that those items are separated by plus signs (+). In addition, the arguments are of different types, so you must convert them using the `str()` function. Python makes it easy to mix and match arguments in this manner. This function also introduces the concept of automatic line continuation. The `print()` function actually appears on two lines, and Python automatically continues the function from the first line to the second.

Next, it's time to test `DisplaySum()`. Of course, you want to try the function using positional arguments first, so type **DisplaySum(2, 3)** and press Enter. You see the expected output of 2 + 3 = 5. Now type **DisplaySum(Value2 = 3, Value1 = 2)** and press Enter. Again, you receive the output 2 + 3 = 5 even though the position of the arguments has been reversed.

Giving function arguments a default value

Whether you make the call using positional arguments or keyword arguments, the functions to this point have required that you supply a value. Sometimes a function can use default values when a common value is available. Default values make the function easier to use and less likely to cause errors when a developer doesn't provide an input. To create a default value, you simply follow the argument name with an equals sign and the default value. To see how this works, open a copy of IPython and type the following code:

```
def SayHello(Greeting = "No Value Supplied"):
    print(Greeting)
```

The `SayHello()` function provides an automatic value for Greeting when a caller doesn't provide one. When someone tries to call `SayHello()` without an argument, it doesn't raise an error. Type **SayHello()** and press Enter to see for yourself — you see the default message. Type **SayHello("Howdy!")** to see a normal response.

Creating functions with a variable number of arguments

In most cases, you know precisely how many arguments to provide with your function. It pays to work toward this goal whenever you can because functions with a fixed number of arguments are easier to troubleshoot later. However, sometimes you simply can't determine how many arguments the function will receive at the outset. For example, when you create a Python application that works at the command line, the user might provide no arguments, the maximum number of arguments (assuming there is one), or any number of arguments in between.

Fortunately, Python provides a technique for sending a variable number of arguments to a function. You simply create an argument that has an asterisk in front of it, such as `*VarArgs`. The usual technique is to provide a second argument that contains the number of arguments passed as an input. To see how this works, open a copy of IPython and type the following code:

```
def DisplayMulti(ArgCount = 0, *VarArgs):
    print('You passed ' + str(ArgCount) + ' arguments.',
    Var Args)
```

Notice that the print() function displays a string and then the list of arguments. Because of the way this function is designed, you can type **DisplayMulti()** and press Enter to see that it's possible to pass zero arguments. To see multiple arguments at work, type **DisplayMulti(3, 'Hello', 1, True)** and press Enter. The output of (`'You passed 3 arguments.'`, (`'Hello', 1, True`)) shows that you need not pass values of any particular type.

Using Conditional and Loop Statements

Computer applications aren't very useful if they perform precisely the same tasks the same number of times every time you run them. Yes, they can perform useful work, but life seldom offers situations in which conditions remain the same. In order to accommodate changing conditions, applications must make decisions and perform tasks a variable number of times. Conditional and loop statements make it possible to perform this task as described in the sections that follow.

Making decisions using the if statement

You use "if" statements regularly in everyday life. For example, you may say to yourself, "If it's Wednesday, I'll eat tuna salad for lunch." The Python if statement is a little less verbose, but it follows precisely the same pattern. To see how this works, open a copy of IPython and type the following code:

```
def TestValue(Value):
    if Value == 5:
        print('Value equals 5!')
    elif Value == 6:
        print('Value equals 6!')
    else:
        print('Value is something else.')
        print('It equals ' + str(Value))
```

Every Python if statement begins, oddly enough, with the word *if*. When Python sees if, it knows that you want it to make a decision. After the word *if* comes a condition. A *condition* simply states what sort of comparison you want Python to make. In this case, you want Python to determine whether Value contains the value 5.

REMEMBER

Notice that the condition uses the relational equality operator, ==, and not the assignment operator, =. A common mistake that developers make is to use the assignment operator rather than the equality operator.

The condition always ends with a colon (:). If you don't provide a colon, Python doesn't know that the condition has ended and will continue to look for additional conditions on which to base its decision. After the colon comes any tasks you want Python to perform.

You may need to perform multiple tasks using a single if statement. The elif clause makes it possible to add an additional condition and associated tasks. A *clause* is an addendum to a previous condition, which is an if statement in this case. The elif clause always provides a condition, just like the if statement, and it has its own associated set of tasks to perform.

Sometimes you need to do something no matter what the condition might be. In this case, you add the else clause. The else clause tells Python to do something in particular when the conditions of the if statement aren't met.

Notice how indenting is becoming more important as the functions become more complex. The function contains an if statement. The if statement contains just one print() statement. The else clause contains two print() statements.

To see this function in action, type **TestValue(1)** and press Enter. You see the output from the else clause. Type **TestValue(5)** and press Enter. The output now reflects the if statement output. Type **TestValue(6)** and press Enter. The output now shows the results of the elif clause. The result is that this function is more flexible than previous functions in the chapter because it can make decisions.

Choosing between multiple options using nested decisions

Nesting is the process of placing a subordinate statement within another statement. You can nest any statement within any other statement in most cases. To see how this works, open a copy of IPython and type the following code:

```python
def SecretNumber():
    One = int(input("Type a number between 1 and 10: "))
    Two = int(input("Type a number between 1 and 10: "))

    if (One >= 1) and (One <= 10):
        if (Two >= 1) and (Two <= 10):
            print('Your secret number is: ' + str(One * Two))
        else:
            print("Incorrect second value!")
    else:
        print("Incorrect first value!")
```

In this case, `SecretNumber()` asks you to provide two inputs. Yes, you can get inputs from a user when needed by using the `input()` function. The `int()` function converts the inputs to a number.

There are two levels of `if` statement this time. The first level checks for the validity of the number in `One`. The second level checks for the validity of the number in `Two`. When both `One` and `Two` have values between 1 and 10, then `SecretNumber()` outputs a secret number for the user.

To see `SecretNumber()` in action, type **SecretNumber()** and press Enter. Type **20** and press Enter when asked for the first input value, and type `10` and press Enter when asked for the second. You see an error message telling you that the first value is incorrect. Type **SecretNumber()** and press Enter again. This time, use values of 10 and 20. The function will tell you that the second input is incorrect. Try the same sequence again using input values of 10 and 10.

Performing repetitive tasks using for

Sometimes you need to perform a task more than one time. You use the `for` loop statement when you need to perform a task a specific number of times. The `for` loop has a definite beginning and a definite end. The number of times that that loop executes depends on the number of elements in the variable you provide. To see how this works, open a copy of IPython and type the following code:

```
def DisplayMulti(*VarArgs):
    for Arg in VarArgs:
        if Arg.upper() == 'CONT':
            continue
            print('Continue Argument: ' + Arg)
        elif Arg.upper() == 'BREAK':
            break
            print('Break Argument: ' + Arg)
        print('Good Argument: ' + Arg)
```

In this case, the `for` loop attempts to process each element in `VarArgs`. Notice that there is a nested `if` statement in the loop and it tests for two ending conditions. In most cases, the code skips the `if` statement and simply prints the argument. However, when the `if` statement finds the words `CONT` or `BREAK` in the input values, it performs one of these two tasks:

 ✔ `continue`: Forces the loop to continue from the current point of execution with the next entry in VarArgs.

 ✔ `break`: Stops the loop from executing.

The keywords can appear capitalized in any way because the `upper()` function converts them to uppercase. The `DisplayMulti()` function can process any number of input strings. To see it in action, type **DisplayMulti('Hello', 'Goodbye', 'First', 'Last')** and press Enter. You see each of the input strings presented on a separate line in the output. Now type **DisplayMulti('Hello', 'Cont', 'Goodbye', 'Break', 'Last')** and press Enter. Notice that the words `Cont` and `Break` don't appear in the output because they're keywords. In addition, the word `Last` doesn't appear in the output because the `for` loop ends before this word is processed.

Using the while statement

The `while` loop statement continues to perform tasks until such time that a condition is no longer true. As with the `for` statement, the `while` statement supports both the `continue` and `break` keywords for ending the loop prematurely. To see how this works, open a copy of IPython and type the following code:

```
def SecretNumber():
    GotIt = False
    while GotIt == False:
        One = int(input("Type a number between 1 and 10: "))
        Two = int(input("Type a number between 1 and 10: "))

        if (One >= 1) and (One <= 10):
            if (Two >= 1) and (Two <= 10):
                print('Secret number is: ' + str(One * Two))
                GotIt = True
                continue
            else:
                print("Incorrect second value!")
        else:
            print("Incorrect first value!")
        print("Try again!")
```

This is an expansion of the `SecretNumber()` function first described in the "Choosing between multiple options using nested decisions" section, earlier in this chapter. However, in this case, the addition of a `while` loop statement means that the function continues to ask for input until it receives a valid response.

To see how the `while` statement works, type **SecretNumber()** and press Enter. Type **20** and press Enter for the first prompt. Type **10** and press Enter for the second prompt. The example tells you that the first number is wrong and then tells you to try again. Try a second time using values of 10 and 20. This time the second number is wrong and you still need to try again. On the third try, use values of 10 and 10. This time you get a secret number. Notice that the use of a `continue` clause means that the application doesn't tell you to try again.

Storing Data Using Sets, Lists, and Tuples

Python provides a host of methods for storing data in memory. Each method has advantages and disadvantages. Choosing the most appropriate method for your particular need is important. The following sections discuss three common techniques used for storing data for data science needs.

Performing operations on sets

Most people have used sets at one time or another in school to create lists of items that belong together. These lists then became the topic of manipulation using math operations such as intersection, union, difference, and symmetric difference. Sets are the best option to choose when you need to perform membership testing and remove duplicates from a list. You can't perform sequence-related tasks using sets, such a indexing or slicing. To see how you can work with sets, start a copy of IPython and type the following code:

```
from sets import Set
SetA = Set(['Red', 'Blue', 'Green', 'Black'])
SetB = Set(['Black', 'Green', 'Yellow', 'Orange'])
SetX = SetA.union(SetB)
SetY = SetA.intersection(SetB)
SetZ = SetA.difference(SetB)
```

Notice that you must import the Set capability into your Python application. The module sets contain a Set class that you import into your application in order to use the resulting functionality. If you try to use the Set class without first importing it, Python displays an error message. The book uses a number of imported libraries, so knowing how to use the import statement is important.

You now have five different sets to play with, each of which has some common elements. To see the results of each math operation, type **print '{0}\n{1}\n{2}'.format(SetX, SetY, SetZ)** and press Enter. You see one set printed on each line, like this:

```
Set(['Blue', 'Yellow', 'Green', 'Orange', 'Black', 'Red'])
Set(['Green', 'Black'])
Set(['Blue', 'Red'])
```

The outputs show the results of the math operations: union(), intersection(), and difference(). (When working with Python 3.4, the output may vary from the Python 2.7 output shown. All output in the book is for Python 2.7, so you may see differences from time to time when using Python 3.4.) Python's fancier print formatting can be useful in working with collections such as sets. The format() function tells Python which objects to place within each of the placeholders in the string. A *placeholder* is a set of curly brackets ({}) with an optional number in it. The *escape character* (essentially a kind of control or special character), /n, provides a newline character between entries. You can read more about fancy formatting at https://docs.python.org/2/tutorial/inputoutput.html.

You can also test relationships between the various sets. For example, type **SetA.issuperset(SetY)** and press Enter. The output value of True tells you that SetA is a superset of SetY. Likewise, if you type **SetA.issubset(SetX)** and press Enter, you find that SetA is a subset of SetX.

It's important to understand that sets are either mutable or immutable. All the sets in this example are mutable, which means that you can add or remove elements from them. For example, if you type **SetA.add('Purple')** and press Enter, SetA receives a new element. If you type **SetA.issubset(SetX)** and press Enter now, you find that SetA is no longer a subset of SetX because SetA has the 'Purple' element in it.

Working with lists

The Python specification defines a list as a kind of sequence. *Sequences* simply provide some means of allowing multiple data items to exist together in a single storage unit, but as separate entities. Think about one of those large mail holders you see in apartment buildings. A single mail holder contains a number of small mailboxes, each of which can contain mail. Python supports other kinds of sequences as well:

- ✔ **Tuples:** A tuple is a collection used to create complex list-like sequences. An advantage of tuples is that you can nest the content of a tuple. This feature lets you create structures that can hold employee records or x-y coordinate pairs.

- ✔ **Dictionaries:** As with the real dictionaries, you create key/value pairs when using the dictionary collection (think of a word and its associated definition). A dictionary provides incredibly fast search times and makes ordering data significantly easier.

✔ **Stacks:** Most programming languages support stacks directly. However, Python doesn't support the stack, although there's a workaround for that. A stack is a first in/first out (LIFO) sequence. Think of a pile of pancakes: You can add new pancakes to the top and also take them off of the top. A stack is an important collection that you can simulate in Python using a list.

✔ **Queues:** A queue is a last in/first out (FIFO) collection. You use it to track items that need to be processed in some way. Think of a queue as a line at the bank. You go into the line, wait your turn, and are eventually called to talk with a teller.

✔ **Deques:** A double-ended queue (deque) is a queue-like structure that lets you add or remove items from either end, but not from the middle. You can use a deque as a queue or a stack or any other kind of collection to which you're adding and from which you're removing items in an orderly manner (in contrast to lists, tuples, and dictionaries, which allow randomized access and management).

Of all the sequences, lists are the easiest to understand and are the most directly related to a real-world object. Working with lists helps you become better able to work with other kinds of sequences that provide greater functionality and improved flexibility. The point is that the data is stored in a list much as you would write it on a piece of paper — one item comes after another. The list has a beginning, a middle, and an end. As shown in the figure, the items are numbered. (Even if you might not normally number them in real life, Python always numbers the items for you.) To see how you can work with lists, start a copy of IPython and type the following code:

```
ListA = [0, 1, 2, 3]
ListB = [4, 5, 6, 7]
ListA.extend(ListB)
ListA
```

When you type the last line of code, you see the output of [0, 1, 2, 3, 4, 5, 6, 7]. The extend() function adds the members of ListB to ListA. Beside extending lists, you can also add to them using the append() function. Type **ListA.append(-5)** and press Enter. When you type **ListA** and press Enter again, you see that Python has added –5 to the end of the list. You may find that you need to remove items again and you do that using the remove() function. For example, type **ListA.remove(-5)** and press Enter. When you list ListA again, you see that the added entry is gone.

Lists also support concatenation using the plus (+) sign. For example, if you type **ListX = ListA + ListB** and press Enter, you find that the newly created ListX contains both ListA and ListB in it with the elements of ListA coming first.

Creating and using Tuples

A tuple is a collection used to create complex lists, in which you can embed one tuple within another. This embedding lets you create hierarchies with tuples. A hierarchy could be something as simple as the directory listing of your hard drive or an organizational chart for your company. The idea is that you can create complex data structures using a tuple.

Tuples are *immutable*, which means you can't change them. You can create a new tuple with the same name and modify it in some way, but you can't modify an existing tuple. Lists are mutable, which means that you can change them. So, a tuple can seem at first to be at a disadvantage, but immutability has all sorts of advantages, such as being more secure as well as faster. In addition, immutable objects are easier to use with multiple processors. To see how you can work with tuples, start a copy of IPython and type the following code:

```
MyTuple = (1, 2, 3, (4, 5, 6, (7, 8, 9)))
```

MyTuple is nested three levels deep. The first level consists of the values 1, 2, and 3, and a tuple. The second level consists of the values 4, 5, and 6, and yet another tuple. The third level consists of the values 7, 8, and 9. To see how this works, type the following code into IPython:

```
for Value1 in MyTuple:
    if type(Value1) == int:
        print Value1
    else:
        for Value2 in Value1:
            if type(Value2) == int:
                print "\t", Value2
            else:
                for Value3 in Value2:
                    print "\t\t", Value3
```

When you run this code, you find that the values really are at three different levels. You can see the indentations showing the level:

```
1
2
3
        4
        5
        6
                7
                8
                9
```

It is possible to perform tasks such as adding new values, but you must do it by adding the original entries and the new values to a new tuple. In addition, you can add tuples to an existing tuple only. To see how this works, type **MyNewTuple = MyTuple.__add__((10, 11, 12, (13, 14, 15)))** and press Enter. `MyNewTuple` contains new entries at both the first and second levels, like this: `(1, 2, 3, (4, 5, 6, (7, 8, 9)), 10, 11, 12, (13, 14, 15))`. If you were to run the previous code against `MyNewTuple`, you'd see entries at the appropriate levels in the output, as shown here.

```
1
2
3
            4
            5
            6
                        7
                        8
                        9
   10
   11
   12
            13
            14
            15
```

Defining Useful Iterators

The chapters that follow use all kinds of techniques to access individual values in various types of data structures. For this section, you use two simple lists, defined as the following:

```
ListA = ['Orange', 'Yellow', 'Green', 'Brown']
ListB = [1, 2, 3, 4]
```

The simplest method of accessing a particular value is to use an index. For example, if you type **ListA[1]** and press Enter, you see `'Yellow'` as the output. All indexes in Python are zero-based, which means that the first entry is 0, not 1.

Ranges present another simple method of accessing values. For example, if you type **ListB[1:3]** and press Enter, the output is `[2, 3]`. You could use the range as input to a `for` loop, such as

```
for Value in ListB[1:3]:
    print Value
```

Instead of the entire list, you see just 2 and 3 as outputs, printed on separate lines. The range has two values separated by a colon. However, the values are optional. For example, ListB[:3] would output [1, 2, 3]. When you leave out a value, the range starts at the beginning or the end of the list, as appropriate.

Sometimes you need to process two lists in parallel. The simplest method of doing this is to use the zip() function. Here's an example of the zip() function in action:

```
for Value1, Value2 in zip(ListA, ListB):
    print Value1, '\t', Value2
```

This code processes both ListA and ListB at the same time. The processing ends when the for loop reaches the shortest of the two lists. In this case, you see the following:

```
Orange   1
Yellow   2
Green    3
Brown    4
```

This is the tip of the iceberg. You see a host of iterator types used throughout the book. The idea is to make it possible to list just the items you want, rather than all of the items in a list or other data structure. Some of the iterators used in upcoming chapters are a little more complicated than what you see here, but this is an important start.

Indexing Data Using Dictionaries

A dictionary is a special kind of sequence that uses a name and value pair. The use of a name makes it easy to access particular values with something other than a numeric index. To create a dictionary, you enclose name and value pairs in curly brackets. Create a test dictionary by typing **MyDict = {'Orange':1, 'Blue':2, 'Pink':3}** and pressing Enter.

To access a particular value, you use the name as an index. For example, type **MyDict['Pink']** and press Enter to see the output value of 3. The use of dictionaries as data structures makes it easy to access incredibly complex data sets using terms that everyone can understand. In many other respects, working with a dictionary is the same as working with any other sequence.

Dictionaries do have some special features. For example, type **MyDict.keys()** and press Enter to see a list of the keys. You can use the values() function to see the list of values in the dictionary.

Part II
Getting Your Hands Dirty with Data

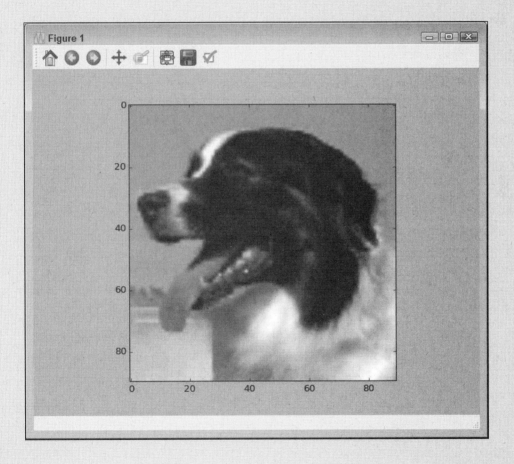

In this part . . .

- ✔ Importing data from various sources
- ✔ Validating your data and making it complete
- ✔ Using only part of the data for analysis
- ✔ Performing data shaping
- ✔ Defining the problem and creating a solution for it

Chapter 5

Working with Real Data

Data science applications require data by definition. It would be nice if you could simply go to a data store somewhere, purchase the data you need in an easy-open package, and then write an application to access that data. However, data is messy. It appears in all sorts of places, in many different forms, and you can interpret it in many different ways. Every organization has a different method of viewing data and stores it in a different manner as well. Even when the data management system used by one company is the same as the data management system used by another company, the chances are slim that the data will appear in the same format or even use the same data types. In short, before you can do any data science work, you must discover how to access the data in all its myriad forms. Real data requires a lot of work to use and fortunately, Python is up to the task of manipulating it as needed.

This chapter helps you understand the techniques required to access data in a number of forms and locations. For example, memory streams represent a form of data storage that your computer supports natively; flat files exist on your hard drive; relational databases commonly appear on networks (although smaller relational databases, such as those found in Access, could appear on your hard drive as well); and web-based data usually appears on the Internet. You won't visit every form of data storage available (such as that stored on a point-of-sale, or POS, system). Quite possibly, an entire book on the topic wouldn't suffice to cover the topic of data formats in any detail.

However, the techniques in this chapter do demonstrate how to access data in the formats you most commonly encounter when working with real-world data.

The Scikit-learn library includes a number of *toy* datasets (small datasets meant for you to play with). These datasets are complex enough to perform a number of tasks, such as experimenting with Python to perform data science tasks. Because this data is readily available, and making the examples too complicated to understand is a bad idea, this book relies on these toy data-sets as input for many of the examples. Even though the book does use these toy datasets for the sake of reducing complexity and making the examples clearer, the techniques that the book demonstrates work equally well on real-world data that you access using the techniques shown in this chapter.

You don't have to type the source code for this chapter in by hand. In fact, it's a lot easier if you use the downloadable source (see the Introduction for download instructions). The source code for this chapter appears in the `P4DS4D; 05; Dataset Load.ipynb` source code file.

It's essential that the `Colors.txt`, `Titanic.csv`, `Values.xls`, and `XMLData.xml` files that come with the downloadable source code appear in the same folder (directory) as your IPython Notebook files. Otherwise, the examples in the following sections fail with an input/output (IO) error. The file location varies according to the platform you're using. For example, on a Windows system, you find the notebooks stored in the `C:\Users\Username\My Documents\IPython Notebooks` folder, where *Username* is your login name. To make the examples work, simply copy the four files from the downloadable source folder into your IPython Notebook folder.

Uploading, Streaming, and Sampling Data

Storing data in local computer memory represents the fastest and most reliable means to access it. The data could reside anywhere. However, you don't actually interact with the data in its storage location. You load the data into memory from the storage location and then interact with it in memory. This is the technique the book uses to access all the toy datasets found in the Scikit-learn library, so you see this technique used relatively often in the book.

Data scientists call the columns in a database *features* or *variables*. The rows are *cases*. Each row represents a collection of variables that you can analyze.

Uploading small amounts of data into memory

The most convenient method that you can use to work with data is to load it directly into memory. This technique shows up a couple of times earlier in the book but uses the toy dataset from the Scikit-learn library. This section uses the `Colors.txt` file, shown in Figure 5-1, for input.

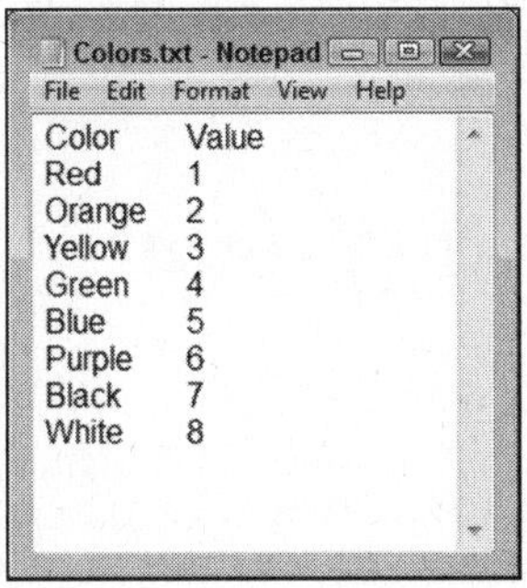

Figure 5-1:
Format
of the
`Colors.`
`txt` file.

The example also relies on native Python functionality to get the task done. When you load a file (of any type), the entire dataset is available at all times and the loading process is quite short. Here is an example of how this technique works.

```
with open("Colors.txt", 'rb') as open_file:
    print 'Colors.txt content:\n' + open_file.read()
```

The example begins by using the `open()` method to obtain a `file` object. The `open()` function accepts the filename and an access mode. In this case, the access mode is read binary (`rb`). (When using Python 3.*x*, you may have to change the mode to read (`r`) in order to avoid error messages.) It then uses the `read()` method of the file object to read all the data in the file. If you were to specify a size argument as part of `read()`, such as `read(15)`, Python would read only the number of characters that you specify or stop when it reaches the End Of File (`EOF`). When you run this example, you see the following output:

```
Colors.txt content:
Color       Value
Red         1
Orange      2
Yellow      3
Green       4
```

```
Blue      5
Purple    6
Black     7
White     8
```

The entire dataset is loaded from the library into free memory. Of course, the loading process will fail if your system lacks sufficient memory to hold the dataset. When this problem occurs, you need to consider other techniques for working with the dataset, such as streaming it or sampling it. In short, before you use this technique, you must ensure that the dataset will actually fit in memory. You won't normally experience any problems when working with the toy datasets in the Scikit-learn library.

Streaming large amounts of data into memory

Some datasets will be so large that you won't be able to fit them entirely in memory at one time. In addition, you may find that some datasets load slowly because they reside on a remote site. Streaming answers both needs by making it possible to work with the data a little at a time. You download individual pieces, making it possible to work with just part of the data and to work with it as you receive it, rather than waiting for the entire dataset to download. Here's an example of how you can stream data using Python:

```
with open("Colors.txt", 'rb') as open_file:
    for observation in open_file:
        print 'Reading Data: ' + observation
```

This example relies on the Colors.txt file, which contains a header, and then a number of records that associate a color name with a value. The open_file file object contains a pointer to the open file.

As the code performs data reads in the for loop, the file pointer moves to the next record. Each record appears one at a time in observation. The code outputs the value in observation using a print statement. You should receive this output:

```
Reading Data: Color     Value

Reading Data: Red       1

Reading Data: Orange    2

Reading Data: Yellow    3
```

```
Reading Data: Green      4

Reading Data: Blue       5

Reading Data: Purple     6

Reading Data: Black      7

Reading Data: White      8
```

Python streams each record from the source. This means that you must perform a read for each record you want.

Sampling data

Data streaming obtains all the records from a data source. You may find that you don't need all the records. You can save time and resources by simply sampling the data. This means retrieving records a set number of records apart, such as every fifth record, or by making random samples. The following code shows how to retrieve every other record in the Colors.txt file:

```
n = 2
with open("Colors.txt", 'rb') as open_file:
    for j, observation in enumerate(open_file):
        if j % n==0:
            print('Reading Line: ' + str(j) +
            ' Content: ' + observation)
```

The basic idea of sampling is the same as streaming. However, in this case, the application uses enumerate() to retrieve a row number. When j % n == 0, the row is one that you want to keep and the application outputs the information. In this case, you see the following output:

```
Reading Line: 0 Content: Color     Value

Reading Line: 2 Content: Orange    2

Reading Line: 4 Content: Green     4

Reading Line: 6 Content: Purple    6

Reading Line: 8 Content: White     8
```

The value of n is important in determining which records appear as part of the dataset. Try changing n to 3. The output will change to sample just the header and rows 3 and 6.

You can perform random sampling as well. All you need to do is randomize the selector, like this:

```
from random import random
sample_size = 0.25
with open("Colors.txt", 'rb') as open_file:
    for j, observation in enumerate(open_file):
        if random()<=sample_size:
            print('Reading Line: ' + str(j) +
                ' Content: ' + observation)
```

To make this form of selection work, you must import the random class. The random() method outputs a value between 0 and 1. However, Python randomizes the output so that you don't know what value you receive. The sample_size variable contains a number between 0 and 1 to determine the sample size. For example, 0.25 selects 25 percent of the items in the file.

The output will still appear in numeric order. For example, you won't see Green come before Orange. However, the items selected are random, and you won't always get precisely the same number of return values. The spaces between return values will differ as well. Here is an example of what you might see as output (although your output will likely vary):

```
Reading Line: 1 Content: Red          1

Reading Line: 4 Content: Green        4

Reading Line: 8 Content: White        8
```

Accessing Data in Structured Flat-File Form

In many cases, the data you need to work with won't appear within a library, such as the toy datasets in the Scikit-learn library. Real-world data usually appears in a file of some type. A flat file presents the easiest kind of file to work with. The data appears as a simple list of entries that you can read one at a time, if desired, into memory. Depending on the requirements for your project, you can read all or part of the file.

A problem with using native Python techniques is that the input isn't intelligent. For example, when a file contains a header, Python simply reads it as yet more data to process, rather than as a header. You can't easily select a particular column of data. The pandas library used in the sections that follow makes it much easier to read and understand flat-file data. Classes and methods in the pandas library interpret (parse) the flat-file data to make it easier to manipulate.

The least formatted and therefore easiest-to-read flat-file format is the text file. However, a text file also treats all data as strings, so you often have to convert numeric data into other forms. A comma-separated value (CSV) file provides more formatting and more information, but it requires a little more effort to read. At the high end of flat-file formatting are custom data formats, such as an Excel file, which contains extensive formatting and could include multiple datasets in a single file.

The following sections describe these three levels of flat-file dataset and show how to use them. These sections assume that the file structures the data in some way. For example, the CSV file uses commas to separate data fields. A text file might rely on tabs to separate data fields. An Excel file uses a complex method to separate data fields and to provide a wealth of information about each field. You can work with unstructured data as well, but working with structured data is much easier because you know where each field begins and ends.

Reading from a text file

Text files can use a variety of storage formats. However, a common format is to have a header line that documents the purpose of each field, followed by another line for each record in the file. The file separates the fields using tabs. Refer to Figure 5-1 for an example of the `Colors.txt` file used for the example in this section.

Native Python provides a wide variety of methods you can use to read such a file. However, it's far easier to let someone else do the work. In this case, you can use the pandas library to perform the task. Within the pandas library, you find a set of *parsers*, code used to read individual bits of data and determine the purpose of each bit according to the format of the entire file. Using the correct parser is essential if you want to make sense of file content. In this case, you use the `read_table()` method to accomplish the task, as shown in the following code:

```
import pandas as pd
color_table = pd.io.parsers.read_table("Colors.txt")
print color_table
```

The code imports the pandas library, uses the `read_table()` method to read `Colors.txt` into a variable named `color_table`, and then displays the resulting memory data onscreen using the `print` function. Here's the output you can expect to see from this example.

```
      Color  Value
0        Red      1
1     Orange      2
2     Yellow      3
3      Green      4
4       Blue      5
5     Purple      6
6      Black      7
7      White      8
```

Notice that the parser correctly interprets the first row as consisting of field names. It numbers the records from 0 through 7. Using `read_table()` method arguments, you can adjust how the parser interprets the input file, but the default settings usually work best. You can read more about the `read_table()` arguments at `http://pandas.pydata.org/pandas-docs/dev/generated/pandas.io.parsers.read_table.html#pandas.io.parsers.read_table`.

Reading CSV delimited format

A CSV file provides more formatting than a simple text file. In fact, CSV files can become quite complicated. There is a standard that defines the format of CSV files, and you can see it at `https://tools.ietf.org/html/rfc4180`. The CSV file used for this example is quite simple:

- ✔ A header defines each of the fields
- ✔ Fields are separated by commas
- ✔ Records are separated by linefeeds
- ✔ Strings are enclosed in double quotes
- ✔ Integers and real numbers appear without double quotes

Figure 5-2 shows the raw format for the `Titanic.csv` file used for this example. You can see the raw format using any text editor.

Applications such as Excel can import and format CSV files so that they become easier to read. Figure 5-3 shows the same file in Excel.

Excel actually recognizes the header as a header. If you were to use features such as data sorting, you could select header columns to obtain the desired

Figure 5-2:
The raw
format of
a CSV file
is still text
and quite
readable.

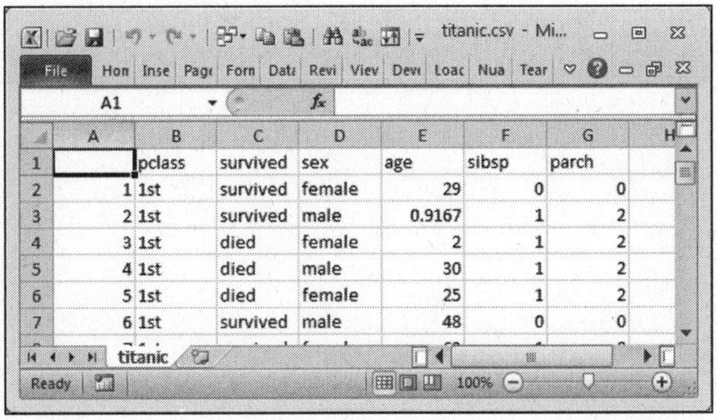

Figure 5-3:
Use an
application
such as
Excel to
create a
formatted
CSV
presentation.

result. Fortunately, pandas also makes it possible to work with the CSV file as formatted data, as shown in the following example:

```
import pandas as pd
titanic = pd.io.parsers.read_csv("Titanic.csv")
X = titanic[['age']]
print X
```

Notice that the parser of choice this time is read_csv(), which understands CSV files and provides you with new options for working with it. (You can read more about this parser at http://pandas.pydata.org/pandas-docs/dev/io.html#io-read-csv-table.) Selecting a specific field is quite easy — you just supply the field name as shown. The output from this example looks like this (some values omitted for the sake of space):

```
            age
0       29.0000
```

```
1          0.9167
2          2.0000
3         30.0000
4         25.0000
5         48.0000
...
1304      14.5000
1305    9999.0000
1306      26.5000
1307      27.0000
1308      29.0000
[1309 rows x 1 columns]
```

Of course, a human readable output like this one is nice when working through an example, but you might also need the output as a list. To create the output as a list, you simply change the third line of code to read X = titanic[['age']].values. Notice the addition of the values property. The output changes to something like this (some values omitted for the sake of space):

```
[[ 29.        ]
 [  0.91670001]
 [  2.        ]
 ...,
 [ 26.5       ]
 [ 27.        ]
 [ 29.        ]]
```

Reading Excel and other Microsoft Office files

Excel and other Microsoft Office applications provide highly formatted content. You can specify every aspect of the information these files contain. The Values.xls file used for this example provides a listing of sine, cosine, and tangent values for a random list of angles. You can see this file in Figure 5-4.

When you work with Excel or other Microsoft Office products, you begin to experience some complexity. For example, an Excel file can contain more than one worksheet, so you need to tell pandas which worksheet to process. In fact, you can choose to process multiple worksheets, if desired. When working with other Office products, you have to be specific about what to process. Just telling pandas to process something isn't good enough. Here's an example of working with the Values.xls file.

Figure 5-4:
An Excel
file is highly
formatted
and might
contain
information
of various
types.

	A	B	C	D	E
1	Angle (Degrees)	Sine	Cosine	Tangent	
2	40.29472	0.646719	0.762728	0.847903	
3	216.71810	-0.597878	-0.801587	0.745868	
4	105.17861	0.965114	-0.261829	-3.686049	
5	97.38824	0.991698	-0.128592	-7.711971	
6	120.87683	0.858272	-0.513194	-1.672413	
7	316.08650	-0.693572	0.720388	-0.962775	
8	317.88761	-0.670587	0.741831	-0.903962	
9	60.82377	0.873124	0.487497	1.791034	
10	34.41988	0.565253	0.824917	0.685224	
11	92.81788	0.998791	-0.049161	-20.316545	

```
import pandas as pd
xls = pd.ExcelFile("Values.xls")
trig_values = xls.parse('Sheet1', index_col=None,
                        na_values=['NA'])
print trig_values
```

The code begins by importing the pandas library as normal. It then creates
a pointer to the Excel file using the `ExcelFile()` constructor. This pointer,
`xls`, lets you access a worksheet, define an index column, and specify how to
present empty values. The index column is the one that the worksheet uses
to index the records. Using a value of `None` means that pandas should generate an index for you. The `parse()` method obtains the values you request.
You can read more about the Excel parser options at `http://pandas.
pydata.org/pandas-docs/dev/io.html#io-excel`.

You don't absolutely have to use the two-step process of obtaining a file
pointer and then parsing the content. You can also perform the task using a
single step like this: `trig_values = pd.read_excel("Values.xls",
'Sheet1', index_col=None, na_values=['NA'])`. Because Excel files
are more complex, using the two-step process is often more convenient and
efficient because you don't have to reopen the file for each read of the data.

Sending Data in Unstructured File Form

Unstructured data files consist of a series of bits. The file doesn't separate
the bits from each other in any way. You can't simply look into the file and
see any structure because there isn't any to see. Unstructured file formats
rely on the file user to know how to interpret the data. For example, each

pixel of a picture file could consist of three 32-bit fields. Knowing that each field is 32-bits is up to you. A header at the beginning of the file may provide clues about interpreting the file, but even so, it's up to you to know how to interact with the file.

The example in this section shows how to work with a picture as an unstructured file. The example image is a public domain offering from `http://commons.wikimedia.org/wiki/Main_Page`. To work with images, you need to access the Scikit-image library (`http://scikit-image.org/`), which is a free-of-charge collection of algorithms used for image processing. You can find a tutorial for this library at `http://scipy-lectures.github.io/packages/scikit-image/`. The first task is to be able to display the image onscreen using the following code. (This code can require a little time to run. The image is ready when the busy indicator disappears from the IPython Notebook tab.)

```
from skimage.io import imread
from skimage.transform import resize
from matplotlib import pyplot as plt
import matplotlib.cm as cm

example_file = ("http://upload.wikimedia.org/" +
    "wikipedia/commons/7/7d/Dog_face.png")
image = imread(example_file, as_grey=True)
plt.imshow(image, cmap=cm.gray)
plt.show()
```

The code begins by importing a number of libraries. It then creates a string that points to the example file online and places it in `example_file`. This string is part of the `imread()` method call, along with `as_grey`, which is set to `True`. The `as_grey` argument tells Python to turn any color images into gray scale. Any images that are already in gray scale remain that way.

Now that you have an image loaded, it's time to render it (make it ready to display onscreen. The `imshow()` function performs the rendering and uses a grayscale color map. The `show()` function actually displays `image` for you, as shown in Figure 5-5.

Close the image when you're finished viewing it. (The asterisk in the In [*]: entry tells you that the code is still running and you can't move on to the next step.) The act of closing the image ends the code segment. You now have an image in memory and you may want to find out more about it. When you run the following code, you discover the image type and size:

```
print("data type: %s, shape: %s" %
      (type(image), image.shape))
```

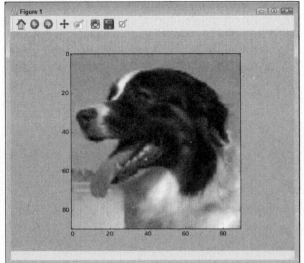

Figure 5-5:
The image
appears
onscreen
after you
render and
show it.

The output from this call tells you that the image type is a `numpy.ndarray` and that the image size is 90 pixels by 90 pixels. The image is actually an array of pixels that you can manipulate in various ways. For example, if you want to crop the image, you can use the following code to manipulate the image array:

```
image2 = image[5:70,0:70]
plt.imshow(image2, cmap=cm.gray)
plt.show()
```

The `numpy.ndarray` in `image2` is smaller than the one in `image`, so the output is smaller as well. Figure 5-6 shows typical results. The purpose of cropping the image is to make it a specific size. Both images must be the same size for you to analyze them. Cropping is one way to ensure that the images are the correct size for analysis.

Another method that you can use to change the image size is to resize it. The following code resizes the image to a specific size for analysis:

```
image3 = resize(image2, (30, 30), mode='nearest')
plt.imshow(image3, cmap=cm.gray)
print("data type: %s, shape: %s" %
      (type(image3), image3.shape))
```

The output from the `print()` function tells you that the image is now 30 pixels by 30 pixels in size. You can compare it to any image with the same dimensions.

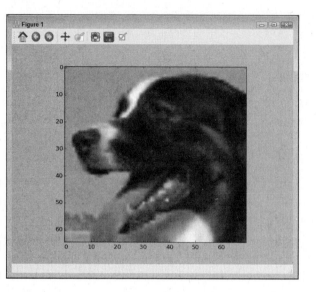

Figure 5-6:
Cropping
the image
makes it
smaller.

After you have all the images the right size, you need to flatten them. A dataset row is always a single dimension, not two dimensions. The image is currently an array of 30 pixels by 30 pixels, so you can't make it part of a dataset. The following code flattens `image3` so that it becomes an array of 900 elements that is stored in `image_row`.

```
image_row = image3.flatten()
print("data type: %s, shape: %s" %
      (type(image_row), image_row.shape))
```

Notice that the type is still a `numpy.ndarray`. You can add this array to a dataset and then use the dataset for analysis purposes. The size is 900 elements, as anticipated.

Managing Data from Relational Databases

Databases come in all sorts of forms. For example, AskSam (`http://asksam.en.softonic.com/`) is a kind of free-form textual database. However, the vast majority of data used by organizations rely on relational databases because these databases provide the means for organizing massive amounts of complex data in an organized manner that makes the data easy to manipulate. The goal of a database manager is to make data easy to manipulate. The focus of most data storage is to make data easy to retrieve.

Relational databases accomplish both the manipulation and data retrieval objectives with relative ease. However, because data storage needs come in all shapes and sizes for a wide range of computing platforms, there are many different relational database products. In fact, for the data scientist, the proliferation of different Database Management Systems (DBMSs) using various data layouts is one of the main problems you encounter with creating a comprehensive dataset for analysis.

The one common denominator between many relational databases is that they all rely on a form of the same language to perform data manipulation, which does make the data scientist's job easier. The Structured Query Language (SQL) lets you perform all sorts of management tasks in a relational database, retrieve data as needed, and even shape it in a particular way so that the need to perform additional shaping is unnecessary.

Creating a connection to a database can be a complex undertaking. For one thing, you need to know how to connect to that particular database. However, you can divide the process into smaller pieces. The first step is to gain access to the database engine. You use two lines of code similar to the following code (but the code presented here is not meant to execute and perform a task):

```
from sqlalchemy import create_engine
engine = create_engine('sqlite:///:memory:')
```

After you have access to an engine, you can use the engine to perform tasks specific to that DBMS. The output of a read method is always a `DataFrame` object that contains the requested data. To write data, you must create a `DataFrame` object or use an existing `DataFrame` object. You normally use these methods to perform most tasks:

- ✔ `read_sql_table()`: Reads data from a SQL table to a `DataFrame` object

- ✔ `read_sql_query()`: Reads data from a database using a SQL query to a `DataFrame` object

- ✔ `read_sql()`: Reads data from either a SQL table or query to a `DataFrame` object

- ✔ `DataFrame.to_sql()`: Writes the content of a `DataFrame` object to the specified tables in the database

The sqlalchemy library provides support for a broad range of SQL databases. The following list contains just a few of them:

- ✔ SQLite
- ✔ MySQL
- ✔ PostgreSQL
- ✔ SQL Server
- ✔ Other relational databases, such as those you can connect to using Open Database Connectivity (ODBC)

You can discover more about working with databases at `http://pandas.pydata.org/pandas-docs/dev/io.html#sql-queries`. The techniques that you discover in this book using the toy databases also work with relational databases.

Interacting with Data from NoSQL Databases

In addition to standard relational databases that rely on SQL, you find a wealth of databases of all sorts that don't have to rely on SQL. These Not only SQL (NoSQL) databases are used in large data storage scenarios in which the relational model can become overly complex or can break down in other ways. The databases generally don't use the relational model. Of course, you find fewer of these DBMSes used in the corporate environment because they require special handling and training. Still, some common DBMSes are used because they provide special functionality or meet unique requirements. The process is essentially the same for using NoSQL databases as it is for relational databases:

1. Import required database engine functionality.

2. Create a database engine.

3. Make any required queries using the database engine and the functionality supported by the DBMS.

The details vary quite a bit, and you need to know which library to use with your particular database product. For example, when working with MongoDB (`https://www.mongodb.org/`), you must obtain a copy of the PyMongo library (`https://api.mongodb.org/python/current/`) and use the `MongoClient` class to create the required engine. The MongoDB engine relies heavily on the `find()` function to locate data. Here's a pseudo-code example of a MongoDB session:

```
import pymongo
import pandas as pd
from pymongo import Connection
connection = Connection()
db = connection.database_name
input_data = db.collection_name
data = pd.DataFrame(list(input_data.find()))
```

Accessing Data from the Web

It would be incredibly difficult (perhaps impossible) to find an organization today that doesn't rely on some sort of web-based data. Most organizations use web services of some type. A *web service* is a kind of web application that provides a means to ask questions and receive answers. Web services usually host a number of input types. In fact, a particular web service may host entire groups of query inputs.

Another type of query system is the microservice. Unlike the web service, *microservices* have a specific focus and provide only one specific query input

APIs and other web entities

A data scientist may have a reason to rely on various web Application Programming Interfaces (APIs) to access and manipulate data. In fact, the focus of an analysis might be the API itself. This book doesn't discuss APIs in any detail because each API is unique, and APIs operate outside the normal scope of what a data scientist might do. For example, you might use a product such as jQuery (http://jquery.com/) to access data and manipulate it in various ways when working with a web application. However, the techniques for doing so are more along the lines of writing an application than employing a data science technique.

It's important to realize that APIs can be data sources and that you might need to use one to achieve some data input or data-shaping goals. In fact, you find many data entities that resemble APIs but don't appear in this book. Windows developers can create Component Object Model (COM) applications that output data onto the web that you could possibly use for analysis purposes. In fact, the number of potential sources is nearly endless. This book focuses on the sources that you use most often and in the most conventional manner. Keeping your eyes open for other possibilities, though, is always a good idea.

and output. Using microservices has specific benefits that are outside the scope of this book to address, but essentially they work like tiny web services, so that's how this book addresses them.

One of the most beneficial data access techniques to know when working with web data is accessing XML. All sorts of content types rely on XML, even some web pages. Working with web services and microservices means working with XML. With this in mind, the example in this section works with XML data found in the XMLData.xml file, shown in Figure 5-7. In this case, the file is simple and uses only a couple of levels. XML is hierarchical and can become quite a few levels deep.

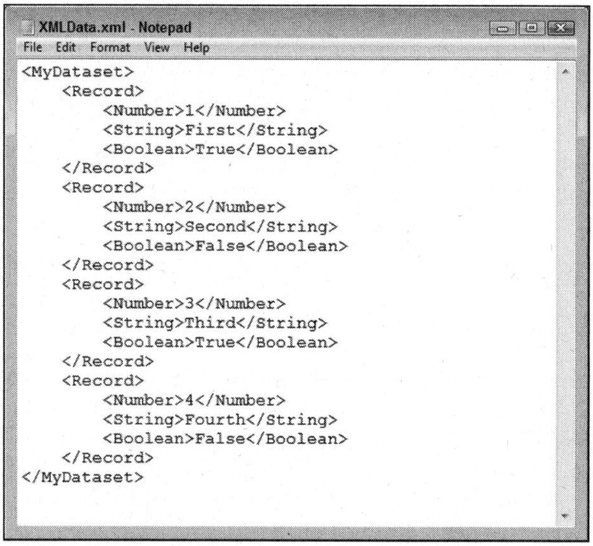

Figure 5-7:
XML is a hierarchical format that can become quite complex.

```
XMLData.xml - Notepad
File  Edit  Format  View  Help
<MyDataset>
    <Record>
        <Number>1</Number>
        <String>First</String>
        <Boolean>True</Boolean>
    </Record>
    <Record>
        <Number>2</Number>
        <String>Second</String>
        <Boolean>False</Boolean>
    </Record>
    <Record>
        <Number>3</Number>
        <String>Third</String>
        <Boolean>True</Boolean>
    </Record>
    <Record>
        <Number>4</Number>
        <String>Fourth</String>
        <Boolean>False</Boolean>
    </Record>
</MyDataset>
```

The technique for working with XML, even simple XML, can be a bit harder than anything else you've worked with so far. Here's the code for this example:

```
from lxml import objectify
import pandas as pd

xml = objectify.parse(open('XMLData.xml'))
root = xml.getroot()

df = pd.DataFrame(columns=('Number', 'String', 'Boolean'))

for i in range(0,4):
    obj = root.getchildren()[i].getchildren()
```

```
        row = dict(zip(['Number', 'String', 'Boolean'],
                    [obj[0].text, obj[1].text,
                    obj[2].text]))
        row_s = pd.Series(row)
        row_s.name = i
        df = df.append(row_s)

print df
```

The example begins by importing libraries and parsing the data file using the `objectify.parse()` method. Every XML document must contain a root node, which is `<MyDataset>` in this case. The root node encapsulates the rest of the content, and every node under it is a child. To do anything practical with the document, you must obtain access to the root node using the `getroot()` method.

The next step is to create an empty `DataFrame` object that contains the correct column names for each record entry: `Number`, `String`, and `Boolean`. As with all other pandas data handling, XML data handling relies on a `DataFrame`. The `for` loop fills the `DataFrame` with the four records from the XML file (each in a `<Record>` node).

The process looks complex but follows a logical order. The `obj` variable contains all the children for one `<Record>` node. These children are loaded into a dictionary object in which the keys are `Number`, `String`, and `Boolean` to match the `DataFrame` columns.

There is now a dictionary object that contains the row data. The code creates an actual row for the `DataFrame` next. It gives the row the value of the current `for` loop iteration. It then appends the row to the `DataFrame`. To see that everything worked as expected, the code prints the result, which looks like this:

```
   Number  String Boolean
0       1   First    True
1       2  Second   False
2       3   Third    True
3       4  Fourth   False
```

Chapter 6

Conditioning Your Data

*T*he characteristics, content, type, and other elements that define your data in its entirety is the data *shape*. The shape of your data determines the kinds of tasks you can perform with it. In order to make your data amenable to certain types of analysis, you must shape it into a different form. Think of the data as clay and you as the potter, because that's the sort of relationship that exists. However, instead of using your hands to shape the data, you rely on functions and algorithms to perform the task. This chapter helps you understand the tools you have available to shape data and the ramifications of shaping it.

Also in this chapter, you consider the problems associated with shaping. For example, you need to know what to do when data is missing from a dataset. It's important to shape the data correctly or you end up with an analysis that simply doesn't make sense. Likewise, some data types, such as dates, can present problems. Again, you need to tread carefully to ensure that you get the desired result so that the dataset becomes more useful and amenable to analysis of various sorts.

The goal of some types of data shaping is to create a larger dataset. In many cases, the data you need to perform an analysis doesn't appear in a single database or in a particular form. You need to shape the data and then combine it so that you have a single dataset in a known format before you can begin the analysis. Combining data successfully can be an art form because data often defies simple analysis or quick fixes.

You don't have to type the source code for this chapter in by hand. In fact, it's a lot easier if you use the downloadable source. The source code for this chapter appears in the P4DS4D; 06; Getting Your Data in Shape. ipynb source code file; see the Introduction for the location of this file.

Juggling between NumPy and pandas

There is no question that you need NumPy at all times. The pandas library is actually built on top of NumPy. However, you do need to make a choice between NumPy and pandas when performing tasks. You need the low-level functionality of NumPy to perform some tasks, but pandas makes things so much easier that you want to use it as often as possible. The following sections describe when to use each library in more detail.

Knowing when to use NumPy

It's essential to realize that developers built pandas on top of NumPy. As a result, every task you perform using pandas also goes through NumPy. To obtain the benefits of pandas, you pay a performance penalty that some testers say is 100 times slower than NumPy for a similar task (see http:// penandpants.com/2014/09/05/performance-of-pandas-series- vs-numpy-arrays/). Given that computer hardware can make up for a lot of performance differences today, the speed issue may not be a concern at times, but when speed is essential, NumPy is always the better choice.

Knowing when to use pandas

You use pandas to make writing code easier and faster. Because pandas does a lot of the work for you, you could make a case for saying that using pandas also reduces the potential for coding errors. The essential consideration, though, is that the pandas library provides rich time-series functionality, data alignment, NA-friendly statistics, groupby, merge, and join methods. Normally, you need to code these features when using NumPy, which means you keep reinventing the wheel.

It's all in the preparation

This book may seem to spend a lot of time massaging data and little time in actually analyzing it. However, the majority of a data scientist's time is actually spent preparing data because the data is seldom in any order to actually perform analysis. To prepare data for use, a data scientist must:

✔ Get the data

✔ Aggregate the data

✔ Create data subsets

✔ Clean the data

✔ Develop a single dataset by merging various datasets together

Fortunately, you don't need to die of boredom while wading your way through these various tasks. Using Python and the various libraries it provides makes the task a lot simpler, faster, and more efficient, which is the point of spending all of the time on seemingly mundane topics in these early chapters. The better you know how to use Python to speed your way through these repetitive tasks, the sooner you begin having fun performing various sorts of analysis on the data.

As the book progresses, you discover just how useful pandas can be performing such tasks as *binning* (a data preprocessing technique designed to reduce the effect of observational errors) and working with a *dataframe* (a two-dimensional labeled data structure with columns that can potentially contain different data types) so that you can calculate statistics on it. For example, in Chapter 8, you discover how to perform both discretization and binning. Chapter 13 shows actual binning examples, such as obtaining a frequency for each categorical variable of a dataset. In fact, many of the examples in Chapter 13 don't work without binning. In other words, don't worry too much right now about knowing precisely what binning is or why you need to use it — examples later in the book discuss the topic in detail. All you really need to know is that pandas does make your work considerably easier.

Validating Your Data

When it comes to data, no one really knows what a large database contains. Yes, everyone has seen bits and pieces of it, but when you consider the size of some databases, viewing it all would be physically impossible. Because you don't know what's in there, you can't be sure that your analysis will actually work as desired and provide valid results. In short, you must validate your data before you use it to ensure that the data is at least close to what you expect it to be. This means performing tasks such as removing duplicate records before you use the data for any sort of analysis (duplicates would unfairly weight the results).

However, you do need to consider what validation actually does for you. It doesn't tell you that the data is correct or that there won't be values outside the expected range. In fact, later chapters help you understand the techniques for handling these sorts of issues. What validation does is ensure that you can perform an analysis of the data and reasonably expect that analysis to succeed. Later, you need to perform additional massaging of the data to obtain the sort of results that you need in order to perform the task you set out to perform in the first place.

Figuring out what's in your data

Figuring out what your data contains is important because checking data by hand is sometimes simply impossible due to the number of observations and variables. In addition, hand verifying the content is time consuming, error prone, and, most important, really boring. Finding duplicates is important because you end up

- ✔ Spending more computational time to process duplicates, which slows your algorithms down.
- ✔ Obtaining false results because duplicates implicitly overweight the results. Because some entries appear more than once, the algorithm considers these entries more important.

As a data scientist, you want your data to enthrall you, so it's time to get it to talk to you — not figuratively, of course, but through the wonders of pandas, as shown in the following example:

```
from lxml import objectify
import pandas as pd

xml = objectify.parse(open('XMLData2.xml'))
root = xml.getroot()
df = pd.DataFrame(columns=('Number', 'String', 'Boolean'))

for i in range(0,4):
    obj = root.getchildren()[i].getchildren()
    row = dict(zip(['Number', 'String', 'Boolean'],
                   [obj[0].text, obj[1].text,
                    obj[2].text]))
    row_s = pd.Series(row)
    row_s.name = i
    df = df.append(row_s)

search = pd.DataFrame.duplicated(df)
```

```
print df
print
print search[search == True]
```

This example shows how to find duplicate rows. It relies on a modified version of the XMLData.xml file, XMLData2.xml, which contains a simple repeated row in it. A real data file contains thousands (or more) of records and possibly hundreds of repeats, but this simple example does the job. The example begins by reading the data file into memory using the same technique you explored in Chapter 5. It then places the data into a DataFrame.

At this point, your data is corrupted because it contains a duplicate row. However, you can get rid of the duplicated row by searching for it. The first task is to create a search object containing a list of duplicated rows by calling pd.DataFrame.duplicated(). The duplicated rows contain a True next to their row number.

Of course, now you have an unordered list of rows that are and aren't duplicated. The easiest way to determine which rows are duplicated is to create an index in which you use search == True as the expression. Following is the output you see from this example. Notice that row 1 is duplicated in the DataFrame output and that row 1 is also called out in the search results:

```
   Number  String Boolean
0       1   First    True
1       1   First    True
2       2  Second   False
3       3   Third    True
1     True
dtype: bool
```

Removing duplicates

To get a clean dataset, you want to remove the duplicates from it. Fortunately, you don't have to write any weird code to get the job done — pandas does it for you, as shown in the following example:

```
from lxml import objectify
import pandas as pd

xml = objectify.parse(open('XMLData2.xml'))
root = xml.getroot()
df = pd.DataFrame(columns=('Number', 'String', 'Boolean'))
```

```
for i in range(0,4):
    obj = root.getchildren()[i].getchildren()
    row = dict(zip(['Number', 'String', 'Boolean'],
                   [obj[0].text, obj[1].text,
                    obj[2].text]))
    row_s = pd.Series(row)
    row_s.name = i
    df = df.append(row_s)

print df.drop_duplicates()
```

As with the previous example, you begin by creating a DataFrame that contains the duplicate record. To remove the errant record, all you need to do is call `drop_duplicates()`. Here's the result you get.

```
  Number  String  Boolean
0      1   First     True
2      2  Second    False
3      3   Third     True
```

Creating a data map and data plan

You need to know about your dataset — that is, how it looks statically. A *data map* is an overview of the dataset. You use it to spot potential problems in your data, such as

✔ Redundant variables

✔ Possible errors

✔ Missing values

✔ Variable transformations

Checking for these problems goes into a *data plan*, which is a list of tasks you have to perform to ensure the integrity of your data. The following example shows a data map, A, with two datasets, B and C:

```
import pandas as pd

df = pd.DataFrame({'A': [0,0,0,0,0,1,1],
                   'B': [1,2,3,5,4,2,5],
                   'C': [5,3,4,1,1,2,3]})

a_group_desc = df.groupby('A').describe()
print a_group_desc
```

In this case, the data map uses 0s for the first series and 1s for the second series. The `groupby()` function places the datasets, B and C, into groups. To determine whether the data map is viable, you obtain statistics using `describe()`. What you end up with is a dataset B, series 0 and 1, and dataset C, series 0 and 1, as shown in the following output.

```
                  B          C
A
0  count    5.000000   5.000000
   mean     3.000000   2.800000
   std      1.581139   1.788854
   min      1.000000   1.000000
   25%      2.000000   1.000000
   50%      3.000000   3.000000
   75%      4.000000   4.000000
   max      5.000000   5.000000
1  count    2.000000   2.000000
   mean     3.500000   2.500000
   std      2.121320   0.707107
   min      2.000000   2.000000
   25%      2.750000   2.250000
   50%      3.500000   2.500000
   75%      4.250000   2.750000
   max      5.000000   3.000000
```

These statistics tell you about the two dataset series. The breakup of the two datasets using specific cases is the *data plan*. As you can see, the statistics tell you that this data plan may not be viable because some statistics are relatively far apart.

The output from `describe()` can be hard to read. The data is crammed together, but you can break it apart, as shown here:

```
unstacked = a_group_desc.unstack()
print unstacked
```

Using `unstack()` creates a new presentation. Here's the output formatted nicely so that you can see it better:

```
        B
     count mean        std min     25%   50%    75% max
A
0        5  3.0   1.581139   1    2.00   3.0   4.00   5
1        2  3.5   2.121320   2    2.75   3.5   4.25   5


        C
     count mean        std min     25%   50%    75% max
A
0        5  2.8   1.788854   1    1.00   3.0   4.00   5
1        2  2.5   0.707107   2    2.25   2.5   2.75   3
```

Of course, you may not want all the data that describe() provides. Perhaps you really just want to see the number of items in each series and their mean. Here's how you reduce the size of the information output:

```
print unstacked.loc[:,(slice(None),['count','mean']),]
```

Using loc lets you obtain specific columns. Here's the final output from the example showing just the information you absolutely need to make a decision:

```
          B              C
      count mean count mean
A
0         5  3.0      5  2.8
1         2  3.5      2  2.5
```

Manipulating Categorical Variables

In data science, a *categorical variable* is one that has a specific value from a limited selection of values. The number of values is usually fixed. Many developers will know categorical variables by the moniker *enumerations*. Each of the potential values that a categorical variable can assume is a *level*.

To understand how categorical variables work, say that you have a variable expressing the color of an object, such as a car, and that the user can select blue, red, or green. To express the car's color in a way that computers can represent and effectively compute, an application assigns each color a numeric value, so blue is 1, red is 2, and green is 3. Normally when you print each color, you see the value rather than the color.

If you use pandas.DataFrame (http://pandas.pydata.org/pandas-docs/dev/generated/pandas.DataFrame.html), you can still see the symbolic value (blue, red, and green), even though the computer stores it as a numeric value. Sometimes you need to rename and combine these named values to create new symbols. Symbolic variables are just a convenient way of representing and storing qualitative data.

When using categorical variables for machine learning, it's important to consider the algorithm used to manipulate the variables. Some algorithms, such as trees and ensembles of three, can work directly with the numeric variables behind the symbols. Other algorithms, such as linear and logistic regression and SVM, require that you encode the categorical values into binary variables. For example, if you have three levels for a color variable (blue, red, and green), you have to create three binary variables:

✔ One for blue (1 when the value is blue, 0 when it is not)

✔ One for red (1 when the value is red, 0 when it is not)

✔ One for green (1 when the value is green, 0 when it is not)

Creating categorical variables

Categorical variables have a specific number of values, which makes them incredibly valuable in performing a number of data science tasks. For example, imagine trying to find values that are out of range in a huge dataset. In this example, you see one method for creating a categorical variable and then using it to check whether some data falls within the specified limits.

```python
import pandas as pd

car_colors = pd.Series(['Blue', 'Red', 'Green'],
        dtype='category')

car_data = pd.Series(
    pd.Categorical(['Yellow', 'Green', 'Red', 'Blue',
            'Purple'],
                categories=car_colors, ordered=False))

find_entries = pd.isnull(car_data)

print car_colors
print
print car_data
print
print find_entries[find_entries == True]
```

Checking your version of pandas

The categorical variable examples in this section depend on your having a minimum version of pandas 0.15.0 installed on your system (using pandas 0.16.0 or above is actually better because it includes a large number of bug fixes). However, your version of Anaconda may have pandas version 0.14.1 installed instead. To check your version of pandas, type **import pandas as pd** and press Enter; then, type **print pd.version.version** and press Enter. You see the version number of pandas you have installed. If you have an older version, download the newest version from http://pandas.pydata.org/ and follow the instructions at http://pandas.pydata.org/pandas-docs/version/0.15.2/install.html to install it.

The example begins by creating a categorical variable, `car_colors`. The variable contains the values `Blue`, `Red`, and `Green` as colors that are acceptable for a car. Notice that you must specify a `dtype` property value of `category`.

The next step is to create another series. This one uses a list of actual car colors, named `car_data`, as input. Not all the car colors match the predefined acceptable values. When this problem occurs, pandas outputs Not a Number (`NaN`) instead of the car color.

Of course, you could search the list manually for the nonconforming cars, but the easiest method is to have pandas do the work for you. In this case, you ask pandas which entries are null using `isnull()` and place them in `find_entries`. You can then output just those entries that are actually null. Here's the output you see from the example:

```
0        Blue
1         Red
2       Green
dtype: category
Categories (3, object): [Blue < Green < Red]

0         NaN
1       Green
2         Red
3        Blue
4         NaN
dtype: category
Categories (3, object): [Blue, Red, Green]

0        True
4        True
dtype: bool
```

Looking at the list of `car_data` outputs, you can see that entries 0 and 4 equal `NaN`. The output from `find_entries` verifies this fact for you. If this were a large dataset, you could quickly locate and correct errant entries in the dataset before performing an analysis on it.

Renaming levels

There are times when the naming of the categories you use is inconvenient or otherwise wrong for a particular need. Fortunately, you can rename the categories as needed using the technique shown in the following example.

```
import pandas as pd

car_colors = pd.Series(['Blue', 'Red', 'Green'],
                        dtype='category')
```

```
car_data = pd.Series(
    pd.Categorical(
        ['Blue', 'Green', 'Red', 'Blue', 'Red'],
        categories=car_colors, ordered=False))


car_colors.cat.categories = ["Purple", "Yellow", "Mauve"]
car_data.cat.categories = car_colors

print car_data
```

All you really need to do is set the `cat.categories` property to a new value, as shown. Here is the output from this example:

```
0      Purple
1      Yellow
2       Mauve
3      Purple
4       Mauve
dtype: category
Categories (3, object): [Purple, Mauve, Yellow]
```

Combining levels

A particular categorical level might be too small to offer significant data for analysis. Perhaps there are only a few of the values, which may not be enough to create a statistical difference. In this case, combining several small categories might offer better analysis results. The following example shows how to combine categories:

```
import pandas as pd

car_colors = pd.Series(['Blue', 'Red', 'Green'],
                       dtype='category')
car_data = pd.Series(
    pd.Categorical(
        ['Blue', 'Green', 'Red', 'Green', 'Red', 'Green'],
        categories=car_colors, ordered=False))

car_data.cat.categories = ["Blue_Red", "Red", "Green"]
print car_data.ix[car_data.isin(['Red'])]

car_data.ix[car_data.isin(['Red'])] = 'Blue_Red'

print
print car_data
```

What this example shows you is that there is only one `Blue` item and only two `Red` items, but there are three `Green` items, which places `Green` in the majority. Combining `Blue` and `Red` together is a two-step process. First, you change the `Blue` category to the `Blue_Red` category so that when you see the output, you know that the two are combined. Then you change the `Red` entries to `Blue_Red`, which creates the combined category.

However, before you can change the `Red` entries to `Blue_Red` entries, you must find them. This is where a combination of calls to `isin()`, which locates the `Red` entries, and `ix[]`, which obtains their index, provides precisely what you need. The first `print` statement shows the result of using this combination. Here's the output from this example.

```
2       Red
4       Red
dtype: category
Categories (3, object): [Blue_Red, Red, Green]

0       Blue_Red
1          Green
2       Blue_Red
3          Green
4       Blue_Red
5          Green
dtype: category
Categories (3, object): [Blue_Red, Red, Green]
```

Notice that there are now three `Blue_Red` entries and three `Green` entries. The `Blue` category no longer exists and the `Red` category is no longer in use. The result is that the levels are now combined as expected.

Dealing with Dates in Your Data

Dates can present problems in data. For one thing, dates are stored as numeric values. However, the precise value of the number depends on the representation for the particular platform and could even depend on the users' preferences. For example, Excel users can choose to start dates in 1900 or 1904 (`https://support.microsoft.com/en-us/kb/180162`). The numeric encoding for each is different, so the same date can have two numeric values depending on the starting date.

In addition to problems of representation, you also need to consider how to work with time values. Creating a time value format that represents a value the user can understand is hard. For example, you might need to use

Greenwich Mean Time (GMT) in some situations but a local time zone in others. Transforming between various times is also problematic. With this in mind, the following sections provide you with details on dealing with time issues.

Formatting date and time values

Obtaining the correct date and time representation can make performing analysis a lot easier. For example, you often have to change the representation to obtain a correct sorting of values. Python provides two common methods of formatting date and time. The first technique is to call `str()`, which simply turns a `datetime` value into a string without any formatting. The `strftime()` function requires more work because you must define how you want the `datetime` value to appear after conversion. When using `strftime()`, you must provide a string containing special directives that define the formatting. You can find a listing of these directives at `http://strftime.org/`.

Now that you have some idea of how time and date conversions work, it's time to see an example. The following example creates a `datetime` object and then converts it into a string using two different approaches:

```
import datetime as dt

now = dt.datetime.now()

print str(now)
print now.strftime('%a, %d %B %Y')
```

In this case, you can see that using `str()` is the easiest approach. However, as shown by the following output, it may not provide the output you need. Using `strftime()` is infinitely more flexible.

```
2015-04-16 17:26:45.986000
Thu, 16 April 2015
```

Using the right time transformation

Time zones and differences in local time can cause all sorts of problems when performing analysis. For that matter, some types of calculations simply require a time shift in order to get the right results. No matter what the reason, you may need to transform one time into another time at some point.

The following examples show some techniques you can employ to perform the task.

```
import datetime as dt

now = dt.datetime.now()
timevalue = now + dt.timedelta(hours=2)

print now.strftime('%H:%M:%S')
print timevalue.strftime('%H:%M:%S')
print timevalue - now
```

The `timedelta()` function makes the time transformation straightforward. You can use any of these parameter names with `timedelta()` to change a time and date value:

✔ days

✔ seconds

✔ microseconds

✔ milliseconds

✔ minutes

✔ hours

✔ weeks

You can also manipulate time by performing addition or subtraction on time values. You can even subtract two time values to determine the difference between them. Here's the output from this example:

```
17:44:40
19:44:40
2:00:00
```

Notice that `now` is the local time, `timevalue` is two time zones different from this one, and there is a two-hour difference between the two times. You can perform all sorts of transformations using these techniques to ensure that your analysis always shows precisely the time-oriented values you need.

Dealing with Missing Data

Sometimes the data you receive is missing information in specific fields. For example, a customer record might be missing an age. If enough records are missing entries, any analysis you perform will be skewed and the results of the analysis weighted in an unpredictable manner. Having a strategy for dealing with missing data is important. The following sections give you some ideas on how to work through these issues and produce better results.

Finding the missing data

It's essential to find missing data in your dataset to avoid getting incorrect results from your analysis. The following code shows how you could obtain a listing of missing values without too much effort.

```
import pandas as pd
import numpy as np

s = pd.Series([1, 2, 3, np.NaN, 5, 6, None])

print s.isnull()

print
print s[s.isnull()]
```

A dataset could represent missing data in several ways. In this example, you see missing data represented as np.NaN (NumPy Not a Number) and the Python None value.

Use the isnull() method to detect the missing values. The output shows True when the value is missing. By adding an index into the dataset, you obtain just the entries that are missing. The example shows the following output:

```
0     False
1     False
2     False
3      True
4     False
5     False
6      True
dtype: bool

3    NaN
6    NaN
dtype: float64
```

Encoding missingness

After you figure out that your dataset is missing information, you need to consider what to do about it. The three possibilities are to ignore the issue, fill in the missing items, or remove (drop) the missing entries from the dataset. Ignoring the problem could lead to all sorts of problems for your analysis, so it's the option you use least often. The following example shows one technique for filling in missing data or dropping the errant entries from the dataset:

```
import pandas as pd
import numpy as np

s = pd.Series([1, 2, 3, np.NaN, 5, 6, None])

print s.fillna(int(s.mean()))
print
print s.dropna()
```

The two methods of interest are `fillna()`, which fills in the missing entries, and `dropna()`, which drops the missing entries. When using `fillna()`, you must provide a value to use for the missing data. This example uses the mean of all the values, but you could choose a number of other approaches. Here's the output from this example:

```
0    1
1    2
2    3
3    3
4    5
5    6
6    3
dtype: float64

0    1
1    2
2    3
4    5
5    6
dtype: float64
```

Working with a series is straightforward because the dataset is so simple. When working with a `DataFrame`, however, the problem becomes significantly more complicated. You still have the option of dropping the entire row. When a column is sparsely populated, you might drop the column instead. Filling in the data also becomes more complex because you must consider the dataset as a whole, in addition to the needs of the individual feature.

Imputing missing data

The previous section hints at the process of imputing missing data (ascribing characteristics based on how the data is used). The technique you use depends on the sort of data you're working with. For example, when working with a tree ensemble (you can find discussions of trees in the "Performing Hierarchical Clustering" section of Chapter 15 and the "Starting with a Plain Decision Tree" section of Chapter 20), you may simply replace missing values with a –1 and rely on the imputer (a transformer algorithm used to complete missing values) to define the best possible value for the missing data. The following example shows a technique you can use to impute missing data values:

```
import pandas as pd
import numpy as np
from sklearn.preprocessing import Imputer

s = pd.Series([1, 2, 3, np.NaN, 5, 6, None])

imp = Imputer(missing_values='NaN',
              strategy='mean', axis=0)

imp.fit([1, 2, 3, 4, 5, 6, 7])

x = pd.Series(imp.transform(s).tolist()[0])

print x
```

In this example, s is missing some values. The code creates an `Imputer` to replace these missing values. The `missing_values` parameter defines what to look for, which is NaN. You set the `axis` parameter to 0 to impute along columns and 1 to impute along rows. The `strategy` parameter defines how to replace the missing values (you can discover more about the Imputer parameters at http://scikit-learn.org/stable/modules/generated/sklearn.preprocessing.Imputer.html):

- ✔ mean: Replaces the values by using the mean along the axis

- ✔ median: Replaces the values by using the medium along the axis

- ✔ most_frequent: Replaces the values by using the most frequent value along the axis

Before you can impute anything, you must provide statistics for the Imputer to use by calling `fit()`. The code then calls `transform()` on s to fill in the missing values. However, the output is no longer a series. To create a series, you must convert the Imputer output to a list and use the resulting list as input to `Series()`. Here's the result of the process with the missing values filled in:

```
0    1
1    2
2    3
3    4
```

```
4    5
5    6
6    7
dtype: float64
```

Slicing and Dicing: Filtering and Selecting Data

You may not need to work with all the data in a dataset. In fact, looking at just one particular column might be beneficial, such as age, or a set of rows with a significant amount of information. You perform two steps to obtain just the data you need to perform a particular task:

1. Filter rows to create a subject of the data that meets the criterion you select (such as all the people between the ages of 5 and 10).

2. Select data columns that contain the data you need to analyze. For example, you probably don't need the individuals' names unless you want to perform some analysis based on name.

The act of slicing and dicing data, gives you a subset of the data suitable for analysis. The following sections describe various ways to obtain specific pieces of data to meet particular needs.

Slicing rows

Slicing can occur in multiple ways when working with data, but the technique of interest in this section is to slice data from a row of 2D or 3D data. A 2D array may contain temperatures (x axis) over a specific timeframe (y axis). Slicing a row would mean seeing the temperatures at a specific time. In some cases, you might associate rows with cases in a dataset.

A 3D array might include an axis for place (x axis), product (y axis), and time (z axis) so that you can see sales for items over time. Perhaps you want to track whether sales of an item are increasing, and specifically where they are increasing. Slicing a row would mean seeing all the sales for one specific product for all locations at any time. The following example demonstrates how to perform this task:

```
x = np.array([[[1, 2, 3],   [4, 5, 6],   [7, 8, 9],],
              [[11,12,13],   [14,15,16],  [17,18,19],],
              [[21,22,23],   [24,25,26],  [27,28,29]]])

x[1]
```

In this case, the example builds a 3D array. It then slices row 1 of that array to produce the following output:

```
array([[11, 12, 13],
       [14, 15, 16],
       [17, 18, 19]])
```

Slicing columns

Using the examples from the previous section, slicing columns would obtain data at a 90-degree angle from rows. In other words, when working with the 2D array, you would want to see the times at which specific temperatures occurred. Likewise, you might want to see the sales of all products for a specific location at any time when working with the 3D array. In some cases, you might associate columns with features in a dataset. The following example demonstrates how to perform this task using the same array as in the previous section:

```
x = np.array([[[1, 2, 3],    [4, 5, 6],    [7, 8, 9],],
              [[11,12,13],    [14,15,16],   [17,18,19],],
              [[21,22,23],    [24,25,26],   [27,28,29]]])

x[:,1]
```

Notice that the indexing now occurs at two levels. The first index refers to the row. Using the colon (:) for the row means to use all the rows. The second index refers to a column. In this case, the output will contain column 1. Here's the output you see:

```
array([[ 4,   5,   6],
       [14,  15,  16],
       [24,  25,  26]])
```

This is a 3D array. Therefore, each of the columns contains all the z axis elements. What you see is every row — 0 through 2 for column 1 with every z axis element 0 through 2 for that column.

Dicing

The act of dicing a dataset means to perform both row and column slicing such that you end up with a data wedge. For example, when working with the 3D array, you might want to see the sales of a specific product in a specific location at any time. The following example demonstrates how to perform this task using the same array as in the previous two sections:

```
x = np.array([[[1, 2, 3],   [4, 5, 6],   [7, 8, 9],],
               [[11,12,13],  [14,15,16],  [17,18,19],],
               [[21,22,23],  [24,25,26],  [27,28,29]]])

print x[1,1]
print x[:,1,1]
print x[1,:,1]
print
print x[1:2, 1:2]
```

This example dices the array in four different ways. First, you get row 1, column 1. Of course, what you may actually want is column 1, z axis 1. If that's not quite right, you could always request row 1, z axis 1 instead. Then again, you may want rows 1 and 2 of columns 1 and 2. Here's the output of all four requests:

```
[14 15 16]
[ 5 15 25]
[12 15 18]

[[[14 15 16]
  [17 18 19]]

 [[24 25 26]
  [27 28 29]]]
```

Concatenating and Transforming

Data used for data science purposes seldom comes in a neat package. You may need to work with multiple databases in various locations — each of which has its own data format. It's impossible to perform analysis on such disparate sources of information with any accuracy. To make the data useful, you must create a single dataset (by *concatenating*, or combining, the data from various sources).

Part of the process is to ensure that each field you create for the combined dataset has the same characteristics. For example, an age field in one database might appear as a string, but another database could use an integer for the same field. For the fields to work together, they must appear as the same type of information.

The following sections help you understand the process involved in concatenating and transforming data from various sources to create a single dataset. After you have a single dataset from these sources, you can begin to perform tasks such as analysis on the data. Of course, the trick is to create a single dataset that truly represents the data in all those disparate datasets — modifying the data would result in skewed results.

Adding new cases and variables

You often find a need to combine datasets in various ways or even to add new information for the sake of analysis purposes. The result is a combined dataset that includes either new cases or variables. The following example shows techniques for performing both tasks:

```
import pandas as pd

df = pd.DataFrame({'A': [2,3,1],
                   'B': [1,2,3],
                   'C': [5,3,4]})

df1 = pd.DataFrame({'A': [4],
                    'B': [4],
                    'C': [4]})

df = df.append(df1)
df = df.reset_index(drop=True)
print df

df.loc[df.last_valid_index() + 1] = [5, 5, 5]
print
print df

df2 = pd.DataFrame({'D': [1, 2, 3, 4, 5]})

df = pd.DataFrame.join(df, df2)
print
print df
```

The easiest way to add more data to an existing DataFrame is to rely on the append() method. You can also use the concat() method (a technique shown in Chapter 13). In this case, the three cases found in df are added to the single case found in df1. To ensure that the data is appended as anticipated, the columns in df and df1 must match. When you append two DataFrame objects in this manner, the new DataFrame contains the old index values. Use the reset_index() method to create a new index to make accessing cases easier.

You can also add another case to an existing `DataFrame` by creating the new case directly. Any time you add a new entry at a position that is one greater than the `last_valid_index()`, you get a new case as a result.

Sometimes you need to add a new variable (column) to the `DataFrame`. In this case, you rely on `join()` to perform the task. The resulting `DataFrame` will match cases with the same index value, so indexing is important. In addition, unless you want blank values, the number of cases in both `DataFrame` objects must match. Here's the output from this example:

```
   A  B  C
0  2  1  5
1  3  2  3
2  1  3  4
3  4  4  4

   A  B  C
0  2  1  5
1  3  2  3
2  1  3  4
3  4  4  4
4  5  5  5

   A  B  C  D
0  2  1  5  1
1  3  2  3  2
2  1  3  4  3
3  4  4  4  4
4  5  5  5  5
```

Removing data

At some point, you may need to remove cases or variables from a dataset because they aren't required for your analysis. In both cases, you rely on the `drop()` method to perform the task. The difference in removing cases or variables is in how you describe what to remove, as shown in the following example:

```python
import pandas as pd

df = pd.DataFrame({'A': [2,3,1],
                   'B': [1,2,3],
                   'C': [5,3,4]})

df = df.drop(df.index[[1]])
print df

df = df.drop('B', 1)
print
print df
```

The example begins by removing a case from `df`. Notice how the code relies on an index to describe what to remove. You can remove just one case (as shown), ranges of cases, or individual cases separated by commas. The main concern is to ensure that you have the correct index numbers for the cases you want to remove.

Removing a column is different. This example shows how to remove a column using a column name. You can also remove a column by using an index. In both cases, you must specify an axis as part of the removal process (normally 1). Here's the output from this example:

```
   A  B  C
0  2  1  5
2  1  3  4

   A  C
0  2  5
2  1  4
```

Sorting and shuffling

Sorting and shuffling are two ends of the same goal — to manage data order. In the first case, you put the data into order, while in the second, you remove any systematic patterning from the order. In general, you don't sort datasets for the purpose of analysis because doing so can cause you to get incorrect results. However, you might want to sort data for presentation purposes. The following example shows both sorting and shuffling:

```
import pandas as pd
import numpy as np

df = pd.DataFrame({'A': [2,1,2,3,3,5,4],
                   'B': [1,2,3,5,4,2,5],
                   'C': [5,3,4,1,1,2,3]})

df = df.sort_index(by=['A', 'B'], ascending=[True, True])
df = df.reset_index(drop=True)
print df

index = df.index.tolist()
np.random.shuffle(index)
df = df.ix[index]
df = df.reset_index(drop=True)
print
print df
```

It turns out that sorting the data is a bit easier than shuffling it. To sort the data, you use the `sort_index()` method and define which columns to use for indexing purposes. You can also determine whether the index is in ascending or descending order. Make sure to always call `reset_index()` when you're done so that the index appears in order for analysis or other purposes.

To shuffle the data, you first acquire the current index using `df.index.tolist()` and place it in `index`. A call to `random.shuffle()` creates a new order for the index. You then apply the new order to `df` using `ix[]`. As always, you call `reset_index()` to finalize the new order. Here's the output from this example:

```
   A  B  C
0  1  2  3
1  2  1  5
2  2  3  4
3  3  4  1
4  3  5  1
5  4  5  3
6  5  2  2

   A  B  C
0  2  3  4
1  3  5  1
2  3  4  1
3  1  2  3
4  4  5  3
5  5  2  2
6  2  1  5
```

Aggregating Data at Any Level

Aggregation is the process of combining or grouping data together into a set, bag, or list. The data may or may not be alike. However, in most cases, an aggregation function combines several rows together statistically using algorithms such as average, count, maximum, median, minimum, mode, or sum. There are several reasons to aggregate data:

✔ Make it easier to analyze

✔ Reduce the ability of anyone to deduce the data of an individual from the dataset for privacy or other reasons

✔ Create a combined data element from one data source that matches a combined data element in another source

The most important use of data aggregation is to promote anonymity in order to meet legal or other concerns. Sometimes even data that should be anonymous turns out to provide identification of an individual using the proper analysis techniques. For example, researchers have found that it's possible to identify individuals based on just three credit card purchases (see http://www.computerworld.com/article/2877935/how-three-small-credit-card-transactions-could-reveal-your-identity.html for details). Here's an example that shows how to perform aggregation tasks:

```
import pandas as pd

df = pd.DataFrame({'Map': [0,0,0,1,1,2,2],
                   'Values': [1,2,3,5,4,2,5]})

df['S'] = df.groupby('Map')['Values'].transform(np.sum)
df['M'] = df.groupby('Map')['Values'].transform(np.mean)
df['V'] = df.groupby('Map')['Values'].transform(np.var)

print df
```

In this case, you have two initial features for this `DataFrame`. The values in `Map` define which elements in `Values` belong together. For example, when calculating a sum for `Map` index 0, you use the `Values` 1, 2, and 3.

To perform the aggregation, you must first call `groupby()` to group the `Map` values. You then index into `Values` and rely on `transform()` to create the aggregated data using one of several algorithms found in NumPy, such as `np.sum`. Here are the results of this calculation:

```
   Map  Values  S    M    V
0   0      1    6  2.0  1.0
1   0      2    6  2.0  1.0
2   0      3    6  2.0  1.0
3   1      5    9  4.5  0.5
4   1      4    9  4.5  0.5
5   2      2    7  3.5  4.5
6   2      5    7  3.5  4.5
```

Chapter 7

Shaping Data

Chapter 6 demonstrates techniques for working with data as an entity — as something you work with in Python. However, data doesn't exist in a vacuum. It doesn't just suddenly appear within Python for absolutely no reason at all. As demonstrated in Chapter 5, you load the data. However, loading may not be enough — you may have to shape the data as part of loading it. That's the purpose of this chapter. You discover how to work with a variety of container types in a way that makes it possible to load data from a number of complex container types, such as HTML pages. In fact, you even work with graphics, images, and sounds.

As you progress through the book, you discover that data takes all kinds of forms and shapes. As far as the computer is concerned, data consists of 0s and 1s. Humans give the data meaning by formatting, storing, and interpreting it in a certain way. The same group of 0s and 1s could be a number, date, or text, depending on the interpretation. The data container provides clues as to how to interpret the data, so that's why this chapter is so important to you as a data scientist using Python to discover data patterns. You find that you can discover patterns in places where you might have thought patterns couldn't exist.

You don't have to type the source code for this chapter manually. In fact, it's a lot easier if you use the downloadable source (see the Introduction for download instructions). The source code for this chapter appears in the `P4DS4D; 07; Shaping Data.ipynb` source code file.

Working with HTML Pages

HTML pages contain data in a hierarchical format. You often find HTML content in a strict HTML form or as XML. The HTML form can present problems because it doesn't always necessarily follow strict formatting rules. XML does follow strict formatting rules because of the standards used to define it, which makes it easier to parse. However, in both cases, you use similar techniques to parse a page. The first section that follows describes how to parse HTML pages in general.

Sometimes you don't need all the data on a page. Instead you need specific data, which is where XPath comes into play. You can use XPath to locate specific data on the HTML page and extract it for your particular needs.

Parsing XML and HTML

Simply extracting data from an XML file as you do in Chapter 5 may not be enough. The data may not be in the correct format. Using the approach in Chapter 5, you end up with a `DataFrame` containing three columns of type `str`. Obviously, you can't perform much data manipulation with strings. The following example shapes the XML data from Chapter 5 to create a new DataFrame containing just the `<Number>` and `<Boolean>` elements in the correct format.

```
from lxml import objectify
import pandas as pd
from distutils import util

xml = objectify.parse(open('XMLData.xml'))
root = xml.getroot()
df = pd.DataFrame(columns=('Number', 'Boolean'))

for i in range(0,4):
    obj = root.getchildren()[i].getchildren()
    row = dict(zip(['Number', 'Boolean'],
                   [obj[0].pyval,
                    bool(util.strtobool(obj[2].text))]))
    row_s = pd.Series(row)
    row_s.name = obj[1].text
    df = df.append(row_s)

print type(df.ix['First']['Number'])
print type(df.ix['First']['Boolean'])
```

Obtaining a numeric value from the `<Number>` element consists of using the `pyval` output, rather than the `text` output. The result isn't an `int`, but it is numeric.

The conversion of the <Boolean> element is a little harder. You must convert the string to a numeric value using the strtobool() function in distutils.util. The output is a 0 for False values and a 1 for True values. However, that's still not a Boolean value. To create a Boolean value, you must convert the 0 or 1 using bool().

This example also shows how to access individual values in the DataFrame. Notice that the name property now uses the <String> element value for easy access. You provide an index value using ix and then access the individual feature using a second index. The output from this example is

```
<type 'numpy.float64'>
<type 'bool'>
```

Using XPath for data extraction

Using XPath to extract data from your dataset can greatly reduce the complexity of your code and potentially make it faster as well. The following example shows an XPath version of the example in the previous section. Notice that this version is shorter and doesn't require the use of a for loop.

```
from lxml import objectify
import pandas as pd
from distutils import util

xml = objectify.parse(open('XMLData.xml'))
root = xml.getroot()

data = zip(map(int, root.xpath('Record/Number')),
           map(bool, map(util.strtobool,
               map(str, root.xpath('Record/Boolean')))))

df = pd.DataFrame(data,
                  columns=('Number', 'Boolean'),
                  index=map(str,
                      root.xpath('Record/String')))

print df
print type(df.ix['First']['Number'])
print type(df.ix['First']['Boolean'])
```

The example begins just like the previous example, with the importing of data and obtaining of the root node. At this point, the example creates a data object that contains record number and Boolean value pairs. Because the XML file entries are all strings, you must use the map() function to convert the strings to the appropriate values. Working with the record number is straightforward — all you do is map it to an int. The xpath() function accepts a path from the root node to the data you need, which is 'Record/ Number' in this case.

Mapping the Boolean value is a little more difficult. As in the previous section, you must use the `util.strtobool()` function to convert the string Boolean values to a number that `bool()` can convert to a Boolean equivalent. However, if you try to perform just a double mapping, you'll encounter an error message saying that lists don't include a required function, `tolower()`. To overcome this obstacle, you perform a triple mapping and convert the data to a string using the `str()` function first.

Creating the `DataFrame` is different, too. Instead of adding individual rows, you add all the rows at one time by using `data`. Setting up the column names is the same as before. However, now you need some way of adding the row names, as in the previous example. This task is accomplished by setting the `index` parameter to a mapped version of the `xpath()` output for the `'Record/String'` path. Here's the output you can expect:

```
        Number Boolean
First        1    True
Second       2   False
Third        3    True
Fourth       4   False
<type 'numpy.int64'>
<type 'numpy.bool_'>
```

Working with Raw Text

Even though it might seem as if raw text wouldn't present a problem in parsing because it doesn't contain any special formatting, you do have to consider how the text is stored and whether it contains special words within it. The multiple forms of Unicode can present interpretation problems that you need to consider as you work through the text. Using regular expressions can help you locate specific information within a raw-text file. You can use regular expressions for both data cleaning and pattern matching. The following sections help you understand the techniques used to shape raw-text files.

Dealing with Unicode

Text files are pure text — this much is certain. The way the text is encoded can differ. For example, a character can use either seven or eight bits for encoding purposes. The use of special characters can differ as well. In short, the interpretation of bits used to create characters differs from encoding to encoding. You can see a host of encodings at `http://www.i18nguy.com/unicode/codepages.html`.

Sometimes you need to work with encodings other than the default encoding set within the Python environment. When working with Python 3.*x*, you must rely on Universal Transformation Format 8-bit (UTF-8) as the encoding used to read and write files. This environment is always set for UTF-8, and trying to change it causes an error message. However, when working with Python 2.*x*, you can choose other encodings. In this case, the default encoding is the American Standard Code for Information Interchange (ASCII), but you can change it to some other encoding.

You can use this technique in any IPython Notebook file, but you won't actually see output from it. In order to see output, you need to work with the IPython prompt. The following steps help you see how to deal with Unicode characters, but only when working with Python 2.*x* (these steps will cause errors in the Python 3.*x* environment).

1. Open a copy of the IPython command prompt.

You see the IPython window.

2. Type the following code, pressing Enter after each line.

```
import sys
sys.getdefaultencoding()
```

You see the default encoding for Python, which is ascii in most cases.

3. Type reload(sys) **and press Enter.**

Python reloads the sys module and makes a special function available.

4. Type sys.setdefaultencoding('utf-8') **and press Enter.**

Python does change the encoding, but you won't know that for certain until after the next step.

5. Type sys.getdefaultencoding() **and press Enter.**

You see that the default encoding has now changed to utf-8.

Changing the default encoding at the wrong time and in the incorrect way can prevent you from performing tasks such as importing modules. Make sure to test your code carefully and completely to ensure that any change in the default encoding won't affect your ability to run the application. Good additional articles to read on this topic appear at `http://blog.notdot.net/2010/07/Getting-unicode-right-in-Python` and `http://web.archive.org/web/20120722170929/http://boodebr.org/main/python/all-about-python-and-unicode`.

Stemming and removing stop words

Stemming is the process of reducing words to their stem (or root) word. This task isn't the same as understanding that some words come from Latin or other roots, but instead makes like words equal to each other for the purpose of comparison or sharing. For example, the words *cats*, *catty*, and *catlike* all have the stem *cat*. The act of stemming helps you analyze sentences by tokenizing them.

Removing suffixes to create stem words and generally tokenizing sentences are only two parts of the process, however, of creating something like a natural language interface. Languages include a great number of glue words that don't mean much to a computer but have significant meaning to humans, such as *a*, *as*, *the*, *that*, and so on in English. These short, less useful words are *stop* words. Sentences don't make sense without them to humans, but for your computer, they can act as a means of stopping sentence analysis.

The act of stemming and removing stop words simplifies the text and reduces the number of textual elements so that just the essential elements remain. In addition, you keep just the terms that are nearest to the true sense of the phrase. By reducing phrases in such a fashion, a computational algorithm can work faster and process the text more effectively.

This example requires the use of the Natural Language Toolkit (NLTK), which Anaconda (see Chapter 3 for details on Anaconda) doesn't install by default. To use this example, you must download and install NLTK using the instructions found at `http://www.nltk.org/install.html` for your platform. Make certain that you install the NLTK for whatever version of Python you're using for this book when you have multiple versions of Python installed on your system. After you install NLTK, you must also install the packages associated with it. The instructions at `http://www.nltk.org/data.html` tell you how to perform this task (install all the packages to ensure you have everything).

The following example demonstrates how to perform stemming and remove stop words from a sentence. It begins by training an algorithm to perform the required analysis using a test sentence. Afterward, the example checks a second sentence for words that appear in the first.

```
import sklearn.feature_extraction.text as ext
from nltk import word_tokenize
from nltk.stem.porter import PorterStemmer

stemmer = PorterStemmer()

def stem_tokens(tokens, stemmer):
    stemmed = []
    for item in tokens:
        stemmed.append(stemmer.stem(item))
```

```
    return stemmed

def tokenize(text):
    tokens = word_tokenize(text)
    stems = stem_tokens(tokens, stemmer)
    return stems

vocab = ['Sam loves swimming so he swims all the time']
vect = ext.CountVectorizer(tokenizer=tokenize,
                           stop_words='english')
vec = vect.fit(vocab)

sentence1 = vec.transform(['George loves swimming too!'])

print vec.get_feature_names()
print sentence1.toarray()
```

At the outset, the example creates a vocabulary using a test sentence and places it in vocab. It then creates a `CountVectorizer`, `vect`, to hold a list of stemmed words, but excludes the stop words. The `tokenizer` parameter defines the function used to stem the words. The `stop_words` parameter refers to a pickle file that contains stop words for a specific language, which is English in this case. There are also files for other languages, such as French and German. (You can see other parameters for the `CountVectorizer()` at `http://scikit-learn.org/stable/modules/generated/sklearn.feature_extraction.text.CountVectorizer.html`.) The vocabulary is fitted into another `CountVectorizer`, `vec`, which is used to perform the actual transformation on a test sentence using the `transform()` function. Here's the output from this example.

```
[u'love', u'sam', u'swim', u'time']
[[1 0 1 0]]
```

The first output shows the stemmed words. Notice that the list contains only *swim*, not *swimming* and *swims*. All the stop words are missing as well. For example, you don't see the words *so*, *he*, *all*, or *the*.

The second output shows how many times each stemmed word appears in the test sentence. In this case, a *love* variant appears once and a *swim* variant appears once as well. The words *sam* and *time* don't appear in the second sentence, so those values are set to 0.

Introducing regular expressions

Regular expressions present the data scientist with an interesting array of tools for parsing raw text. At first, it may seem daunting to figure out precisely how regular expressions work. However, sites such as `http://regexr.com/` let you play with regular expressions so that you can see how the use of various expressions performs specific types of pattern matching. Of course, the first requirement is to discover *pattern matching*, which is the use of special characters to tell a parsing engine what to find in the raw text file. Table 7-1 provides a list of pattern-matching characters and tells you how to use them.

Table 7-1	Pattern-Matching Characters Used in Python
Character	*Interpretation*
(re)	Groups regular expressions and remembers the matched text
(?: re)	Groups regular expressions without remembering matched text
(?#...)	Indicates a comment, which isn't processed
re?	Matches 0 or 1 occurrence of preceding expression (but no more than 0 or 1 occurrence)
re*	Matches 0 or more occurrences of the preceding expression
re+	Matches 1 or more occurrences of the preceding expression
(?> re)	Matches an independent pattern without backtracking
.	Matches any single character except the newline (\n) character (adding the m option allows it to match the newline character as well)
[^...]	Matches any single character or range of characters not found within the brackets
[...]	Matches any single character or range of characters that appears within the brackets
re{ n, m}	Matches at least n and at most m occurrences of the preceding expression
\n, \t, etc.	Matches control characters such as newlines (\n), carriage returns (\r), and tabs (\t)
\d	Matches digits (which is equivalent to using [0-9])
a|b	Matches either a or b
re{ n}	Matches exactly the number of occurrences of preceding expression specified by n
re{ n, }	Matches n or more occurrences of the preceding expression
\D	Matches nondigits
\S	Matches nonwhitespace
\B	Matches nonword boundaries
\W	Matches nonword characters

Character	Interpretation
`\1...\9`	Matches nth grouped subexpression
`\10`	Matches nth grouped subexpression if it matched already (otherwise the pattern refers to the octal representation of a character code)
`\A`	Matches the beginning of a string
`^`	Matches the beginning of the line
`\z`	Matches the end of a string
`\Z`	Matches the end of string (when a newline exists, it matches just before newline)
`$`	Matches the end of the line
`\G`	Matches the point where the last match finished
`\s`	Matches whitespace (which is equivalent to using [\t\n\r\f])
`\b`	Matches word boundaries when outside the brackets Matches the backspace (0x08) when inside the brackets
`\w`	Matches word characters
`(?= re)`	Specifies a position using a pattern (this pattern doesn't have a range)
`(?! re)`	Specifies a position using pattern negation (this pattern doesn't have a range)
`(?-imx)`	Toggles the i, m, or x options temporarily off within a regular expression (when this pattern appears in parentheses, only the area within the parentheses is affected)
`(?imx)`	Toggles the i, m, or x options temporarily on within a regular expression (when this pattern appears in parentheses, only the area within the parentheses is affected)
`(?-imx: re)`	Toggles the i, m, or x options within parentheses temporarily off
`(?imx: re)`	Toggles the i, m, or x options within parentheses temporarily on

Using regular expressions helps you manipulate complex text before using other techniques described in this chapter. In the following example, you see how to extract a telephone number from a sentence no matter where the telephone number appears. This sort of manipulation is helpful when you have to work with text of various origins and in irregular format. You can see some additional telephone number manipulation routines at `http://www.diveintopython.net/regular_expressions/phone_numbers.html`. The big thing is that this example helps you understand how to extract any text you need from text you don't.

```
import re

data1 = 'My phone number is: 800-555-1212.'
data2 = '800-555-1234 is my phone number.'

pattern = re.compile(r'(\d{3})-(\d{3})-(\d{4})')

dmatch1 = pattern.search(data1).groups()
dmatch2 = pattern.search(data2).groups()

print dmatch1
print dmatch2
```

The example begins with two telephone numbers placed in sentences in various locations. Before you can do much, you need to create a pattern. Always read a pattern from left to right. In this case, the pattern is looking for three digits, followed by a dash, three more digits, followed by another dash, and finally four digits.

To make the process faster and easier, the code calls the `compile()` function to create a compiled version of the pattern so that Python doesn't have to recreate the pattern every time you need it. The compiled pattern appears in `pattern`.

The `search()` function looks for the pattern in each of the test sentences. It then places any matched text that it finds into groups and outputs a tuple into one of two variables. Here's the output from this example.

```
('800', '555', '1212')
('800', '555', '1234')
```

Using the Bag of Words Model and Beyond

The goal of most data imports is to perform some type of analysis. Before you can perform analysis on textual data, you must tokenize every word within the dataset. The act of tokenizing the words creates a *bag of words*. You can then use the bag of words to train *classifiers*, a special kind of algorithm used to break words down into categories. The following section provides additional insights into the bag of words model and shows how to work with it.

Getting the 20 Newsgroups dataset

The examples in the sections that follow rely on the 20 Newsgroups dataset (`http://qwone.com/~jason/20Newsgroups/`) that's part of the Scikit-learn installation. The host site provides some additional information about the dataset, but essentially it's a good dataset to use to demonstrate various kinds of text analysis.

You don't have to do anything special to work with the dataset because Scikit-learn already knows about it. However, when you run the first example, you see the message "WARNING:sklearn.datasets.twenty_

newsgroups:Downloading dataset from `http://people.csail.mit.edu/jrennie/20Newsgroups/20news-bydate.tar.gz` (14 MB)." All this message tells you is that you need to wait for the data download to complete. There is nothing wrong with your system. Look at the left side of the code cell in IPython Notebook and you see the familiar In [*]: entry. When this entry changes to show a number, the download is complete. The message doesn't go away until the next time you run the cell.

Understanding the bag of words model

As mentioned in the introduction, in order to perform textual analysis of various sorts, you need to first tokenize the words and create a bag of words from them. The bag of words uses numbers to represent words, word frequencies, and word locations that you can manipulate mathematically to see patterns in the way that the words are structured and used. The bag of words model ignores grammar and even word order — the focus is on simplifying the text so that you can easily analyze it.

The creation of a bag of words revolves around Natural Language Processing (NLP) and Information Retrieval (IR). Before you perform this sort of processing, you normally remove any special characters (such as HTML formatting from a web source), remove the stop words, and possibly perform stemming as well (as described in the "Stemming and removing stop words" section, earlier this chapter). For the purpose of this example, you use the 20 Newsgroups dataset directly. Here's an example of how you can obtain textual input and create a bag of words from it:

```
from sklearn.datasets import fetch_20newsgroups
import sklearn.feature_extraction.text as ext

categories = ['comp.graphics', 'misc.forsale',
              'rec.autos', 'sci.space']
twenty_train = fetch_20newsgroups(subset='train',
                                  categories=categories,
```

```
                                    shuffle=True,
                                    random_state=42)

count_vect = ext.CountVectorizer()
X_train_counts = count_vect.fit_transform(
    twenty_train.data)

print X_train_counts.shape
```

A number of the examples you see online are unclear as to where the list of categories they use come from. The host site at http://qwone. com/~jason/20Newsgroups/ provides you with a listing of the categories you can use. The category list doesn't come from a magic hat somewhere, but many examples online simply don't bother to document some information sources. Always refer to the host site when you have questions about issues such as dataset categories.

The call to fetch_20newsgroups() loads the dataset into memory. You see the resulting training object, twenty_train, described as a *bunch*. At this point, you have an object that contains a listing of categories and associated data, but the application hasn't tokenized the data, and the algorithm used to work with the data isn't trained.

Now that you have a bunch of data to use, you can begin creating a bag of words with it. The bag of words process begins by assigning an integer value (an index of a sort) to each unique word in the training set. In addition, each document receives an integer value. The next step is to count every occurrence of these words in each document and create a list of document and count pairs so that you know which words appear how often in each document.

Naturally, some words from the master list aren't used in some documents, thereby creating a *high-dimensional sparse dataset*. The scipy.sparse matrix is a data structure that lets you store only the nonzero elements of the list in order to save memory. When the code makes the call to count_vect. fit_transform(), it places the resulting bag of words into X_train_ counts. You can see the resulting number of entries by accessing the shape property. The result, using the categories defined for this example, is

```
(2356, 34750)
```

Working with n-grams

An *n-gram* is a continuous sequence of items in the text you want to analyze. The items are phonemes, syllables, letters, words, or base pairs. The *n* in n-gram refers to a size. An n-gram that has a size of one, for example, is a unigram. The example in this section uses a size of three, making a trigram. You use n-grams in a probabilistic manner to perform tasks such as predicting the next sequence in a series, which wouldn't seem very useful until you start thinking about applications such as search engines that try to predict the word you want to type based on the previous letters you've supplied. However, the technique has all sorts of applications, such as in DNA sequencing and data compression. The following example shows how to create n-grams from the 20 Newsgroups dataset.

```
from sklearn.datasets import fetch_20newsgroups
import sklearn.feature_extraction.text as ext

categories = ['sci.space']

twenty_train = fetch_20newsgroups(subset='train',
        categories=categories,
        remove=('headers', 'footers', 'quotes'),
        shuffle=True,
        random_state=42)

count_chars = ext.CountVectorizer(analyzer='char_wb',
        ngram_range=(3,3),
        max_features=10).fit(twenty_train['data'])
count_words = ext.CountVectorizer(analyzer='word',
        ngram_range=(2,2),
        max_features=10,
        stop_words='english').fit(twenty_train['data'])
X = count_chars.transform(twenty_train.data)

print count_words.get_feature_names()
print X[1].todense()
print count_words.get_feature_names()
```

The beginning code is the same as in the previous section. You still begin by fetching the dataset and placing it into a bunch. However, in this case, the vectorization process takes on new meaning. The arguments process the data in a special way.

In this case, the `analyzer` parameter determines how the application creates the n-grams. You can choose words (`word`), characters (`char`), or characters within word boundaries (`char_wb`). The `ngram_range` parameter requires two inputs in the form of a tuple: The first determines the minimum n-gram size and the second determines the maximum n-gram size. The third argument, `max_features`, determines how many features the vectorizer returns. In the second vectorizer call, the `stop_words` argument removes the terms contained in the English pickle (see the "Stemming and removing stop words" section, earlier in the chapter, for details). At this point, the application fits the data to the transformation algorithm.

The example provides three outputs. The first shows the top ten trigrams for characters from the document. The second is the n-gram for the first document. It shows the frequency of the top ten trigrams. The third is the top ten trigrams for words. Here's the output from this example:

```
[u'ax ax', u'ax max', u'distribution world', u'don know',
 u'edu organization', u'max ax', u'nntp posting',
 u'organization university', u'posting host',
 u'writes article']
[[0 0 5 1 0 0 4 2 5 1]]
[u'ax ax', u'ax max', u'distribution world', u'don know',
 u'edu organization', u'max ax', u'nntp posting',
 u'organization university', u'posting host',
 u'writes article']
```

Implementing TF-IDF transformations

The *Term Frequency times Inverse Document Frequency (TF-IDF)* transformation is a technique used to help compensate for the lengths of different documents. A short document and a long document might discuss the same topics, but the long document will have higher bag of word counts because it contains more words. When performing a comparison between the short and long document, the long document will receive unfair weighting without this transformation. Search engines often need to weigh documents equally, so you see this transformation used quite often in search engine applications.

However, what this transformation is really telling you is the importance of a particular word to a document. The greater the frequency of a word in a document, the more important it is to that document. However, the measurement is offset by the document size — the total number of words the document contains. The TF part of the equation determines how frequently the term appears in the document, while the IDF part of the equation determines the term's importance. You can see some actual calculations of this particular measure at http://www.tfidf.com/. Here's an example of how you'd calculate TF-IDF using Python:

```
from sklearn.datasets import fetch_20newsgroups
import sklearn.feature_extraction.text as ext

categories = ['sci.space']

twenty_train = fetch_20newsgroups(subset='train',
        categories=categories,
        remove=('headers', 'footers', 'quotes'),
        shuffle=True,
        random_state=42)
```

```
count_vect = ext.CountVectorizer()
X_train_counts = count_vect.fit_transform(
    twenty_train.data)

tfidf = ext.TfidfTransformer().fit(X_train_counts)
X_train_tfidf = tfidf.transform(X_train_counts)

print X_train_tfidf.shape
```

This example begins much like the other examples in this section have, by fetching the 20 Newsgroups dataset. It then creates a word bag, much like the example in the "Understanding the bag of words model" section, earlier in this chapter. However, now you see something you can do with the word bag.

In this case, the code calls upon `TfidfTransformer()` to convert the raw newsgroup documents into a matrix of TF-IDF features. The `use_idf` controls the use of inverse-document-frequency reweighting, which it turned off in this case. The vectorized data is fitted to the transformation algorithm. The next step, calling `tf_transformer.transform()`, performs the actual transformation process. Here's the result you get from this example:

```
(593, 13564)
```

TF-IDF helps you to locate the most important word or n-grams and exclude the least important ones. It is also very helpful as an input for linear models, because they work better with TF-IDF scores than word counts. At this point, you normally train a classifier and perform various sorts of analysis. Don't worry about this next part of the process just yet. Starting with Chapters 12 and 15, you get introduced to classifiers. In Chapter 17, you begin working with classifiers in earnest.

Working with Graph Data

Imagine data points that are connected to other data points, such as how one web page is connected to another web page through hyperlinks. Each of these data points is a *node*. The nodes connect to each other using *links*. Not every node links to every other node, so the node connections become important. By analyzing the nodes and their links, you can perform all sorts of interesting tasks in data science, such as defining the best way to get from work to your home using streets and highways. The following sections describe how graphs work and how to perform basic tasks with them.

Understanding the adjacency matrix

An *adjacency matrix* represents the connections between nodes of a graph. When there is a connection between one node and another, the matrix indicates it as a value greater than 0. The precise representation of connections in the matrix depends on whether the graph is directed (where the direction of the connection matters) or undirected.

A problem with many online examples is that the authors keep them simple for explanation purposes. However, real-world graphs are often immense and defy easy analysis simply through visualization. Just think about the number of nodes that even a small city would have when considering street intersections (with the links being the streets themselves). Many other graphs are far larger, and simply looking at them will never reveal any interesting patterns. Data scientists call the problem in presenting any complex graph using an adjacency matrix a *hairball*.

One key to analyzing adjacency matrices is to sort them in specific ways. For example, you might choose to sort the data according to properties other than the actual connections. A graph of street connections might include the date the street was last paved with the data, making it possible for you to look for patterns that direct someone based on the streets that are in the best repair. In short, making the graph data useful becomes a matter of manipulating the organization of that data in specific ways.

Using NetworkX basics

Working with graphs could become difficult if you had to write all the code from scratch. Fortunately, the NetworkX package for Python makes it easy to create, manipulate, and study the structure, dynamics, and functions of complex networks (or graphs). Even though this book covers only graphs, you can use the package to work with digraphs and multigraphs as well.

The main emphasis of NetworkX is to avoid the whole issue of hairballs. The use of simple calls hides much of the complexity of working with graphs and adjacency matrices from view. The following example shows how to create a basic adjacency matrix from one of the NetworkX-supplied graphs:

```
import networkx as nx

G = nx.cycle_graph(10)
A = nx.adjacency_matrix(G)

print(A.todense())
```

The example begins by importing the required package. It then creates a graph using the `cycle_graph()` template. The graph contains ten nodes. Calling `adjacency_matrix()` creates the adjacency matrix from the graph. The final step is to print the output as a matrix, as shown here:

```
[[0 1 0 0 0 0 0 0 0 1]
 [1 0 1 0 0 0 0 0 0 0]
 [0 1 0 1 0 0 0 0 0 0]
 [0 0 1 0 1 0 0 0 0 0]
 [0 0 0 1 0 1 0 0 0 0]
 [0 0 0 0 1 0 1 0 0 0]
 [0 0 0 0 0 1 0 1 0 0]
 [0 0 0 0 0 0 1 0 1 0]
 [0 0 0 0 0 0 0 1 0 1]
 [1 0 0 0 0 0 0 0 1 0]]
```

You don't have to build your own graph from scratch for testing purposes. The NetworkX site documents a number of standard graph types that you can use, all of which are available within IPython. The list appears at `https://networkx.github.io/documentation/latest/reference/generators.html`.

It's interesting to see how the graph looks after you generate it. The following code displays the graph for you. Figure 7-1 shows the result of the plot.

```
import matplotlib.pyplot as plt
nx.draw_networkx(G)
plt.show()
```

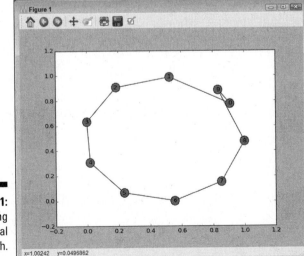

Figure 7-1:
Plotting
the original
graph.

The plot shows that you can add an edge between nodes 1 and 5. Here's the code needed to perform this task using the add_edge() function. Figure 7-2 shows the result.

```
G.add_edge(1,5)
nx.draw_networkx(G)
plt.show()
```

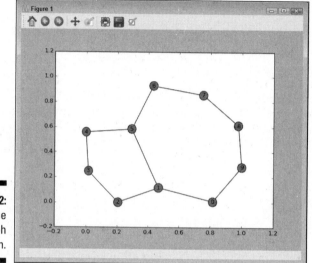

Figure 7-2:
Plotting the graph addition.

Chapter 8

Putting What You Know in Action

*P*revious chapters have all been preparatory in nature. You have discovered how to perform essential data science tasks using Python. In addition, you spent time working with the various tools that Python provides to make data science tasks easier. All this information is essential, but it doesn't help you see the big picture — where all the pieces go. This chapter shows you how to employ the techniques you discovered in previous chapters to solve real data science problems.

This chapter isn't the end of the journey — it's the beginning. Think of previous chapters in the same way as you think about packing your bags, making reservations, and creating an itinerary before you go on a trip. This chapter is the trip to the airport, during which you start to see everything come together.

The chapter begins by looking at the aspects you normally have to consider when trying to solve a data science problem. You can't just jump in and start performing an analysis; you must understand the problem first, as well as consider the resources (in the form of data, algorithms, computational resources) to solve it. Putting the problem into a context, a setting of a sort, helps you understand the problem and define how the data relates to that problem. The context is essential because, like language, context alters the meaning of both the problem and its associated data. For example, when you say, "I have a red rose" to your significant other, the meaning behind the sentence has one connotation. If you say the same sentence to a fellow gardener, the connotation is different. The rose is a sort of data and the person you're speaking to is the context. There is no meaning to saying, "I have a red rose." unless you know the context in which the statement is made. Likewise, data has no meaning; it doesn't answer any question until you know the context in which the data is used. Saying "I have data" expresses a question, "What does the data mean?"

In the end, you'll need one or more datasets. Two dimensional data tables (datasets) consist of *cases* (the rows) and *features* (the columns). You can also refer to features as *variables* when using a statistical terminology. The features you decide to use for any given dataset determine the kinds of analysis you can perform, the ways in which you can manipulate the data, and ultimately the sorts of results you obtain. Determining what sorts of features you can create from source data and how you must transform the data to ensure that it works for the analysis you want to perform is an essential part of developing a data science solution.

After you get a picture of what your problem is, the resources you have to solve it, and the inputs you need to work with to solve it, you're ready to perform some actual work. The last section of this chapter shows you how to perform simple tasks efficiently. You can usually perform tasks using more than one methodology, but when working with big data, the fastest routes are better. By working with arrays and matrices to perform specific tasks, you'll notice that certain operations can take a long time unless you leverage some computational tricks. Using computational tricks is one of the most basic forms of manipulation you perform, but knowing about them from the beginning is essential. Applying these techniques paves the road to later chapters when you start to look at the magic that data science can truly accomplish in helping you see more in the data you have than is nominally apparent.

You don't have to type the source code for this chapter manually. In fact, it's a lot easier if you use the downloadable source (see the Introduction for download instructions). The source code for this chapter appears in the `P4DS4D; 08; Operations on Arrays and Matrices.ipynb` source code file.

Contextualizing Problems and Data

Putting your problem in the correct context is an essential part of developing a data science solution for any given problem and associated data. Data science is definitively applied science, and abstract manual approaches may not work all that well on your specific situation. Running a Hadoop cluster or building a deep neural network may sound cool in front of fellow colleagues and make you feel you are doing great data science projects, but they may not provide what you need to solve your problem. Putting the problem in the correct context isn't just a matter of deliberating whether to use a certain algorithm or that you must transform the data in a certain way — it's the art of critically examining the problem and the available resources and creating an environment in which to solve the problem and obtain a desired solution.

The key point here is the *desired* solution, in that you could come up with solutions that aren't desirable because they don't tell you what you need to know — or, even when they do tell you what you need to know, they waste too much time and resources. The following sections provide an overview of the process you follow to contextualize both problems and data.

Evaluating a data science problem

When working through a data science problem, you need to start by considering your goal and the resources you have available for achieving that goal. The resources are data, computational resources such as available memory, CPUs, and disk space. In the real world, no one will hand you ready-made data and tell you to perform a particular analysis on it. Most of the time, you have to face completely new problems, and you have to build your solution from scratch. During your first evaluation of a data science problem, you need to consider the following:

- ✔ **The data available in terms of accessibility, quantity, and quality.** You must also consider the data in terms of possible biases that could influence or even distort its characteristics and content. Data never contains absolute truths, only relative truths that offer you a more or less useful view of a problem. Always be aware of the truthfulness of data and apply critical reasoning as part of your analysis of it.

- ✔ **The methods you can feasibly use to analyze the dataset.** Consider whether the methods are simple or complex. You must also decide how well you know a particular methodology. Start by using simple approaches, and never fall in love with any particular technique. There are neither free lunches nor Holy Grails in data science.

- ✔ **The questions you want to answer by performing your analysis and how you can quantitatively measure whether you achieved a satisfactory answer to them.** "If you can not measure it, you can not improve it," as Lord Kelvin stated (see http://zapatopi.net/kelvin/quotes/). If you can measure performance, you can determine the impact of your work and even make a monetary estimation. Stakeholders will be delighted to know that you've figured out what to do and what benefits your data science project will bring about.

Researching solutions

Data science is a complex system of knowledge at the intersection of computer science, math, statistics, and business. Very few people can know everything about it, and, if someone has already faced the same problem or dilemmas as you face, reinventing the wheel makes little sense. Now that you have contextualized your project, you know what you're looking for and you can search for it in different ways.

- **Check the Python documentation.** You might be able to find examples that suggest a possible solution. NumPy (`http://docs.scipy.org/doc/numpy/user/`), SciPy (`http://docs.scipy.org/doc/`), pandas (`http://pandas.pydata.org/pandas-docs/version/0.15.2/`), and especially Scikit-learn (`http://scikit-learn.org/stable/user_guide.html`) have detailed in-line and online documentation with plenty of data science–related examples.

- **Seek out online articles and blogs that hint at how other practitioners solved similar problems.** Q&A websites such as Quora (`http://www.quora.com/`), Stack Overflow (`http://stackoverflow.com/`), and Cross Validated (`http://stats.stackexchange.com/`) can provide you with plenty of answers to similar problems.

- **Consult academic papers.** For example, you can query your problem on Google Scholar at `https://scholar.google.it/` or Microsoft Academic Search at `http://academic.research.microsoft.com/`. You can find a series of scientific papers that can tell you about preparing the data or detail the kind of algorithms that work better for a particular problem.

It may seem trivial, but the solutions you create have to reflect the problem you're trying to solve. As you research solutions, you may find that some of them seem promising at first, but then you can't successfully apply them to your case because something in their context is different. For instance, your dataset may be incomplete or may not provide enough input to solve the problem. In addition, the analysis model you select may not actually provide the answer you need or the answer might prove inaccurate. As you work through the problem, don't be afraid to perform your research multiple times as you discover, test, and evaluate possible solutions that you could apply given the resources available and your actual constraints.

Formulating a hypothesis

At some point, you have everything you think you need to solve the problem. Of course, it's a mistake to assume now that the solutions you create can actually solve the problem. You have a hypothesis, rather than a solution, because you have to demonstrate the efficacy of the potential solution in a scientific way. In order to form and test a hypothesis, you must train a model using a training dataset and then test it using an entirely different dataset. Later chapters in the book spend a great deal of time helping you through the process of training and testing the algorithms used to perform analysis, so don't worry too much if you don't understand this aspect of the process right now.

Preparing your data

After you have some idea of the problem and its solution, you know the inputs required to make the algorithm work. Unfortunately, your data probably appears in multiple forms, you get it from multiple sources, and some data is missing entirely. Moreover, the developers of the features that existing data sources provide may have devised them for different purposes (such as accountancy or marketing) than yours and you have to transform them so that you can use your algorithm at its fullest power. To make the algorithm work, you must prepare the data. This means checking for missing data, creating new features as needed, and possibly manipulating the dataset to get it into a form that your algorithm can actually use to make a prediction.

Considering the Art of Feature Creation

Features have to do with the columns in your dataset. Of course, you need to determine what those columns should contain. They might not end up looking precisely like the data in the original data source. The original data source may present the data in a form that leads to inaccurate analysis or even prevent you from getting a desired outcome because it's not completely suited to your algorithm or your objectives. For example, the data may contain too much information redundancy inside multiple variables, which is a problem called *multivariate correlation*. The task of making the columns work in the best manner for data analysis purposes is *feature creation* (also called feature engineering). The following sections help you understand feature creation and why it's important. (Future chapters provide all sorts of examples of how you actually employ feature creation to perform analysis.)

Defining feature creation

Feature creation may seem a bit like magic or weird science to some people, but it really does have a firm basis in math. The task is to take existing data and transform it into something that you can work with to perform an analysis. For example, numeric data could appear as strings in the original data source. To perform an analysis, you must convert the string data to numeric values in many cases. The immediate goal of feature creation is to achieve better performance from the algorithms used to accomplish the analysis than you can when using the original data.

In many cases, the transformation is less than straightforward. You may have to combine values in some way or perform math operations on them. The information you can access may appear in all sorts of forms, and the transformation process lets you work with the data in new ways so that you can see patterns in it. For example, consider this popular Kaggle competition: `http://www.kaggle.com/c/march-machine-learning-mania-2015`. The goal is to use all sorts of statistics to determine who will win the NCAA Basketball Tournament. Imagine trying to derive disparate measures from public information on a match, such as the geographic location the team will travel to or the unavailability of key players, and you can begin to grasp the need to create features in a dataset.

As you might imagine, feature creation truly is an art form, and everyone has an opinion on precisely how to perform it. This book provides you with some good basic information on feature creation as well as a number of examples, but it leaves advanced techniques to experimentation and trial. As Pedro Domingos, professor at Washington University, stated in his Data Science paper, "A Few Useful Things to Know about Machine Learning" (see `http://homes.cs.washington.edu/~pedrod/papers/cacm12.pdf`), feature engineering is "easily the most important factor" in determining the success or failure of a machine-learning project, and nothing can really replace the "smarts you put into feature engineering."

Combining variables

Data often comes in a form that doesn't work at all for an algorithm. Consider a simple real-life situation in which you need to determine whether one person can lift a board at a lumber yard. You receive two data tables. The first contains the height, width, thickness, and wood types of boards. The second contains a list of wood types and the amount they weigh per board foot (a piece of wood 12" x 12" x 1"). Not every wood type comes in every size, and some shipments come unmarked, so you don't actually know what type of wood you're working with. The goal is to create a prediction so that the company knows how many people to send to work with the shipments.

In this case, you create a two-dimensional dataset by combining variables. The resulting dataset contains only two features. The first feature contains just the length of the boards. It's reasonable to expect a single person to carry a board that is up to ten feet long, but you want two people carrying a board ten feet or longer. The second feature is the weight of the board. A board that is 10 feet long, 12 inches wide, and 2 inches thick contains 20 board feet. If the board is made of ponderosa pine (with a board foot rating of 2.67), the overall weight of the board is 53.4 pounds — one person could probably lift it. However, when the board is made of hickory (with a board foot rating of 4.25), the overall weight is now 85 pounds. Unless you have the Hulk working for you, you really do need two people lifting that board, even though the board is short enough for one person to lift.

Getting the first feature for your dataset is easy. All you need is the lengths of each of the boards that you stock. However, the second feature requires that you combine variables from both tables: length in feet * width in feet * thickness in inches * board foot rating. The resulting dataset will contain the weight for each length of each kind of wood you stock. Having this information means that you can create a model that predicts whether a particular task will require one, two, or even three people to perform.

Understanding binning and discretization

In order to perform some types of analysis, you need to break numeric values into classes. For example, you might have a dataset that includes entries for people from ages 0 to 80. To derive statistics that work in this case (such as running the Naïve Bayes algorithm), you might want to view the variable as a series of levels in ten-year increments. The process of breaking the dataset up into these ten-year increments is *binning*. Each bin is a numeric category that you can use.

Binning may improve the accuracy of predictive models by reducing noise or by helping model nonlinearity. In addition, it allows easy identification of *outliers* (values outside the expected range) and invalid or missing values of numerical variables.

Binning works exclusively with single numeric features. *Discretization* is a more complex process, in which you place combinations of values from different features in a bucket — limiting the number of states in any given bucket. In contrast to binning, discretization works with both numeric and string values. It's a more generalized method of creating categories. For example, you can obtain a discretization as a byproduct of cluster analysis.

Using indicator variables

Indicator variables are features that can take on a value of 0 or 1. Another name for indicator variables is dummy variables. No matter what you call them, these variables serve an important purpose in making data easier to work with. For example, if you want to create a dataset in which individuals under 25 are treated one way and individuals 25 and over are treated another, you could replace the age feature with an indicator variable that contains a 0 when the individual is under 25 or a 1 when the individual is 25 and older.

Using an indicator variable lets you perform analysis faster and categorize cases with greater accuracy than you can without this variable. The indicator variable removes shades of gray from the dataset. Someone is either under 25 or 25 and older — there is no middle ground. Because the data is simplified, the algorithm can perform its task faster, and you have less ambiguity to contend with.

Transforming distributions

A *distribution* is an arrangement of the values of a variable that shows the frequency at which various values occur. After you know how the values are distributed, you can begin to understand the data better. All sorts of distributions exist (see a gallery of distributions at http://www.itl.nist.gov/div898/handbook/eda/section3/eda366.htm), and most algorithms can easily deal with them. However, you must match the algorithm to the distribution.

Pay particular attention to uniform and skewed distributions. They are quite difficult to deal with for different reasons. The bell-shaped curve, the normal distribution, is always your friend. When you see a distribution shaped differently from a bell distribution, you should think about performing a transformation.

When working with distributions, you might find that the distribution of values is skewed in some way and that, because of the skewed values, any algorithm applied to the set of values produces output that simply won't match your expectations. Transforming a distribution means to apply some sort of function to the values in order to achieve specific objectives, such as fixing the data skew, so that the output of your algorithm is closer to what you expected. In addition, transformation helps make the distribution friendlier, such as when you transform a dataset to appear as a normal distribution. Transformations that you should always try on your numeric features are

- Logarithm np.log(x) and exponential np.exp(x)
- Inverse 1/x, square root np.sqrt(x), and cube root x**(1.0/3.0)
- Polynomial transformations such as, x**2, x**3, and so on.

Performing Operations on Arrays

A basic form of data manipulation is to place the data in an array or matrix and then use standard math-based techniques to modify its form. Using this approach puts the data in a convenient form to perform other operations done at the level of every single observation, such as in iterations, because they can leverage your computer architecture and some highly optimized numerical linear algebra routines present in CPUs. These routines are callable from every operating system. The larger the data and the computations, the more time you can save. In addition, using these techniques also spare you writing long and complex Python code. The following sections describe how to work with arrays for data science purposes.

Using vectorization

Your computer provides you with powerful routine calculations, and you can use them when your data is in the right format. NumPy's `ndarray` is a multidimensional data storage structure that you can use as a dimensional datatable. In fact, you can use it as a cube or even a hypercube when there are more than three dimensions.

Using `ndarray` makes computations easy and fast. The following example creates a dataset of three observations with seven features for each observation. In this case, the example obtains the maximum value for each observation and subtracts it from the minimum value to obtain the range of values for each observation.

```
import numpy as np
dataset = np.array([[2, 4, 6, 8, 3, 2, 5],
                    [7, 5, 3, 1, 6, 8, 0],
                    [1, 3, 2, 1, 0, 0, 8]])
print np.max(dataset, axis=1) - np.min(dataset, axis=1)
```

The print statement obtains the maximum value from each observation using `np.max()` and then subtracts it from the minimum value using `np.min()`. The maximum value in each observation is `[8 8 8]`. The minimum value for each observation is `[2 0 0]`. As a result, you get the following output:

```
[6 8 8]
```

Performing simple arithmetic on vectors and matrices

Most operations and functions from NumPy that you apply to arrays leverage vectorization, so they're fast and efficient — much more efficient than any other solution or handmade code. Even the simplest operations such as additions or divisions can take advantage of vectorization.

For instance, many times, the form of the data in your dataset won't quite match the form you need. A list of numbers could represent percentages as whole numbers when you really need them as fractional values. In this case, you can usually perform some type of simple math to solve the problem, as shown here:

```
import numpy as np
a = np.array([15.0, 20.0, 22.0, 75.0, 40.0, 35.0])
a = a*.01
print a
```

The example creates an array, fills it with whole number percentages, and then uses 0.01 as a multiplier to create fractional percentages. You can then multiply these fractional values against other numbers to determine how the percentage affects that number. The output from this example is

```
[ 0.15  0.2   0.22  0.75  0.4   0.35]
```

Performing matrix vector multiplication

The most efficient vectorization operations are matrix manipulations in which you add and multiply multiple values against other multiple values. NumPy makes performing multiplication of a vector by a matrix easy, which is handy if you have to estimate a value for each observation as a weighted summation of the features. Here's an example of this technique:

```
import numpy as np
a = np.array([2, 4, 6, 8])
b = np.array([[1, 2, 3, 4],
              [2, 3, 4, 5],
              [3, 4, 5, 6],
              [4, 5, 6, 7]])
c = np.dot(a, b)
print c
```

Notice that the `array` formatted as a vector must appear before the `array` formatted as a matrix in the multiplication or you get an error. The example outputs these values:

```
[60 80 100 120]
```

To obtain the values shown, you multiply every value in the `array` against the matching `column` in the matrix — you multiply the first value in the `array` against the first column, first row of the `matrix`. For example, the first value in the output is 2 * 1 + 4 * 2 + 6 * 3 + 8 * 4, which equals 60.

Performing matrix multiplication

You can also multiply one matrix against another. In this case, the output is the result of multiplying rows in the first matrix against columns in the second matrix. Here is an example of how you multiply one NumPy matrix against another:

```
import numpy as np

a = np.array([[2, 4, 6, 8],
              [1, 3, 5, 7]])
b = np.array ([[1, 2],
               [2, 3],
               [3, 4],
               [4, 5]])
c = np.dot(a, b)
print c
```

In this case, you end up with a 2 x 2 matrix as output. Here are the values you should see when you run the application:

```
[[60 80]
 [50 66]]
```

Each row in the first matrix is multiplied by each column of the second matrix. For example, to get the value 50 shown in row 2, column 1 of the output, you match up the values in row two of matrix a with column 1 of matrix b, like this: 1 * 1 + 3 * 2 + 5 * 3 + 7 * 4.

Part III
Visualizing the Invisible

See an example of how you can plot a sound file at http://www.dummies.com/extras/pythonfordatascience.

In this part . . .

- ✔ Creating graphs and charts
- ✔ Changing the appearance of graphs and charts
- ✔ Using scatterplots effectively
- ✔ Working with geographical data and other nontraditional data types
- ✔ Using the IPython tools to your advantage

Chapter 9

Getting a Crash Course in MatPlotLib

. . . .

In This Chapter

▶ Creating a basic graph

▶ Adding measurement lines to your graph

▶ Dressing your graph up with styles and color

▶ Documenting your graph with labels, annotations, and legends

. . . .

Most people visualize information better when they see it in graphic, versus textual, format. Graphics help people see relationships and make comparisons with greater ease. Even if you can deal with the abstraction of textual data with ease, performing data analysis is all about communication. Unless you can communicate your ideas to other people, the act of obtaining, shaping, and analyzing the data has little value beyond your own personal needs. Fortunately, Python makes the task of converting your textual data into graphics relatively easy using MatPlotLib, which is actually a simulation of the MATLAB application. You can see a comparison of the two at `http://www.pyzo.org/python_vs_matlab.html`.

If you already know how to use MATLAB (see my book, *MATLAB For Dummies*, published by John Wiley & Sons, Inc., if you'd like to learn), moving over to MatPlotLib is relatively easy because they both use the same sort of state machine to perform tasks and they have a similar method of defining graphic elements. A number of people feel that MatPlotLib is superior to MATLAB because you can do things like perform tasks using less code when working with MatPlotLib than when using MATLAB (see `http://phillipmfeldman.org/Python/Advantages_of_Python_Over_Matlab.html`). Others have noted that the transition from MATLAB to MatPlotLib is relatively straightforward (see `https://vnoel.wordpress.com/2008/05/03/bye-matlab-hello-python-thanks-sage/`). However, what matters most is what you think. You may find that you like to experiment with data using MATLAB and then create applications based on your findings using Python with MatPlotLib. It's a matter of personal taste rather than one of a strict correct answer.

This chapter focuses on getting you up to speed quickly with MatPlotLib. You do use MatPlotLib quite a few times later in the book, so this short overview of how it works is important, even if you already know how to work with MATLAB. That said, the MATLAB experience will be incredibly helpful as you progress through the chapter, and you may find that you can simply skim through some sections. Make sure to keep this chapter in mind as you start working with MatPlotLib in more detail later in the book.

You don't have to type the source code for this chapter manually. In fact, it's a lot easier if you use the downloadable source code. The source code for this chapter appears in the P4DS4D; 09; Getting a Crash Course in MatPlotLib.ipynb source code file (see the Introduction for where to find this code).

Starting with a Graph

A graph or chart is simply a visual representation of numeric data. MatPlotLib makes a large number of graph and chart types available to you. Of course, you can choose any of the common graph and graph types such as bar charts, line graphs, or pie charts. As with MATLAB, you also have access to a huge number of statistical plot types, such as box plots, error bar charts, and histograms. You can see a gallery of the various graph types that MatPlotLib supports at http://matplotlib.org/gallery.html. However, it's important to remember that you can combine graphic elements in an almost infinite number of ways to create your own presentation of data no matter how complex that data might be. The following sections describe how to create a basic graph, but remember that you have access to a lot more functionality than these sections tell you about.

Defining the plot

Plots show graphically what you've defined numerically. To define a plot, you need some values, the matplotlib.pyplot module, and an idea of what you want to display, as shown in the following code.

```
values = [1, 5, 8, 9, 2, 0, 3, 10, 4, 7]
import matplotlib.pyplot as plt
plt.plot(range(1,11), values)
plt.show()
```

In this case, the code tells the plt.plot() function to create a plot using x-axis values between 1 and 11 and y-axis values as they appear in values. Calling plot.show() displays the plot in a separate dialog box, as shown in Figure 9-1. Notice that the output is a line graph. Chapter 10 shows you how to create other chart and graph types.

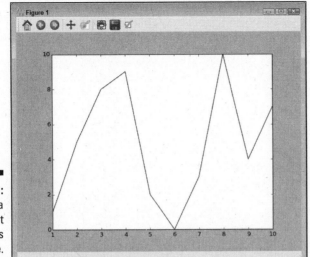

Figure 9-1:
Creating a
basic plot
that shows
just one line.

Drawing multiple lines and plots

You encounter many situations in which you must use multiple plot lines,
such as when comparing two sets of values. To create such plots using
MatPlotLib, you simply call `plt.plot()` multiple times — once for each plot
line, as shown in the following example.

```
values = [1, 5, 8, 9, 2, 0, 3, 10, 4, 7]
values2 = [3, 8, 9, 2, 1, 2, 4, 7, 6, 6]
import matplotlib.pyplot as plt
plt.plot(range(1,11), values)
plt.plot(range(1,11), values2)
plt.show()
```

When you run this example, you see two plot lines, as shown in Figure 9-2.
Even though you can't see it in the printed book, the line graphs are different
colors so that you can tell them apart.

Saving your work

Often you need to save a copy of your work to disk for later reference or to
use as part of a larger report. The easiest way to accomplish this task is to
click Save the Figure (the floppy disk icon in Figure 9-2). You see a dialog box
that you can use to save the figure to disk.

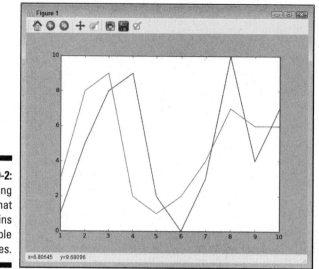

Figure 9-2:
Defining
a plot that
contains
multiple
lines.

However, you sometimes need to save the graphic automatically rather than wait for the user to do it. In this case, you can save it programmatically using the `plt.savefig()` function, as shown in the following code:

```
values = [1, 5, 8, 9, 2, 0, 3, 10, 4, 7]
import matplotlib.pyplot as plt
plt.plot(range(1,11), values)
plt.savefig('MySamplePlot.png', format='png')
```

In this case, you must provide a minimum of two inputs. The first input is the filename. You may optionally include a path for saving the file. The second input is the file format. In this case, the example saves the file in Portable Network Graphic (PNG) format, but you have other options: Portable Document Format (PDF), Postscript (PS), Encapsulated Postscript (EPS), and Scalable Vector Graphics (SVG).

Setting the Axis, Ticks, Grids

It's hard to know what the data actually means unless you provide a unit of measure or at least some means of performing comparisons. The use of axes, ticks, and grids make it possible to illustrate graphically the relative size of data elements so that the viewer gains an appreciation of comparative measure. You won't use these features with every graphic, and you may employ the features differently based on viewer needs, but it's important to know that these features exist and how you can use them to help document your data within the graphic environment.

Getting the axes

The axes define the x and y plane of the graphic. The x axis runs horizontally, and the y axis runs vertically. In many cases, you can allow MatPlotLib to perform any required formatting for you. However, sometimes you need to obtain access to the axes and format them manually. The following code shows how to obtain access to the axes for a plot:

```
values = [0, 5, 8, 9, 2, 0, 3, 10, 4, 7]
import matplotlib.pyplot as plt
ax = plt.axes()
plt.plot(range(1,11), values)
plt.show()
```

The reason you place the axes in a variable, ax, instead of manipulating them directly is to make writing the code simpler and more efficient. In this case, you simply turn on the default axes by calling plt.axes(); then you place a handle to the axes in ax. A *handle* is a sort of pointer to the axes. Think of it as you would a frying pan. You wouldn't lift the frying pan directly but would instead use its handle when picking it up.

Formatting the axes

Simply displaying the axes won't be enough in many cases. You want to change the way MatPlotLib displays them. For example, you may not want the highest value t to reach to the top of the graph. The following example shows just a small number of tasks you can perform after you have access to the axes:

```
values = [0, 5, 8, 9, 2, 0, 3, 10, 4, 7]
import matplotlib.pyplot as plt
ax = plt.axes()
ax.set_xlim([0, 11])
ax.set_ylim([-1, 11])
ax.set_xticks([1, 2, 3, 4, 5, 6, 7, 8, 9, 10])
ax.set_yticks([0, 1, 2, 3, 4, 5, 6, 7, 8, 9, 10])
plt.plot(range(1,11), values)
plt.show()
```

In this case, the set_xlim() and set_ylim() calls change the axes limits — the length of each axis. The set_xticks() and set_yticks() calls change the ticks used to display data. The ways in which you can change a graph using these calls can become quite detailed. For example, you can choose to change individual tick labels if you want. Figure 9-3 shows the output from this example. Notice how the changes affect how the line graph displays.

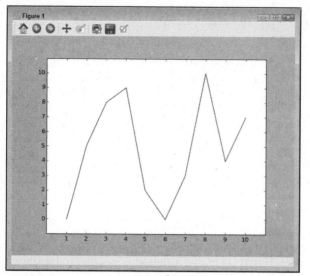

Adding grids

Grid lines make it possible to see the precise value of each element of a graph. You can more quickly determine both the x and y coordinate, which allow you to perform comparisons of individual points with greater ease. Of course, grids also add noise and make seeing the actual flow of data harder. The point is that you can use grids to good effect to create particular effects. The following code shows how to add a grid to the graph in the previous section:

```
values = [0, 5, 8, 9, 2, 0, 3, 10, 4, 7]
import matplotlib.pyplot as plt
ax = plt.axes()
ax.set_xlim([0, 11])
ax.set_ylim([-1, 11])
ax.set_xticks([1, 2, 3, 4, 5, 6, 7, 8, 9, 10])
ax.set_yticks([0, 1, 2, 3, 4, 5, 6, 7, 8, 9, 10])
ax.grid()
plt.plot(range(1,11), values)
plt.show()
```

All you really need to do is call the `grid()` function. As with many other MatPlotLib functions, you can add parameters to create the grid precisely as you want to see it. For example, you can choose whether to add the x grid lines, y grid lines, or both. The output from this example appears in Figure 9-4.

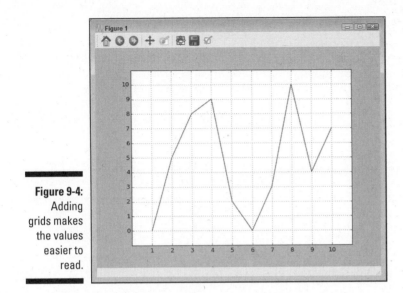

Figure 9-4: Adding grids makes the values easier to read.

Defining the Line Appearance

Just drawing lines on a page won't do much for you if you need to help the viewer understand the importance of your data. In most cases, you need to use different line styles to ensure that the viewer can tell one data grouping from another. However, to emphasize the importance or value of a particular data grouping, you need to employ color. The use of color communicates all sorts of ideas to the viewer. For example, green often denotes that something is safe, while red communicates danger. The following sections help you understand how to work with line style and color to communicate ideas and concepts to the viewer without using any text.

Making graphics accessible

Avoiding assumptions about someone's ability to see your graphic presentation is essential. For example, someone who is color blind may not be able to tell that one line is green and the other red. Likewise, someone with low-vision problems may not be able to distinguish between a line that is dashed and one that has a combination of dashes and dots. Using multiple methods to distinguish each line helps ensure that everyone can see your data in a manner that is comfortable to each person.

Working with line styles

Line styles help differentiate graphs by drawing the lines in various ways. Using a unique presentation for each line helps you distinguish each line so that you can call it out (even when the printout is in shades of gray). You could also call out a particular line graph by using a different line style for it (and using the same style for the other lines). Table 9-1 shows the various MatPlotLib line styles.

Table 9-1	MatPlotLib Line Styles
Character	*Line Style*
'-'	Solid line
'--'	Dashed line
'-.'	Dash-dot line
':'	Dotted line

The line style appears as a third argument to the `plot()` function call. You simply provide the desired string for the line type, as shown in the following example.

```
values = [1, 5, 8, 9, 2, 0, 3, 10, 4, 7]
values2 = [3, 8, 9, 2, 1, 2, 4, 7, 6, 6]
import matplotlib.pyplot as plt
plt.plot(range(1,11), values, '--')
plt.plot(range(1,11), values2, ':')
plt.show()
```

In this case, the first line graph uses a dashed line style, while the second line graph uses a dotted line style. You can see the results of the changes in Figure 9-5.

Using colors

Color is another way in which to differentiate line graphs. Of course, this method has certain problems. The most significant problem occurs when someone makes a black-and-white copy of your colored graph — hiding the color differences as shades of gray. Another problem is that someone with color blindness may not be able to tell one line from the other. All this said, color does make for a brighter, eye-grabbing presentation. Table 9-2 shows the colors that MatPlotLib supports.

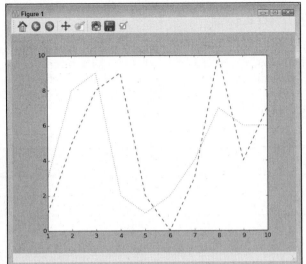

Figure 9-5:
Line styles
help
differentiate
between
plots.

Table 9-2	MatPlotLib Colors
Character	*Color*
'b'	Blue
'g'	Green
'r'	Red
'c'	Cyan
'm'	Magenta
'y'	Yellow
'k'	Black
'w'	White

As with line styles, the color appears in a string as the third argument to the
plot() function call. In this case, the viewer sees two lines — one in red
and the other in magenta. The actual presentation looks like Figure 9-2, but
with specific colors, rather than the default colors used in that screenshot.
If you're reading the printed version of the book, Figure 9-2 actually uses
shades of gray.

```
values = [1, 5, 8, 9, 2, 0, 3, 10, 4, 7]
values2 = [3, 8, 9, 2, 1, 2, 4, 7, 6, 6]
import matplotlib.pyplot as plt
plt.plot(range(1,11), values, 'r')
plt.plot(range(1,11), values2, 'm')
plt.show()
```

Adding markers

Markers add a special symbol to each data point in a line graph. Unlike line style and color, markers tend to be a little less susceptible to accessibility and printing issues. Even when the specific marker isn't clear, people can usually differentiate one marker from the other. Table 9-3 shows the list of markers that MatPlotLib provides.

Table 9-3	MatPlotLib Markers
Character	*Marker Type*
'.'	Point
','	Pixel
'o'	Circle
'v'	Triangle 1 down
'^'	Triangle 1 up
'<'	Triangle 1 left
'>'	Triangle 1 right
'1'	Triangle 2 down
'2'	Triangle 2 up
'3'	Triangle 2 left
'4'	Triangle 2 right
's'	Square
'p'	Pentagon
'*'	Star
'h'	Hexagon style 1
'H'	Hexagon style 2
'+'	Plus
'x'	X
'D'	Diamond
'd'	Thin diamond
'|'	Vertical line
'_'	Horizontal line

As with line style and color, you add markers as the third argument to a
`plot()` call. In the following example, you see the effects of combining line
style with a marker to provide a unique line graph presentation.

```
values = [1, 5, 8, 9, 2, 0, 3, 10, 4, 7]
values2 = [3, 8, 9, 2, 1, 2, 4, 7, 6, 6]
import matplotlib.pyplot as plt
plt.plot(range(1,11), values, 'o--')
plt.plot(range(1,11), values2, 'v:')
plt.show()
```

Notice how the combination of line style and marker makes each line stand
out in Figure 9-6. Even when printed in black and white, you can easily differentiate one line from the other, which is why you usually want to combine
presentation techniques.

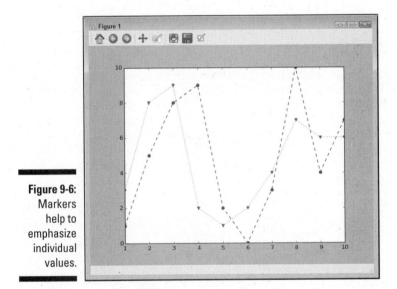

Figure 9-6:
Markers
help to
emphasize
individual
values.

Using Labels, Annotations, and Legends

To fully document your graph, you usually have to resort to labels, annotations,
and legends. Each of these elements has a different purpose, as follows:

- **Label:** Provides positive identification of a particular data element or
  grouping. The purpose is to make it easy for the viewer to know the
  name or kind of data illustrated.

✔ **Annotation:** Augments the information the viewer can immediately see about the data with notes, sources, or other useful information. In contrast to a label, the purpose of annotation is to help extend the viewer's knowledge of the data rather than simply identify it.

✔ **Legend:** Presents a listing of the data groups within the graph and often provides cues (such as line type or color) to make identification of the data group easier. For example, all the red points may belong to group A, while all the blue points may belong to group B.

The following sections help you understand the purpose and usage of various documentation aids provided with MatPlotLib. These documentation aids help you create an environment in which the viewer is certain as to the source, purpose, and usage of data elements. Some graphs work just fine without any documentation aids, but in other cases, you might find that you need to use all three in order to communicate with your viewer fully.

Adding labels

Labels help people understand the significance of each axis of any graph you create. Without labels, the values portrayed don't have any significance. In addition to a moniker, such as rainfall, you can also add units of measure, such as inches or centimeters, so that your audience knows how to interpret the data shown. The following example shows how to add labels to your graph:

```
values = [1, 5, 8, 9, 2, 0, 3, 10, 4, 7]
import matplotlib.pyplot as plt
plt.xlabel('Entries')
plt.ylabel('Values')
plt.plot(range(1,11), values)
plt.show()
```

The call to xlabel() documents the x axis of your graph, while the call the ylabel() documents the y axis of your graph. Figure 9-7 shows the output of this example.

Annotating the chart

You use annotation to draw special attention to points of interest on a graph. For example, you may want to point out that a specific data point is outside the usual range expected for a particular dataset. The following example shows how to add annotation to a graph.

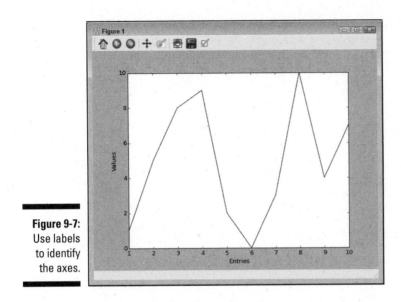

```
values = [1, 5, 8, 9, 2, 0, 3, 10, 4, 7]
import matplotlib.pyplot as plt
plt.annotate(xy=[1,1], s='First Entry')
plt.plot(range(1,11), values)
plt.show()
```

The call to `annotate()` provides the labeling you need. You must provide a location for the annotation by using the `xy` parameter, as well as provide text to place at the location by using the `s` parameter. The `annotate()` function also provides other parameters that you can use to create special formatting or placement onscreen. Figure 9-8 shows the output from this example.

Creating a legend

A legend documents the individual elements of a plot. Each line is presented in a table that contains a label for it so that people can differentiate between each line. For example, one line may represent sales in 2014 and another line may represent sales in 2015, so you include an entry in the legend for each line that is labeled 2014 and 2015. The following example shows how to add a legend to your plot.

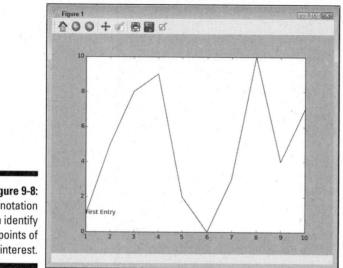

Figure 9-8:
Annotation
can identify
points of
interest.

```
values = [1, 5, 8, 9, 2, 0, 3, 10, 4, 7]
values2 = [3, 8, 9, 2, 1, 2, 4, 7, 6, 6]
import matplotlib.pyplot as plt
line1 = plt.plot(range(1,11), values)
line2 = plt.plot(range(1,11), values2)
plt.legend(['First', 'Second'], loc=4)
plt.show()
```

The call to legend() occurs after you create the plots, not before, as with
some of the other functions described in this chapter. You must provide a
handle to each of the plots. Notice how line1 is set equal to the first plot()
call and line2 is set equal to the second plot() call.

The default location for the legend is the upper-right corner of the plot,
which proved inconvenient for this particular example. Adding the loc
parameter lets you place the legend in a different location. See the legend()
function documentation at http://matplotlib.org/api/pyplot_api.
html#matplotlib.pyplot.legend for additional legend locations.
Figure 9-9 shows the output from this example.

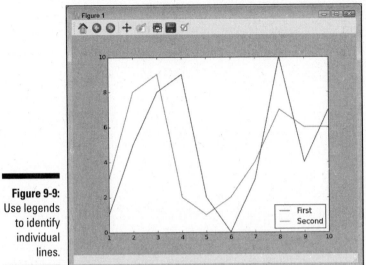

Figure 9-9:
Use legends
to identify
individual
lines.

Chapter 10

Visualizing the Data

* * *

In This Chapter

▶ Selecting the right graph for the job

▶ Working with advanced scatterplots

▶ Exploring time-related data

▶ Exploring geographical data

▶ Creating graphs

* * *

Chapter 9 helped you understand the mechanics of working with MatPlotLib, which is an important first step toward using it. This chapter takes the next step in helping you use MatPlotLib to perform useful work. The main goal of this chapter is to help you visualize your data in various ways. Creating a graphic presentation of your data is essential if you want to help other people understand what you're trying to say. Even though you can see what the numbers mean in your mind, other people will likely need graphics to see what point you're trying to make by manipulating data in various ways.

The chapter starts by looking at some basic graph types that MatPlotLib supports. You don't find the full list of graphs and plots listed in this chapter — it could take an entire book to explore them all in detail. However, you do find the most common types.

In the remainder of the chapter, you begin exploring specific sorts of plotting as it relates to data science. Of course, no book on data science would be complete without exploring scatterplots, which are used to help people see patterns in seemingly unrelated data points. Because much of the data that you work with today is time related or geographic in nature, the chapter devotes two special sections to these topics. You also get to work with both directed and undirected graphs, which is fine for social media analysis.

You don't have to type the source code for this chapter manually. In fact, it's a lot easier if you use the downloadable source. The source code for this chapter appears in the P4DS4D; 10; Visualizing the Data.ipynb source code file (see the Introduction for details on how to find that source file).

Choosing the Right Graph

The kind of graph you choose determines how people view the associated data, so choosing the right graph from the outset is important. For example, if you want to show how various data elements contribute toward a whole, you really need to use a pie chart. On the other hand, when you want people to form opinions on how data elements compare, you use a bar chart. The idea is to choose a graph that naturally leads people to draw the conclusion that you need them to draw about the data that you've carefully massaged from various data sources. (You also have the option of using line graphs — a technique demonstrated in Chapter 9.) The following sections describe the various graph types and provide you with basic examples of how to use them.

Showing parts of a whole with pie charts

Pie charts focus on showing parts of a whole. The entire pie would be 100 percent. The question is how much of that percentage each value occupies. The following example shows how to create a pie chart with many of the special features in place:

```python
import matplotlib.pyplot as plt

values = [5, 8, 9, 10, 4, 7]
colors = ['b', 'g', 'r', 'c', 'm', 'y']
labels = ['A', 'B', 'C', 'D', 'E', 'F']
explode = (0, 0.2, 0, 0, 0, 0)

plt.pie(values, colors=colors, labels=labels,
        explode=explode, autopct='%1.1f%%',
        counterclock=False, shadow=True)
plt.title('Values')

plt.show()
```

The essential part of a pie chart is the values. You could create a basic pie chart using just the values as input.

The `colors` parameter lets you choose custom colors for each pie wedge. You use the `labels` parameter to identify each wedge. In many cases, you need to make one wedge stand out from the others, so you add the `explode` parameter with list of explode values. A value of 0 keeps the wedge in place — any other value moves the wedge out from the center of the pie.

Each pie wedge can show various kinds of information. This example shows the percentage occupied by each wedge with the `autopct` parameter. You must provide a format string to format the percentages.

Some parameters affect how the pie chart is drawn. Use the `counterclock` parameter to determine the direction of the wedges. The `shadow` parameter determines whether the pie appears with a shadow beneath it (for a 3D effect). You can find other parameters at `http://matplotlib.org/api/pyplot_api.html`.

In most cases, you also want to give your pie chart a title so that others know what it represents. You do this using the `title()` function. Figure 10-1 shows the output from this example.

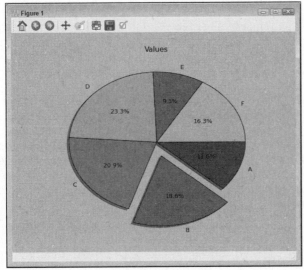

Figure 10-1:
Pie charts
show a
percentage
of the
whole.

Creating comparisons with bar charts

Bar charts make comparing values easy. The wide bars and segregated measurements emphasize the differences between values, rather than the flow of one value to another as a line graph would do. Fortunately, you have all sorts of methods at your disposal for emphasizing specific values and performing other tricks. The following example shows just some of the things you can do with a vertical bar chart.

```
import matplotlib.pyplot as plt

values = [5, 8, 9, 10, 4, 7]
widths = [0.7, 0.8, 0.7, 0.7, 0.7, 0.7]
colors = ['b', 'r', 'b', 'b', 'b', 'b']
plt.bar(range(0, 6), values, width=widths,
        color=colors, align='center')

plt.show()
```

To create even a basic bar chart, you must provide a series of x coordinates and the heights of the bars. The example uses the `range()` function to create the x coordinates, and `values` contains the heights.

Of course, you may want more than a basic bar chart, and MatPlotLib provides a number of ways to get the job done. In this case, the example uses the `width` parameter to control the width of each bar, emphasizing the second bar by making it slightly larger. The larger width would show up even in a black-and-white printout. It also uses the `color` parameter to change the color of the target bar to red (the rest are blue).

As with other chart types, the bar chart provides some special features that you can use to make your presentation stand out. The example uses the `align` parameter to center the data on the x coordinate (the standard position is to the left). You can also use other parameters, such as `hatch`, to enhance the visual appearance of your bar chart. Figure 10-2 shows the output of this example.

This chapter helps you get started using MatPlotLib to create a variety of chart and graph types. Of course, more examples are better, so you can also find some more advanced examples on the MatPlotLib site at `http://matplotlib.org/1.2.1/examples/index.html`. Some of the examples, such as those that demonstrate animation techniques, become quite advanced, but with practice you can use any of them to improve your own charts and graphs.

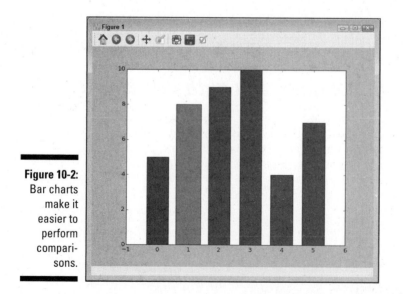

Figure 10-2:
Bar charts
make it
easier to
perform
compari-
sons.

Showing distributions using histograms

Histograms categorize data by breaking it into *bins*, where each bin contains a subset of the data range. A histogram then displays the number of items in each bin so that you can see the distribution of data and the progression of data from bin to bin. In most cases, you see a curve of some type, such as a bell curve. The following example shows how to create a histogram with randomized data:

```
import numpy as np
import matplotlib.pyplot as plt

x = 20 * np.random.randn(10000)

plt.hist(x, 25, range=(-50, 50), histtype='stepfilled',
         align='mid', color='g', label='Test Data')
plt.legend()
plt.title('Step Filled Histogram')
plt.show()
```

In this case, the input values are a series of random numbers. The distribution of these numbers should show a type of bell curve. As a minimum, you must provide a series of values, x in this case, to plot. The second argument contains the number of bins to use when creating the data intervals. The default value is 10. Using the `range` parameter helps you focus the histogram on the relevant data and exclude any outliers.

You can create multiple histogram types. The default setting creates a bar chart. You can also create a stacked bar chart, stepped graph, or filled stepped graph (the type shown in the example). In addition, it's possible to control the orientation of the output, with vertical as the default.

As with most other charts and graphs in this chapter, you can add special features to the output. For example, the `align` parameter determines the alignment of each bar along the baseline. Use the `color` parameter to control the colors of the bars. The `label` parameter doesn't actually appear unless you also create a legend (as shown in this example). Figure 10-3 shows typical output from this example.

Random data varies call by call. Every time you run the example, you see slightly different results because the random-generation process differs.

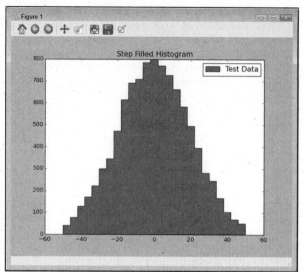

Figure 10-3:
Histograms
let you see
distributions
of numbers.

Depicting groups using box plots

Box plots provide a means of depicting groups of numbers through their *quartiles* (three points dividing a group into four equal parts). A box plot may also have lines, called *whiskers*, indicating data outside the upper and lower quartiles. The spacing shown within a box plot helps indicate the skew and dispersion of the data. The following example shows how to create a box plot with randomized data.

```
import numpy as np
import matplotlib.pyplot as plt

spread = 100 * np.random.rand(100)
center = np.ones(50) * 50
flier_high = 100 * np.random.rand(10) + 100
flier_low = -100 * np.random.rand(10)
data = np.concatenate((spread, center,
                       flier_high, flier_low))

plt.boxplot(data, sym='gx', widths=.75, notch=True)
plt.show()
```

To create a usable dataset, you need to combine several different number-generation techniques, as shown at the beginning of the example. Here are how these techniques work:

✔ `spread`: Contains a set of random numbers between 0 and 100

✔ `center`: Provides 50 values directly in the center of the range of 50

✔ flier_high: Simulates outliers between 100 and 200

✔ flier_low: Simulates outliers between 0 and –100

The code combines all these values into a single dataset using concatenate().
Being randomly generated with specific characteristics (such as a large number
of points in the middle), the output will show specific characteristics but will
work fine for the example.

The call to boxplot() requires only data as input. All other parameters
have default settings. In this case, the code sets the presentation of outliers
to green *X*s by setting the sym parameter. You use widths to modify the
size of the box (made extra large in this case to make the box easier to see).
Finally, you can create a square box or a box with a notch using the notch
parameter (which normally defaults to False). Figure 10-4 shows typical
output from this example.

The box shows the three data points as the box, with the red line in the middle
being the median. The two black horizontal lines connected to the box by
whiskers show the upper and lower limits (for four quartiles). The outliers
appear above and below the upper and lower limit lines as green Xs.

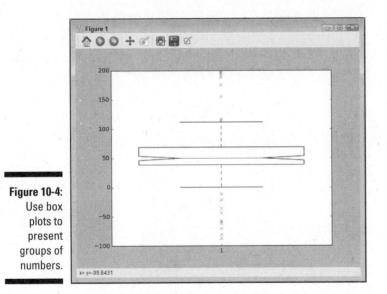

Figure 10-4:
Use box
plots to
present
groups of
numbers.

Seeing data patterns using scatterplots

Scatterplots show clusters of data rather than trends (as with line graphs) or
discrete values (as with bar charts). The purpose of a scatterplot is to help

you see data patterns. The following example shows how to create a scatter-plot using randomized data:

```
import numpy as np
import matplotlib.pyplot as plt

x1 = 5 * np.random.rand(40)
x2 = 5 * np.random.rand(40) + 25
x3 = 25 * np.random.rand(20)
x = np.concatenate((x1, x2, x3))

y1 = 5 * np.random.rand(40)
y2 = 5 * np.random.rand(40) + 25
y3 = 25 * np.random.rand(20)
y = np.concatenate((y1, y2, y3))

plt.scatter(x, y, s=[100], marker='^', c='m')
plt.show()
```

The example begins by generating random x and y coordinates. For each x coordinate, you must have a corresponding y coordinate. It's possible to create a scatterplot using just the x and y coordinates.

It's possible to dress up a scatterplot in a number of ways. In this case, the s parameter determines the size of each data point. The marker parameter determines the data point shape. You use the c parameter to define the colors for all the data points, or you can define a separate color for individual data points. Figure 10-5 shows the output from this example.

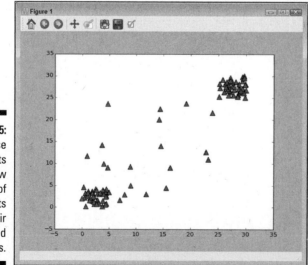

Figure 10-5: Use scatterplots to show groups of data points and their associated patterns.

Creating Advanced Scatterplots

Scatterplots are especially important for data science because they can show data patterns that aren't obvious when viewed in other ways. You can see data groupings with relative ease and help the viewer understand when data belongs to a particular group. You can also show overlaps between groups and even demonstrate when certain data is outside the expected range. Showing these various kinds of relationships in the data is an advanced technique that you need to know in order to make the best use of MatPlotLib. The following sections demonstrate how to perform these advanced techniques on the scatterplot you created earlier in the chapter.

Depicting groups

Color is the third axis when working with a scatterplot. Using color lets you highlight groups so that others can see them with greater ease. The following example shows how you can use color to show groups within a scatterplot:

```
import numpy as np
import matplotlib.pyplot as plt

x1 = 5 * np.random.rand(50)
x2 = 5 * np.random.rand(50) + 25
x3 = 30 * np.random.rand(25)
x = np.concatenate((x1, x2, x3))

y1 = 5 * np.random.rand(50)
y2 = 5 * np.random.rand(50) + 25
y3 = 30 * np.random.rand(25)
y = np.concatenate((y1, y2, y3))

color_array = ['b'] * 50 + ['g'] * 50 + ['r'] * 25

plt.scatter(x, y, s=[50], marker='D', c=color_array)
plt.show()
```

The example works essentially the same as the scatterplot example in the previous section, except that this example uses an array for the colors. Unfortunately, if you're seeing this in the printed book, the differences between the shades of gray in Figure 10-6 will be hard to see. However, the first group is blue, followed by green for the second group. Any outliers appear in red.

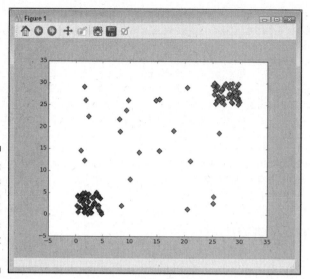

Figure 10-6:
Color arrays can make the scatterplot groups stand out better.

Showing correlations

In some cases, you need to know the general direction that your data is taking when looking at a scatterplot. Even if you create a clear depiction of the groups, the actual direction that the data is taking as a whole may not be clear. In this case, you add a trendline to the output. Here's an example of adding a trendline to a scatterplot that includes groups but isn't quite as clear as the scatterplot shown previously in Figure 10-6.

```
import numpy as np
import matplotlib.pyplot as plt
import matplotlib.pylab as plb

x1 = 15 * np.random.rand(50)
x2 = 15 * np.random.rand(50) + 15
x3 = 30 * np.random.rand(30)
x = np.concatenate((x1, x2, x3))

y1 = 15 * np.random.rand(50)
y2 = 15 * np.random.rand(50) + 15
y3 = 30 * np.random.rand(30)
y = np.concatenate((y1, y2, y3))

color_array = ['b'] * 50 + ['g'] * 50 + ['r'] * 25

plt.scatter(x, y, s=[90], marker='*', c=color_array)
```

```
z = np.polyfit(x, y, 1)
p = np.poly1d(z)
plb.plot(x, p(x), 'm-')

plt.show()
```

The code for creating the scatterplot is essentially the same as in the example in the "Depicting groups" section, earlier in the chapter, but the plot doesn't define the groups as clearly. Adding a trendline means calling the NumPy polyfit() function with the data, which returns a vector of coefficients, p, that minimizes the least squares error. (Least square regression is a method for finding a line that summarizes the relationship between two variables, x and y in this case, at least within the domain of the explanatory variable x. The third polyfit() parameter expresses the degree of the polynomial fit.)

The vector output of polyfit() is used as input to poly1d(), which calculates the actual y-axis data points. The call to plot() creates the trendline on the scatterplot. You can see a typical result of this example in Figure 10-7.

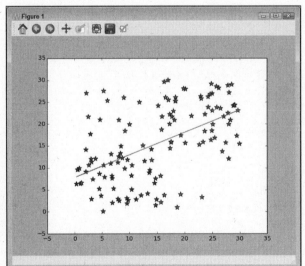

Figure 10-7:
Scatterplot trendlines can show you the general data direction.

Plotting Time Series

Nothing is truly static. When you view most data, you see an instant of time — a snapshot of how the data appeared at one particular moment. Of course, such views are both common and useful. However, sometimes you need to view data as it moves through time — to see it as it changes. Only by viewing the data as it changes can you expect to understand the underlying forces that shape it. The following sections describe how to work with data on a time-related basis.

Representing time on axes

Many times, you need to present data over time. The data could come in many forms, but generally you have some type of time tick (one unit of time), followed by one or more features that describe what happens during that particular tick. The following example shows a simple set of days and sales on those days for a particular item in whole (integer) amounts.

```
import datetime as dt
import pandas as pd
import matplotlib.pyplot as plt

df = pd.DataFrame(columns=('Time', 'Sales'))

start_date = dt.datetime(2015, 7,1)
end_date = dt.datetime(2015, 7,10)
daterange = pd.date_range(start_date, end_date)

for single_date in daterange:
    row = dict(zip(['Time', 'Sales'],
                   [single_date,
                    int(50*np.random.rand(1))]))
    row_s = pd.Series(row)
    row_s.name = single_date.strftime('%b %d')
    df = df.append(row_s)

df.ix['Jul 01':'Jul 07', ['Time', 'Sales']].plot()
plt.ylim(0, 50)
plt.xlabel('Sales Date')
plt.ylabel('Sale Value')
plt.title('Plotting Time')
plt.show()
```

The example begins by creating a `DataFrame` to hold the information. The source of the information could be anything, but the example generates it randomly. Notice that the example creates a `date_range` to hold the starting and ending date time frame for easier processing using a `for` loop.

An essential part of this example is the creation of individual rows. Each row has an actual time value so that you don't lose information. However, notice that the index (`row_s.name` property) is a string. This string should appear in the form that you want the dates to appear when presented in the plot.

Using ix[] lets you select a range of dates from the total number of entries available. Notice that this example uses only some of the generated data for output. It then adds some amplifying information about the plot and displays it onscreen. Figure 10-8 show typical output from the randomly generated data.

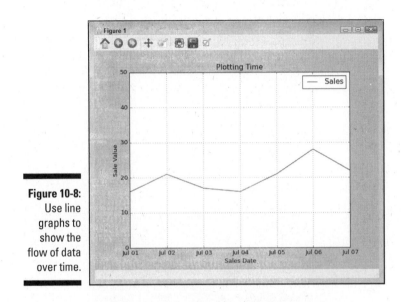

Figure 10-8:
Use line graphs to show the flow of data over time.

Plotting trends over time

As with any other data presentation, sometimes you really can't see what direction the data is headed in without help. The following example starts with the plot from the previous section and adds a trendline to it:

```
import datetime as dt
import pandas as pd
import matplotlib.pyplot as plt
import numpy as np
import matplotlib.pylab as plb

df = pd.DataFrame(columns=('Time', 'Sales'))

start_date = dt.datetime(2015, 7,1)
end_date = dt.datetime(2015, 7,10)
daterange = pd.date_range(start_date, end_date)

for single_date in daterange:
    row = dict(zip(['Time', 'Sales'],
                   [single_date,
                    int(50*np.random.rand(1))]))
```

```
    row_s = pd.Series(row)
    row_s.name = single_date.strftime('%b %d')
    df = df.append(row_s)

df.ix['Jul 01':'Jul 10', ['Time', 'Sales']].plot()

z = np.polyfit(range(0, 10),
            df.as_matrix(['Sales']).flatten(), 1)

p = np.poly1d(z)
plb.plot(df.as_matrix(['Sales']),
        p(df.as_matrix(['Sales'])), 'm-')

plt.ylim(0, 50)
plt.xlabel('Sales Date')
plt.ylabel('Sale Value')
plt.title('Plotting Time')
plt.legend(['Sales', 'Trend'])
plt.show()
```

The technique for adding the trendline is the same as for the example in the "Showing correlations" section, earlier in this chapter, with some interesting differences. Because the data appears within a `DataFrame`, you must export it using `as_matrix()` and then flatten the resulting array using `flatten()` before you can use it as input to `polyfit()`. Likewise, you must export the data before you can call `plot()` to display the trendline onscreen.

When you plot the initial data, the call to `plot()` automatically generates a legend for you. MatPlotLib doesn't automatically add the trendline, so you must also create a new legend for the plot. Figure 10-9 shows typical output from this example using randomly generated data.

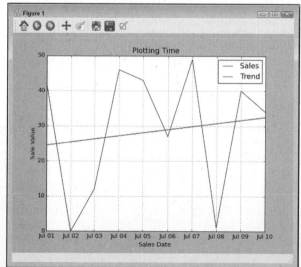

Figure 10-9: Add a trend-line to show the average direction of change in a chart or graph.

Plotting Geographical Data

Knowing where data comes from or how it applies to a specific place can
be important. For example, if you want to know where food shortages have
occurred and plan how to deal with them, you need to match the data you
have to geographical locations. The same holds true for predicting where
future sales will occur. You may find that you need to use existing data to
determine where to put new stores. Otherwise, you could put a store in a
location that won't receive much in the way of sales, and the effort will lose
money rather than make it. The following example shows how to draw a map
and place pointers to specific locations on it:

```
import numpy as np
import matplotlib.pyplot as plt
from mpl_toolkits.basemap import Basemap

austin = (-97.75, 30.25)
hawaii = (-157.8, 21.3)
washington = (-77.01, 38.90)
chicago = (-87.68, 41.83)
losangeles = (-118.25, 34.05)

m = Basemap(projection='merc',llcrnrlat=10,urcrnrlat=50,
            llcrnrlon=-160,urcrnrlon=-60)

m.drawcoastlines()
m.fillcontinents(color='lightgray',lake_color='lightblue')
m.drawparallels(np.arange(-90.,91.,30.))
m.drawmeridians(np.arange(-180.,181.,60.))
m.drawmapboundary(fill_color='aqua')

m.drawcountries()

x, y = m(*zip(*[hawaii, austin, washington,
                chicago, losangeles]))
m.plot(x, y, marker='o', markersize=6,
       markerfacecolor='red', linewidth=0)

plt.title("Mercator Projection")
plt.show()
```

The example begins by defining the longitude and latitude for various cities.
It then creates the basic map. The projection parameter defines the
basic map appearance. The next four parameters, llcrnrlat, urcrnrlat,
llcrnrlon, and urcrnrlon define the sides of the map. You can define
other parameters, but these parameters generally create a useful map.

Getting the Basemap Toolkit

Before you can work with mapping data, you need a library that supports the required mapping functionality. A number of such packages are available, but the easiest to work with and install is the Basemap Toolkit. You can obtain this toolkit from `http://matplotlib.org/basemap/users/intro.html`. The site includes supplementary information about the toolkit and provides download instructions. Unlike some other packages, this one does include instructions for Mac, Windows, and Linux users. In addition, you can obtain a Windows-specific installer. Make sure to also check out the usage video at `http://nbviewer.ipython.org/github/mqlaql/geospatial-data/blob/master/Geospatial-Data-with-Python.ipynb`.

The next set of calls defines the map particulars. For example, `drawcoastlines()` determines whether the coastlines are highlighted to make them easy to see. To make landmasses easy to discern from water, you want to call `fillcontinents()` with the colors of your choice. When working with specific locations, as the example does, you want to call `drawcountries()` to ensure that the country boundaries appear on the map. At this point, you have a map that's ready to fill in with data.

In this case, the example creates x and y coordinates using the previously stored longitude and latitude values. It then plots these locations on the map in a contrasting color so that you can easily see them. The final step is to display the map, as shown in Figure 10-10.

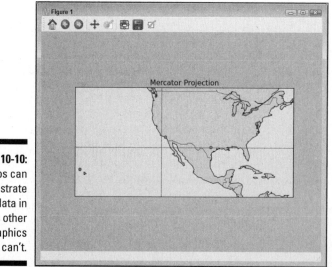

Figure 10-10:
Maps can illustrate data in ways other graphics can't.

Visualizing Graphs

A *graph* is a depiction of data showing the connections between data points using lines. The purpose is to show that some data points relate to other data points, but not all the data points that appear on the graph. Think about a map of a subway system. Each of the stations connects to other stations, but no single station connects to all the stations in the subway system. Graphs are a popular data science topic because of their use in social media analysis. When performing social media analysis, you depict and analyze networks of relationships, such as friends or business connections, from social hubs such as Facebook, Google+, Twitter, or LinkedIn.

 The two common depictions of graphs are *undirected*, where the graph simply shows lines between data elements, and *directed*, where arrows added to the line show that data flows in a particular direction. For example, consider a depiction of a water system. The water would flow in just one direction in most cases, so you could use a directed graph to depict not only the connections between sources and targets for the water but also to show water direction by using arrows. The following sections help you understand the two types of graphs better and show you how to create them.

Developing undirected graphs

As previously stated, an undirected graph simply shows connections between nodes. The output doesn't provide a direction from one node to the next. For example, when establishing connectivity between web pages, no direction is implied. The following example shows how to create an undirected graph.

```
import networkx as nx
import matplotlib.pyplot as plt

G = nx.Graph()
H = nx.Graph()
G.add_node(1)
G.add_nodes_from([2, 3])
G.add_nodes_from(range(4, 7))
H.add_node(7)
G.add_nodes_from(H)

G.add_edge(1, 2)
G.add_edge(1, 1)
G.add_edges_from([(2,3), (3,6), (4,6), (5,6)])
H.add_edges_from([(4,7), (5,7), (6,7)])
G.add_edges_from(H.edges())

nx.draw_networkx(G)
plt.show()
```

In contrast to the canned example found in the "Using NetworkX basics" section of Chapter 7, this example builds the graph using a number of different techniques. It begins by importing the Networkx package you use in Chapter 7. To create a new undirected graph, the code calls the `Graph()` constructor, which can take a number of input arguments to use as attributes. However, you can build a perfectly usable graph without using attributes, which is what this example does.

The easiest way to add a node is to call `add_node()` with a node number. You can also add a list, dictionary, or `range()` of nodes using `add_nodes_from()`. In fact, you can import nodes from other graphs if you want.

Even though the nodes used in the example rely on numbers, you don't have to use numbers for your nodes. A node can use a single letter, a string, or even a date. Nodes do have some restrictions. For example, you can't create a node using a Boolean value.

Nodes don't have any connectivity at the outset. You must define connections (edges) between them. To add a single edge, you call `add_edge()` with the numbers of the nodes that you want to add. As with nodes, you can use `add_edges_from()` to create more than one edge using a list, dictionary, or another graph as input. Figure 10-11 shows the output from this example (your output may differ slightly but should have the same connections).

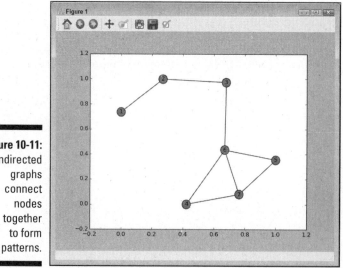

Figure 10-11:
Undirected graphs connect nodes together to form patterns.

Developing directed graphs

You use directed graphs when you need to show a direction, say from a start point to an end point. When you get a map that shows you how to get from one specific point to another, the starting node and ending node are marked as such and the lines between these nodes (and all the intermediate nodes), show direction.

Your graphs need not be boring. You can dress them up in all sorts of ways so that the viewer gains additional information in different ways. For example, you can create custom labels, use specific colors for certain nodes, or rely on color to help people see the meaning behind your graphs. You can also change edge line weight and use other techniques to mark a specific path between nodes as the better one to choose. The following example shows many (but not nearly all) the ways in which you can dress up a directed graph and make it more interesting:

```
import networkx as nx
import matplotlib.pyplot as plt

G = nx.DiGraph()

G.add_node(1)
G.add_nodes_from([2, 3])
G.add_nodes_from(range(4, 6))
G.add_path([6, 7, 8])

G.add_edge(1, 2)
G.add_edges_from([(1,4), (4,5), (2,3), (3,6), (5,6)])

colors = ['r', 'g', 'g', 'g', 'g', 'm', 'm', 'r']
labels = {1:'Start', 2:'2', 3:'3', 4:'4',
          5:'5', 6:'6', 7:'7', 8:'End'}
sizes = [800, 300, 300, 300, 300, 600, 300, 800]

nx.draw_networkx(G, node_color=colors, node_shape='D',
                 with_labels=True, labels=labels,
                 node_size=sizes)
plt.show()
```

The example begins by creating a directional graph using the `DiGraph()` constructor. You should note that the NetworkX package also supports `MultiGraph()` and `MultiDiGraph()` graph types. You can see a listing of all the graph types at `http://networkx.lanl.gov/reference/classes.html`.

Adding nodes is much like working with an undirected graph. You can add single nodes using `add_node()` and multiple nodes using `add_nodes_from()`. The `add_path()` call lets you create nodes and edges at the same time. The order of nodes in the call is important. The flow from one node to another is from left to right in the list supplied to the call.

Adding edges is much the same as working with an undirected graph, too. You can use `add_edge()` to add a single edge or `add_edges_from()` to add multiple edges at one time. However, the order of the node numbers is important. The flow goes from the left node to the right node in each pair.

This example adds special node colors, labels, shape (only one shape is used), and sizes to the output. You still call on `draw_networkx()` to perform the task. However, adding the parameters shown changes the appearance of the graph. Note that you must set `with_labels` to `True` in order to see the labels provided by the `labels` parameter. Figure 10-12 shows the output from this example.

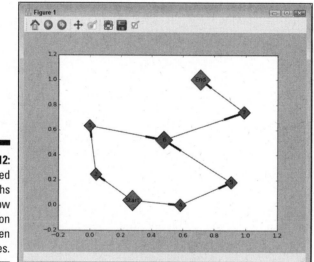

Figure 10-12: Use directed graphs to show direction between nodes.

Chapter 11

Understanding the Tools

In This Chapter

▶ Working with the IPython console

▶ Working with IPython Notebook

▶ Interacting with multimedia and graphics

Up to this point, the book spends a lot of time working with Python to perform data science tasks without actually engaging the tools provided by Anaconda much. Yes, a good deal of what you do involves typing in code and seeing what happens. However, if you don't actually know how to use your tools well, you miss opportunities to perform tasks easier and faster. Automation is an essential part of performing data science tasks in Python.

This chapter is about working with the two main Anaconda tools, IPython console and IPython Notebook. Earlier chapters give you some experience with both tools, but those chapters don't explore either tool in any detail, and you need to know these tools a lot better for upcoming chapters. The skills you develop in this chapter will help you perform tasks in later chapters with greater speed and far less effort.

The chapter also looks at tasks you can perform with your newfound skills. You develop even more skills as the book progresses, but these tasks help put your new skills into perspective and appreciate how you can use them to make working with Python even easier.

You don't have to manually type the source code for this chapter. In fact, it's a lot easier if you use the downloadable source. The source code for this chapter appears in the `P4DS4D; 11; Understanding the Tools.ipynb` source code file. (See the Introduction for details on where to locate this file.)

Using the IPython Console

The Python console is where you can experiment with data science interactively. You can try things and see the results immediately. If you make a mistake, you can simply close the console and create a new one. The console is for playing around and considering what might be possible. The following sections help you understand what you can do to make your IPython console experience better.

The standard Python console and the IPython console look similar, and you can perform many of the same tasks using them. If you already know how to use the Python console, you have an advantage when it comes to working with the IPython console. However, they also have differences. The IPython console provides enhancements that don't come with the Python console. In addition, performing certain tasks, such as pasting large amounts of text, differs between the two consoles, so even if you know how to use the Python console, reading the sections that follow will help you.

Interacting with screen text

When you first start IPython, you see a screen similar to the one shown in Figure 11-1. The screen seems loaded with text, but all of it provides useful information. The top three lines tell you about your version of Python and Anaconda. Below that are three help terms (copyright, credits, and license) that you can type to obtain more information about your version of these two products. For example, when you type **credits** and press Enter, you see a listing of the contributors to this version of the product.

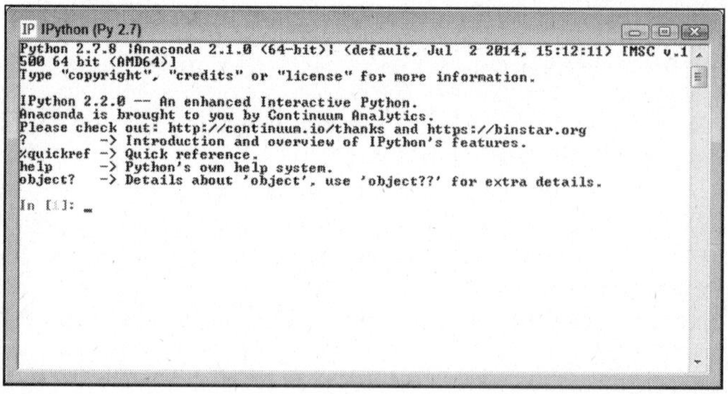

Figure 11-1:
The opening screen provides information on where to get additional help.

```
IP IPython (Py 2.7)
Python 2.7.8 |Anaconda 2.1.0 (64-bit)| (default, Jul  2 2014, 15:12:11) [MSC v.1
500 64 bit (AMD64)]
Type "copyright", "credits" or "license" for more information.

IPython 2.2.0 -- An enhanced Interactive Python.
Anaconda is brought to you by Continuum Analytics.
Please check out: http://continuum.io/thanks and https://binstar.org
?         -> Introduction and overview of IPython's features.
%quickref -> Quick reference.
help      -> Python's own help system.
object?   -> Details about 'object', use 'object??' for extra details.

In [1]:
```

Below the product text, you see another text area containing information about IPython. The four commands that follow, `?`, `%quickref`, `help`, and `object?` tell you how to obtain additional information about

- ✔ Using IPython to perform useful work
- ✔ Obtaining information about the magic functions that IPython provides
- ✔ Learning about the Python programming language
- ✔ Discovering facts about the packages, objects, and methods you use in Python to interact with data

Depending on your operating system, you should be able to right-click the IPython window and see a context menu containing options for working with the text in the window. Figure 11-2 shows the context menu for Windows. This menu is important because it lets you interact with the text and copy the results of your experimentation in a more permanent form.

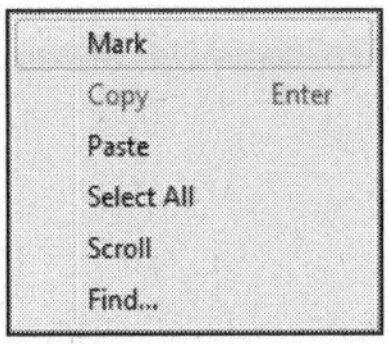

Figure 11-2:
You can cut, copy, and paste text using this context menu.

Mark	
Copy	Enter
Paste	
Select All	
Scroll	
Find...	

You can obtain access to the same menu of options by choosing the System menu (click the icon in the upper-left corner of the window) and selecting the Edit menu. The options you commonly see are the following:

- ✔ **Mark:** Selects the specific text you want to copy.
- ✔ **Copy:** Places the text you have marked onto the Clipboard (you can also press Enter after marking the text to perform a copy).
- ✔ **Paste:** Moves text from the Clipboard to the window. Unfortunately, this command doesn't work right with IPython for copying multiple lines of text. Use the `%paste` magic function to copy multiple lines of text instead.
- ✔ **Select All:** Performs a mark on all the text visible in the window.
- ✔ **Scroll:** Makes it possible to scroll the window when using the arrow keys. Press Enter to stop scrolling.
- ✔ **Find:** Displays a Find dialog box that you can use to locate text anywhere in the screen buffer. This is actually an exceptionally useful command because you can quickly locate text that you previously entered and want to reuse in some way.

One feature that IPython provides that you don't find when working with the standard Python console is cls, or clear screen. To clear the screen and make typing new commands easier, simply type **cls** and press Enter.

Changing the window appearance

The Windows console lets you change the IPython window appearance with ease. Depending on the console and platform you use, you may find that you have other options as well. If your console doesn't provide any flexibility in changing the IPython appearance, you can still do so using a magic function as described in the "Using magic functions" section later in the chapter to change the window appearance.

To change the Windows console, click the system menu and choose Properties. You see a dialog box like the one shown in Figure 11-3.

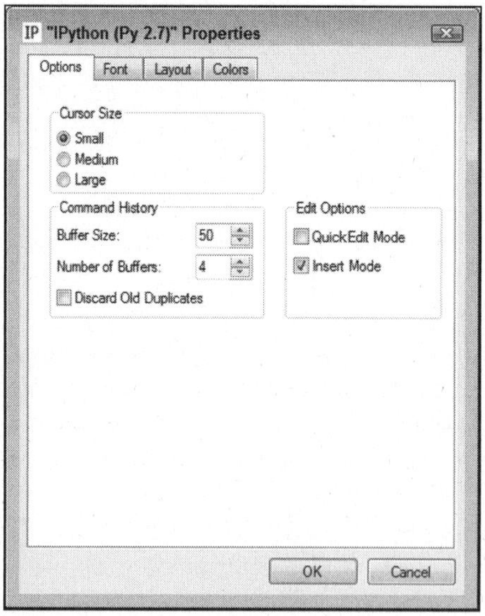

Figure 11-3:
The Properties dialog box makes it possible to control the appearance of your window.

Each tab controls a different aspect of the window appearance. Even though you're working with IPython, the underlying console still affects what you see. Here are the purposes for each of the tabs shown in Figure 11-3:

- ✔ **Options:** Determines the size of the cursor (a large cursor works better in bright settings), how many commands the window remembers, and how editing works (such as whether you're in Insert mode).

- ✔ **Font:** Defines the font used to display text in the window. The Raster Fonts option appears to work best for most people, but trying other font options may help you see the text better under certain conditions.

✔ **Layout:** Specifies the window size, position onscreen, and size of the buffer used to hold information that scrolls out of view. If you find that old commands scroll off too quickly, increasing the size of the window can help. Likewise, if you find that you can't locate older commands, increasing the size of the buffer can help.

✔ **Colors:** Determines the basic color settings for the window. The default setting of a black background with gray text is hard for many people to use. Using a white background with black text is much easier. However, you need to choose the color settings that work best for you. These colors are augmented by the colors used by the `%colors` magic function.

Getting Python help

No one can remember absolutely everything about a programming language. Even the best coders have memory lapses. This is why having language-specific help is so important. Without this help, programmers would spend a great deal of time researching packages, classes, methods, and properties online. Yes, they've used them in the past, but they can't quite bring the required information to mind today.

The Python portion of the IPython console provides two methods of getting help: help mode and interactive help. You use help mode when you want to explore the language and plan to spend some while doing it. Interactive help is better when you know specifically what you need help with and don't want to spend a lot of time looking at other sorts of information. The following sections tell you how to get help on the Python language whenever you need it.

Entering help mode

To enter help mode, type **help()** and press Enter. The console enters a new mode, in which you can type help-related commands as needed to discover more about Python. You can't type Python commands in this mode. The prompt changes to a help> prompt, as shown in Figure 11-4, to remind you that you're in help mode.

Figure 11-4: Help mode relies on a special help> prompt.

```
IP IPython (Py 2.7)

In [?]: help()

Welcome to Python 2.7!  This is the online help utility.

If this is your first time using Python, you should definitely check out
the tutorial on the Internet at http://docs.python.org/2.7/tutorial/.

Enter the name of any module, keyword, or topic to get help on writing
Python programs and using Python modules.  To quit this help utility and
return to the interpreter, just type "quit".

To get a list of available modules, keywords, or topics, type "modules",
"keywords", or "topics".  Each module also comes with a one-line summary
of what it does; to list the modules whose summaries contain a given word
such as "spam", type "modules spam".

help> _
```

To obtain help about any object or command, simply type the object or command name and press Enter. You can also type any of the following commands to obtain a listing of other topics of discussion.

- ✔ `modules`: Compiles a list of the currently loaded modules. This list varies by how your copy of Python is configured at any given time, so the list won't be the same every time you use this command. The command can take a while to execute, and the output list is usually quite large (unlike the standard Python console, in which the list is relatively small). In some cases, the command actually fails because of the way in which Anaconda interacts with Python.

- ✔ `keywords`: Presents a list of Python keywords that you can ask about. For example, you can type **assert** and learn more about the `assert` keyword.

- ✔ `topics`: Displays a list of general Python topics, such as CONVERSIONS. The topics appear in uppercase rather than lowercase.

Requesting help in help mode

To obtain help in help mode, you simply type the name of the module, keyword, or topic you want to learn more about and press Enter. Help mode is Python specific, which means that you can ask about a `list`, but not an object based on a list named `mylist`. You also can't ask about IPython-specific features, such as the `cls` command.

When working with features that are part of a module, you need to include the module name. For example, if you want to find out about the `version()` method within the `sys` module, you type **sys.version** and press Enter at the help prompt, rather than just type **version**.

If a help topic is too large to present as a single screen of information, you see `-- More --` at the bottom of the display. Press Enter to advance the help information one line at a time or the spacebar to advance the help information a full screen a time. You can't go backward in the help listing. Pressing Q ends the help information immediately.

Exiting help mode

After you finish exploring help, you need to get back to the Python prompt to type more commands. Simply press Enter without entering anything at the help prompt or type **quit** and press Enter at the help prompt.

Getting interactive help

Sometimes you don't want to leave the Python prompt to get help. In this case, you can type `help('<topic>')` and press Enter to obtain help information. For example, to receive help on the print command, you type **help('print')** and press Enter. Notice that the help topic is in single quotation marks. If you try to request help without enclosing the topic in single quotation marks, you see an error message.

Interactive help works with any module, keyword, or topic that Python supports. For example, you can type **help('CONVERSIONS')** and press Enter to receive help about the CONVERSIONS topic. It's important to note that case is still important when working with interactive help. Typing **help('conversions')** and pressing Enter displays a message telling you that help isn't available.

Getting IPython help

Getting help with IPython is different from getting help with Python. When you obtain IPython help, you work with the development environment rather than the programming language. To obtain IPython help, type **?** and press Enter. You see a long listing of the various ways in which you can use IPython help.

Some of the more essential forms of help rely on typing a keyword with a question mark. For example, if you want to learn more about the cls command, you type cls? or ?cls and press Enter. It doesn't matter whether the question mark appears before or after the command.

Interestingly enough, you can kick IPython help up a notch. If you want to obtain more details about a command or other IPython feature, use two question marks. For example, ??cls displays the source code for the cls command. The double question mark (??) may not always return additional information if there isn't any more information to find.

If you want to stop displaying IPython information early, press Q to quit. Otherwise, you can press Space or Enter to display each screen of information until the help system has displayed everything available.

Using magic functions

It's amazing to think that you really can get magic on your computer! IPython provides a special feature called magic functions. The functions let you perform all sorts of amazing tasks with your IPython console. The following sections provide an overview of the magic functions. You do see some of them used later in the book as well. However, it pays to spend some time checking out these functions for yourself.

Obtaining the magic functions list

The best way to start working with magic functions is to obtain a list of them by typing **%quickref** and pressing Enter. What you see is a help screen similar to the one shown in Figure 11-5. The listing can be a little confusing to read, so make sure you take your time with it.

Working with magic functions

Most magic functions start with either a single percent sign (%) or two percent signs (%%). Those with a single percent sign work at the command-line level, while those that have two percent signs work at the cell level. The IPython Notebook discussion later in the chapter talks more about cells. For now, all you really need to know is that you generally use magic functions with a single percent sign within the IPython console.

Most of the magic functions display status information when you use them by themselves. For example, when you type **%cd** and press Enter, you see the current directory. To change directories, you type %cd plus the new directory location on your system. There are some exceptions to this rule, however. For example, %cls clears the screen when used alone because it doesn't take any parameters.

One of the more interesting magic functions is %colors. You can use this function to change the colors used to display information onscreen, which is helpful when you use various devices. The available options are NoColor (everything is in black and white), Linux (the default setting), and LightBG (which uses a blue-and-green color scheme). This particular function is another exception to the rule. Typing %colors alone doesn't display the current color scheme but displays an error message instead.

Discovering objects

Python is all about objects. In fact, you can't do anything in Python without working with some sort of object. With this in mind, it's a good idea to know how to discover precisely what object you're working with and what features it provides. The following sections help you discover the Python objects you use as you code.

Getting object help

With IPython, you can request information about specific objects using the object name and a question mark (?). For example, if you want to know more about a `list` object named `mylist`, simply type **mylist?** and press Enter. You see output showing the `mylist` type, content in string form, length, and a document string providing a quick overview of `mylist`.

When you need detailed help about `mylist`, you type **help(mylist)** and press Enter instead. You see the same help that you should when requesting information about the Python `list`. However, you receive the information that's appropriate to the particular object you need help with, rather than having to first discover the object type and then request information for that object.

Obtaining object specifics

The `dir()` function is often overlooked, but it's an essential way to learn about object specifics. To see a list of properties and methods associated with any object, use `dir(<object name>)`. For example, if you create a list called `mylist` and want to know what sorts of things you can do with it, **type dir(mylist)** and press Enter. IPython displays a list of methods and properties that are specific to `mylist`.

Using IPython object help

Python provides one level of help about your objects — and IPython provides another. When you want to know more about your object than Python tells you, try using the question mark with it. For example, when working with a `list` named `mylist`, you can type **mylist?** and press Enter to discover the object type, content, length, and associated `docstring`. The `docstring` provides you with a quick overview of usage information for the type — enough that you can find more details with what you now know about the object.

Using a single question mark does cause IPython to clip long content. If you want to obtain the full content for an object, you need to use the double question mark (??). For example, type **mylist??** and press Enter to see any clipped details (although there may not be any additional details). Whenever possible, IPython provides you with the full source code for the object (assuming that the source code is available).

You can use magic functions with objects as well. These functions simplify the help output and provide only the information you need, as shown here:

- ✔ `%pdoc`: Displays the `docstring` for the object
- ✔ `%pdef`: Shows how to call the object (assuming that the object is callable)
- ✔ `%source`: Displays the source code for the object (assuming that the source is available)
- ✔ `%file`: Outputs the name of the file that contains the source code for the object
- ✔ `%pinfo`: Displays detailed information about the object (often more than provided by help alone)
- ✔ `%pinfo2`: Displays extra detailed information about the object (when available)

Using IPython Notebook

So far, the chapter has told you about using IPython Notebook to input code, and that's about it. Of course, it works fine for that purpose. However, the IDE can do more for you. The following sections help you understand some of the interesting things that IPython Notebook can help you do.

Working with styles

One of the ways in which IPython Notebook excels over just about any other Integrated Development Environment (IDE) you'll ever use is that you can use it to create nice-looking output. Rather than have a screen full of a whole bunch of plain old code, you can use iPython to create sections and add styles so that the output is nicely formatted. What you can end up with is a good-looking report that just happens to contain executable code. The reason for this improved output is the use of styles.

When you type code into IPython Notebook, you place the code in a cell. Each section of code you create goes into a separate cell. When you need to create a new cell, you click Insert Cell Below (the button with a plus sign in a black circle) on the toolbar. Likewise, when you decide that you no longer need a cell, you select it and then click Cut Cell (the button with a scissors).

The default style for a cell is Code. However, when you click the down arrow next to the Code entry, you see a listing of styles, as shown in Figure 11-6.

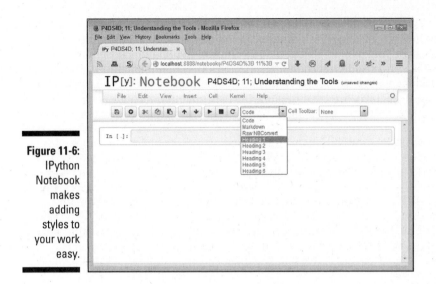

Figure 11-6:
IPython
Notebook
makes
adding
styles to
your work
easy.

The various styles shown help you format content in various ways. The headings are most definitely used to separate varies entries. To try it for yourself, type the heading for this main chapter section, **Using IPython Notebook**, in the first cell; next, select Heading 1 from the drop-down list and click Run Cell. The content changes to a heading. Now add another cell by clicking Insert Cell Below and type **Working with styles** as a Heading 2. Figure 11-7 shows that the two entries are indeed headings and that the second entry is smaller than the first.

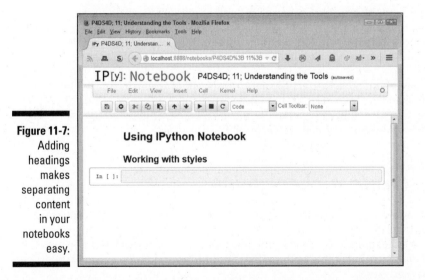

Figure 11-7:
Adding
headings
makes
separating
content
in your
notebooks
easy.

You can add HTML content to your documents as well. Simply select the Markdown style. The HTML content can contain anything a web page contains with regard to standard HTML tags. In general, you use this style to provide documentation and links to outside material. Relying on HTML tags makes it possible to include things like lists or even pictures. In short, you can actually include an HTML document fragment as part of your notebook, which makes an IPython Notebook much more than a simple means of writing down code.

The use of the Raw NBConvert formatting option is outside the scope of this book. However, it provides you the means for included information that shouldn't be modified by the notebook converter (NBConvert). You can output IPython Notebooks in a variety of formats, and NBConvert performs this task for you. You can read about this feature at `https://ipython.org/ipython-doc/dev/notebook/nbconvert.html#nbconvert`. The goal of the Raw NBConvert style is to allow you to include special content, such as Lamport TeX (LaTeX) content. The LaTeX document system isn't tied to a particular editor — it's simply a means of encoding scientific documents.

Restarting the kernel

Every time you perform a task in your notebook, you create variables, import modules, and perform a wealth of other tasks that corrupt the environment. At some point, you can't really be sure that something is working as it should. To overcome this problem, you click Restart Kernel after saving your document by clicking Save and Checkpoint. You can then run your code again to ensure that it does work as you thought it would.

Sometimes an error also causes the kernel to crash. Your document starts acting oddly, updates slowly, or shows other signs of corruption. Again, the answer is to restart the kernel to ensure that you have a clean environment and that the kernel is running as it should.

Whenever you click Restart Kernel, you see the warning message shown in Figure 11-8. Make certain that you pay attention to the warning because you could lose temporary changes during a kernel restart. Always save your document before you restart the kernel.

Restoring a checkpoint

At some point, you may find that you made a mistake. IPython Notebook is notably missing an Undo button: You won't find one anywhere. Instead, you create checkpoints each time you finish a task. Creating checkpoints when your document is stable and working properly helps you recover faster from mistakes.

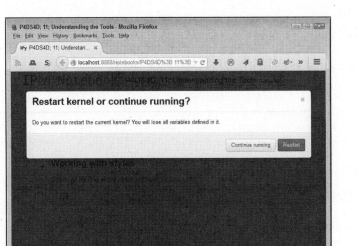

Figure 11-8:
Save your
document
before
restarting
the kernel.

To restore your setup to the condition contained in a checkpoint, choose
File⇨Revert to Checkpoint. You see a listing of available checkpoints. Simply
select the one you want to use. When you select the checkpoint, you see a
warning message like the one shown in Figure 11-9. When you click Revert,
any old information is gone and the information found in the checkpoint
becomes the current information.

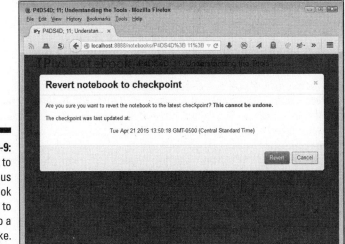

Figure 11-9:
Revert to
a previous
notebook
setup to
undo a
mistake.

Performing Multimedia and Graphic Integration

Pictures say a lot of things that words can't say (or at least they do it with far less effort). IPython Notebook is both a coding platform and a presentation platform. You may be surprised at just what you can do with it. The following sections provide a brief overview of some of the more interesting features.

Embedding plots and other images

At some point, you might have spotted an IPython Notebook with multimedia or graphics embedded into it and wondered why you didn't see the same effects in your own files. In fact, all the graphics examples to this point in the book have appeared as separate figures and not part of the code. Fortunately, you cam perform some more magic by using the `%matplotlib` magic function. The possible values for this function are: `'gtk'`, `'gtk3'`, `'inline'`, `'nbagg'`, `'osx'`, `'qt'`, `'qt4'`, `'qt5'`, `'tk'`, and `'wx'`, each of which defines a different plotting backend (the code used to actually render the plot) used to present information onscreen.

When you run `%matplotlib inline`, any plots you create appear as part of the document. When you try this technique with the "Showing parts of a whole with pie charts" example from Chapter 10, you get the output shown in Figure 11-10.

Loading examples from online sites

Because some examples you see online can be hard to understand unless you have them loaded on your own system, you should also keep the `%load` magic function in mind. All you need is the URL of an example you want to see on your system. For example, try `%load http://matplotlib.sourceforge.net/mpl_examples/pylab_examples/integral_demo.py`. When you click Run Cell, IPython Notebook loads the example directly below the cell. You can then run the example and see the output from it on your own system.

Obtaining online graphics and multimedia

A lot of the functionality required to perform special multimedia and graphics processing appears within `IPython.display`. By importing a required

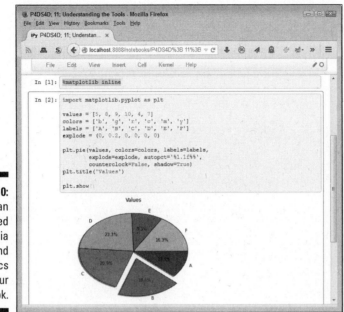

Figure 11-10: You can embed multimedia and graphics into your notebook.

class, you can perform tasks such as embedding images into your notebook. Here's an example of embedding one of the pictures from the author's blog into the notebook for this chapter:

```
from IPython.display import Image
Embed = Image(
    'http://blog.johnmuellerbooks.com/' +
    'wp-content/uploads/2015/04/Layer-Hens.jpg')
Embed
```

The code begins by importing the required class, Image, and then using features from it to first define what to embed and then actually embed the image. The output you see from this example appears in Figure 11-11.

If you expect an image to change over time, you might want to create a link to it instead of embedding it. You must refresh a link because the content in the notebook is only a reference rather than the actual image. However, as the image changes, you see the change in your notebook as well. To accomplish this task, you use `SoftLinked = Image(url='http://blog.johnmuellerbooks.com/wp-content/uploads/2015/04/Layer-Hens.jpg')` instead of `Embed`.

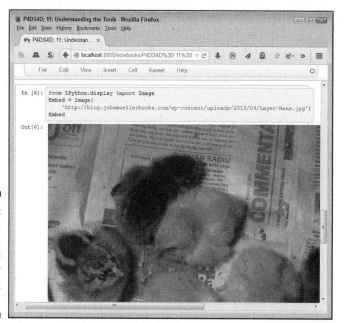

Figure 11-11:
Embedding
images
can dress
up your
notebook
presentation.

When working with embedded images on a regular basis, you might want to set the form in which the images are embedded. For example, you may prefer to embed them as PDFs. To perform this task, you use code similar to this:

```
from IPython.display import set_matplotlib_formats
set_matplotlib_formats('pdf', 'svg')
```

You have access to a wide number of formats when working with a notebook. The commonly supported formats are 'png', 'retina', 'jpeg', 'svg', and 'pdf'.

The IPython display system is nothing short of amazing, and this section hasn't even begun to tap the surface for you. For example, you can import a YouTube video and place it directly into your notebook as part of your presentation if you want. You can see quite a few more of the display features demonstrated at http://nbviewer.ipython.org/github/ipython/ipython/blob/1.x/examples/notebooks/Part 5 - Rich Display System.ipynb.

Part IV
Wrangling Data

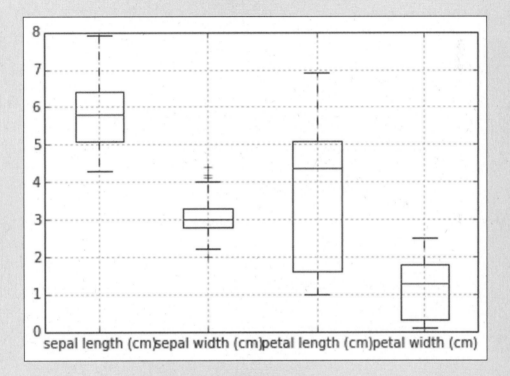

See an example of how you can analyze a sound file using a Fast Fourier Transform (FFT) at http://www.dummies.com/extras/pythonfordatascience.

In this part . . .

- ✔ Using programming tricks to solve data science problems
- ✔ Performing data analysis
- ✔ Making data easier to analyze
- ✔ Developing merged datasets
- ✔ Finding data that lies outside the predicted range

Chapter 12

Stretching Python's Capabilities

*I*f you've gone through the previous chapters, by this point you've dealt with all the basic data loading and manipulation methods offered by Python. Now it's time to start using some more complex instruments for data wrangling (or munging) and for machine learning. The final step of most data science projects is to build a data tool able to automatically summarize, predict, and recommend directly from your data.

Before taking that final step, you still have to massage your data by enforcing transformations that are even more radical. That's the *data wrangling* or *data munging* part, where sophisticated transformations are followed by visual and statistical explorations, and then again by further transformations. In the following sections, you learn how to handle huge streams of text, explore the basic characteristics of a dataset, optimize the speed of your experiments, compress data and create new synthetic features, generate new groups and classifications, and detect unexpected or exceptional cases that may cause your project to go wrong.

From here onward, you use the Scikit-learn package more and more (which means knowing more about it — the full documentation appears at http://scikit-learn.org/stable/documentation.html). The Scikit-learn package, in fact, offers a single repository containing almost all the tools that you need to be a data scientist and for your data science project to be successful. In this chapter, you discover important characteristics of Scikit-learn, structured in modules, classes, and functions, and some advanced Python time savers for improving performance with big unstructured data and highly time-consuming computational operations.

You don't have to type the source code for this chapter in by hand. In fact, it's a lot easier if you use the downloadable source (see the Introduction for download instructions). The source code for this chapter appears in the `P4DS4D; 12; Stretching Pythons Capabilities.ipynb` source code file.

Playing with Scikit-learn

Sometimes the best way to discover how to use something is to spend time playing with it. The more complex a tool, the more important play becomes. Given the complex math tasks you perform using Scikit-learn, playing becomes especially important. The following sections use the idea of playing with Scikit-learn to help you discover important concepts in using Scikit-learn to perform amazing feats of data science work.

Understanding classes in Scikit-learn

Understanding how classes work is an important prerequisite for being able to use the Scikit-learn package appropriately. Scikit-learn is the package for machine learning and data science experimentation favored by most data scientists. It contains a wide range of well-established learning algorithms, error functions, and testing procedures.

At its core, Scikit-learn features some base classes on which all the algorithms are built. Apart from `BaseEstimator`, the class from which all other classes inherit, there are four class types covering all the basic machine-learning functionalities:

- Classifying
- Regressing
- Grouping by clusters
- Transforming data

Even though each base class has specific methods and attributes, the core functionalities for data processing and machine learning are guaranteed by one or more series of methods and attributes called interfaces. The interfaces provide a uniform Application Programming Interface (API) to enforce similarity of methods and attributes between all the different algorithms present in the package. There are four Scikit-learn object-based interfaces:

- ✔ `estimator`: For fitting parameters, learning them from data, according to the algorithm
- ✔ `predictor`: For generating predictions from the fitted parameters
- ✔ `transformer`: For transforming data, implementing the fitted parameters
- ✔ `model`: For reporting goodness of fit or other score measures

The package groups the algorithms built on base classes and one or more object interfaces into modules, each module displaying a specialization in a particular type of machine-learning solution. For example, the `linear_model` module is for linear modeling, and `metrics` is for score and loss measure.

In order to find a specific algorithm in Scikit-learn, you must first find the module containing the same kind of algorithm that interests you, and then select it from the list of contents of the module. The algorithm is typically a class itself, whose methods and attributes are already known because they're common to other algorithms in Scikit-learn.

Getting accustomed to the Scikit-learn class approach may take some time. However, the API is the same for all the tools available in the package, so learning one class necessarily tells you about all the other classes. The best approach is to learn one class completely and then apply what you know to other classes.

Defining applications for data science

Figuring out ways to use data science to obtain constructive results is important. For example, you can apply the estimator interface to a

- ✔ **Classification problem:** Guessing that a new observation is from a certain group
- ✔ **Regression problem:** Guessing the value of a new observation

It works with the method `fit(X,y)` where `X` is the bidimensional array of predictors (the set of observations to learn) and `y` is the target outcome (another array, unidimensional).

By applying `fit`, the information in `X` is related to `y`, so that, knowing some new information with the same characteristics of `X`, we can guess correctly `y`.

In the process, some parameters are estimated internally by the `fit` method. Using `fit` makes it possible to distinguish between parameters, which are learned, and hyper-parameters, which instead are fixed by you when you instantiate the learner.

Instantiation involves assigning a Scikit-learn class to a Python variable. In addition to hyper-parameters, you can also fix other working parameters, such as requiring normalization or setting a random seed to reproduce the same results for each call, given the same input data.

Here is an example with linear regression, a very basic and common machine-learning algorithm. You must upload some data to use this example, and Scikit-learn provides some useful examples. The Boston dataset, for instance, contains predictor variables that the example code can match against house prices, which helps build a predictor that can figure out the value of a house given some characteristics of it.

```
from sklearn.datasets import load_boston
boston = load_boston()
X, y = boston.data,boston.target
print X.shape, y.shape

(506L, 13L) (506L,)
```

The output specifies that both arrays have the same row number and that the X has 13 features. The `shape` method performs the analysis on the arrays and reports their dimensions.

The rows of X have to be of the same length as y. You also have to take care that X and y correspond, because learning from data happens when the algorithm matches the rows of X with the corresponding element of y. If you shuffle the two arrays, no learning is possible.

The characteristics of X, expressed as X's columns, are called variables (a more statistical term) or features (a term more related to machine learning).

Now, after importing the `LinearRegression` class, we can instantiate a variable called `hypothesis` and set a parameter indicating the algorithm to standardize (that is to set mean zero and unit standard deviation for all the variables, a statistical operation for having all the variables at a similar level) before estimating the parameters to learn.

```
from sklearn.linear_model import LinearRegression
hypothesis = LinearRegression(normalize=True)
hypothesis.fit(X,y)
print hypothesis.coef_
```

```
[ -1.07170557e-01    4.63952195e-02    2.08602395e-02
   2.68856140e+00   -1.77957587e+01    3.80475246e+00
   7.51061703e-04   -1.47575880e+00    3.05655038e-01
  -1.23293463e-02   -9.53463555e-01    9.39251272e-03
  -5.25466633e-01]
```

After fitting, `hypothesis` holds the learned parameters, and you can visualize them using the `coef_` method, which is typical of all the linear models (where the model output is a summation of variables weighted by coefficients). You can also call this fitting activity training (as in, "training a machine learning algorithm").

A *hypothesis* is a way to describe a learning algorithm trained with data. The hypothesis defines a possible representation of y given X that you test for validity. Therefore, it's a hypothesis in both scientific and machine-learning language.

Apart from the estimator class, the predictor and the model object classes are also important. The predictor class, which predicts the probability of a certain result, obtains the result of new observations using the `predict` and `predict_proba` methods, as in this script:

```
import numpy as np
new_observation = np.array(
    [1,0,1,0,0.5,7,59,6,3,200,20,350,4],
        dtype=float)
print hypothesis.predict(new_observation)

25.8972783977
```

Make sure that new observations have the same feature number and order as in the training X; otherwise, the prediction will be incorrect.

The class model provides information about the quality of the fit using the `score` method, as shown here:

```
hypothesis.score(X,y)

0.74060774286494291
```

In this case, `score` returns the coefficient of determination R^2 of the prediction. R^2 is a measure ranging from 0 to 1, comparing our predictor to a simple mean. Higher values show that the predictor is working well. Different learning algorithms may use different scoring functions. Please consult the online documentation of each algorithm or ask for help on the Python console:

```
help(LinearRegression)
```

The transform class applies transformations derived from the fitting phase to other data arrays. `LinearRegression` doesn't have a transform method, but most preprocessing algorithms do. For example, `MinMaxScaler`, from the Scikit-learn `preprocessing` module, can transform values in a specific range of minimum and maximum values, learning the transformation formula from an example array.

```
from sklearn.preprocessing import MinMaxScaler
scaler = MinMaxScaler(feature_range=(0, 1))
scaler.fit(X)
print scaler.transform(new_observation)

[ 0.01116872  0.          0.01979472  0.
  0.23662551  0.65893849  0.57775489  0.44288845
  0.08695652  0.02480916  0.78723404  0.88173887
  0.06263797]
```

In this case, the code applies the `min` and `max` values learned from X to the `new_observation` variable, and returns a transformation.

Performing the Hashing Trick

Scikit-learn provides you with most of the data structures and functionality you need to complete your data science project. There are even classes for the trickiest and most advanced problems.

For instance, when dealing with text, one of the most useful solutions provided by the Scikit-learn package is the hashing trick. You discover how to work with text by using the bag of words model (as shown in the "Using the Bag of Words Model and Beyond" section of Chapter 7) and weighting them with the TF-IDF. All these powerful transformations can operate properly only if all your text is known and available in the memory of your computer.

A more serious data science challenge is to analyze online-generated text flows, such as from social networks or large online text repositories. This scenario poses quite a challenge when trying to turn the text into a data matrix suitable for analysis. When working through such problems, knowing the hashing trick can give you quite a few advantages:

- ✔ Handling large data matrices based on text on the fly
- ✔ Fixing unexpected values or variables in your textual data
- ✔ Building scalable algorithms for large collections of documents

Using hash functions

Hash functions can transform any input into an output whose characteristics are predictable. Usually they return a value where the output is bound at a specific interval — whose extremities range from negative to positive numbers or just span through positive numbers. You can imagine them as enforcing a standard on your data — no matter what values you provide, they always return a specific data product.

Their most useful hash function characteristic is that, given a certain input, they always provide the same numeric output value. Consequently, they're called deterministic functions. For example, input a word like *dog* and the hashing function always returns the same number.

In a certain sense, hash functions are like a secret code, transforming everything into numbers. Unlike secret codes, however, you can't convert the hashed code to its original value. In addition, in some rare cases, different words generate the same hashed result (also called a hash collision).

Demonstrating the hashing trick

There are many hash functions, with MD5 (often used to check file integrity, because you can hash entire files) and SHA (used in cryptography) being the most popular. Python possesses a built-in hash function named `hash` that you can use to compare data objects before storing them in dictionaries. For instance, you can test how Python hashes its name:

```
hash('Python')
-539294296
```

The Python session on your computer may return a different value than the one shown on the preceding line. Don't worry — the built-in hash functions aren't always consistent across computers. When you need consistent output, rely on the Scikit-learn hash functions instead because the output is consistent across machines.

A Scikit-learn hash function can also return an index in a specific positive range. You can obtain something similar using a built-in hash by employing standard division and its remainder:

```
abs(hash('Python')) % 1000
296
```

When you ask for the remainder of the absolute number of the result from the hash function, you get a number that never exceeds the value you used for the division.

To see how this works, pretend that you want to transform a text string from the Internet into a numeric vector (a feature vector) so that you can use it for starting a machine-learning project. A good strategy for managing this data science task is to employ one-hot-encoding, which produces a bag of words. Here are the steps for one-hot-encoding a string ("Python for data science") into a vector.

1. Assign a number to each word, for instance, Python=0 for=1 data=2 science=3.

2. Initialize the vector, counting the number of unique words that you assigned a code in Step 1.

3. Use the codes assigned in Step 1 as indexes for populating the vector with values, assigning a 1 where there is a coincidence with a word existing in the phrase.

The resulting feature vector is expressed as the sequence `[1,1,1,1]` and made of exactly four elements. You have started the machine-learning process, telling the program to expect sequences of four text features, when suddenly a new phrase arrives and you must vectorize the following text as well: "Python for machine learning". Now you have two new words — "machine learning" — to work with. The following steps help you create the new vectors:

1. Assign these new codes: machine=4 learning=5.

2. Enlarge the previous vector to include the new words: `[1,1,1,1,0,0]`.

3. Compute the vector for the new string: `[1,1,0,0,1,1]`.

One-hot-encoding is quite optimal because it creates efficient and ordered feature vectors. Unfortunately, one-hot-encoding fails and becomes difficult to handle when your project experiences a lot of variability with regard to its inputs. This is a common situation in data science projects working with text or other symbolic features where flow from the Internet or other online environments can suddenly create or add to your initial data. Using hash functions is a smarter way to handle unpredictability in your inputs:

1. Define a range for the hash function outputs. All your feature vectors will use that range. The example uses a range of values from 0 to 24.

2. Compute an index for each word in your string using the hash function.

3. Assign a unit value to vector's positions according to word indexes.

In Python, you can define a simple hashing trick by creating a function and checking the results using the two test strings:

```
def hashing_trick(input_string, vector_size=20):
    feature_vector = [0] * vector_size
    for word in input_string.split(' '):
        index = abs(hash(word)) % vector_size
        feature_vector[index] = 1
    return feature_vector
```

Now you can test both strings.

```
hashing_trick(input_string='Python for data science',
    vector_size=20)
[1, 0, 0, 0, 0, 1, 0, 0, 0, 0, 0, 0, 0, 0, 0, 0, 1, 0, 1,
    0]
hashing_trick(input_string='Python for machine learning',
    vector_size=20)
[0, 0, 0, 0, 0, 0, 0, 0, 0, 0, 1, 0, 1, 0, 0, 0, 1, 0, 1,
    0]
```

When viewing the feature vectors, you should notice that:

- ✔ You don't know where each word is located. When it's important to be able to reverse the process of assigning words to indexes, you must store the relationship between words and their hashed value separately (for example, you can use a dictionary where the keys are the hashed values and the values are the words).

- ✔ For small values of the `vector_size` function parameter (for example, `vector_size=10`), many words overlap in the same positions in the list representing the feature vector. To keep the overlap to a minimum, you must create hash function boundaries that are greater than the number of elements you plan to index later.

The feature vectors in this example are made mostly of zero entries, representing a waste of memory when compared to the more memory-efficient one-hot-encoding. One of the ways in which you can solve this problem is to rely on sparse matrices, as described in the next section.

Working with deterministic selection

Sparse matrices are the answer when dealing with data that has few values, that is, when most of the matrix values are zeroes. Sparse matrices store just the coordinates of the cells and their values, instead of storing the information for all the cells in the matrix. When an application requests data from an empty cell, the sparse matrix will return a zero value after looking for the coordinates and not finding them. Here's an example vector:

```
[1, 0, 0, 0, 0, 1, 0, 0, 0, 0, 0, 0, 0, 0, 0, 0, 1, 0, 1,
 0]
```

The following code turns it into a sparse matrix.

```
from scipy.sparse import csc_matrix
print csc_matrix([1, 0, 0, 0, 0, 1, 0, 0, 0, 0, 0, 0, 0,
                 0, 0, 0, 1, 0, 1, 0])

   (0, 0)        1
   (0, 5)        1
   (0, 16)       1
   (0, 18)       1
```

Notice that the data representation is in coordinates (expressed in a tuple of row and column index) and the cell value.

The package SciPy offers a large variety of sparse matrix structures — each one storing the data in a different way and each one performing in a different way. (Some are good with slicing; some others are better for computations.) Usually the `csc_matrix` (a compressed matrix based on rows) is a good choice because most Scikit-learn algorithms accept it as input and it's optimal for matrix operations.

As a data scientist, you don't have to worry about programming your own version of the hashing trick unless you would like some special implementation of the idea. Scikit-learn offers `HashingVectorizer`, a class that rapidly transforms any collection of text into a sparse data matrix using the hashing trick. Here's an example script that replicates the previous example:

```
import sklearn.feature_extraction.text as txt
one_hot_enconder = txt.CountVectorizer()
one_hot_enconded = one_hot_enconder.fit_transform(
    ['Python for data science',
     'Python for machine learning'])

<2x6 sparse matrix of type '<type 'numpy.int64'>'
with 8 stored elements in Compressed Sparse Row format>
```

As soon as new text arrives, `CountVectorizer` stops working:

```
one_hot_enconded.transform(['New text has arrived'])
AttributeError: transform not found
```

Using `HashingVectorizer`, there is always a place for new words in the data matrix. At worst, a word settles in an already occupied position, causing a word collision.

```
sklearn_hashing_trick = txt.HashingVectorizer(
    n_features=20, binary=True, norm=None)
text_vector = sklearn_hashing_trick.transform(
    ['Python for data science',
     'Python for machine learning'])
text_vector
<2x20 sparse matrix of type '<type 'numpy.float64'>'
with 8 stored elements in Compressed Sparse Row format>
```

```
sklearn_hashing_trick.transform(['New text has arrived'])
<1x20 sparse matrix of type '<type 'numpy.float64'>'
with 4 stored elements in Compressed Sparse Row format>
```

`HashingVectorizer` is the perfect function to use when your data can't fit into memory and its features aren't fixed. In the other cases, consider using the more intuitive `CountVectorizer`.

Considering Timing and Performance

As the book introduces more and more complex themes, such as Scikit-learn machine-learning classes and SciPy sparse matrices, you may start to wonder how all this processing might influence application speed. The increased processing requirements affect both running time and available memory.

Managing the best use of machine resources is indeed an art, the art of optimization, and it requires time to master. However, you can start immediately becoming proficient in it by doing some accurate speed measurement and realizing what your problems really are. Profiling the time that operations require, measuring how much memory adding more data takes, or performing a transformation on your data can help you to spot the bottlenecks in your code and start looking for alternative solutions.

As described in Chapter 11, IPython is the perfect environment for experimenting, tweaking, and improving your code. Working on blocks of code, recording the results and outputs, and writing additional notes and comments will help your data science solutions take shape in a controlled and reproducible way.

Benchmarking with timeit

While working through the hashing trick example in the "Performing the Hashing Trick" section, earlier in this chapter, we compare two alternatives for encoding textual information into a data matrix that can address different needs:

- ✔ CountVectorizer: Optimally encodes text into a data matrix but cannot address subsequent novelties in text.

- ✔ HashingVectorizer: Provides flexibility in situations when it is likely that the application will receive new data, but is less optimal than techniques based on hashing functions.

Although their advantages are quite clear in terms of how they handle the data, you may wonder what impact using one or the other has on your data processing in terms of speed and memory feasibility.

Concerning speed, IPython offers an easy, out-of-the-box solution, the line magic %timeit and the cell magic %%timeit:

- ✔ %timeit: Calculates the best performance time for an instruction.

- ✔ %%timeit: Calculates the best time performance for all the instructions in a cell, apart from the one placed on the same cell line as the cell magic (which could therefore be an initialization instruction).

Both magic commands report the best performance in r trials repeated for n loops. When you add the –r and –n parameters, IPython chooses the number automatically in order to provide a fast answer.

Here is an example of testing whether it is faster to assign a list 10**6 ordinal values by using list comprehension or by appending the values in a for loop:

```
%timeit l = [k for k in range(10**6)]

10 loops, best of 3: 94.8 ms per loop
```

The result for the list comprehension can be tested by incrementing both the sample performance and repetitions of the test:

```
%timeit -n 20 -r 5 l = [k for k in range(10**6)]

20 loops, best of 5: 95.6 ms per loop
```

Since the `for` loop requires an entire cell, the example uses the cell magic, `%%timeit`, call. Notice that the first line that assigns the value of 10**6 to a variable is not considered in the performance.

```
%%timeit limit = 10**6
l = list()
for k in range(limit):
    l.append(k)

10 loops, best of 3: 176 ms per loop
```

The results show that list comprehension is about 50 percent faster than using a `for` loop. You can then repeat the test using different text encoding strategies:

```
import sklearn.feature_extraction.text as txt
sklearn_hashing_trick = txt.HashingVectorizer(
    n_features=20, binary=True, norm=None)
enconder = txt.CountVectorizer()
texts = ['Python for data science',
        'Python for machine learning']
```

After performing initial loading of the classes and instantiating them, you can test the two solutions:

```
%timeit enconded = enconder.fit_transform(texts)

1000 loops, best of 3: 1.27 ms per loop
```

```
%timeit  hashing = sklearn_hashing_trick.transform(texts)

10000 loops, best of 3: 158 µs per loop
```

The hashing trick is faster than one hot encoder, and it's possible to explain the difference by noting that the latter is an optimized algorithm that keeps track of how the words are encoded, something that the hashing trick doesn't do.

IPython is the best environment to benchmark the speed of your data science solution code. If you'd like to track performance on the command line or in a script running from an IDE, you can import the `timeit` class and use the `timeit` function for tracking performance of the command by providing the input parameter as a string.

If your command needs variables, classes, or functions that aren't available in the base Python (such as the Scikit-learn classes), you can provide them as a second input parameter. You formulate a string in which Python imports all the necessary objects from the main environment, as shown in the following example:

```
import timeit
cumulative_time = timeit.timeit(
    "hashing = sklearn_hashing_trick.transform(texts)",
    "from __main__ import sklearn_hashing_trick,texts",
    number=10000)
print cumulative_time / 10000.0
```

Working with the memory profiler

As you've seen when testing your application code for performance (speed) characteristics, you can obtain analogous information about memory usage. Keeping track of memory consumption could tell you about possible problems in the way data is processed or transmitted to the learning algorithms. The memory_profiler package implements the required functionality. This package is not provided as a default Python or IPython package and it requires installation. Use the following commands to install the package and its dependencies from the command line:

```
ipython -m pip install psutil
ipython -m pip install memory_profiler
```

Using the preferred installer program (pip)

Python provides a huge number of packages that you can install. Many of these packages come as separate, downloadable modules. Some of them have an executable suitable for a platform such as Windows, which means you can easily install the package. However, many other packages rely on pip, which is a feature that you can access directly from the command line when using later versions of Python, including both 2.7.9 and 3.4.

When working with older versions of Python, you must first install pip by installing a package such as distribute (https://pypi.python.org/pypi/distribute). When working on some Linux or Mac systems, you can also rely on sudo to get the job done

by typing **sudo apt-get install python3-pip** and pressing Enter. You may find that neither of these techniques works for you, so try the instructions found at https://pip.pypa.io/en/latest/installing.html as well.

To use pip, you open a command line or terminal. This book uses IPython as its environment. When you want to install a new feature, you type **ipython** to start a copy of IPython, **–m** to load a module, **pip** to start pip, **install** to tell pip what action to take, and the name of the package you want to install. For example, to install psutil later in the chapter, you type **ipython –m pip install psutil** and press Enter.

Use the following command for each IPython session you want to monitor:

```
%load_ext memory_profiler
```

After performing these tasks, you can easily track how much memory a command consumes:

```
hashing = sklearn_hashing_trick.transform(texts)
%memit dense_hashing = hashing.toarray()
peak memory: 68.79 MiB, increment: 0.14 MiB
```

Obtaining a complete overview of memory consumption is possible by saving an IPython cell to disk and then profiling it using the line magic %mprun on an externally imported function. (The line magic works only by operating with external Python scripts.) Profiling produces a detailed report, command by command, as shown in the following example:

```
%%writefile example_code.py
import sklearn.feature_extraction.text as txt
def comparison_test():
    sklearn_hashing_trick = txt.HashingVectorizer(
        n_features=20, binary=True, norm=None)
    one_hot_enconder = txt.CountVectorizer()
    texts = ['Python for data science',
             'Python for machine learning']
    one_hot_enconded = one_hot_enconder.fit_transform(
        texts)
    hashing = sklearn_hashing_trick.transform(texts)

from example_code import comparison_test
%mprun -f comparison_test comparison_test()

Line # Mem usage Increment Line Contents
================================================
     2  68.5 MiB   0.0 MiB  def comparison_test():
     3  68.5 MiB   0.0 MiB      HashingVectorizer(...)
     4  68.5 MiB   0.0 MiB      CountVectorizer(...)
     5  68.5 MiB   0.0 MiB      texts = [...]
     6  68.7 MiB   0.2 MiB      one_hot_enconder.fit_t(...)
     7  68.7 MiB   0.0 MiB      sklearn_hashing_trick.(...)
```

The resulting report details the memory usage from every line in the function, pointing out the major increments.

Running in Parallel

Most computers today are multicore (two or more processors in a single package), some with multiple physical CPUs. One of the most important limitations of Python is that it uses a single core by default. (It was created in a time when single cores were the norm.)

Data science projects require quite a lot of computations. In particular, a part of the scientific aspect of data science relies on repeated tests and experiments on different data matrices. Don't forget that working with huge data quantities means that most time-consuming transformations repeat observation after observation (for example, identical and not related operations on different parts of a matrix).

Using more CPU cores accelerates a computation by a factor that almost matches the number of cores. For example, having four cores would mean working at best four times faster. You don't receive a full fourfold increase because there is overhead when starting a parallel process — new running Python instances have to be set up with the right in-memory information and launched; consequently, the improvement will be less than potentially achievable but still significant. Knowing how to use more than one CPU is therefore an advanced but incredibly useful skill for increasing the number of analyses completed, and for speeding up your operations both when setting up and when using your data products.

Multiprocessing works by replicating the same code and memory content in various new Python instances (the workers), calculating the result for each of them, and returning the pooled results to the main original console. If your original instance already occupies much of the available RAM memory, it won't be possible to create new instances, and your machine may run out of memory.

Performing multicore parallelism

To perform multicore parallelism with Python, you integrate the Scikit-learn package with the joblib package for time-consuming operations, such as replicating models for validating results or for looking for the best hyper-parameters. In particular, Scikit-learn allows multiprocessing when

- **Cross-validating:** Testing the results of a machine-learning hypothesis using different training and testing data
- **Grid-searching:** Systematically changing the hyper-parameters of a machine-learning hypothesis and testing the consequent results

✔ **Multilabel prediction:** Running an algorithm multiple times against multiple targets when there are many different target outcomes to predict at the same time

✔ **Ensemble machine-learning methods:** Modeling a large host of classifiers, each one independent from the other, such as when using `RandomForest`-based modeling

You don't have to do anything special to take advantage of parallel computations — you can activate parallelism by setting the `n_jobs` parameter to a number of cores more than 1 or by setting the value to –1, which means you want to use all the available CPU instances.

If you aren't running your code from the console or from an IPython Notebook, it is extremely important that you separate your code from any package import or global variable assignment in your script by using the `if __name__=='__main__':` command at the beginning of any code that executes multicore parallelism. The `if` statement checks whether the program is directly run or is called by an already-running Python console, avoiding any confusion or error by the multiparallel process (such as recursively calling the parallelism).

Demonstrating multiprocessing

It's a good idea to use IPython when you run a demonstration of how multiprocessing can really save you time during data science projects. Using IPython provides the advantage of using the `%timeit` magic command for timing execution. You start by loading a multiclass dataset, a complex machine-learning algorithm (the Support Vector Classifier, or SVC), and a cross-validation procedure for estimating reliable resulting scores from all the procedures. You find details about all these tools later in the book. The most important thing to know is that the procedures become quite large because the SVC produces 10 models, which it repeats 10 times each using cross-validation, for a total of 100 models.

```
from sklearn.datasets import load_digits
digits = load_digits()
X, y = digits.data,digits.target
from sklearn.svm import SVC
from sklearn.cross_validation import cross_val_score
%timeit single_core_learning = cross_val_score(SVC(), X,
    y, cv=20, n_jobs=1)

Out [1] : 1 loops, best of 3: 17.9 s per loop
```

After this test, you need to activate the multicore parallelism and time the results using the following commands:

```
%timeit multi_core_learning = cross_val_score(SVC(), X, y,
    cv=20, n_jobs=-1)
Out [2] : 1 loops, best of 3: 11.7 s per loop
```

The example machine demonstrates a positive advantage using multicore processing, despite using a small dataset where Python spends most of the time starting consoles and running a part of the code in each one. This overhead, a few seconds, is still significant given that the total execution extends for a handful of seconds. Just imagine what would happen if you worked with larger sets of data — your execution time could be easily cut by two or three times.

Although the code works fine with IPython, putting it down in a script and asking Python to run it in a console or using an IDE may cause errors because of the internal operations of a multicore task. The solution, as mentioned before, is to put all the code under an if statement, which checks whether the program started directly and wasn't called afterward. Here's an example script:

```
from sklearn.datasets import load_digits
from sklearn.svm import SVC
from sklearn.cross_validation import cross_val_score
if __name__ == '__main__':
    digits = load_digits()
    X, y = digits.data,digits.target
    multi_core_learning = cross_val_score(SVC(), X, y,
        cv=20, n_jobs=-1)
```

Chapter 13

Exploring Data Analysis

Data science relies on complex algorithms for building predictions and spotting important signals in data, and each algorithm presents different strong and weak points. In short, you select a range of algorithms, you have them run on the data, you optimize their parameters as much as you can, and finally you decide which one will best help you build your data product or generate insight into your problem.

It sounds a little bit automatic and, partially, it is, thanks to powerful analytical software and scripting languages like Python. Learning algorithms are complex, and their sophisticated procedures naturally seem automatic and a bit opaque to you. However, even if some of these tools seem like black or even magic boxes, keep this simple acronym in mind: GIGO. GIGO stands for "Garbage In/Garbage Out." It has been a well-known adage in statistics (and computer science) for a long time. No matter how powerful the machine-learning algorithms you use, you won't obtain good results if your data has something wrong in it.

Exploratory Data Analysis (EDA) is a general approach to exploring datasets by means of simple summary statistics and graphic visualizations in order to gain a deeper understanding of data. EDA helps you become more effective in the subsequent data analysis and modeling. In this chapter, you discover all the necessary and indispensable basic descriptions of the data and see how those descriptions can help you decide how to proceed using the most appropriate data transformation and solutions.

You don't have to type the source code for this chapter manually. In fact, it's a lot easier if you use the downloadable source. The source code for this chapter appears in the P4DS4D; 13; Exploring Data Analysis.ipynb source code file. (See the Introduction for details on where to locate this file.)

The EDA Approach

EDA was developed at Bell Labs by John Tukey, a mathematician and statistician who wanted to promote more questions and actions on data based on the data itself (the exploratory motif) in contrast to the dominant confirmatory approach of the time. A confirmatory approach relies on the use of a theory or procedure — the data is just there for testing and application. EDA emerged at the end of the 70s, long before the big data flood appeared. Tukey could already see that certain activities, such as testing and modeling, were easy to make automatic. In one of his famous writings, Tukey said:

> *"The only way humans can do BETTER than computers is to take a chance of doing WORSE than them."*

This statement explains why, as a data scientist, your role and tools aren't limited to automatic learning algorithms but also to manual and creative exploratory tasks. Computers are unbeatable at optimizing, but humans are strong at discovery by taking unexpected routes and trying unlikely but very effective solutions.

If you've been through the examples in the previous chapters, you have already worked on quite a bit of data, but using EDA is a bit different because it checks beyond the basic assumptions about data workability, which actually comprises the Initial Data Analysis (IDA). Up to now, the book has shown how to

✔ Complete observations or mark missing cases by appropriate features

✔ Transform text or categorical variables

✔ Create new features based on domain knowledge of the data problem

✔ Have at hand a numeric dataset where rows are observations and columns are variables

EDA goes further than IDA. It's moved by a different attitude: going beyond basic assumptions. With EDA, you

✔ Describe of your data

✔ Closely explore data distributions

✔ Understand the relations between variables

✔ Notice unusual or unexpected situations

✔ Place the data into groups

✔ Notice unexpected patterns within groups

✔ Take note of group differences

Defining Descriptive Statistics for Numeric Data

The first actions that you can take with the data are to produce some synthetic measures to help figure out what is going in it. You acquire knowledge of measures such as maximum and minimum values, and you define which intervals are the best place to start.

During your exploration, you use a simple but useful dataset that is used in previous chapters, the Fisher's Iris dataset. You can load it from the Scikit-learn package by using the following code:

```
from sklearn.datasets import load_iris
iris = load_iris()
```

Having loaded the Iris dataset into a variable of a custom Scikit-learn class, you can derive a NumPy `nparray` and a pandas `DataFrame` from it:

```
import pandas as pd
import numpy as np
print 'Your pandas version is: %s' % pd.__version__
print 'Your NumPy version is %s' % np.__version__
iris_nparray = iris.data
iris_dataframe = pd.DataFrame(iris.data, columns=iris.feature_names)
iris_dataframe['group'] = pd.Series([iris.target_names[k] for k in iris.target],
    dtype="category")

Your pandas version is: 0.15.2
Your NumPy version is 1.8.1
```

NumPy, Scikit-learn, and especially pandas are packages under constant development, so before you start working with EDA, it's a good idea to check the product version numbers. Using an old version could cause your output to differ from that shown in the book or cause some commands to fail.

This chapter presents a series of `pandas` and NumPy commands that help you explore the structure of data. Even though applying single explorative commands grants you more freedom in your analysis, it's nice to know that you can obtain most of these statistics using the `describe` method applied to your `pandas` `DataFrame`: such as, `print iris_dataframe.describe()`, when you're in a hurry in your data science project.

Measuring central tendency

Mean and median are the first measures to calculate for numeric variables when starting EDA. They can provide you with an estimate of EDA when the variables are centered and somehow symmetric.

Using `pandas`, you can quickly compute both means and medians. Here is the command for getting the mean from the Iris `DataFrame`:

```
print iris_dataframe.mean(numeric_only=True)

sepal length (cm)    5.843333
sepal width (cm)     3.054000
petal length (cm)    3.758667
petal width (cm)     1.198667
```

Similarly, here is the command that will output the median:

```
print iris_dataframe.median(numeric_only=True)

sepal length (cm)    5.80
sepal width (cm)     3.00
petal length (cm)    4.35
petal width (cm)     1.30
```

The median provides the central position in the series of values. When creating a variable, it is a measure less influenced by anomalous cases or by an asymmetric distribution of values around the mean. What you should notice here is that the means are not centered (no variable is zero mean) and that the median of petal length is quite different from the mean, requiring further inspection.

When checking for central tendency measures, you should:

✔ Verify whether means are zero

✔ Check whether they are different from each other

✔ Notice whether the median is different from the mean

Measuring variance and range

As a next step, you should check the variance by squaring the value of its standard deviation. The variance is a good indicator of whether a mean is a suitable indicator of the variable distribution.

```
print iris_dataframe.std()

sepal length (cm)    0.828066
sepal width (cm)     0.433594
petal length (cm)    1.764420
petal width (cm)     0.763161
```

In addition, the range, which is the difference between the maximum and minimum value for each quantitative variable, is quite informative.

```
print iris_dataframe.max(numeric_only=True)-iris_dataframe.min(numeric_only=True)

sepal length (cm)    3.6
sepal width (cm)     2.4
petal length (cm)    5.9
petal width (cm)     2.4
```

Take notice of the standard deviation and the range with respect to the mean and median. A standard deviation or range that is too high with respect to the measures of centrality (mean and median) may point to a possible problem, with extremely unusual values affecting the calculation.

Working with percentiles

Because the median is the value in the central position of your distribution of values, you may need to consider other notable positions. Apart from the minimum and maximum, the position at 25 percent of your values (the lower quartile) and the position at 75 percent (the upper quartile) are useful for figuring how the data distribution works, and they are the basis of an illustrative graph called a *boxplot*, which is one of the topics we cover in this chapter.

```
print iris_dataframe.quantile(np.array([0,.25,.50,.75,1]))
```

	sepal length (cm)	sepal width (cm)	petal length (cm)	petal width (cm)
0.00	4.3	2.0	1.00	0.1
0.25	5.1	2.8	1.60	0.3
0.50	5.8	3.0	4.35	1.3
0.75	6.4	3.3	5.10	1.8
1.00	7.9	4.4	6.90	2.5

The difference between the upper and lower percentile constitutes the inter-quartile range (IQR) which is a measure of the scale of variables that are of highest interest. You don't need to calculate it, but you will find it in the boxplot because it helps to determinate the plausible limits of your distribution. What lies between the lower quartile and the minimum, and the upper quartile and the maximum, are exceptionally rare values that can negatively affect the results of your analysis. Such rare cases are outliers — and they're the topic of Chapter 16.

Defining measures of normality

The last indicative measures of how the numeric variables used for these examples are structured are skewness and kurtosis:

- *Skewness* defines the asymmetry of data with respect to the mean. If the skew is negative, the left tail is too long and the mass of the observations are on the right side of the distribution. If it is positive, it is exactly the opposite.

- *Kurtosis* shows whether the data distribution, especially the peak and the tails, are of the right shape. If the kurtosis is above zero, the distribution has a marked peak. If it is below zero, the distribution is too flat instead.

Although reading the numbers can help you determine the shape of the data, taking notice of such measures presents a formal test to select the variables that may need some adjustment or transformation in order to become more similar to the Gaussian distribution. Remember that you also visualize the data later, so this is a first step in a longer process.

As an example, a previous illustration in this chapter shows that the petal length feature presents differences between the mean and the median (see "Measuring variance and range," earlier in this chapter). In this section, you test the same example for kurtosis and skewness in order to determine whether the variable requires intervention.

When performing the kurtosis and skewness tests, you determine whether the p-value is less than or equal 0.05. If so, you have to reject normality, which implies that you could obtain better results if you try to transform the variable into a normal one. The following code shows how to perform the required test:

```
from scipy.stats import kurtosis, kurtosistest
k = kurtosis(iris_dataframe['petal length (cm)'])
zscore, pvalue = kurtosistest(iris_dataframe['petal length (cm)'])
print 'Kurtosis %0.3f z-score %0.3f p-value %0.3f' % (k, zscore, pvalue)
```

```
Kurtosis -1.395 z-score -14.811 p-value 0.000

from scipy.stats import skew, skewtest
s = skew(iris_dataframe['petal length (cm)'])
zscore, pvalue = skewtest(iris_dataframe['petal length (cm)'])
print 'Skewness %0.3f z-score %0.3f p-value %0.3f' % (s, zscore, pvalue)

Skewness -0.272 z-score -1.398 p-value 0.162
```

The test results tell you that the data is slightly skewed to the left, but not enough to make it unusable. The real problem is that the curve is much too flat to be bell shaped, so you should investigate the matter further.

It's a good practice to test all variables for kurtosis and skewness automatically. You should then proceed to inspect those whose values are the highest visually. Non-normality of a distribution may also conceal different issues, such as outliers to groups that you can perceive only by a graphical visualization.

Counting for Categorical Data

The Iris dataset is made of four metric variables and a qualitative target outcome. Just as you use means and variance as descriptive measures for metric variables, so do frequencies strictly relate to qualitative ones.

Because the dataset is made up of metric measurements (width and lengths in centimeters), you must render it qualitative by dividing it into bins according to specific intervals. The pandas package features two useful functions, cut and qcut, that can transform a metric variable into a qualitative one:

✔ cut expects a series of edge values used to cut the measurements or an integer number of groups used to cut the variables into equal-width bins.

✔ qcut expects a series of percentiles used to cut the variable.

You can obtain a new categorical DataFrame using the following command, which concatenates a binning (see the "Understanding binning and discretization" section of Chapter 8 for details) for each variable:

```
iris_binned = pd.concat([
pd.qcut(iris_dataframe.ix[:,0], [0, .25, .5, .75, 1]),
pd.qcut(iris_dataframe.ix[:,1], [0, .25, .5, .75, 1]),
pd.qcut(iris_dataframe.ix[:,2], [0, .25, .5, .75, 1]),
pd.qcut(iris_dataframe.ix[:,3], [0, .25, .5, .75, 1]),
], join='outer', axis = 1)
```

This example relies on binning. However, it could also help to explore when the variable is above or below a singular hurdle value, usually the mean or the median. In this case, you set pd.qcut to the 0.5 percentile or pd.cut to the mean value of the variable.

Binning transforms numerical variables into categorical ones. This transformation can improve your understanding of data and the machine-learning phase that follows by reducing the noise (outliers) or nonlinearity of the transformed variable.

Understanding frequencies

You can obtain a frequency for each categorical variable of the dataset, both for the predictive variable and for the outcome, by using the following code:

```
print iris_dataframe['group'].value_counts()

virginica     50
versicolor    50
setosa        50

print iris_binned['petal length (cm)'].value_counts()

[1, 1.6]        44
(4.35, 5.1]     41
(5.1, 6.9]      34
(1.6, 4.35]     31
```

This example provides you with some basic frequency information as well, such as the number of unique values in each variable and the mode of the frequency (top and freq rows in the output).

```
print iris_binned.describe()

        sepal length (cm) sepal width (cm) petal length (cm) petal width (cm)
count                 150              150               150              150
unique                  4                4                 4                4
top           [4.3, 5.1]         [2, 2.8]          [1, 1.6]       [0.1, 0.3]
freq                   41               47                44               41
```

Frequencies can signal a number of interesting characteristics of qualitative features:

✔ The mode of the frequency distribution that is the most frequent category

✔ The other most frequent categories, especially when they are comparable with the mode (bimodal distribution) or if there is a large difference between them

✔ The distribution of frequencies among categories, if rapidly decreasing or equally distributed

✔ Rare categories that gather together

Creating contingency tables

By matching different categorical frequency distributions, you can display the relationship between qualitative variables. The `pandas.crosstab` function can match variables or groups of variables, helping to locate possible data structures or relationships.

In the following example, you check how the outcome variable is related to petal length and observe how certain outcomes and petal binned classes never appear together:

```
print pd.crosstab(iris_dataframe['group'], iris_binned['petal length (cm)'])

petal length (cm)  (1.6, 4.35]  (4.35, 5.1]  (5.1, 6.9]  [1, 1.6]
group
setosa                       6            0           0        44
versicolor                  25           25           0         0
virginica                    0           16          34         0
```

The `pandas.crosstab` function ignores categorical variable ordering and always displays the row and column categories according to their alphabetical order. This nuisance is still present in the pandas version used for this book, 0.15.2, but it may be resolved in the future.

Creating Applied Visualization for EDA

Up to now, the chapter has explored variables by looking at each one separately. Technically, if you've followed along with the examples, you have created a *univariate* (that is, you've paid attention to stand-alone variations of the data only) description of the data. The data is rich in information because it offers a perspective that goes beyond the single variable, presenting more variables with their reciprocal variations. The way to use more of the data is to create a *bivariate* (seeing how couples of variables relate to each other) exploration. This is also the basis for complex data analysis based on a *multivariate* (simultaneously considering all the existent relations between variables) approach.

If the univariate approach inspected a limited number of descriptive statistics, then matching different variables or groups of variables increases the number of possibilities. Such exploration overloads the data scientist with different tests and bivariate analysis. Using visualization is a rapid way to limit test and analysis to only interesting traces and hints. Visualizations, using a few informative graphics, can convey the variety of statistical characteristics of the variables and their reciprocal relationships with greater ease.

Inspecting boxplots

Boxplots provide a way to represent distributions and their extreme ranges, signaling whether some observations are too far from the core of the data — a problematic situation for some learning algorithms. The following code shows how to create a basic boxplot using the iris dataset:

```
boxplots = iris_dataframe.boxplot(return_type='axes')
```

In Figure 13-1, you see the structure of each variable's distribution at its core, represented by the 25° and 75° percentile (the sides of the box) and the median (at the center of the box). The lines, the so-called whiskers, represent 1.5 times the IQR from the box sides (or by the distance to the most extreme value, if within 1.5 times the IQR). The boxplot marks every observation outside the whisker (deemed an unusual value) by a sign.

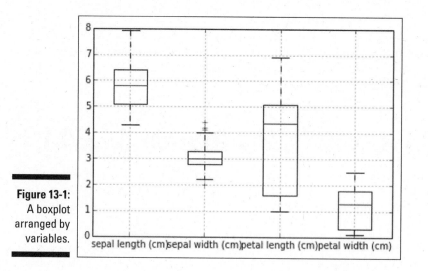

Figure 13-1:
A boxplot arranged by variables.

Boxplots are also extremely useful for visually checking group differences. Note in Figure 13-2 how a boxplot can hint that the three groups, setosa, versicolor, and virginica, have different petal lengths, with only partially overlapping values at the fringes of the last two of them.

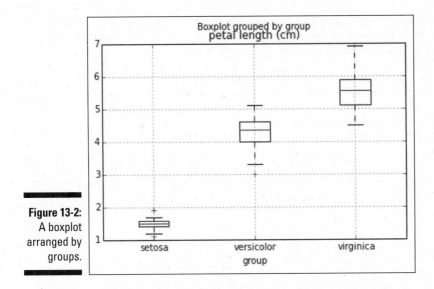

Figure 13-2:
A boxplot
arranged by
groups.

Performing t-tests after boxplots

After you have spotted a possible group difference relative to a variable, a
t-test (you use a t-test in situations in which the sampled population has an
exact normal distribution) or a one-way Analysis Of Variance (ANOVA) can
provide you with a statistical verification of the significance of the difference
between the groups' means.

```
from scipy.stats import ttest_ind
group0 = iris_dataframe['group'] == 'setosa'
group1 = iris_dataframe['group'] == 'versicolor'
group2 = iris_dataframe['group'] == 'virginica'
print 'var1 %0.3f var2 %03f' % (iris_dataframe['petal length (cm)'][group1].
            var(),
    iris_dataframe['petal length (cm)'][group2].var())

var1 0.221 var2 0.304588
```

The t-test compares two groups at a time, and it requires that you define
whether the groups have similar variance or not. So it is necessary to calculate the variance beforehand, like this:

```
t, pvalue = ttest_ind(iris_dataframe[sepal width (cm)'][group1],
    iris_dataframe['sepal width (cm)'][group2], axis=0, equal_var=False)
print 't statistic %0.3f p-value %0.3f' % (t, pvalue)

t statistic -3.206 p-value 0.002
```

You interpret the `pvalue` as the probability that the calculated `t` statistic difference is just due to chance. Usually, when it is below 0.05, you can confirm that the groups' means are significantly different.

You can simultaneously check more than two groups using the one-way ANOVA test. In this case, the `pvalue` has an interpretation similar to the t-test:

```
from scipy.stats import f_oneway
f, pvalue = f_oneway(iris_dataframe['sepal width (cm)'][group0],
                     iris_dataframe['sepal width (cm)'][group1],
                     iris_dataframe['sepal width (cm)'][group2])
print "One-way ANOVA F-value %0.3f p-value %0.3f" % (f,pvalue)

One-way ANOVA F-value 47.364 p-value 0.000
```

Observing parallel coordinates

Parallel coordinates can help spot which groups in the outcome variable you could easily separate from the other. It is a truly multivariate plot, because at a glance it represents all your data at the same time. The following example shows how to use parallel coordinates.

```
from pandas.tools.plotting import parallel_coordinates
iris_dataframe['labels'] = [iris.target_names[k] for k in
iris_dataframe['group']]
pll = parallel_coordinates(iris_dataframe,'labels')
```

As shown in Figure 13-3, on the abscissa axis you find all the quantitative variables aligned. On the ordinate, you find all the observations, carefully represented as parallel lines, each one of a different color given its ownership to a different group.

Figure 13-3:
Parallel coordinates anticipate whether groups are easily separable.

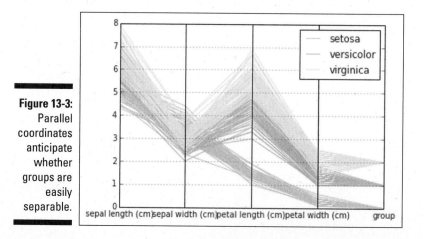

If the parallel lines of each group stream together along the visualization in a separate part of the graph far from other groups, the group is easily separable. The visualization also provides the means to assert the capability of certain features to separate the groups.

Graphing distributions

You usually render the information that boxplot and descriptive statistics provide into a curve or a histogram, which shows an overview of the complete distribution of values. The output shown in Figure 13-4 represents all the distributions in the dataset. Different variable scales and shapes are immediately visible, such as the fact that petals' features display two peaks.

```
densityplot = iris_dataframe[iris_dataframe.columns[:4]].plot(kind='density')
```

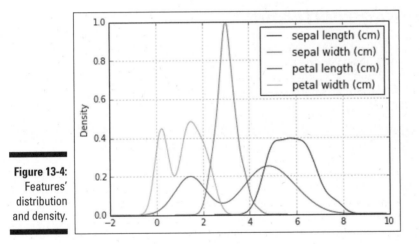

Figure 13-4: Features' distribution and density.

Histograms present another, more detailed, view over distributions:

```
single_distribution = iris_dataframe['petal length (cm)'].plot(kind='hist')
```

Figure 13-5 shows the histogram of petal length. It reveals a gap in the distribution that could be a promising discovery if you can relate it to a certain group of Iris flowers.

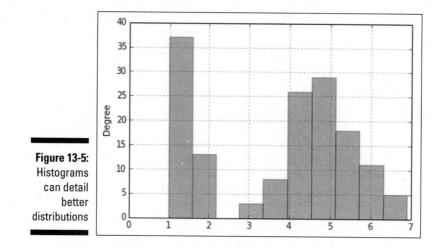

Figure 13-5:
Histograms
can detail
better
distributions

Plotting scatterplots

In scatterplots, the two compared variables provide the coordinates for plotting the observations as points on a plane. The result is usually a cloud of points. When the cloud is elongated and resembles a line, you can perceive the variables as correlated. The following example demonstrates this principle.

```
colors_palette = {0: 'red', 1: 'yellow', 2:'blue'}
colors = [colors_palette[c] for c in iris_dataframe['group']]
simple_scatterplot = iris_dataframe.plot(kind='scatter',
    x='petal length (cm)', y='petal width (cm)', c=colors)
```

This simple scatterplot, represented in Figure 13-6, compares length and width of petals. The scatterplot highlights different groups using different colors. The elongated shape described by the points hints at a strong correlation between the two observed variables, and the division of the cloud into groups suggests a possible separability of the groups.

Because the number of variables isn't too large, you can also generate all the scatterplots automatically from the combination of the variables. This representation is a matrix of scatterplots. The following example demonstrates how to create one:

```
from pandas.tools.plotting import scatter_matrix
colors_palette = {0: "red", 1: "yellow", 2: "blue"}
colors = [colors_palette[c] for c in iris_dataframe['group']]
matrix_of_scatterplots = scatter_matrix(iris_dataframe,
    figsize=(6, 6), color=colors, diagonal='kde')
```

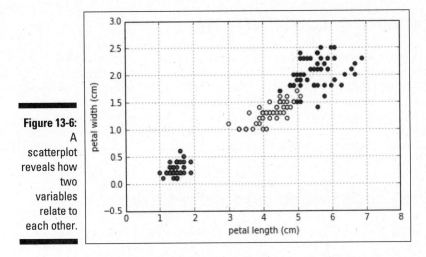

Figure 13-6:
A scatterplot reveals how two variables relate to each other.

In Figure 13-7, you can see the resulting visualization for the Iris dataset. The diagonal representing the density estimation can be replaced by a histogram using the parameter `diagonal='hist'`.

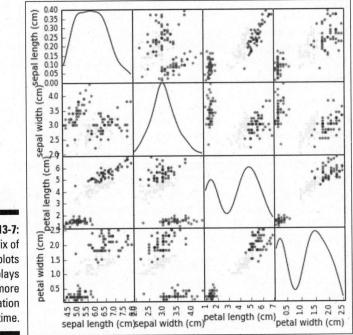

Figure 13-7:
A matrix of scatterplots displays more information at one time.

Understanding Correlation

Just as the relationship between variables is graphically representable, it is also measurable by a statistical estimate. When working with numeric variables, the estimate is a correlation, and the Pearson's correlation is the most famous. The Pearson's correlation is the foundation for complex linear estimation models. When you work with categorical variables, the estimate is an association, and the chi-square statistic is the most frequently used tool for measuring association between features.

Using covariance and correlation

Covariance is the first measure of the relationship of two variables. It determines whether both variables have a coincident behavior with respect to their mean. If the single values of two variables are usually above or below their respective averages, the two variables have a positive association. It means that they tend to agree, and you can figure out the behavior of one of the two by looking at the other. In such a case, their covariance will be a positive number, and the higher the number, the higher the agreement.

If, instead, one variable is usually above and the other variable usually below their respective averages, the two variables are negatively associated. Even though the two disagree, it's an interesting situation for making predictions, because by observing the state of one of them, you can figure out the likely state of the other (albeit they're opposite). In this case, their covariance will be a negative number.

A third state is that the two variables don't systematically agree or disagree with each other. In this case, the covariance will tend to be zero, a sign that the variables don't share much and have independent behaviors.

Ideally, when you have a numeric target variable, you want the target variable to have a high positive or negative covariance with the predictive variables. Having a high positive or negative covariance among the predictive variables is a sign of information redundancy. *Information redundancy* signals that the variables point to the same data — that is, the variables are telling us the same thing in slightly different ways.

Computing a covariance matrix is straightforward using `pandas`. You can immediately apply it to the `DataFrame` of the Iris dataset as shown here:

```
iris_dataframe.cov()
                sepal length (cm)  sepal width (cm)  petal length (cm)  \
```

sepal length (cm)	0.685694	-0.039268	1.273682
sepal width (cm)	-0.039268	0.188004	-0.321713
petal length (cm)	1.273682	-0.321713	3.113179
petal width (cm)	0.516904	-0.117981	1.296387

	petal width (cm)
sepal length (cm)	0.516904
sepal width (cm)	-0.117981
petal length (cm)	1.296387
petal width (cm)	0.582414

This matrix output shows variables present on both rows and columns. By observing different row and column combinations, you can determine the value of covariance between the variables chosen. After observing these results, you can immediately understand that little relationship exists between sepal length and sepal width, meaning that they're different informative values. However, there could be a special relationship between petal width and petal length, but the example doesn't tell what this relationship is because the measure is not easily interpretable.

The scale of the variables you observe influences covariance, so you should use a different, but standard, measure. The solution is to use correlation, which is the covariance estimation after having standardized the variables. Here is an example of obtaining a correlation using a simple pandas method:

```
print iris_dataframe.corr()
                sepal length (cm)  sepal width (cm)  petal length (cm) \
sepal length (cm)     1.000000         -0.109369          0.871754
sepal width (cm)     -0.109369          1.000000         -0.420516
petal length (cm)     0.871754         -0.420516          1.000000
petal width (cm)      0.817954         -0.356544          0.962757

                petal width (cm)
sepal length (cm)     0.817954
sepal width (cm)     -0.356544
petal length (cm)     0.962757
petal width (cm)      1.000000
```

Now that's even more interesting, because correlation values are bound between values of –1 and +1, so the relationship between petal width and length is positive and, with a 0.96, it is almost the maximum possible.

You can compute covariance and correlation matrices also by means of NumPy commands, as shown here:

```
covariance_matrix = np.cov(iris_nparray, rowvar=0, bias=1)
correlation_matrix= np.corrcoef(iris_nparray, rowvar=0, bias=1)
```

In statistics, this kind of correlation is a *Pearson correlation,* and its coefficient is a *Pearson's r.*

Another nice trick is to square the correlation. By squaring it, you lose the sign of the relationship. The new number tells you the percentage of the information shared by two variables. In this example, a correlation of 0.96 implies that 96 percent of the information is shared. You can obtain a squared correlation matrix using this command: `print iris_dataframe.corr()**2`.

Something important to remember is that covariance and correlation are based on means, so they tend to represent relationships that you can express using linear formulations. Variables in real-life datasets usually don't have nice linear formulations. Instead they are highly nonlinear, with curves and bends. You can rely on mathematical transformations to make the relationships linear between variables anyway. A good rule to remember is to use correlations only to assert relationships between variables, not to exclude them.

Using nonparametric correlation

Correlations can work fine when your variables are numeric and their relationship is strictly linear. Sometimes, your feature could be ordinal (a numeric variable but with orderings) or you may suspect some nonlinearity due to non-normal distributions in your data. A possible solution is to test the doubtful correlations with a nonparametric correlation, such as a Spearman correlation (which means that it has fewer requirements in terms of distribution of considered variables). A *Spearman correlation* transforms your numeric values into rankings and then correlates the rankings, thus minimizing the influence of any nonlinear relationship between the two variables under scrutiny.

As an example, you verify the relationship between sepals' length and width whose Pearson correlation was quite weak:

```
from scipy.stats import spearmanr
from scipy.stats.stats import pearsonr
spearmanr_coef, spearmanr_p = spearmanr(iris_dataframe['sepal length (cm)'],
    iris_dataframe['sepal width (cm)'])
pearsonr_coef, pearsonr_p = pearsonr(iris_dataframe['sepal length (cm)'],
    iris_dataframe['sepal width (cm)'])
print 'Pearson correlation %0.3f | Spearman correlation %0.3f' % (pearsonr_coef,
    spearmanr_coef)
Pearson correlation -0.109 | Spearman correlation -0.159
```

In this case, the code confirms the weak association between the two variables using the nonparametric test.

Considering chi-square for tables

You can apply another nonparametric test for relationship when working with cross-tables. This test is applicable to both categorical and numeric data (after it has been discretized into bins). The chi-square statistic tells you when the table distribution of two variables is statistically comparable to a table in which the two variables are hypothesized as not related to each other (the so-called independence hypothesis). Here is an example of how you use this technique:

```
from scipy.stats import chi2_contingency
table = pd.crosstab(iris_dataframe['group'], iris_binned['petal length (cm)'])
chi2, p, dof, expected = chi2_contingency(table.values)
print 'Chi-square %0.2f p-value %0.3f' % (chi2, p)

Chi-square 212.43 p-value 0.000
```

As seen before, the p-value is the chance that the chi-square difference is just by chance.

The chi-square measure value depends on how many cells the table has. Do not use the chi-square measure to compare different chi-square tests unless you know for sure that the tables in comparison share the same structure.

The chi-square is particularly interesting for assessing the relationships between binned numeric variables, even in the presence of strong nonlinearity that can fool Person's r. Contrary to correlation measures, it can inform you of a possible association, but it won't provide clear details of its direction or absolute magnitude.

Modifying Data Distributions

As a by-product of data exploration, in an EDA phase you can do the following:

- Obtain new feature creation from the combination of different but related variables
- Spot hidden groups or strange values lurking in your data
- Try some useful modifications of your data distributions by binning (or other discretizations such as binary variables)

When performing EDA, you need to consider the importance of data transformation in preparation for the learning phase, which also means using certain mathematical formulas. The following sections present an overview of the most common mathematical formulas used for EDA (such as linear regression). The data transformation you choose depends on the distribution of your data, with a normal distribution being the most common. In addition, these sections highlight the need to match the transformation process to the mathematical formula you use.

Using the normal distribution

The normal, or Gaussian, distribution is the most useful distribution in statistics thanks to its frequent recurrence and particular mathematical properties. It's essentially the foundation of many statistical tests and models, with some of them, such as the linear regression, widely used in data science.

During data science practice, you'll meet with a wide range of different distributions — with some of them named by probabilistic theory, others not. For some distributions, the assumption that they should behave as a normal distribution may hold, but for others, it may not, and that could be a problem depending on what algorithms you use for the learning process. As a general rule, if your model is a linear regression or part of the linear model family because it boils down to a summation of coefficients, then both variable standardization and distribution transformation should be considered.

Creating a Z-score standardization

In your EDA process, you may have realized that your variables have different scales and are heterogeneous in their distributions. As a consequence of your analysis, you need to transform the variables in a way that makes them easily comparable:

```
from sklearn.preprocessing import scale
stand_sepal_width = scale(iris_dataframe['sepal width (cm)'])
```

Transforming other notable distributions

When you check variables with high skewness and kurtosis for their correlation, the results may disappoint you. As you find out earlier in this chapter, using a nonparametric measure of correlation, such as Spearman's, may tell you more about two variables than Pearson's r may tell you. In this case, you should transform your insight into a new, transformed feature:

```
tranformations = {'x': lambda x: x, '1/x': lambda x: 1/x, 'x**2': lambda x:
          x**2,
  'x**3': lambda x: x**3, 'log(x)': lambda x: np.log(x)}
for transformation in tranformations:
    pearsonr_coef, pearsonr_p = pearsonr(iris_dataframe['sepal length (cm)'],
       tranformations[transformation](iris_dataframe['sepal width (cm)']))
    print 'Transformation: %s \t Pearson\'s r: %0.3f' % (transformation,
            pearsonr_coef)


Transformation: x          Pearson's r: -0.109
Transformation: x**2       Pearson's r: -0.122
Transformation: x**3       Pearson's r: -0.131
Transformation: log(x)     Pearson's r: -0.093
Transformation: 1/x        Pearson's r:  0.073
```

In exploring various possible transformations, using a `for` loop may tell you that a power transformation will increase the correlation between the two variables, thus increasing the performance of a linear machine-learning algorithm. You may also try other, further transformations such as square root `np.sqrt(x)`, exponential `np.exp(x)`, and various combinations of all the transformations, such as log inverse `np.log(1/x)`.

Chapter 14

Reducing Dimensionality

ig data is defined as a collection of datasets that is so huge that it becomes difficult to process using traditional techniques. The manipulation of big data differentiates statistical problems, which are based on small samples, from data science problems. You typically use traditional statistical techniques on small problems and data science techniques on big problems.

Data may be viewed as big because it consists of many examples, and this is the first kind of big that spontaneously comes to mind. Analyzing a database of millions of customers and interacting with them all simultaneously is really challenging, but that isn't the only possible perspective of big data.

Another potential view of big data relates to its production and velocity, that is, the time dimension. Even if your observations are few, producing data points for an extended time frame results in a huge stack of information. The dataset reports each instant's persistency or change of your cases.

A third view of big data is data dimensionality, which refers to how many aspects of the cases an application tracks. Data with high dimensionality may offer many features (variables) — often hundreds or thousands of them. And that may turn into a real problem. Even if you're observing only a few cases for a short time, dealing with too many features can make most analysis intractable.

The complexity of working with so many dimensions drives the necessity for various data techniques to filter the information — keeping the data that seems to solve the problem better. The filter reduces dimensionality by removing redundant information in high-dimension datasets.

The focus in this chapter is on reducing data dimensions when the data has too many repetitions of the same information. You can view this reduction as a kind of information compression, which is similar to compressing files on a hard disk in order to save space.

You don't have to type the source code for this chapter manually. In fact, it's a lot easier if you use the downloadable source (see the Introduction for download instructions). The source code for this chapter appears in the `P4DS4D; 14; Reducing Dimensionality.ipynb` source code file.

Understanding SVD

The core of data reduction magic lies in a form of linear algebra called Singular Value Decomposition (SVD). *SVD* is a mathematical method that takes data as input in the form of a single matrix and gives back three resulting matrices that, multiplied together, return the original input matrix. The formula of SVD is

M = U * s * Vh

Here is a short explanation of the letters used in the equation:

- **U:** Contains all the information about the rows (your observations)
- **Vh:** Contains all the information about the columns (your features)
- **s:** Records the SVD process (it is kind of a log record)

Creating three matrices out of one seems counterproductive when the goal is to reduce data dimensions. It would seem that using SVD should be called data explosion, not reduction! However, SVD conceals the magic in the process, because as it builds these new matrices, it separates the information regarding the rows from the columns of the original matrix. As a result, it compresses all the valuable information into the first columns of the new data.

The resulting matrix s shows how the compression happened. The sum of all the values in s tells you how much information was previously stored in your original matrix, and each value in r reports how much data has accumulated in each respective column of U and Vh.

To understand how this all works, you need to look at individual values. For instance, if the sum of s is 100 and the first value of s is 99, that means that 99 percent of the information is now stored in the first column of U and Vh. Therefore, you can happily discard all the remaining columns after the first column without losing any important information for your data science knowledge discovery process.

Looking for dimensionality reduction

It's time to see how Python can help you reduce data complexity. The following example demonstrates a method for reducing your big data. You can use this technique in many other interesting applications, too.

```
import numpy as np
M = np.array([[1, 3, 4], [2, 3, 5], [1, 2, 3], [5, 4, 6]])
print(M)


[[1 3 4]
 [2 3 5]
 [1 2 3]
 [5 4 6]]
```

Let's say you have a matrix, M, that contains the data that you want to reduce. M is made of four observations containing three features each. Using the module linalg from NumPy, you can access the svd function that exactly splits your original matrix into three variables: U, s, and Vh.

```
U, s, Vh = np.linalg.svd(M, full_matrices=False)
print np.shape(U), np.shape(s),np.shape(Vh)
print s


(4L, 3L) (3L,) (3L, 3L)
[ 12.26362747   2.11085464   0.38436189]
```

The matrix U, representing the rows, has four row values. The matrix Vh is a square matrix, and its three rows represent the original columns. The matrix s is a diagonal matrix. A diagonal matrix contains zeros in every element but its diagonal. The length of its diagonal is exactly that of the three original columns. Inside s, you find that most of the values are in the first elements, indicating that the first column is what holds the most information (more than 80 percent), the second has some values (about 14 percent), and the third contains the residual values.

You can check whether the SVD keeps its promises by viewing the example output. The example reconstructs the original matrix using the dot NumPy function to multiply U, s (diagonal), and Vh. The dot function performs matrix multiplication, which is a multiplication procedure slightly different from the arithmetic one.

```
print np.dot(np.dot(U, np.diag(s)), Vh) # Full matrix reconstruction


[[ 1.   3.   4.]
 [ 2.   3.   5.]
 [ 1.   2.   3.]
 [ 5.   4.   6.]]
```

The reconstruction is perfect. Now it's time to play with the results a little. For example, you might want to see what happens when you exclude the third column, the less important of the three. The following example shows what happens when you cut the last column from all three matrices.

```
print np.round(np.dot(np.dot(U[:,:2], np.diag(s[:2])), Vh[:2,:]),1) # k=2
        reconstruction

[[ 1.   2.8  4.1]
 [ 2.   3.2  4.8]
 [ 1.   2.   3. ]
 [ 5.   3.9  6. ]]
```

The output is almost perfect. There are a few decimal points of difference. To take the example further, the following code removes both the second and third columns.

```
print np.round(np.dot(np.dot(U[:,:1], np.diag(s[:1])), Vh[:1,:]),1) # k=1
        reconstruction

[[ 2.1  2.5  3.7]
 [ 2.6  3.1  4.6]
 [ 1.6  1.8  2.8]
 [ 3.7  4.3  6.5]]
```

Now there are more errors. Some elements of the matrix are missing more than a few decimal points. However, you can see that most of the numeric information is intact. Just imagine the potential of using such a technique on a larger matrix, a matrix with hundreds of columns.

One of the difficult issues to consider is determining how many columns to keep. Creating a cumulated sum of the diagonal matrix s (using the NumPy cumsum function is perfect for this task) is useful for keeping track of how information is expressed, and by how many columns. As a general rule, you should consider solutions maintaining from 70 to 99 percent of the original information; however, that's not a strict rule — it really depends on how important it is for you to be able to reconstruct the original dataset.

Using SVD to measure the invisible

A property of SVD is to compress the original data at such a level and in such a smart way that, in certain situations, the technique can really create new meaningful and useful features, not just compressed variables. Therefore, you could have used the three columns of the U matrix in the previous example as new features.

If your data contains hints and clues about a hidden cause or motif, an SVD can put them together and offer you proper answers and insights. That is especially true when your data is made up of interesting pieces of information like the ones in the following list:

- ✔ **Text in documents hints at ideas and meaningful categories.** Just as you can make up your mind about treated themes by reading blogs and newsgroups, so also can SVD help you deduce a meaningful classification of groups of documents or the specific topics being written about in each of them.

- ✔ **Reviews of specific movies or books hint at your personal preferences and at larger product categories.** So if you say that you loved the original *Star Trek* series collection on a rating site, it becomes easy to determine what you like in terms of other films, consumer products, or even personality types.

An example of a method based on SVD is Latent Semantic Indexing (LSI), which has been successfully used to associate documents and words on the basis of the idea that words, though different, tend to have the same meaning when placed in similar contexts. This type of analysis suggests not only synonymous words but also higher grouping concepts. For example, an LSI analysis on some sample sports news may group together baseball teams of the Major League based solely on the co-occurrence of team names in similar articles, without any previous knowledge of what a baseball team or the Major League are.

Performing Factor and Principal Component Analysis

SVD operates directly on the numeric values in data, but you can also express data as a relationship between variables. Each feature has a certain variation. You can calculate the variability as the variance measure around the mean. The more the variance, the more the information contained inside the variable. In addition, if you place the variable into a set, you can compare the variance of two variables to determine whether they correlate, which is a measure of how strongly they have similar values.

Checking all the possible correlations of a variable with the others in the set, you can discover that you may have two types of variance:

- ✔ **Unique variance:** Some variance is unique to the variable under examination. It cannot be associated to what happens to any other variable.

- ✔ **Shared variance:** Some variance is shared with one or more other variables, creating redundancy in the data. Redundancy implies that you can find the same information, with slightly different values, in various features and across many observations.

Of course, the next step is to determine the reason for shared variance. Trying to answer such a question, as well as determining how to deal with unique and shared variances, led to the creation of factor and principal component analysis.

Considering the psychometric model

Long before many machine-learning algorithms were thought up, *psychometrics*, the discipline in psychology that is concerned with psychological measurement, tried to find a statistical solution to effectively measure dimensions in personality. Our personality, as with other aspects of ourselves, is not directly measurable. For example, it isn't possible to measure precisely how much a person is introverted or intelligent. Questionnaires and psychological tests only hint at these values.

Psychologists knew of SVD and tried to apply it to the problem. Shared variance attracted their attention: If some variables are almost the same, they should have the same root cause, they thought. Psychologists created *factor analysis* to perform this task! Instead of applying SVD directly to data, they applied it to a newly created matrix tracking the common variance, in the hope of condensing all the information and recovering new useful features called *factors*.

Looking for hidden factors

A good way to show how to use factor analysis is to start with the Iris dataset.

```
from sklearn.datasets import load_iris
from sklearn.decomposition import FactorAnalysis
iris = load_iris()
X, y = iris.data, iris.target
factor = FactorAnalysis(n_components=4, , random_state=101).fit(X)
```

After loading the data and having stored all the predictive features, the `FactorAnalysis` class is initialized with a request to look for four factors. The data is then fitted. You can explore the results by observing the `components_` attribute, which returns an array containing measures of the relationship between the newly created factors, placed in rows, and the original features, placed in columns. At the intersection of each factor and feature, a positive number indicates that a positive proportion exists between the two; a negative number, instead, points out that they diverge and one is the contrary to the other.

You'll have to test different values of `n_components` because it isn't possible to know how many factors exist in the data. If the algorithm is required for more factors than exist, it will generate factors with low values in the `components_` array.

```
import pandas as pd
print pd.DataFrame(factor.components_,columns=iris.feature_names)

    sepal length (cm)  sepal width (cm)  petal length (cm)  petal width (cm)
0            0.707227         -0.153147           1.653151          0.701569
1            0.114676          0.159763          -0.045604         -0.014052
2            0.000000         -0.000000          -0.000000         -0.000000
3           -0.000000          0.000000           0.000000         -0.000000
```

In the test on the Iris dataset, for example, the resulting factors should be a maximum of 2, not 4, because only two factors have significant connections with the original features. You can use these two factors as new variables in your project because they reflect an unseen but important feature that the previously available data only hinted at.

Using components, not factors

If an SVD could be successfully applied to the common variance, you might wonder why you can't apply it to all the variances. Using a slightly modified starting matrix, all the relationships in the data could be reduced and compressed in a similar way to how SVD does it. The results of this process, which are quite similar to SVD, are called *principal components analysis* (PCA). The newly created features are named *components*. In contrast to factors, components aren't described as the root cause of the data structure but are just restructured data, so you can view them as a big, smart summation of selected variables.

For data science applications, PCA and SVD are quite similar. However, PCA isn't affected by the scale of the original features (because it works on correlation measures that are all bound between −1 and +1 values) and PCA focuses on rebuilding the relationship between the variables, thus offering different results from SVD.

Achieving dimensionality reduction

The procedure to obtain a PCA is quite similar to the factor analysis. The difference is that you don't specify the number of components to extract. You decide later how many components to keep after checking the `explained_variance_ratio_` attribute, which provides quantification (in percentage) of the informative value of each extracted component. The following example shows how to perform this task:

```
from sklearn.decomposition import PCA
import pandas as pd
pca = PCA().fit(X)
print 'Explained variance by component: %s' % pca.explained_variance_ratio_
print pd.DataFrame(pca.components_,columns=iris.feature_names)

Explained variance by component: [ 0.92461621  0.05301557  0.01718514
            0.00518309]
     sepal length (cm)  sepal width (cm)  petal length (cm)  petal width (cm)
0             0.361590         -0.082269           0.856572          0.358844
1            -0.656540         -0.729712           0.175767          0.074706
2             0.580997         -0.596418          -0.072524         -0.549061
3             0.317255         -0.324094          -0.479719          0.751121
```

In this decomposition of the Iris dataset, the vector array provided by `explained_variance_ratio_` indicates that most of the information is concentrated into the first component (92.5 percent). You saw this same sort of result after the factor analysis. It's therefore possible to reduce the entire dataset to just two components, providing a reduction of noise and redundant information from the original dataset.

Understanding Some Applications

Understanding the algorithms that compose the family of SVD-derived data decomposition techniques is complex because of its mathematical complexity and its numerous variants (such as Factor, PCA, and SVD). A few applications may instead help you understand the best ways to employ these powerful data science tools.

In the following paragraphs, you work with some algorithms that you likely have seen in action when

✔ Performing a search by images on a search engine or publishing an image on a social network

✔ Automatically labeling blog posts or questions to Q&A websites

✔ Receiving recommendations for your purchases on e-commerce websites.

Recognizing faces with PCA

Our first example deals with images, and more precisely with facial images. You may have wondered how social networks manage to tag images with the appropriate label or name. The following example demonstrates how to perform this task.

```
from sklearn.datasets import fetch_olivetti_faces
dataset = fetch_olivetti_faces(shuffle=True, random_state=101)
train_faces = dataset.data[:350,:]
test_faces  = dataset.data[350:,:]
train_answers = dataset.target[:350]
test_answers  = dataset.target[350:]
```

The example begins by using the Olivetti faces dataset, a set of images readily available from Scikit-learn. For this experiment, the code divides the set of labeled images into a training and a test set. You need to pretend that you know the labels of the training set but don't know anything from the test set. As a result, you want to associate images from the test set to the most similar image from the training set.

```
print dataset.DESCR
```

The Olivetti dataset consists of 400 photos taken from 40 people (so there are 10 photos of each person). Even though the photos represent the same person, each photo has been taken at different times during the day, with different light and facial expressions or details (for example, with glasses and without). The images are 64 x 64 pixels, so unfolding all the pixels into features creates a dataset made of 400 cases and 4,096 variables.

```
from sklearn.decomposition import RandomizedPCA
n_components = 25
Rpca = RandomizedPCA(n_components=n_components, whiten=True,
    random_state=101).fit(train_faces)
print 'Explained variance by %i components: %0.3f' % (n_components,
    np.sum(Rpca.explained_variance_ratio_))
compressed_train_faces = Rpca.transform(train_faces)
compressed_test_faces  = Rpca.transform(test_faces)

Explained variance by 25 components: 0.794
```

The `RandomizedPCA` class is an approximate PCA version, which works better when the dataset is large (many rows and variables). The decomposition creates 25 new variables (`n_components` parameter) and whitening (`whiten=True`), thus removing some constant noise (created by textual and photo granularity) from images. The resulting decomposition uses 25 components, which is about 80 percent of information held in 4,096 features.

```
import matplotlib.pyplot as plt
photo = 17 # This is the photo in the test set we want to know about
print 'We are looking for face id=%i' % test_answers[photo]
plt.subplot(1, 2, 1)
plt.axis('off')
plt.title('Unknown face '+str(photo)+' in test set')
plt.imshow(test_faces[photo].reshape(64,64), cmap=plt.cm.gray,
           interpolation='nearest')
```

Figure 14-1 represents the chosen photo from the test set. It is subject number 34.

Figure 14-1:
The example application would like to find similar photos.

After the decomposition of the test set, the example takes the data relative only to photo 17 and subtracts it from the decomposition of the training set. Now the training set is made of differences with respect to the example photo. The code squares them (to remove negative values) and sums them by row. That results in a series of summed errors. The most similar photos are the ones with the least-squared errors, the ones whose differences are the least.

```
mask = compressed_test_faces[photo,] #Just the vector of value components of our
           photo
squared_errors = np.sum((compressed_train_faces - mask)**2,axis=1)
minimum_error_face = argmin(squared_errors)
most_resembling = list(np.where(squared_errors < 20)[0])
print 'Best resembling face in train test: %i' % train_answers[minimum_error_
           face]

Best resembling face in train test: 34
```

As it did before, the code can now display photo 17, which is the photo that best resembles images from the training set.

```
import matplotlib.pyplot as plt
plt.subplot(2, 2, 1)
plt.axis('off')
plt.title('Unknown face '+str(photo)+' in test set')
plt.imshow(test_faces[photo].reshape(64,64), cmap=plt.cm.gray,
           interpolation='nearest')
for k,m in enumerate(most_resembling[:3]):
    plt.subplot(2, 2, 2+k)
    plt.title('Match in train set no. '+str(m))
    plt.axis('off')
    plt.imshow(train_faces[m].reshape(64,64), cmap=plt.cm.gray,
               interpolation='nearest')
plt.show()
```

Figure 14-2:
The output
shows the
results that
resemble
the test
image.

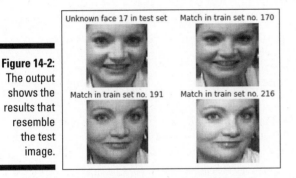

Even though the most similar photo is similar (it's just scaled slightly differently), the other two photos are quite different. However, even though those photos don't match the text image as well, they really do show the same person as in photo 17.

Extracting Topics with NMF

Textual data is another field of application for the family of data reduction algorithms. The idea that prompted such application is that if a group of people talks or writes about something, those people tend to use words from a limited set because they refer or are related to the same topic; they share some meaning or are part of the same group. Consequently, if you have a collection of texts and don't know what topics the text references, you can reverse the previous reasoning — you can simply look for groups of words that tend to associate together, so their newly formed group by dimensionality reduction may hint at the topics you'd like to know about.

This is a perfect application for the SVD family, because by reducing the number of columns, the features (in a document, the words are the features) will gather in dimensions, and you can discover the topics by checking high-scoring words. SVD and PCA provide features to relate both positively and negatively with the newly created dimensions. So a resulting topic may be expressed by the presence of a word (high positive value) or by the absence of it (high negative value), making interpretation both tricky and counter-intuitive for humans. Luckily, Scikit-learn includes the Non-Negative Matrix Factorization (NMF) decomposition class, which allows an original feature to relate only positively with the resulting dimensions.

This example starts with a new experiment after loading the 20newsgroups dataset, selecting only the posts regarding objects for sale and automatically removing headers, footers, and quotes.

```
from sklearn.datasets import fetch_20newsgroups
dataset = fetch_20newsgroups(shuffle=True, categories = ['misc.forsale'],
    remove=('headers', 'footers', 'quotes'), random_state=101)
print 'Posts: %i' % len(dataset.data)

Posts: 585
```

The `TfidVectorizer` class is imported and set up to remove stop words (common words such as *the* or *and*) and keep only distinctive words, producing a matrix whose columns point to distinct words.

```
from sklearn.feature_extraction.text import TfidfVectorizer
vectorizer = TfidfVectorizer(max_df=0.95, min_df=2, stop_words='english')
tfidf = vectorizer.fit_transform(dataset.data)

from sklearn.decomposition import NMF
n_topics = 5
nmf = NMF(n_components=n_topics, random_state=101).fit(tfidf)
```

Term frequency-inverse document frequency (Tf-idf) is a simple calculation based on the frequency of a word in document. It is weighted by the rarity of the word between all the documents available. Weighting words is an effective way to rule out words that cannot help you to classify or to identify the document when processing text. For example, you can eliminate common parts of speech or other common words.

As with other algorithms from the `sklearn.decomposition` module, the `n_components` parameter indicates the number of desired components. If you'd like to look for more topics, you use a higher number. As the required number of topics increases, the `reconstruction_err_` method reports lower error rates. It's up to you to decide when to stop given the trade-off between more time spent on computations and more topics.

The last part of the script outputs the resulting five topics. By reading the printed words, you can decide on the meaning of the extracted topics, thanks to product characteristics (for instance, the words *drive*, *hard*, *card*, and *floppy* refer to computers) or the exact product (for instance, *comics*, *car*, *stereo*, *games*).

```
feature_names = vectorizer.get_feature_names()
n_top_words = 15
for topic_idx, topic in enumerate(nmf.components_):
    print "Topic #%d:" % (topic_idx+1),
    print " ".join([feature_names[i] for i in topic.argsort()[:-n_top_words -
            1:-1]])


Topic #1: drive hard card floppy monitor meg ram disk motherboard vga scsi brand
            color
    internal modem
Topic #2: 00 50 dos 20 10 15 cover 1st new 25 price man 40 shipping comics
Topic #3: condition excellent offer asking best car old sale good new miles 10
            000 tape
    cd
Topic #4: shipping vcr stereo works obo included amp plus great volume vhs unc
            mathes
    gibbs radley
Topic #5: email looking games game mail interested send like thanks price
            package list
    sale want know
```

You can explore the resulting model by looking into the attribute `compo-nents_` from the trained `NMF` model. It consists of a NumPy `ndarray` holding positive values for words connected to the topic. By using the `argsort` method, you can get the indexes of the top associations, whose high values indicate that they are the most representative words.

```
print nmf.components_[0,:].argsort()[:-n_top_words-1:-1] # Gets top words for
            topic 0
[1337 1749  889 1572 2342 2263 2803 1290 2353 3615 3017  806 1022 1938 2334]
```

Decoding the words' indexes creates readable strings by calling them from the array derived from the `get_feature_names` method applied to the `TfidfVectorizer` that was previously fitted.

```
print vectorizer.get_feature_names()[1337] # transform indexes into words
drive
```

Recommending movies

Other interesting applications for data reduction are systems for generating recommendations about the things you may like to buy or know more about. You likely have quite a few occasions to see recommenders in action. On most e-commerce websites, after logging-in, visiting some product pages, and rating or putting a product into your electronic basket, you see other buying opportunities based on other customers' previous experiences (the method is called *collaborative filtering*).

You can implement collaborative recommendations based on simple means or frequencies calculated on other customers' set of purchased items or on ratings using SVD. This approach helps you reliably generate recommendations even in the case of products the vendor seldom sells or that are quite new to users.

For this example, you use a well-known database created by the MovieLens website, collected from its users' ratings of a movie they liked or disliked. Because this is an external dataset, you first have to download it from its Internet location:

```
http://files.grouplens.org/datasets/movielens/ml-1m.zip
```

After downloading it, you have to extract it into your Python working directory. You can discover what your working directory is by using these commands:

```
import os
print os.getcwd()
```

Take note of the displayed directory and extract the ml-1m database there. Then execute the following code.

```
import pandas as pd
from scipy.sparse import csr_matrix
users = pd.read_table('ml-1m/users.dat', sep='::', header=None,
            names=['user_id',
    'gender', 'age', 'occupation', 'zip'])
ratings = pd.read_table('ml-1m/ratings.dat', sep='::', header=None,
            names=['user_id',
    'movie_id', 'rating', 'timestamp'])
movies = pd.read_table('ml-1m/movies.dat', sep='::', header=None,
            names=['movie_id',
    'title', 'genres'])
MovieLens = pd.merge(pd.merge(ratings, users), movies)
```

Using `pandas`, the code loads the different data tables and then merges them on the basis of the features with the same name (the `user_id` and `movie_id` variables).

```
ratings_mtx_df = MovieLens.pivot_table(values='rating', rows='user_id',
            cols='title',
    fill_value=0)
movie_index = ratings_mtx_df.columns
```

`pandas` will also help create a data table crossing information on rows about users and in columns about movie titles. A movie index will keep track about what movie each column represents.

```
from sklearn.decomposition import TruncatedSVD
recom = TruncatedSVD(n_components=10, random_state=101)
R = recom.fit_transform(ratings_mtx_df.values.T)
```

The `TruncatedSVD` class reduces the data table to ten components. This class offers a more scalable algorithm than SciPy's `linalg.svd` used in earlier examples. `TruncatedSVD` computes result matrices of exactly the shape you decide by the `n_components` parameter (the full resulting matrices are not calculated), resulting in a faster output and less memory usage.

By calculating the `Vh` matrix, you can reduce the ratings of different but similar users (each user's scores are expressed by row) into compressed dimensions that reconstruct general tastes and preferences. Please also notice that because you're interested in the `Vh` matrix (the columns/movies reduction) but the algorithm provides you with only the `U` matrix (the decomposition based on rows), you need to input the transposition of the data table (using this approach, columns become rows and you obtain `TruncatedSVD` output, which is the `Vh` matrix).

```
# 1196::Star Wars: Episode V - The Empire Strikes Back
# (1980)::Action|Adventure|Drama|Sci-Fi|War
favoured_movie_idx = list(movie_index).index(
    'Star Wars: Episode V - The Empire Strikes Back (1980)')
print R[favoured_movie_idx]

[ 184.72254552  -17.7761415    47.33483561  -51.46669814  -47.9152707
 -17.65000951  -14.34294204  -12.88678007  -17.48586358   -5.38370224]
```

Using the movie label (in such cases, you look for suggestions based on preference for a Star Wars episode), you can find out what column the movie is in (column index 3154 in this case) and print the values of the 10 components. This sequence provides the movie profile. You could try to interpret it, but the focus is on other movies that are similar based on the users' ratings. These movies have similar scores to the target movie and therefore are highly correlated with it. A good strategy is to calculate a correlation matrix of all movies, get the slice related to your movie, and find out inside it what are the most related (characterized by high positive correlation — say at least 0.98) movie titles using indexing as shown in the following code.

```
import numpy as np
correlation_matrix = np.corrcoef(R)
P = correlation_matrix[favoured_movie_idx]
print list(movie_index[(P > 0.98) & (P < 1.0)])


['Raiders of the Lost Ark (1981)', 'Star Wars: Episode IV - A New Hope (1977)',
 'Star Wars: Episode VI - Return of the Jedi (1983)']
```

It seems there are quite a few titles that fans would like, such as Star Wars Episodes IV and VI (of course). In addition, fans might like Raiders of the Lost Ark, maybe because they like the actor Harrison Ford, who is the main character in all these films.

SVD will always find the best way to relate a row or column in your data, discovering complex interactions or relations you didn't imagine before. You don't need to imagine anything in advance; it's fully a data-driven approach.

Chapter 15

Clustering

- -

- -

One of the basic abilities that humans have exercised since primitive times is to divide the known world into separate classes where individual objects share common features deemed important by the classifier. Starting with primitive cave dwellers classifying the natural world they lived in, distinguishing plants and animals useful or dangerous for their survival, we arrive at modern times in which marketing departments classify consumers into target segments and then act with proper marketing plans.

Classifying is crucial to our process of building new knowledge because, by gathering similar objects, we can

✔ Mention all the items in a class by the same denomination

✔ Summarize relevant features by an exemplificative class type

✔ Associate particular actions or recall specific knowledge automatically

Dealing with big data streams today requires the same classificatory ability, but on a different scale. To spot unknown groups of signals present in the data, we need specialized algorithms that are both able to learn how to assign examples to certain given classes (the *supervised* approach) and to spot new interesting classes that we weren't aware of (*unsupervised* learning).

Even though your main routine as a data scientist will be to put into practice your predictive skills, you'll also have to provide useful insight into possible structured information present in your data. For example, you'll often need to locate new features in order to strengthen the predictive power of your models, find an easy way to make complex comparisons inside the data, and discover communities in social networks.

A data-driven approach to classification, called *clustering*, will prove to be of great help in achieving success for your data project when you need to provide new insights from scratch.

Clustering techniques are a set of *unsupervised classification* methods that can create meaningful classes by directly processing your data, without any previous knowledge or hypothesis about the groups that may be present. If all supervised algorithms need labeled examples (class labels), unsupervised ones can figure out by themselves what the most appropriate labels could be.

There are a few kinds of clustering techniques. You can distinguish between them using the guidelines in the following list:

- ✔ Assigning every example to a unique group (partitioning) or to multiple ones (fuzzy clustering)
- ✔ Determining the heuristic — that is, the rule of thumb — that they use to figure out whether an example is part of a group
- ✔ Specifying how they quantify the difference between observations, that is, the so-called distance measure

Most of the time you use *partition-clustering techniques* (a data point can be part of only one group, so the groups don't overlap; their membership is distinct) and among partitioning methods, you use K-means the most. But other useful methods are mentioned in this chapter, which are based on agglomerative methods and on data density.

Agglomerative methods link data points into clusters based on their distance. *Data density approaches* take advantage of the idea that groups are very dense and continuous, so if you notice a decrease in density when exploring a part of a group of points, it could mean that you arrived at one of its borders.

Because you normally don't know what you're looking for, different methods can provide you with different solutions and points of view on the data. The secret of a successful clustering is to try as many of the recipes as possible, compare the results, and try to find a reason why you can consider certain observations as a group in respect to others.

You don't have to type the source code for this chapter manually. In fact, it's a lot easier if you use the downloadable source (see the Introduction for download instructions). The source code for this chapter appears in the `P4DS4D; 15; Clustering.ipynb` source code file.

Clustering with K-means

K-means is an iterative algorithm that has become very popular in machine learning because of its simplicity, speed, and scalability to a large number of data points. The K-means algorithm relies on the idea that there are a specific number of data groups, called *clusters*. Each data group is scattered around a central point with which they share some key characteristics.

You can actually imagine the central point of a cluster, called a *centroid,* as a sun. The data points distribute around the centroid like planets. Clusters are also expected to clearly separate from each other, so, as groups of points they are both internally homogeneous and different from each other.

The K-means algorithm expects to find clusters in your data. Therefore, it will find them even when none exist! It's important to check inside the groups to determine whether the group is a true gold nugget.

Given such assumptions, all you have to do is to specify the number of groups you expect (you can use a guess or try a number of possible desirable solutions), and the K-means algorithm will look for them, using a heuristic in order to recover the position of the central points.

The cluster centroids should be evident by their different characteristics and positions from each other. Even if you start by randomly guessing where they could be, in the end, after a few corrections, you always find them by using the many data points that gravitate around them.

Understanding centroid-based algorithms

The procedure for finding the centroids is straightforward:

1. Guess a K number of clusters.

   K centroids are picked randomly from your data points or chosen so that they are placed in your data in very distant positions from each other. All the other points are assigned to their nearest centroid based on the Euclidean distance.

2. Form the initial clusters.

3. Reiterate the clusters until you notice that your solution doesn't change anymore.

   You recalculate the centroids as an average of all the points present in the group. All the data points are reassigned to the groups based on the distance from the new centroids.

The iterative process of assigning cases to the most plausible centroid and then averaging the assigned ones to find a new centroid will slowly shift the centroid position toward the areas where most data points gravitate. The result is that you end up with the true centroid position.

The procedure has only two weak points that you need to consider. First, you choose the initial centroids randomly, which means that you could start from a bad starting point. As a result, the iterative process will stop at some unlikely solution — for example, having a centroid in the middle of two groups. To ensure that your solution is the most probable, you have to try the algorithm a few times and track the results. The more often you try, the more likely you are to confirm the right solution. The Python Scikit-learn implementation of K-means will do that for you, so you just have to decide how many times you intend to try. (The trade-off is that more iterations produce better results, but each iteration consumes valuable time.)

The second weak point is due to the distance that K-means uses, the *Euclidean distance*, which is the distance between two points on a plane (a concept that you likely studied at school). In a K-means application, each data point is a vector of features, so when comparing the distance of two points, you do the following:

1. Create a list containing the differences of the elements in the two vectors.

2. Square all the elements of the difference vector.

3. Calculate the square root of the summed elements.

You can try a simple example in Python. Pretend that you have two points, A and B, and they have three numeric features. If A and B are the data representation of two persons, their distinguishing features could be measured in height (cm), weight (kg), and age (years), as shown in the following code:

```
import numpy as np
A = np.array([165, 50, 22])
B = np.array([185, 80, 21])
```

The following example shows how to calculate the differences between the three elements, square all the resulting elements, and determine the square root of the squared values:

```
D = (A-B)
D = D**2
D = np.sqrt(np.sum(D))
print D

45.0
```

In the end, the Euclidean distance is really just a big sum. When the variables making up the difference vector are significantly different in scale from each other (in our example, the height could have been expressed in meters), you end up with a distance dominated by the elements with the largest scale. It is very important to rescale the variables so that they use a similar scale before applying the K-means algorithm. You can use a fixed range or a statistical normalization with zero mean and unit variance to achieve this goal.

Another problem that may arise, apart from scale, is due to correlation between variables, causing redundancy of information. If two variables are highly correlated, that means that a part of their information content is repeated. Replication implies counting the same information more than once in the summation used to calculate the distance. If you're not aware of the correlation issue, some variables will dominate your distance measure calculation — a situation that may lead to not finding the useful clusters that you want. The solution is to remove the correlation thanks to a dimensionality reduction algorithm such as Principle Component Analysis (PCA). Scikit-learn has a function in the preprocessing module that can correctly scale your variable, as well as a function for PCA, but it is up to you to remember to use these functions before employing K-means and other clustering techniques using distance measure.

Creating an example with image data

An example with image data demonstrates how to apply the tool and how to get insight from clusters. An ideal example is clustering the handwritten digits dataset provided by the Scikit-learn package. Hand-written numbers are naturally different from each other — they possess variability in that there are several ways to write certain numbers. Of course, we all have different writing styles, so it is natural that each person's numbers differ slightly. The following code shows how to import the image data.

```
from sklearn.datasets import load_digits
digits = load_digits()
X = digits.data
ground_truth = digits.target
```

The example begins by importing the digits dataset from Scikit-learn and assigning the data to a variable. It then stores the labels in another variable for later verification. The next step is to process the data using a PCA.

```
from sklearn.decomposition import PCA
from sklearn.preprocessing import scale
pca = PCA(n_components=40)
Cx = pca.fit_transform(scale(X))
print 'Explained variance %0.3f'
    % sum(pca.explained_variance_ratio_)

Explained variance 0.951
```

By applying a PCA on scaled data, the code addresses the problems of scale and correlation. Even though PCA can recreate the same number of variables as in the input data, the example code drops a few using the n_components parameter. The decision to use 40 components, as compared to the original 64 variables, allows the example to retain most of the original information (95 percent of the original variation in data) and simplify the dataset by removing correlation and some noise.

In this example, the PCA-transformed data appears in the Cx variable. After importing the KMeans class, the code defines its main parameters:

- n_clusters is the K number of centroids to find
- n_init is the number of times to try the K-means with different starting centroids. The code needs to test the procedure a sufficient number of times, such as 10, as shown here.

```
from sklearn.cluster import KMeans
clustering = KMeans(n_clusters=10, n_init=10,
    random_state=1)
clustering.fit(Cx)
```

After creating the parameters, the clustering class is ready for use. You can apply the fit() method to the Cx variable, which produces a scaled and dimensionally reduced dataset.

Looking for optimal solutions

As mentioned in the previous section, the example is clustering ten different numbers. It's time to start looking for a solution with K = 10. The following code compares the clustering result to the *ground truth* — the true labels — in order to determine whether there is any correspondence.

```
import numpy as np
import pandas as pd
ms = np.column_stack((ground_truth,clustering.labels_))
df = pd.DataFrame(ms,
    columns = ['Ground truth','Clusters'])
pd.crosstab(df['Ground truth'], df['Clusters'],
    margins=True)
```

Converting our solution, given by the labels variable internal to the clustering class, into a pandas DataFrame allows us to apply a cross tabulation and compare the original labels with the labels derived from clustering. You can observe the results in Figure 15-1. Because rows represent ground truth, you can look for numbers whose majority of observations are split among different clusters. These observations are the handwritten examples that are more difficult to figure out by K-means.

Clusters	0	1	2	3	4	5	6	7	8	9	All
Ground truth											
0	0	0	0	0	2	0	0	176	0	0	178
1	107	0	0	0	47	0	0	0	27	1	182
2	20	6	0	1	3	0	3	0	45	99	177
3	6	155	0	0	0	0	11	0	1	10	183
4	0	0	0	3	154	9	15	0	0	0	181
5	6	74	2	0	4	0	48	0	0	48	182
6	6	0	174	0	0	0	0	1	0	0	181
7	1	0	0	0	3	17	150	0	0	8	179
8	90	51	2	0	3	0	15	0	0	13	174
9	1	146	0	0	14	4	14	0	0	1	180
All	237	432	178	4	230	30	256	177	73	180	1797

Figure 15-1:
Cross-tabulation of ground truth and K-means clusters.

Notice how numbers such as seven or zero are concentrated into their own cluster, but others, such as 3 and 9, tend to gather together into the same group, the cluster 1. From such a discovery, you can deduce that certain handwritten numbers are easy to guess, while others aren't.

Representing the centroids is also useful. You can use statistics to perform this task. However, because the data is made up of pixels, you can visualize the cases that are nearest to each centroid. The following code shows how to perform this task.

```
import matplotlib.pyplot as plt
for k,img in enumerate(np.argmin(dist,axis=0)):
    cluster = clustering.labels_[img]
    plt.subplot(2, 5, cluster)
    plt.imshow(digits.images[img],cmap='binary',
        interpolation='none')
    plt.title('cl '+str(cluster))
plt.show()
```

Observing the depicted centroids can make clear why the cluster 1 contains most of the numbers 3 and 9 and how a number 8 could be mistaken for a number 1 in cluster 0. In general, reasoning using clusters' centroids is indeed easy because we have reduced thousands of cases into a few clusters to study and compare.

Clustering can help you to summarize huge quantities of data. It is an effective technique for presenting data to a nontechnical audience and for feeding a supervised algorithm with group variables, thus providing them with concentrated, significant information.

Another observation you can make is that even though there are just ten numbers in this example, there are more types of handwritten forms of each, hence the necessity of finding more clusters. Of course, the problem is to determine just how many clusters you need.

You use inertia to measure the viability of a cluster. *Inertia* is the sum of all the differences between every cluster member and its centroid. If the examples in the group are similar to the centroid, the difference is small and so is the inertia. Inertia as an individual measure reveals little. Moreover, when comparing inertia from different clusters in general, you notice that the more groups you have, the less the inertia. What you want to do instead of using inertia directly is to compare the inertia of a cluster solution with the previous cluster solution. This comparison provides you with the rate of change, a more interpretable measure. To obtain the inertia rate of change in Python, you will have to create a loop. Try progressive cluster solutions inside the loop, recording their value. Here is a script for the handwritten digit example:

```python
inertia = list()
delta_inertia = list()
for k in range(1,21):
    clustering = KMeans(n_clusters=k, n_init=10,
        random_state=1)
    clustering.fit(Cx)
    if inertia: # So we won't compare the solution k==1
        delta_inertia.append(
            inertia[-1] - clustering.inertia_)
    inertia.append(clustering.inertia_)
```

You use the `inertia` variable inside the clustering class after fitting the clustering. The inertia variable is a list containing the rate of change of inertia between a solution and the previous one. Here is some code that prints a line graph of the rate of change, as depicted by Figure 15-2.

```python
import matplotlib.pyplot as plt
plt.figure()
plt.plot([k for k in range(2,21)], delta_inertia, 'ko-')
plt.xlabel('Number of clusters')
plt.ylabel('Rate of change of inertia')
plt.show()
```

When examining `inertia`'s rate of change, look for jumps in the rate itself. If the rate jumps up, it means that adding a cluster more than the previous solution brings much more benefit than expected; if it jumps down instead, you're likely forcing a cluster more than necessary. All the cluster solutions before a jump down may be a good candidate, according to the principle of parsimony (the jump signals a sophistication in our analysis, but the right solutions are usually the simplest). In the example, the first jump downward is at K=14, so the first solution to evaluate is K=13. You can see another interesting jump at K=18, so you should also evaluate K=17, which is a peak.

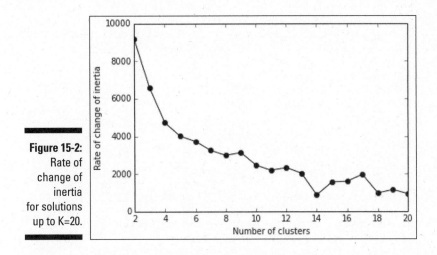

The rate of change in inertia will provide you with just a few tips where there could be good cluster solutions. It is up to you to decide which to pick if you need to get some extra insight on data. If, instead, clustering is just a step in a complex data science project, you can just pass the entire solution to the next machine-learning algorithm.

Clustering big data

K-means is a way to reduce the complexity of your data by summarizing the many examples in your dataset. To perform this task, you load the data into your computer's memory, and that won't always be feasible, especially if you are working with big data. Scikit-learn offers an alternative way to apply K-means — the MiniBatchKMeans is a variant that can progressively cluster separated chunks of data. In fact, a batch learning procedure usually processes the data part by part. There are only two differences between the standard K-means function and MiniBatchKMeans:

- ✔ You cannot automatically test different starting centroids unless you try running the analysis again.

- ✔ The analysis will start when there is a batch made of at least a minimum number of cases. This value is usually set to 100 (but the more cases there are, the better the result) by the batch_size parameter.

A simple demonstration on the previous handwritten dataset shows how effective and easy it is to use the MiniBatchKMeans clustering class.

```
from sklearn.cluster import MiniBatchKMeans
batch_clustering = MiniBatchKMeans(n_clusters=10,
    random_state=1)
batch = 100
guessed_labels = list()
inertia = 0
for row in range(0,len(Cx),batch):
    if row+batch < len(Cx):
        feed = Cx[row:row+batch,:]
    else:
        feed = Cx[row:,:]
    batch_clustering.partial_fit(feed)
    # We have to stack results in a list, because
    # MiniBatchKMean does not take track of all the
    # batches
    guessed_labels.append(batch_clustering.labels_)
    inertia += batch_clustering.inertia_
# NumPy hstack turns a list of arrays into an array
# by inspecting the variable guess_labels you can know
# the assigned cluster
guessed_labels = np.hstack(guessed_labels)
print "Kmeans inertia: %0.1f\n" +
    "MiniBatchKmeans inertia: %0.1f"
    % (clustering.inertia_,inertia)

Kmeans inertia: 48591.7
MiniBatchKmeans inertia: 67027.5
```

This script iterates through the indexes of the previously scaled and PCA simplified dataset (Cx), creating batches of 100 observations each. Using the `partial_fit` method, it fits a K-means clustering on each batch, using the centroids found by the previous call. The algorithm stops when it runs out of data. It then reports its inertia for a 10-clusters solution, comparing it with the same solution's inertia by the standard K-means class. Usually `MiniBatchKmeans` results in a higher inertia than a standard algorithm, so reserve this solution for those times when you cannot work with in-memory datasets.

Performing Hierarchical Clustering

If the K-means algorithm is concerned with centroids, hierarchical (also known as agglomerative) clustering tries to link each data point, by a distance measure, to its nearest neighbor, creating a cluster. Reiterating the algorithm using different linkage methods, the algorithm gathers all the available points into a rapidly diminishing number of clusters, until in the end all the points reunite into a single group.

The results, if visualized, will closely resemble the biological classifications of living beings that you may have studied in school or seen on posters at the local natural history museum, an upside-down tree whose branches are all converging into a trunk. Such a figurative tree is a *dendrogram,* and you see it used in medical and biological research. Scikit-learn implementation of agglomerative clustering does not offer the possibility of depicting a dendrogram from your data because such a visualization technique works fine with only a few cases, whereas you can expect to work on many examples.

Compared to K-means, agglomerative algorithms are more cumbersome and do not scale well to large datasets. Agglomerative algorithms are more suitable for statistical studies (they can be easily found in natural sciences, archeology, and sometimes psychology and economics). These algorithms do offer the advantage of creating a complete range of nested cluster solutions, so you just need to pick the right one for your purpose.

To use agglomerative clustering effectively, you have to know about the different linkage methods (the heuristics for clustering) and the distance metrics. There are three linkage methods:

- **Ward:** Tends to look for spherical clusters, very cohesive inside and extremely differentiated from other groups. Another nice characteristic is that the method tends to find clusters of similar size. It works only with the Euclidean distance.

- **Complete:** Links clusters using their furthest observations, that is, their most dissimilar data points. Consequently, clusters created using this method tend to be comprised of highly similar observations, making the resulting groups quite compact.

- **Average:** Links clusters using their centroids and ignoring their boundaries. The method creates larger groups than the complete method. In addition, the clusters can be different sizes and shapes, contrary to the Ward's solutions. Consequently, this average, multipurpose, approach sees successful use in the field of biological sciences.

There are also three distance metrics:

- **Euclidean (euclidean or l2):** As seen in K-means

- **Manhattan (manhattan or l1):** Similar to Euclidean, but the distance is calculated by summing the absolute value of the difference between the dimensions. In a map, if the Euclidean distance is the shortest route between two points, the Manhattan distance implies moving straight, first along one axis and then along the other — as a car in the city would, reaching a destination by driving along city blocks (the distance is also known as city block distance).

✔ **Cosine (cosine):** A good choice when there are too many variables and you worry that some variable may not be significant (just noise). Cosine distance reduces noise by taking the shape of the variables, more than their values, into account. It tends to associate observations that have the same maximum and minimum variables, regardless of their effective value.

If your dataset doesn't contain too many observations, it's worth trying agglomerative clustering with all the combinations of linkage and distance and then comparing the results carefully. In clustering, you rarely already know right answers, and agglomerative clustering can provide you with another useful potential solution. For example, you can recreate the previous analysis with K-means and handwritten digits, using the ward linkage and the Euclidean distance as follows:

```
from sklearn.cluster import AgglomerativeClustering
# Affinity = {"euclidean", "l1", "l2", "manhattan",
# "cosine"}
# Linkage = {"ward", "complete", "average"}
Hclustering = AgglomerativeClustering(n_clusters=10,
    affinity='euclidean', linkage='ward')
Hclustering.fit(Cx)
ms = np.column_stack((ground_truth,Hclustering.labels_))
df = pd.DataFrame(ms,
    columns = ['Ground truth','Clusters'])
pd.crosstab(df['Ground truth'], df['Clusters'],
    margins=True)
```

The results, in this case, are comparable to K-means, although, you may have noticed that completing the analysis using this approach takes longer than using K-means. When working with a large number of observations, the computations for a hierarchical cluster solution may take hours to complete, making this solution less feasible. You can get around the time issue by using two-phase clustering, which is faster and provides you with a hierarchical solution even when you are working with large datasets.

To implement the two-phase clustering solution, you process the original observations using K-means with a large number of clusters. A good rule of thumb is to take the square root of the number of observations and use that figure, but you always have to keep the number of clusters in the range of 100–200 for the second phase, based on hierarchical clustering, to work well. The following example uses 100 clusters.

```
from sklearn.cluster import KMeans
clustering = KMeans(n_clusters=100, n_init=10,
    random_state=1)
clustering.fit(Cx)
```

At this point, the tricky part is to keep track of what case has been assigned to what cluster derived from K-means. You can use a dictionary for such a purpose.

```
Kx = clustering.cluster_centers_
Kx_mapping = {case:cluster for case,
    cluster in enumerate(clustering.labels_)}
```

The new dataset is Kx, which is made up of the cluster centroids that the K-means algorithm has discovered. You can think of each cluster as a well-represented summary of the original data. If you cluster the summary now, it will be almost the same as clustering the original data.

```
from sklearn.cluster import AgglomerativeClustering
Hclustering = AgglomerativeClustering(n_clusters=10,
    affinity='cosine', linkage='complete')
Hclustering.fit(Kx)
```

You now map the results to the centroids you originally used so that you can easily determine whether a hierarchical cluster is made of certain K-means centroids. The result consists of the observations making up the K-means clusters having those centroids.

```
H_mapping = {case:cluster for case,
    cluster in enumerate(Hclustering.labels_)}
final_mapping = {case:H_mapping[Kx_mapping[case]]
    for case in Kx_mapping}
```

Now you can evaluate the solution you obtained using a similar confusion matrix as you did before for both K-means and hierarchical clustering.

```
ms = np.column_stack((ground_truth,
  [final_mapping[n] for n in range(max(final_mapping)+1)]))
df = pd.DataFrame(ms,
    columns = ['Ground truth','Clusters'])
pd.crosstab(df['Ground truth'], df['Clusters'],
    margins=True)
```

The solution you obtain is analogous to the previous solutions. The result proves that this approach is a viable method for handling large datasets or even big data datasets, reducing them to a smaller representations and then operating with less scalable clustering, but more varied and precise techniques. The two-phase approach also presents another advantage because it operates well with noisy or outlying data — the initial K-means phase filters out such problems well and relegates them to separate cluster solutions.

Moving Beyond the Round-Shaped Clusters: DBScan

Both K-means and agglomerative clustering, especially if you are using the Ward's linkage criteria, will produce cohesive groups, similar to bubbles, equally spread in all directions.

Reality can sometimes produce complex and unsettling results — groups may have strange forms far from the canonical bubble. The Scikit-learns's datasets module offers a wide range of mind-teasing shapes that you can't successfully crunch using either K-means or agglomerative clustering: large circles containing smaller ones, interleaved small circles, and spiraling Swiss roll datasets (named after the sponge cake roll because of how the data points are arranged).

DBScan is another clustering algorithm based on a smart intuition that can solve even the most difficult problems. DBScan relies on the idea that clusters are dense, so to start exploring the data space in every direction and mark a cluster boundary when the density decreases should be sufficient. Areas of the data space with insufficient density of points are just considered empty, and all the points there are noise or *outliers*, that is, points characterized by unusual or strange values.

DBScan is more complex and requires more running time than K-means (but it is faster than agglomerative clustering). It automatically guesses the number of clusters and points out strange data that doesn't easily fit into any class. This makes DBScan different from the previous algorithms that try to force every observation into a class.

Replicating the handwritten digit clustering requires just a few lines of Python code:

```
from sklearn.cluster import DBSCAN
DB = DBSCAN(eps=4.35, min_samples=25, random_state=1)
DB.fit(Cx)
```

Using DBScan, you won't have to set a K number of expected clusters; the algorithm will find them by itself. Apparently, the lack of a K number seems to simplify the usage of DBScan; in reality, the algorithm requires you to fix two essential parameters, `eps` and `min_sample`, in order to work properly:

- `eps`: The maximum distance between two observations that allows them to be part of the same neighborhood.

- `min_sample`: The minimum number of observations in a neighborhood that transform them into a core point.

The algorithm works by walking around the data and building clusters by linking observations arranged into neighborhoods. A *neighborhood* is a small cluster of data points all within a distance value of eps. If the number of points in the neighborhood is less than the number min_sample, then DBScan doesn't form the neighborhood.

No matter what the shape of the cluster, DBScan links all the neighborhoods together if they are near enough (under the distance value of eps). When no more neighborhoods are within reach, DBScan tries to aggregate to group even single data points, if they are within eps distance. The data points that aren't associated with any group are treated as noisy points (too particular to be part of a group).

Try many values of eps and min_sample. The resulting clusters may also change drastically with respect to the values set into these two parameters.

Start with a low number of min_samples. Using a lower number allows many neighborhoods to cluster together. The default number 5 is fine. Then try different numbers for eps, starting from 0.1 upward. Don't be disappointed if you can't get a viable result initially — keep trying different combinations.

Getting back to the example, after this brief explanation of DBScan details, some data exploration can allow you to observe the results under the right point of view. First, count the clusters:

```
from collections import Counter
print Counter(DB.labels_)

Counter({-1: 913, 4: 222, 1: 176, 3: 162, 0: 134, 2: 104,
    5: 86})
```

A large number of observations are assigned to the cluster labeled -1, which represents the noise (noise is defined as examples that are too unusual to group). Likely, given the high number of dimensions (40 uncorrelated variables from a PCA analysis) in our data and its high variability (after all, they are handwritten samples), many cases do not naturally fall together into the same group.

At this point, print a visual representation of some example characteristics of the six clusters (as shown in Figure 15-3):

```
import matplotlib.pyplot as plt
for k,cl in enumerate(np.unique(DB.labels_)):
    if cl >= 0:
        example = np.min(np.where(DB.labels_==cl))
        plt.subplot(2, 3, k)
        plt.imshow(digits.images[example],
```

```
                  cmap='binary',interpolation='none')
              plt.title('cl '+str(cl))
plt.show()
ms = np.column_stack((ground_truth,DB.labels_))
df = pd.DataFrame(ms,
    columns = ['Ground truth','Clusters'])
pd.crosstab(df['Ground truth'], df['Clusters'],
    margins=True)
```

(a)

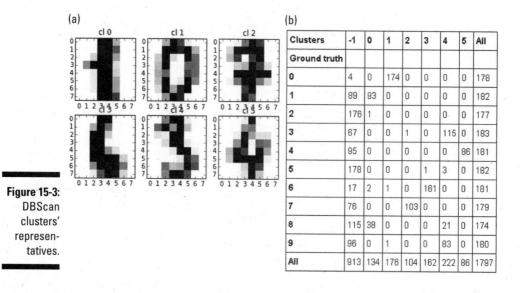

(b)

Clusters	-1	0	1	2	3	4	5	All
Ground truth								
0	4	0	174	0	0	0	0	178
1	89	93	0	0	0	0	0	182
2	176	1	0	0	0	0	0	177
3	67	0	0	1	0	115	0	183
4	95	0	0	0	0	0	86	181
5	178	0	0	0	1	3	0	182
6	17	2	1	0	161	0	0	181
7	76	0	0	103	0	0	0	179
8	115	38	0	0	0	21	0	174
9	96	0	1	0	0	83	0	180
All	913	134	176	104	162	222	86	1797

Figure 15-3:
DBScan
clusters'
represen-
tatives.

The six examples in Figure 15-3 show the numbers 1, 0, 7, 6, 3, and 4 quite clearly. Also, the cross tabulation of cluster ownership with the real labels indicate that DBScan succeeded in finding the numbers precisely and didn't mix different numbers together.

The strength of DBScan is to provide reliable, consistent clusters. After all, DBScan isn't forced, as are K-means and agglomerative clustering, to reach a solution with a certain number of clusters, even when such a solution does not exist.

Chapter 16

Detecting Outliers in Data

• •

• •

*E*rrors happen when you least expect, and that's also true in regard to your data. In addition, data errors are difficult to spot, especially when your dataset contains many variables of different types and scale (a high-dimensionality data structure).

Data errors can take a number of forms. For example, the values may be systematically missing on certain variables, erroneous numbers could appear here and there, and the data could include outliers. A red flag has to be raised when the following characteristics are met:

✔ Missing values on certain groups of cases or variables imply that some specific cause is generating the error.

✔ Erroneous values depend on how the application has produced or manipulated the data. For instance, you need to know whether the application has obtained data from a measurement instrument. External conditions and human error can affect the reliability of instruments.

✔ The case is apparently valid, but quite different from the usual values that characterize that variable. When you can't explain the reason for the difference, you could be observing an outlier.

Among the illustrated errors, the trickiest problem to solve is when your dataset has outliers, because you don't always have a unique definition of outliers, or a clear reason to have them in your data. As a result, much is left to your investigation and evaluation. The good news is that Python offers you quite a few tools for spotting outliers and other kinds of unexpected values, so at least you won't be looking for a needle in a haystack.

You don't have to type the source code for this chapter manually. In fact, it's a lot easier if you use the downloadable source (see the Introduction for download instructions). The source code for this chapter appears in the P4DS4D; 16; Outliers.ipynb source code file.

Considering Detection of Outliers

As a general definition, *outliers* are data that differ significantly (they're distant) from other data in a sample. The reason they're distant is that one or more values are too high or too low when compared to the majority of the values. They could also display an almost unique combination of values. For instance, if you are analyzing records of students enlisted in a university, students who are too young or too old may catch you attention. Students studying unusual mixes of different subjects would also require scrutiny.

Outliers skew your data distributions and affect all your basic central tendency statistics. Means are pushed upward or downward, influencing all other descriptive measures. An outlier will always inflate variance and modify correlations, so you may obtain incorrect assumptions about your data and the relationships between variables.

This simple example can display the effect (on a small scale) of a single outlier with respect to more than one thousand regular observations:

```
import numpy as np
from scipy.stats.stats import pearsonr
np.random.seed(101)
normal = np.random.normal(loc=0.0, scale= 1.0, size=1000)
print 'Mean: %0.3f Median: %0.3f Variance: %0.3f' % (np.mean(normal),
            np.median(normal),
            np.var(normal))

Mean: 0.026 Median: 0.032 Variance: 1.109
```

Using the NumPy random generator, we created the variable named normal, which contains 1000 observation derived from a standard normal distribution. Basic descriptive statistics (mean, median, variance) do not show anything unexpected.

Now we change a single value by inserting an outlying value:

```
outlying = normal.copy()
outlying[0] = 50.0
print 'Mean: %0.3f Median: %0.3f Variance: %0.3f' % (np.mean(outlying),
    np.median(outlying), np.var(outlying))
print 'Pearson''s correlation coefficient: %0.3f p-value: %0.3f' % pearsonr(
    normal,outlying)
Mean: 0.074 Median: 0.032 Variance: 3.597
Pearsons correlation coefficient: 0.619 p-value: 0.000
```

We call this new variable `outlying` and put an outlier into it (at index 0, we have a positive value of 50.0). Now, as for as basic statistics go, the mean has a value three times higher than before, and so does variance. Only the median, which relies on position (it tells you the value occupying the middle position when all the observations are arranged in order) is not affected by the change.

More significant, the correlation of the original variable and the outlying variable is quite far from being +1.0 (the correlation value of a variable in respect of itself), indicating that the measure of linear relationship between the two variables has been seriously damaged.

Finding more things that can go wrong

Outliers do not simply shift key measures in your explorative statistics — they also change the structure of the relationships between variables in your data. Outliers can affect machine-learning algorithms in two ways:

- ✔ Algorithms based on coefficients may take the wrong coefficient in order to minimize their inability to understand the outlying cases. Linear models are a clear example (they are sums of coefficients), but they are not the only ones. Outliers can also influence tree-based learners such as Adaboost or Gradient Boosting Machines.

- ✔ Because algorithms learn from data samples, outliers may induce the algorithm to overweight the likelihood of extremely low or high values given a certain variable configuration.

Both situations limit the capacity of a learning algorithm to generalize well to new data. In other words, they make your learning process overfit to the present dataset.

There are a few remedies for outliers — some of them require that you modify your present data and others that you choose a suitable error function for your machine-learning algorithm. (Some algorithms offer you the possibility to pick a different error function as a parameter when setting up the learning procedure.)

Most machine learning algorithms can accept different error functions. The error function is important because it helps the algorithm to learn by understanding errors and enforcing adjustments in the learning process. Some error functions are extremely sensitive to outliers, while others are quite resistant to them. When illustrating the different machine-learning classes that the Scikit-learn package offers, the chapter points out the available error functions or other learning parameters that can increase resistance to extreme cases.

Understanding anomalies and novel data

Because outliers occur as mistakes or in extremely rare cases, detecting an outlier is never an easy job; it is, however, an important one for obtaining effective results from your data science project. In certain fields, detecting anomalies is itself the purpose of data science: fraud detection in insurance and banking, fault detection in manufacturing, system monitoring in health and other critical applications, and event detection in security systems and for early warning.

An important distinction is when we are looking for existing outliers in data, or when we are checking to see whether any new data contains anomalies with respect to the existent one. Maybe we spent a lot of time cleaning our data or we have developed a machine-learning application based on available data, so it would be critical to figure out whether the new data we are providing is similar to the old data and whether our algorithms will keep up the good job in classification or prediction. In such cases, we instead talk of novelty detection, because what we are interested in is to know how much the new data resembles the old. Being exceptionally new is considered an anomaly: Novelty may conceal a significant event or may risk preventing our algorithm from working properly. When working with new data, the algorithm should be retrained.

Examining a Simple Univariate Method

When looking for outliers, a good start, no matter how many variables you have in your data, is to look at every single variable by itself, using both graphical and statistical inspection. This is the univariate approach, which allows you to spot an outlier given an incongruous value on a variable. The `pandas` package can make spotting outliers quite easy thanks to

✔ A straightforward `describe` method that informs you on mean, variance, quartiles, and extremes of your numeric values for each variable

✔ A system of automatic boxplot visualizations

Using both techniques in conjunction makes it easy to know when you have outliers and where to look for them. The diabetes dataset, from the Scikit-learn datasets module, is a good example to start with.

```
from sklearn.datasets import load_diabetes
diabetes = load_diabetes()
X,y = diabetes.data, diabetes.target
```

All the data is in the X variable, a NumPy `ndarray`. We transform it into a `pandas` DataFrame.

```
import pandas as pd
pd.options.display.float_format = '{:.2f}'.format
df = pd.DataFrame(X)
print df.describe()

            0      1      2      3      4      5      6      7      8      9
count  442.00 442.00 442.00 442.00 442.00 442.00 442.00 442.00 442.00 442.00
mean    -0.00   0.00  -0.00   0.00  -0.00   0.00  -0.00   0.00  -0.00  -0.00
std      0.05   0.05   0.05   0.05   0.05   0.05   0.05   0.05   0.05   0.05
min     -0.11  -0.04  -0.09  -0.11  -0.13  -0.12  -0.10  -0.08  -0.13  -0.14
25%     -0.04  -0.04  -0.03  -0.04  -0.03  -0.03  -0.04  -0.04  -0.03  -0.03
50%      0.01  -0.04  -0.01  -0.01  -0.00  -0.00  -0.01  -0.00  -0.00  -0.00
75%      0.04   0.05   0.03   0.04   0.03   0.03   0.03   0.03   0.03   0.03
max      0.11   0.05   0.17   0.13   0.15   0.20   0.18   0.19   0.13   0.14
[8 rows x 10 columns]
```

You can spot the problematic variables by looking at the extremities of the distribution. For example, you must consider whether the minimum and maximum values lie respectively far from the 25th and 75th percentile. As shown in the output, many variables have suspect large maximum values. A boxplot analysis will clarify the situation. The following command creates the boxplot of all variables shown in Figure 16-1.

```
box_plots = df.boxplot()
```

Boxplots generated from `pandas` DataFrame will have whiskers set to plus or minus 1.5 IQR (*interquartile range* or the distance between the lower and upper quartile) with respect to the upper and lower side of the box (the upper and lower quartiles). This boxplot style is called the Tukey boxplot (from the name of statistician John Tukey, who created and promoted it among statisticians together with other explanatory data techniques) and it allows a visualization of the presence of cases outside the whiskers. (All points outside these whiskers are deemed outliers.)

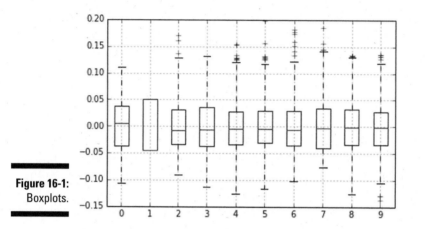

Figure 16-1:
Boxplots.

Leveraging on the Gaussian distribution

Another fast check for outliers in your data is accomplished by leveraging the normal distribution. Even if your data isn't normally distributed, standardizing it will allow you to assume certain probabilities of finding anomalous values. For instance, 99.7% in a standardized normal distribution should be inside the range of +3 and –3 standard deviations from the mean, as shown in the following code.

```
from sklearn.preprocessing import StandardScaler
Xs = StandardScaler().fit_transform(X)
o_idx = np.where(np.abs(Xs)>3)
# .any(1) method will avoid duplicating
print df[(np.abs(Xs)>3).any(1)]

          0     1     2     3     4     5     6     7     8     9
58     0.04 -0.04 -0.06  0.04  0.01 -0.06  0.18 -0.08 -0.00 -0.05
123    0.01  0.05  0.03 -0.00  0.15  0.20 -0.06  0.19  0.02  0.07
216    0.01  0.05  0.04  0.05  0.05  0.07 -0.07  0.15  0.05  0.05
...
[12 rows x 10 columns]
```

The Scikit-learn module provides an easy way to standardize your data and to record all the transformations for later use on different datasets. This means that all your data, no matter whether it's for machine-learning training or for performance test purposes, is standardized in the same way.

The 68-95-99.7 rule says that in a standardized normal distribution, 68 percent of values are within one standard deviation, 95 percent are within two standard deviations, and 99.7 percent are within three. When working with skewed data, the 68-95-99.7 rule may not hold true, and in such an occurrence, you may need some more conservative estimate, such as Chebyshev's inequality. *Chebyshev's inequality* relies on a formula that says that for k standard deviations around the mean, no more cases than a percentage of $1/k^2$ should be over the mean. Therefore, at seven standard deviations around the mean, your probability of finding a legitimate value is at most two percent, no matter what the distribution is (two percent is a low probability; your case could be an outlier).

Chebyshev's inequality is conservative. A high probability of being an outlier corresponds to seven or more standard deviations away from the mean. Use it when it may be costly to deem a value an outlier when it isn't. For all other applications, the 68-95-99.7 rule will suffice.

Making assumptions and checking out

Having found some possible univariate outliers, you now have to decide how to deal with them. If you completely distrust the outlying cases, under the assumption that they were unfortunate errors or mistakes, you could just delete them. (In Python, you can just deselect them using fancy indexing.)

Modifying the values in your data or deciding to exclude certain values is a decision to make after you understand why there are some outliers in your data. You can rule out unusual values or cases for which you presume that some error in measurement has occurred, in recording or previous handling of the data. If instead you realize that the outlying case is a legitimate, though rare, one, the best approach would be to underweight it (if your learning algorithms use weight for the observations) or to increase the size of your data sample.

In our case, deciding to keep the data and having standardized it, we could just cap the outlying values by using a simple multiplier of the standard deviation:

```
Xs_c = Xs.copy()
Xs_c[o_idx] = np.sign(Xs[o_idx]) * 3
```

In the proposed code, the sign function from NumPy recovers the sign of the outlying observation (+1 or –1), which is then multiplied by the value of 3 and then assigned to the respective data point recovered by a Boolean indexing of the standardized array.

This approach does have a limitation. Being the standard deviation used both for high and low values, it implies symmetry in your data distribution, an assumption often unverified in real data. As an alternative, you can use a bit more sophisticated approach called winsorizing. When using *winsorizing*, the values deemed outliers are clipped to the value of specific percentiles that act as value limits (usually the fifth percentile for the lower bound, the 95th for the upper):

```
from scipy.stats.mstats import winsorize
Xs_w = winsorize(Xs, limits=(0.05, 0.95))
```

In this way, you create a different hurdle value for larger and smaller values — taking into account any asymmetry in the data distribution. Whatever you decide for capping (by standard deviation or by winsorizing), your data is now ready for further processing and analysis, and you can cross-validate or test the decision of how to deal with outlying data as it is done for machine learning models (testing decisions and your hypothesis are part of the data science process).

Developing a Multivariate Approach

Working on single variables allows you to spot a large number of outlying observations. However, outliers do not necessarily display values too far from the norm. Sometimes outliers are made of unusual combinations of values in more variables. They are rare, but influential, combinations that can especially trick machine learning algorithms.

In such cases, the precise inspection of every single variable won't suffice to rule out anomalous cases from your dataset. Only a few selected techniques, taking in consideration more variables at a time, will manage to reveal problems in your data.

The presented techniques approach the problem from different points of view:

- Dimensionality reduction
- Density clustering
- Nonlinear distribution modeling

Using these techniques allows you to compare their results, taking notice of the recurring signals on particular cases — sometimes already located by the univariate exploration, sometimes as yet unknown.

Using principal component analysis

Principal component analysis can completely restructure the data, removing redundancies and ordering newly obtained components according to the amount of the original variance that they express. This type of analysis offers a synthetic and complete view over data distribution, making multivariate outliers particularly evident.

The first two components, being the most informative in term of variance, can depict the general distribution of the data if visualized. The output provides a good hint at possible evident outliers.

The last two components, being the most residual, depict all the information that could not be otherwise fitted by the PCA method. They can also provide a suggestion about possible but less evident outliers.

```
from sklearn.decomposition import PCA
from sklearn.preprocessing import scale
from pandas.tools.plotting import scatter_matrix
dim_reduction = PCA()
Xc = dim_reduction.fit_transform(scale(X))
print 'variance explained by the first 2 components: %0.1f%%' % (
    sum(dim_reduction.explained_variance_ratio_[:2]*100))
print 'variance explained by the last 2 components: %0.1f%%' % (
    sum(dim_reduction.explained_variance_ratio_[-2:]*100))
df = pd.DataFrame(Xc, columns=['comp_'+str(j+1) for j in range(10)])
first_two = df.plot(kind='scatter', x='comp_1', y='comp_2', c='DarkGray', s=50)
last_two  = df.plot(kind='scatter', x='comp_9', y='comp_10', c='DarkGray', s=50)
```

Figure 16-2 shows two scatterplots of the first and last components. Pay particular attention to the data points along the axis (where the x axis defines the independent variable and the y axis defines the dependent variable). You can see a possible threshold to use for separating regular data from suspect data.

Using the two last components, you can locate a few points to investigate using the threshold of –0.3 for the tenth component and of –1.0 for the ninth. All cases below these values are possible outliers.

```
outlying = (Xc[:,-1] < -0.3) | (Xc[:,-2] < -1.0)
print df[outlying]
```

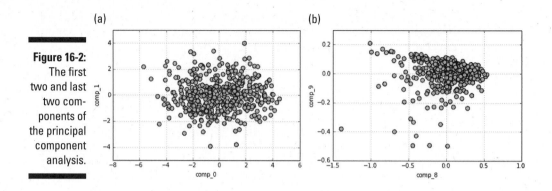

Using cluster analysis

Outliers are isolated points in the space of variables, and DBScan is a cluster-ing algorithm that links dense data parts together and marks the too-sparse parts. DBScan is therefore an ideal tool for an automated exploration of your data for possible outliers to verify.

```
from sklearn.cluster import DBSCAN
DB = DBSCAN(eps=2.5, min_samples=25, random_state=101)
DB.fit(Xc)
from collections import Counter
print Counter(DB.labels_),'\n'
print df[DB.labels_==-1]
Counter({0: 414, -1: 28})

        0     1     2     3     4     5     6     7     8     9
15  -0.05  0.05 -0.02  0.08  0.09  0.11 -0.04  0.11  0.04 -0.04
23   0.05  0.05  0.06  0.03  0.03 -0.05 -0.05  0.07  0.13  0.14
29   0.07  0.05 -0.01  0.06 -0.04 -0.10  0.05 -0.08  0.06  0.05
... (results partially omitted)
[28 rows x 10 columns]
```

However, `DBSCAN` requires two parameters, `eps` and `min_samples`. These two parameters require multiple tries to locate the right values, making using the parameters a little tricky.

As hinted in the previous chapter, start with a low value of `min_samples` and try growing the values of `eps` from 0.1 upward. After every trial with modified parameters, check the situation by counting the number of observa-tions in the class –1 inside the attribute `labels`, and stop when the number of outliers seems reasonable for a visual inspection.

There will always be points on the fringe of the dense parts' distribution, so it is hard to provide you with a threshold for the number of cases that might be classified in the –1 class. Normally, outliers should not be more than 5 percent of cases, so use this indication as a generic rule of thumb.

Automating outliers detection with SVM

Support Vector Machines (SVM) is a powerful machine learning technique that's extensively illustrated in Chapter 19 of the book. OneClassSVM is an algorithm that specializes in learning the expected distributions in a dataset. OneClassSVM is especially useful as a novelty detector method if you can first provide data cleaned from outliers; otherwise, it's effective as a detector of multivariate outliers. In order to have OneClassSVM work properly, you have two key parameters to fix:

- gamma, telling the algorithm whether to follow or approximate the dataset distributions. For novelty detection, it is better to have a value of 0 or superior (follow the distribution); for outlier detection values, smaller than 0 values are preferred (approximate the distribution).

- nu, which can be calculated by the following formula: nu_estimate = 0.95 * f + 0.05, where f is the percentage of expected outliers (a number from 1 to 0). If your purpose is novelty detection, f will be 0.

Executing the following script, you will get a OneClassSVM working as an outlier detection system:

```
from sklearn import svm
outliers_fraction = 0.01 #
nu_estimate = 0.95 * outliers_fraction + 0.05
auto_detection = svm.OneClassSVM(kernel="rbf", gamma=0.01, degree=3,
            nu=nu_estimate)
auto_detection.fit(Xc)
evaluation = auto_detection.predict(Xc)
print df[evaluation==-1]
          0     1     2     3     4     5     6     7     8     9
10   -0.10 -0.04 -0.08  0.01 -0.10 -0.09 -0.01 -0.08 -0.06 -0.03
23    0.05  0.05  0.06  0.03  0.03 -0.05 -0.05  0.07  0.13  0.14
32    0.03  0.05  0.13  0.03 -0.05 -0.01 -0.10  0.11  0.00  0.03
... (results partially omitted)
[25 rows x 10 columns]
```

OneClassSVM, like all the family of SVM, works better if you rescale your variables using the sklearn.preprocessing function scale or the class StandardScaler.

Part V
Learning from Data

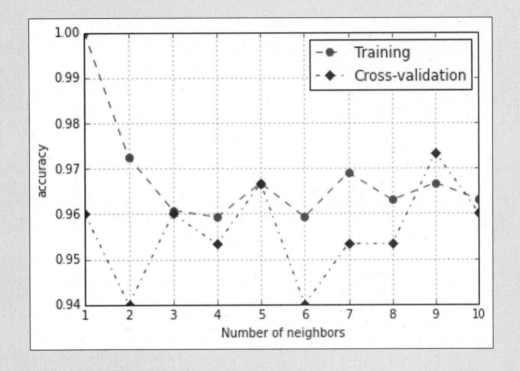

See an example of how you can perform a Twitter sentiment analysis at
`http://www.dummies.com/extras/pythonfordatascience`.

In this part . . .

✔ Using four major algorithms to analyze your data

✔ Validating, selecting, and optimizing the data analysis process

✔ Employing linear and nonlinear tricks to increase complexity

✔ Creating applications using the power of many

Chapter 17

Exploring Four Simple and Effective Algorithms

In This Chapter

▶ Using linear and logistic regression

▶ Understanding Bayes theorem and using it for naive classification

▶ Predicting on the basis of cases being similar with kNN

*I*n this new part, you start to explore all the algorithms and tools necessary for learning from data (the training phase) and being capable of predicting a numeric estimate (for example, house pricing) or a class (for instance, the species of an Iris flower) given a new example that you didn't have before. In this chapter, you start with the simplest algorithms and work toward more complex ones.

Simple and complex aren't absolute values in machine learning — they're relative to the algorithm's construction. Some algorithms are simple summations while others require complex calculations (and Python deals with both the simple and complex algorithms for you). It's the data that makes the difference: For some problems, simple algorithms are better; other problems may instead require complex algorithms.

You don't have to type the source code for this chapter manually. In fact, it's a lot easier if you use the downloadable source (see the Introduction for download instructions). The source code for this chapter appears in the `P4DS4D; 17; Exploring Four Simple and Effective Algorithms. ipynb` source code file.

Guessing the Number: Linear Regression

Regression has a long history in statistics, from building simple but effective linear models of economic, psychological, social, or political data, to hypothesis testing for understanding group differences, to modeling more complex problems with ordinal values, binary and multiple classes, count data, and hierarchical relationships.

Regression is also a common tool in data science. Stripped of most of its statistical properties, data science practitioners see linear regression as a simple, understandable, yet effective algorithm for estimations, and, in its logistic regression version, for classification as well.

Defining the family of linear models

Linear regression is a statistical model that defines the relationship between a target variable and a set of predictive features. It does so using a formula of the following type:

```
y = a + bx.
```

You can translate this formula into something readable and useful for many problems. For instance, if you're trying to guess your sales based on historical results and available data about advertising expenditures, the same preceding formula becomes

```
sales = a + b * (advertising expenditure)
```

You may already have encountered this formula during high school because it's also the formula of a line in a bidimensional plane, which is made of an x axis (the abscissa) and a y axis (the ordinate).

You can demystify the formula by explaining its components: a is the value of the intercept (the value of y when x is zero) and b is a coefficient that expresses the slope of the line (the relationship between x and y). If b is positive, y increases and decreases as x increases and decreases — when b is negative, y behaves in the opposite manner. You can understand b as the unit change in y given a unit change in x. When the value of b is near zero, the effect of x on y is slight, but if the value of b is high, either positive or negative, the effect of changes in x on y are great.

Linear regression, therefore, can find the best $y = a + bx$ and represent the relationship between your target variable, y, with respect to your predictive feature, x. Both a (alpha) and b (beta coefficient) are estimated on the basis of the data and they are found using the linear regression algorithm so that the difference between all the real y target values and all the y values derived from the linear regression formula are the minimum possible.

You can express this relationship graphically as the sum of the square of all the vertical distances between all the data points and the regression line. Such a sum is always the minimum possible when you calculate the regression line correctly using an estimation called ordinary least squares, which is derived from statistics or the equivalent gradient descent, a machine-learning method. The differences between the real y values and the regression line (the predicted y values) are defined as residuals (because they are what are left after a regression: the errors).

Using more variables

When using a single variable for predicting y, you use simple linear regression, but when working with many variables, you use multiple linear regression. When you have many variables, their scale isn't important in creating precise linear regression predictions. But a good habit is to standardize X because the scale of the variables is quite important for some variants of regression (that you see later on) and it is insightful for your understanding of data to compare coefficients according to their impact on y.

The following example relies on the Boston dataset from Scikit-learn. It tries to guess Boston housing prices using a linear regression. The example also tries to determine which variables influence the result more, so the example standardizes the predictors.

```
from sklearn.datasets import load_boston
from sklearn.preprocessing import scale
boston = load_boston()
X, y = scale(boston.data), boston.target
```

The regression class in Scikit-learn is part of the linear_model module. Having previously scaled the X variable, you have no other preparations or special parameters to decide when using this algorithm.

```
from sklearn.linear_model import LinearRegression
regression = LinearRegression()
regression.fit(X,y)
```

Now that the algorithm is fitted, you can use the `score` method to report the *R2* measure, which is a measure that ranges from 0 to 1 and points out how using a particular regression model is better in predicting y than using a simple mean would be. You can also see R2 as being the quantity of target information explained by the model (the same as the squared correlation), so getting near 1 means being able to explain most of the y variable using the model.

```
print regression.score(X,y)

0.740607742865
```

In this case, R2 on the previously fitted data is 0.74, a good result for a simple model.

Calculating R2 on the same set of data used for the training is common in statistics. In data science and machine-learning, it's always better to test scores on data that has not been used for training. Algorithms of greater complexity can memorize the data better than they learn from it, but this statement can be also true sometimes for simpler models, such as linear regression.

To understand what drives the estimates in the multiple regression model, you have to look at the `coefficients_` attribute, which is an array containing the regression beta coefficients. Printing at the same time, the `boston.DESCR` attribute helps you understand which variable the coefficients reference. The `zip` function will generate an iterable of both attributes, and you can print it for reporting.

```
print [a+':'+str(round(b,1)) for a, b in zip(
    boston.feature_names, regression.coef_,)]

['CRIM:-0.9', 'ZN:1.1', 'INDUS:0.1', 'CHAS:0.7',
 'NOX:-2.1', 'RM:2.7', 'AGE:0.0', 'DIS:-3.1',
 'RAD:2.7', 'TAX:-2.1', 'PTRATIO:-2.1', 'B:0.9',
 'LSTAT:-3.7']
```

`DIS` is the weighted distances to five employment centers. It shows the major absolute unit change. For example, in real estate, a house that's too far from people's interests (such as work) lowers the value. As a contrast, `AGE` and `INDUS`, with both proportions describing building age and showing whether nonretail activities are available in the area, don't influence the result as much because the absolute value of their beta coefficients is lower than `DIS`.

Understanding limitations and problems

Although linear regression is a simple yet effective estimation tool, it has quite a few problems. The problems can reduce the benefit of using linear regressions in some cases, but it really depends on the data. You determine whether any problems exist by employing the method and testing its efficacy. Unless you work hard on data (see Chapter 19), you may encounter these limitations:

- ✔ Linear regression can model only quantitative data. When modeling categories as response, you need to modify the data into a logistic regression.

- ✔ If data is missing and you don't deal with it properly, the model stops working. It's important to impute the missing values or, using the value of zero for the variable, to create an additional binary variable pointing out that a value is missing.

- ✔ Also, outliers are quite disruptive for a linear regression because linear regression tries to minimize the square value of the residuals, and outliers have big residuals, forcing the algorithm to focus more on them than on the mass of regular points.

- ✔ The relation between the target and each predictor variable is based on a single coefficient — there isn't an automatic way to represent complex relations like a parabola (there is a unique value of x maximizing y) or exponential growth. The only way you can manage to model such relations is to use mathematical transformations of x (and sometimes y) or add new variables. Chapter 19 explores both the use of transformations and the addition of variables.

- ✔ The greatest limitation is that linear regression provides a summation of terms, which can vary independently of each other. It's hard to figure out how to represent the effect of certain variables that affect the result in very different ways according to their value. In short, you can't represent complex situations with your data, just simple ones.

Moving to Logistic Regression

Linear regression is well suited for estimating values, but it isn't the best tool for predicting the class of an observation. In spite of the statistical theory that advises against it, you can actually try to classify a binary class by scoring one class as 1 and the other as 0. The results are disappointing most of the time, so the statistical theory wasn't wrong!

The fact is that linear regression works on a continuum of numeric estimates. In order to classify correctly, you need a more suitable measure, such as the probability of class ownership. Thanks to the following formula, you can transform a linear regression numeric estimate into a probability that is more apt to describe how a class fits an observation:

probability of a class = exp(r) / (1+exp(r))

r is the regression result (the sum of the variables weighted by the coefficients) and exp is the exponential function. exp(r) corresponds to Euler's number e elevated to the power of r. A linear regression using such a formula (also called a link function) for transforming its results into probabilities is a logistic regression.

Applying logistic regression

Logistic regression is similar to linear regression, with the only difference being the y data, which should contain integer values indicating the class relative to the observation. Using the Iris dataset from the Scikit-learn datasets module, you can use the values 0, 1, and 2 to denote three classes that correspond to three species:

```
from sklearn.datasets import load_iris
iris = load_iris()
X, y = iris.data[:-1,:], iris.target[:-1]
```

To make the example easier to work with, leave a single value out so that later you can use this value to test the efficacy of the logistic regression model on it.

```
from sklearn.linear_model import LogisticRegression
logistic = LogisticRegression()
logistic.fit(X,y)
print 'Predicted class %s, real class %s' % (
    logistic.predict(iris.data[-1,:]),iris.target[-1])
print 'Probabilities for each class from 0 to 2: %s'
    % logistic.predict_proba(iris.data[-1,:])

Predicted class [2], real class 2
Probabilities for each class from 0 to 2:
   [[ 0.00168787  0.28720074  0.71111138]]
```

Contrary to linear regression, logistic regression doesn't just output the resulting class (in this case, the class 2), but it also estimates the probability of the observation's being part of all three classes. Based on the observation used for prediction, logistic regression estimates a probability of 71 percent of its being from class 2 — a high probability, but not a perfect score, therefore leaving a margin of uncertainty.

Using probabilities lets you guess the most probable class, but you can also order the predictions with respect to being part of that class. This is especially useful for medical purposes: Ranking a prediction in terms of likelihood with respect to others can reveal what patients are at most risk of getting or already having a disease.

Considering when classes are more

The previous problem, logistic regression, automatically handles a multiple class problem (it started with three iris species to guess). Most algorithms provided by Scikit-learn that predict probabilities or a score for class can automatically handle multiclass problems using two different strategies:

✔ **One versus rest:** The algorithm compares every class with all the remaining classes, building a model for every class. If you have ten classes to guess, you have ten models. This approach relies on the OneVsRestClassifier class from Scikit-learn.

✔ **One versus one:** The algorithm compares every class against every individual remaining class, building a number of models equivalent to n * (n-1) / 2, where n is the number of classes. If you have ten classes, you have 45 models. This approach relies on the OneVsOneClassifier class from Scikit-learn.

In the case of logistic regression, the default multiclass strategy is the one versus rest. The example in this section shows how to use both the strategies with the handwritten digit dataset, containing a class for numbers from 0 to 9. The following code loads the data and places it into variables.

```
from sklearn.datasets import load_digits
digits = load_digits()
X, y = digits.data[:1700,:], digits.target[:1700]
tX, ty = digits.data[1700:,:], digits.target[1700:]
```

The observations are actually a grid of pixel values. The grid's dimensions are 8 pixels by 8 pixels. To make the data easier to learn by machine-learning algorithms, the code aligns them into a list of 64 elements. The example reserves a part of the available examples for a test.

```
from sklearn.multiclass import OneVsRestClassifier
from sklearn.multiclass import OneVsOneClassifier
OVR = OneVsRestClassifier(LogisticRegression()).fit(X,y)
OVO = OneVsOneClassifier(LogisticRegression()).fit(X,y)
print 'One vs rest accuracy: %.3f' % OVR.score(tX,ty)
print 'One vs one accuracy: %.3f' % OVO.score(tX,ty)

One vs rest accuracy: 0.938
One vs one accuracy: 0.969
```

The two multiclass classes `OneVsRestClassifier` and `OneVsOne Classifier` operate by incorporating the estimator (in this case, `Logistic Regression`). After incorporation, they usually work just like any other learning algorithm in Scikit-learn. Interestingly, the one-versus-one strategy obtained the best accuracy thanks to its high number of models in competition.

When working with Anaconda and Python version 3.4, you may receive a deprecation warning when working with this example. You're safe to ignore the deprecation warning — the example should work as normal. All the deprecation warning tells you is that one of the features used in the example is due for an update or will become unavailable in a future version of Python.

Making Things as Simple as Naïve Bayes

You might wonder why anyone would name an algorithm Naïve Bayes. The naïve part comes from its formulation — it makes some extreme simplifications to standard probability calculations. The reference to Bayes in its name relates to the Reverend Bayes and his theorem on probability.

Reverend Thomas Bayes was a statistician and a philosopher who formulated his theorem during the first half of the eighteenth century. The theorem was never published while he was alive. It has deeply revolutionized the theory of probability by introducing the idea of conditional probability — that is, probability conditioned by evidence.

Of course, it helps to start from the beginning — probability itself. Probability tells you the likelihood of an event and is expressed in a numeric form. The probability of an event is measured in the range from 0 to 1 (from 0 percent to 100 percent) and it's empirically derived from counting the number of times the specific event happened with respect to all the events. You can calculate it from data!

When you observe events (for example, when a feature has a certain characteristic), and you want to estimate the probability associated with the event, you count the number of times the characteristic appears in the data and divide that figure by the total number of observations available. The result is a number ranging from 0 to 1, which expresses the probability.

When you estimate the probability of an event, you tend to believe that you can apply the probability in each situation. The term for this belief is *a priori* because it constitutes the first estimate of probability with regard to an event (the one that comes to mind first). For example, if you estimate the probability of a person being a female you might say, after some counting, that it's 50 percent, which is the prior, the first probability you will stick with.

The prior probability can change in the face of evidence, that is, something that can radically modify your expectations. For example, the evidence of whether a person is male or female could be that the person's hair is long or short. You can estimate having long hair as an event with 35 percent probability for the general population, but within the female population, it's 60 percent. If the percentage is so high in the female population, contrary to the general probability (the prior for having long hair), there should be some useful information that you can use!

Imagine that you have to guess whether a person is male or female and the evidence is that the person has long hair. This sounds like a predictive problem, and in the end, this situation is really similar to predicting a categorical variable from data: We have a target variable with different categories and you have to guess the probability of each category on the basis of evidence, the data. Reverend Bayes provided a useful formula:

$$P(A|B) = P(B|A)*P(A) / P(B)$$

The formula looks like statistical jargon and is a bit counterintuitive, so it needs to be explained in depth. Reading the formula using the previous example as input makes the meaning behind the formula quite a bit clearer:

- $P(A|B)$ is the probability of being a female (event A) given long hair (evidence B). This part of the formula defines what you want to predict. In short, it says to predict y given x where y is an outcome (male or female) and x is the evidence (long or short hair).
- $P(B|A)$ is the probability of having long hair when the person is a female. In this case, you already know that it's 60 percent. In every data problem, you can obtain this figure easily by simple cross-tabulation of the features against the target outcome.
- $P(A)$ is the probability of being a female, a 50 percent general chance (a prior).
- $P(B)$ is the probability of having long hair, which is 35 percent (another prior).

When reading parts of the formula such as P(A|B), you should read them as follows: probability of A given B. The | symbol translates as given. A probability expressed in this way is a conditional probability, because it's the probability of A conditioned by the evidence presented by B. In this example, plugging the numbers into the formula translates into: 60% * 50% / 35% = 85.7%

Therefore, even if being a female is a 50 percent probability, just knowing evidence like long hair takes it up to 85.7 percent, which is a more favorable chance for the guess. You can be more confident in guessing that the person with long hair is a female because you have a bit less than a 15 percent chance of being wrong.

Finding out that Naïve Bayes isn't so naïve

Naive Bayes, leveraging the simple Bayes' rule, takes advantage of all the evidence available in order to modify the prior base probability of your predictions. Because your data contains so much evidence — that is, it has many features — the data makes a big sum of all the probabilities derived from a simplified Naïve Bayes formula.

As discussed in the "Guessing the number: linear regression" section, earlier in this chapter, summing variables implies that the model takes them as separate and unique pieces of information. But this isn't true in reality, because applications exist in a world of interconnections, with every piece of information connecting to many other pieces. Using one piece of information more than once means giving more emphasis to that particular piece.

Because you don't know (or simply ignore) the relationships between each piece of evidence, you probably just plug all of them in to Naïve Bayes. The simple and naïve move of throwing everything that you know at the formula works well indeed, and many studies report good performance despite the fact that you make a naïve assumption. It's okay to use everything for prediction, even though it seems as though it shouldn't be okay given the strong association between variables. Here are some of the ways in which you commonly see Naïve Bayes used:

- ✔ Building spam detectors (catching all annoying emails in your inbox)
- ✔ Sentiment analysis (guessing whether a text contains positive or negative attitudes with respect to a topic, and detecting the mood of the speaker)
- ✔ Text-processing tasks such as spell correction, or guessing the language used to write or classify the text into a larger category

Naïve Bayes is also popular because it doesn't need as much data to work. It can naturally handle multiple classes. With some slight variable modifications (transforming them into classes), it can also handle numeric variables. Scikit-learn provides three Naïve Bayes classes in the `sklearn.naive_bayes` module:

✔ `MultinomialNB`: Uses the probabilities derived from a feature's presence. When a feature is present, it assigns a certain probability to the outcome, which the textual data indicates for the prediction.

✔ `BernoulliNB`: Provides the multinomial functionality of Naïve Bayes, but it penalizes the absence of a feature. It assigns a different probability when the feature is present than when it's absent. In fact, it treats all features as dichotomous variables (the distribution of a dichotomous variable is a Bernoulli distribution). You can also use it with textual data.

✔ `GaussianNB`: Defines a version of Naïve Bayes that expects a normal distribution of all the features. Hence, this class is suboptimal for textual data in which words are sparse (use the multinomial or Bernoulli distributions instead). If your variables have positive and negative values, this is the best choice.

Predicting text classifications

Naïve Bayes is particularly popular for document classification. In textual problems, you often have millions of features involved, one for each word spelled correctly or incorrectly. Sometimes the text is associated with other nearby words in *n-grams*, that is, sequences of consecutive words. Naïve Bayes can learn the textual features quickly and provide fast predictions based on the input.

This section tests text classifications using the binomial and multinomial Naïve Bayes models offered by Scikit-learn. The examples rely on the `20newsgroups` dataset, which contains a large number of posts from 20 kinds of newsgroups. The dataset is divided into a training set, for building your textual models, and a test set, which is comprised of posts that temporally follow the training set. You use the test set to test the accuracy of your predictions.

```
from sklearn.datasets import fetch_20newsgroups
newsgroups_train = fetch_20newsgroups(subset='train',
    remove=('headers', 'footers', 'quotes'))
newsgroups_test = fetch_20newsgroups(subset='test',
    remove=('headers', 'footers', 'quotes'))
```

After loading the two sets into memory, you import the two Naïve Bayes and instantiate them. At this point, you set alpha values, which are useful for avoiding a zero probability for rare features (a zero probability would exclude these features from the analysis). You typically use a small value for alpha, as shown in the following code:

```
from sklearn.naive_bayes import BernoulliNB, MultinomialNB
Bernoulli = BernoulliNB(alpha=0.01)
Multinomial = MultinomialNB(alpha=0.01)
```

In Chapter 12, you use the hashing trick to model textual data without fear of encountering new words when using the model after the training phase. You can use two different hashing tricks, one counting the words (for the multinomial approach) and one recording whether a word appeared in a binary variable (the binomial approach). You can also remove *stop words*, that is, common words found in the English language, such as "a," "the," "in," and so on.

```
import sklearn.feature_extraction.text as txt
multinomial_hashing_trick = txt.HashingVectorizer(
    stop_words='english', binary=False, norm=None,
    non_negative=True)
binary_hashing_trick = txt.HashingVectorizer(
    stop_words='english', binary=True, norm=None,
    non_negative=True)
```

At this point, you can train the two classifiers and test them on the test set, which is a set of posts that temporally appear after the training set. The test measure is accuracy, which is the percentage of right guesses that the algorithm makes.

```
Multinomial.fit(multinomial_hashing_trick.transform(
    newsgroups_train.data), newsgroups_train.target)
Bernoulli.fit(binary_hashing_trick.transform(
    newsgroups_train.data), newsgroups_train.target)
from sklearn.metrics import accuracy_score
for m, h in [(Bernoulli, binary_hashing_trick),
    (Multinomial, multinomial_hashing_trick)]:
    print 'Accuracy for %s: %.3f' % (m,
        accuracy_score(y_true=newsgroups_test.target,
            y_pred=m.predict(h.transform(
                newsgroups_test.data))))

Accuracy for BernoulliNB(alpha=0.01, binarize=0.0,
    class_prior=None, fit_prior=True): 0.570
Accuracy for MultinomialNB(alpha=0.01, class_prior=None,
    fit_prior=True): 0.651
```

You might notice that it won't take long for both models to train and report their predictions on the test set. Consider that the training set is made up of more than 11,000 posts containing 300,000 words, and the test set contains about 7,500 other posts.

```
print 'number of posts in training: %i' % len(
    newsgroups_train.data)
D={word:True for post in newsgroups_train.data for word
    in post.split(' ')}
print 'number of distinct words in training: %i' % len(D)
print 'number of posts in test: %i' % len(
    newsgroups_test.data)
number of posts in training: 11314
number of distinct words in training: 300972
number of posts in test: 7532
```

Learning Lazily with Nearest Neighbors

k-Nearest Neighbors (kNN) is not about building rules from data based on coefficients or probability. kNN works on the basis of similarities. When you have to predict something like a class, it may be the best to find the most similar observations to the one you want to classify or estimate. You can then derive the answer you need from the similar cases.

Observing how many observations are similar doesn't imply learning something, but rather measuring. Because kNN isn't learning anything, it's considered lazy, and you'll hear it referenced as a lazy learner or an instance-based learner. The idea is that similar premises usually provide similar results, and it's important not to forget to get such low-hanging fruit before trying to climb the tree!

The algorithm is fast during training because it only has to memorize data about the observations. It actually calculates more during predictions. When there are too many observations, the algorithm can become slow and memory consuming. You're best advised not to use it with big data or it may take almost forever to predict anything! Moreover, this simple and effective algorithm works better when you have distinct data groups without too many variables involved because the algorithm is also sensitive to the dimensionality curse.

The curse of dimensionality happens as the number of variables increases. Consider a situation in which you're measuring the distance between observations and, as the space becomes larger and larger, it becomes difficult to find real neighbors — a problem for kNN, which sometimes mistakes a far observation for a near one. Rendering the idea is just like playing chess on a multidimensional chessboard. When playing on the classic 2D board, most pieces are near and you can more easily spot opportunities and menaces for your pawns when you have 32 pieces and 64 positions. However, when you start playing on a 3D board, such as those found in some sci-fi films, your 32 pieces can become lost in 512 possible positions. Now just imagine playing with a 12D chessboard. You can easily misunderstand what is near and what is far, which is what happens with kNN.

You can still make kNN smart in detecting similarities between observations by removing redundant information and simplifying the data dimensionality using data the reduction techniques, as explained in Chapter 14.

Predicting after observing neighbors

For an example showing how to use kNN, you can start with the digit dataset again. kNN is particularly useful, just like Naïve Bayes, when you have to predict many classes, or in situations that would require you to build too many models or rely on a complex model.

```
from sklearn.datasets import load_digits
from sklearn.decomposition import PCA
digits = load_digits()
pca = PCA(n_components=25)
pca.fit(digits.data[:1700,:])
X, y = pca.transform(digits.data[:1700,:]),
    digits.target[:1700]
tX, ty = pca.transform(digits.data[1700:,:]),
    digits.target[1700:]
```

kNN is an algorithm that's quite sensitive to outliers. Moreover, you have to rescale your variables and remove some redundant information. In this example, you use PCA. Rescaling is not necessary because the data represents pixels, which means that it's already scaled.

You can avoid the problem with outliers by keeping the neighborhood small, that is, by not looking too far for similar examples.

Knowing the data type can save you a lot of time and many mistakes. For example, in this case, you know that the data represents pixel values. Doing EDA (as described in Chapter 13) is always the first step and can provide you with useful insights, but getting additional information about how the data was obtained and what the data represents is also a good practice and can be just as useful. To see this task in action, you reserve cases in tX and try a few cases that kNN won't look up when looking for neighbors.

```
from sklearn.neighbors import KNeighborsClassifier
kNN = KNeighborsClassifier(n_neighbors=5)
kNN.fit(X,y)
```

kNN uses a distance measure in order to determine which observations to consider as possible neighbors for the target case. You can easily change the predefined distance using the p parameter:

✔ When p is 2, use the Euclidean distance (discussed as part of the clustering topic in Chapter 15).

✔ When p is 1, use the Manhattan distance metric, which is the absolute distance between observations. In a 2D square, when you go from one corner to the opposite one, the Manhattan distance is the same as walking the perimeter, whereas Euclidean is like walking on the diagonal. Although the Manhattan distance isn't the shortest route, it's a more realistic measure than Euclidean distance, and it's less sensitive to noise and high dimensionality.

Usually, the Euclidean distance is the right measure, but sometimes it can give you worse results, especially when the analysis involves many correlated variables. The following code shows that the analysis seems fine with it.

```
print 'Accuracy: %.3f' % kNN.score(tX,ty)
print 'Prediction: %s actual: %s' %
    (kNN.predict(tX[:10,:]),ty[:10])

Accuracy: 0.990
Prediction: [5 6 5 0 9 8 9 8 4 1]
    actual: [5 6 5 0 9 8 9 8 4 1]
```

Choosing your k parameter wisely

A critical parameter that you have to define in kNN is k. As k increases, kNN considers more points for its predictions, and the decisions are less influenced by noisy instances that could exercise an undue influence. Your decisions are based on an average of more observations, and they become more solid. When the k value you use is too large, you start considering neighbors that are too far, sharing less and less with the case you have to predict.

It's an important trade-off. When the value of k is less, you consider a more homogeneous pool of neighbors but can more easily make an error by taking the few similar cases for granted. When the value of k is more, you consider more cases at a higher risk of observing neighbors that are too far or that are outliers. Getting back to the previous example with handwritten digit data, you can experiment with changing the k value, as shown in the following code:

```
for k in [1, 5, 10, 100, 200]:
    kNN = KNeighborsClassifier(n_neighbors=k).fit(X,y)
    print 'for k= %3i accuracy is %.3f' %
        (k, kNN.score(tX,ty))

for k=   1 accuracy is 0.979
for k=   5 accuracy is 0.990
for k=  10 accuracy is 0.969
for k= 100 accuracy is 0.959
for k= 200 accuracy is 0.907
```

Through experimentation, you find that setting n_neighbors (the parameter representing k) to 5 is the optimum choice, resulting in the highest accuracy. Using just the nearest neighbor (n_neighbors =1) isn't a bad choice, but setting the value above 5 instead brings decreasing results in the classification task.

As a rule of thumb, when your dataset doesn't have many observations, set k as a number near the squared number of available observations. However, there is no general rule, and trying different k values is always a good way to optimize your kNN performance. Always start from low values and work toward higher values.

Chapter 18

Performing Cross-Validation, Selection, and Optimization

. . . .

In This Chapter

▶ Learning about overfitting and underfitting

▶ Choosing the right metric to monitor

▶ Cross-validating our results

▶ Selecting the best features for machine-learning

▶ Optimizing hyperparameters

. . . .

Machine-learning algorithms can indeed learn from data. For instance, the four algorithms presented in the previous chapter, although quite simple, can effectively estimate a class or a value after being presented with examples associated with outcomes. It is all a matter of learning by induction, which is the process of extracting general rules from specific exemplifications. From childhood, humans commonly learn by seeing examples, deriving some general rules or ideas from them, and then successfully applying the derived rule to new situations as we grow up. For example, if we see someone being burned after touching fire, we understand that fire is dangerous, and we don't need to touch it ourselves to know that.

Learning by example using machine algorithms has pitfalls. Here are a few issues that might arise:

✔ There aren't enough examples to make a judgment about a rule, no matter what machine-learning algorithm you are using.

✔ The machine-learning application is presented with the wrong examples and consequently cannot reason correctly.

> ✔ Even when the application sees enough right examples, it still can't figure out rules because they're too complex. Sir Isaac Newton, the father of modern physics, narrated the story that he was inspired by the fall of an apple from a tree in his formulation of gravity. Unfortunately, deriving a universal law from a series of observations is not an automatic consequence for most of us and the same applies to algorithms.

It's important to consider these pitfalls when delving into machine learning! The quantity of data, its quality, and the characteristics of the learning algorithm decide whether a machine-learning application can generalize well to new cases. If anything is wrong with any of them, they can pose some serious limits. As a data science practitioner, you must recognize and learn to avoid these types of pitfalls in your data science experiments.

You don't have to type the source code for this chapter manually. In fact, it's a lot easier if you use the downloadable source (see the Introduction for download instructions). The source code for this chapter appears in the P4DS4D; 18; Performing Cross Validation, Selection and Optimization.ipynb source code file.

Pondering the Problem of Fitting a Model

Fitting a model implies learning from data a representation of the rules that generated the data in the first place. From a mathematical perspective, fitting a model is analogous to guessing an unknown function of the kind you faced in high school, such as, y=4x^2+2x, just by observing its y results. Therefore, under the hood, machine-learning algorithms generate mathematical formulations that should represent how reality works.

Demonstrating whether such formulations are real is beyond the scope of data science. What is most important is that they work by producing exact predictions. For example, even though you can describe much of the physical world using mathematical functions, you often can't describe social and economic dynamics this way — but people try guessing them anyway.

To summarize, as a data scientist, you should always strive to approximate the real functions underlying the problems you face using the best information available. The result of your work is evaluated based on your capacity to predict specific outcomes (the target outcome) given certain premises (the data) thanks to a useful range of algorithms (the machine-learning algorithms).

Earlier in the book, you see something akin to a real function or law when the book presents linear regression, which has its own formulation. The linear formula y=a + Bx, which mathematically represents a line on a plane, can often approximate training data well, even if the data is not representing a line or something similar to a line. As with linear regression, all other machine-learning algorithms have an internal formulation themselves (and many are indeed available). The linear regression's formulation is one of the simplest ones; formulations from other learning algorithms can appear quite complex. You don't need to know exactly how they work. You do need to have an idea of how complex they are, whether they are representing a line or a curve, and whether they can sense outliers or noisy data. When planning to learn from data, you should address these problematic aspects based on the formulation you intend to use:

1. Whether the learning algorithm is the best one that can approximate the unknown function that you imagine behind the data you are using. In order to make such a decision, you must consider the learning algorithm's formulation performance on the data at hand and compare it with other, alternative formulations from other algorithms.

2. Whether the specific formulation of the learning algorithm is too simple, with respect to the hidden function, to make an estimate (this is called a bias problem).

3. Whether the specific formulation of the learning algorithm is too complex, with respect to the hidden function to be guessed (leading to the variance problem).

Not all algorithms are suitable for every data problem. If you don't have enough data or the data is full of erroneous information, it may be too difficult for some formulations to figure out the real function.

Understanding bias and variance

If your chosen learning algorithm can't learn properly from data and is not performing well, the cause is bias or variance in its estimates.

- ✔ **Bias:** Given the simplicity of formulation, your algorithm tends to overestimate or understimate the real rules behind the data and is systematically wrong in certain situations. Simple algorithms have high bias; having few internal parameters, they tend to represent only simple formulations well.

- ✔ **Variance:** Given the complexity of formulation, your algorithm tends to learn too much information from the data and detect rules that don't exist, which causes its predictions to be erratic when faced with new data. You can think of variance as a problem connected to memorization. Complex algorithms can memorize data features thanks to the algorithms' high number of internal parameters.

Bias and variance depend on the complexity of the formulation at the core of the learning algorithm with respect to the complexity of the formulation that is presumed to have generated the data you are observing. However, when you consider a specific problem using the available data rules, you're better off having high bias or variance when

- ✔ **You have few observations:** Simpler algorithms perform better, no matter what the unknown function is. Complex algorithms tend to learn too much from data, estimating with inaccuracy.

- ✔ **You have many observations:** Complex algorithms always reduce variance. The reduction occurs because even complex algorithms can't learn all that much from data, so they learn just the rules, not any erratic noise.

- ✔ **You have many variables:** Provided that you also have many observations, simpler algorithms tend to find a way to approximate even complex hidden functions.

Defining a strategy for picking models

When faced with a machine-learning problem, you usually know little about the problem and don't know whether a particular algorithm will manage it well. Consequently, you don't really know whether the source of a problem is caused by bias or variance — although you can usually use the rule of thumb that if an algorithm is simple, it will have high bias, and if it is complex, it will have high variance. Even when working with common, well-documented data science applications, you'll notice that what works in other situations (as described in academic and industry papers) often doesn't operate very well for your own application because the data is different.

You can summarize this situation using the famous no-free-lunch theorem of the mathematician David Wolpert: Any two machine-learning algorithms are equivalent in performance when tested across all possible problems. Consequently, it isn't possible to say that one algorithm is always better than another; it can be better than another one only when used to solve specific problems. You can view the concept in another way: For every problem, there is never a fixed recipe! The best and only strategy is just to try everything you can and verify the results using a controlled scientific experiment. Using this approach ensures that what seems to work is what really works and, most important, what will keep on working with new data. Although you may have more confidence when using some learners over others, you can never tell what machine-learning algorithm is the best before trying it and measuring its performance on your problem.

At this point, you must consider a critical, yet underrated, necessary aspect to decide upon for the success of your data project. For a best model and greatest results, it's essential to define an evaluation metric that distinguishes a good model from a bad one with respect to the business or scientific problem that you want to solve. In fact, for some projects, you may need to avoid predicting negative cases when they are positive; for others, you may want to absolutely spot all the positive ones; and for still others, all you need to do is order them so that positive ones come before the negative ones and you don't need to check them all.

By picking an algorithm, you automatically also pick an optimization process ruled by an evaluation metric that reports its performance to the algorithm so that the algorithm can better adjust its parameters. For instance, when using a linear regression, the metric is the mean squared error given by the vertical distance of the observations from the regression line. Therefore, it is automatic, and you can more easily accept the algorithm performance provided by such a default evaluation metric.

Apart from accepting the default metric, some algorithms do let you choose a preferred evaluation function. In other cases, when you can't point out a favorite evaluation function, you can still influence the existing evaluation metric by appropriately fixing some of its hyperparameters, thus optimizing the algorithm indirectly for another, different, metric.

Before starting to train your data and create predictions, always consider what could be the best performance measure for your project. Scikit-learn offers access to a wide range of measures for both classification and regression problems. The `sklearn.metrics` module allows you to call the optimization procedures using a simple string or by calling an error function from its modules. Table 18-1 shows the measures commonly used for regression problems.

Table 18-1	Regression Evaluation Measures
callable string	*function*
mean_absolute_error	sklearn.metrics.mean_absolute_error
mean_squared_error	sklearn.metrics.mean_squared_error
r2	sklearn.metrics.r2_score

The `r2` string specifies a statistical measure for linear regression called R squared. It expresses how the model compares in predictive power with respect to a simple mean. Machine-learning applications seldom use this measure because it doesn't explicitly report errors made by the model, although high R squared values imply fewer errors; more viable metrics for regression models are the mean squared errors and the mean absolute errors.

Squared errors penalize extreme values more, whereas absolute error weights all the errors the same. So it is really a matter of considering the trade-off between reducing the error on extreme observations as much as possible (squared error) or trying to reduce the error for the majority of the observations (absolute error). The choice you make depends on the application. When extreme values represent critical situations for your application, a squared error measure is better. However, when your concern is to minimize the common and usual observations, as often happens in forecasting sales problems, you should use a mean absolute error as the reference. The choices are even for complex classification problems, as you can see in Table 18-2.

Table 18-2	Classification Evaluation Measures
callable string	*function*
accuracy	sklearn.metrics.accuracy_score
precision	sklearn.metrics.precision_score
recall	sklearn.metrics.recall_score
f1	sklearn.metrics.f1_score
roc_auc	sklearn.metrics.roc_auc_score

Accuracy is the simplest error measure in classification, counting (as a percentage) how many of the predictions are correct. It takes into account whether the machine-learning algorithm has guessed the right class. This measure works with both binary and multiclass problems. Even though it's a simple measure, optimizing accuracy may cause problems when an imbalance exists between classes. For example, it could be a problem when the class is frequent or preponderant, such as in fraud detection, where most transactions are actually legitimate with respect to a few criminal transactions. In such situations, machine-learning algorithms optimized for accuracy tend to guess in favor of the preponderant class and be wrong most of time with the minor classes, which is an undesirable behavior for an algorithm that you expect to guess all the classes correctly, not just a few selected ones.

Precision and recall, and their conjoint optimization by F1 score, can solve problems not addressed by accuracy. Precision is about being precise when guessing. It tracks the percentage of times, when forecasting a class, that a class was right. For example, you can use precision when diagnosing cancer in patients after evaluating data about their exams. Your precision in this case is the percentage of patients who really have cancer among those diagnosed with cancer. Therefore, if you have diagnosed ten ill patients and nine are truly ill, your precision is 90 percent.

You face different consequences when you don't diagnose cancer in a patient who has it or you do diagnose it in a healthy patient. Precision tells just a part of the story, because there are patients with cancer that you have diagnosed as healthy, and that's a terrible problem. The recall measure tells the second part of the story. It reports, among an entire class, your percentage of correct guesses. For example, when reviewing the previous example, the recall metric is the percentage of patients that you correctly guessed have cancer. If there are 20 patients with cancer and you have diagnosed just 9 of them, your recall will be 45 percent.

When using your model, you can be accurate but still have low recall, or have a high recall but lose accuracy in the process. Fortunately, precision and recall can be maximized together using the F1 score, which uses the formula: `F1 = 2 * (precision * recall) / (precision + recall)`. Using the F1 score ensures that you always get the best precision and recall combined.

Receiver Operating Characteristic Area Under Curve (ROC AUC) is useful when you want to order your classifications according to their probability of being correct. Therefore, when optimizing ROC AUC in the previous example, the learning algorithm will first try to order (sort) patients starting from those most likely to have cancer to those least likely to have cancer. The ROC AUC is higher when the ordering is good and low when it is bad. If your model has a high ROC AUC, you need to check the most likely ill patients. Another example is in a fraud detection problem, when you want to order customers according to the risk of being fraudulent. If your model has a good ROC AUC, you need to check just the riskiest customers closely.

Dividing between training and test sets

Having explored how to decide among the different error metrics for classification and regression, the next step in the strategy for choosing the best model is to experiment and evaluate the solutions by viewing their ability to generalize to new cases. As an example of correct procedures for experimenting with machine-learning algorithms, begin by loading the Boston dataset (a popular example dataset created in the 1970s), which consists of Boston housing prices, various house characteristic measurements, and measures of the residential area where each house is located.

```
from sklearn.datasets import load_boston
boston = load_boston()
X, y = boston.data, boston.target
print X.shape, y.shape

(506L, 13L) (506L,)
```

Notice that the dataset contains more than 500 observations and 13 features. The target is a price measure, so you decide to use linear regression and to optimize the result using the mean squared error. The objective is to ensure that a linear regression is a good model for the Boston dataset and to quantify how good it is using the mean squared error (which lets you compare it with alternative models).

```
from sklearn.linear_model import LinearRegression
from sklearn.metrics import mean_squared_error
regression = LinearRegression()
regression.fit(X,y)
print 'Mean squared error: %.2f' % mean_squared_error(
    y_true=y, y_pred=regression.predict(X))

Mean squared error: 21.90
```

After having fitted the model with the data (which is called the training data because it provides examples to learn from), the `mean_squared_error` error function reports the data prediction error. The mean squared error is 21.90, apparently a good measure but calculated directly on the training set, so you cannot be sure if it could work as well with new data (machine-learning algorithms are both good at learning and at memorizing from examples).

Ideally, you need to perform a test on data that the algorithm has never seen in order to exclude any memorization. Only in this way can you discover whether your algorithm works well when new data arrives. To perform this task, you wait for new data, make the predictions on it, and then confront predictions and reality. But, performing the task this way may take a long time and be very risky and expensive, depending on the type of problem you want to solve by machine learning (for example, some applications such as cancer detection can be very costly to experiment with because lives are at a stake).

Luckily, there's another way to obtain the same result. In order to simulate having new data, you can divide the observations into test and training cases. It's quite common in data science to have a test size of 25 to 30 percent of the available data and to train the predictive model on the remaining 70–75 percent.

```
from sklearn.cross_validation import train_test_split
X_train, X_test, y_train, y_test = train_test_split(X, y,
    test_size=0.30, random_state=5)
print X_train.shape, X_test.shape

(354L, 13L) (152L, 13L)
```

The example separates training and test X and y variables into distinct variables using the train_test_split function. test_size parameter indicates a test set made of 30 percent of available observations. The function always chooses the test sample randomly.

```
regression.fit(X_train,y_train)
print 'Train mean squared error: %.2f'
    % mean_squared_error(y_true=y_train,
        y_pred=regression.predict(X_train))

Train mean squared error: 19.07
```

At this point, you fit the model again and the code reports a new training error of 19.07, which is somehow different from before. However, the error you really have to refer to comes from the test set you reserved.

```
print 'Test mean squared error: %.2f'
    % mean_squared_error(y_true=y_test,
        y_pred=regression.predict(X_test))

Test mean squared error: 30.70
```

When you the estimate the error on the test set, the results show that the reported value is 30.70. What a difference, indeed! Somehow, the estimate on the training set was too optimistic. Using the test set, while more realistic in error estimation, really makes your result depend on a small portion of the data. If you change that small portion, the test result will also change.

```
X_train, X_test, y_train, y_test = train_test_split(X, y,
    test_size=0.30, random_state=6)
regression.fit(X_train,y_train)
print 'Train mean squared error: %.2f'
    % mean_squared_error(y_true=y_train,
        y_pred=regression.predict(X_train))
print 'Test mean squared error: %.2f'
    % mean_squared_error(y_true=y_test,
        y_pred=regression.predict(X_test))

Train mean squared error: 19.48
Test mean squared error: 28.33
```

What you have experienced in this section is a common problem with machine-learning algorithms. You know that each algorithm has a certain bias or variance in predicting an outcome; the problem is that you can't estimate its impact for sure. Moreover, if you have to make choices with regard to the algorithm, you can't be sure of which decision might be the most effective one.

Using training data is always unsuitable because the learning algorithm can actually predict the training data better. This is especially true when an algorithm has a low bias because of its complexity. In this case, you can expect a low error when predicting the training data, which means that you get an overly optimistic result that doesn't compare it fairly with other algorithms (which may have a different bias/variance profile), nor are the results useful for our evaluation. You can sample test data differently, on the other hand, and, by reserving a certain portion of data for test purposes, you can actually reduce the number of examples used to train the algorithm in an effective way.

Cross-Validating

If test sets can provide unstable results because of sampling, the solution is to systematically sample a certain number of test sets and then average the results. It is a statistical approach (to observe many results and take an average of them), and that's the basis of cross-validation. The recipe is straightforward:

1. Divide your data into folds (each *fold* is a container that holds an even distribution of the cases), usually 10, but fold sizes of 3, 5, and 20 are viable alternative options.

2. Hold out one fold as a test set and use the others as training sets.

3. Train and record the test set result. If you have little data, it's better to use a larger number of folds, because the quantity of data and the use of additional folds positively affects the quality of training.

4. Perform Steps 2 and 3 again, using each fold in turn as a test set.

5. Calculate the average and the standard deviation of all the folds' test results. The average is a reliable estimator of the quality of your predictor. The standard deviation will tell you the predictor reliability (if it is too high, the cross-validation error could be imprecise). Expect that predictors with high variance will have a high cross-validation standard deviation.

Even though this technique may appear complicated, Scikit-learn handles it using a single class:

```
>>> from sklearn.cross_validation import cross_val_score
```

Using cross-validation on k folds

In order to run cross-validation, you first have to initialize an iterator. KFold is the iterator that implements k folds cross-validation. There are other iterators available from the `sklearn.cross_validation` module, mostly derived from the statistical practice, but KFolds is the most widely used in data science practice.

KFolds requires you to specify how many observations are in your sample (the n parameter), specify the n_folds number, and indicate whether you want to shuffle the data (by using the `shuffle` parameter). As a rule, the higher the expected variance, the more that increasing the number of folds can provide you a better mean estimate. It's a good idea to shuffle the data because ordered data can introduce confusion into the learning processes if the first observations are different from the last ones.

After setting KFolds, call the `cross_val_score` function, which returns an array of results containing a score (from the scoring function) for each cross-validation fold. You have to provide `cross_val_score` with your data (both X and y) as an input, your estimator (the regression class), and the previously instantiated KFolds iterator (the cv parameter). In a matter of a few seconds or minutes, depending on the number of folds and data processed, the function returns the results. You average these results to obtain a mean estimate, and you can also compute the standard deviation to check how stable the mean is.

```
crossvalidation = KFold(n=X.shape[0], n_folds=10,
    shuffle=True, random_state=1)
scores = cross_val_score(regression, X, y,
    scoring='mean_squared_error', cv=crossvalidation,
    n_jobs=1)
print 'Folds: %i, mean squared error: %.2f std: %.2f'
    %(len(scores),np.mean(np.abs(scores)),np.std(scores))

Folds: 10, mean squared error: 23.76 std: 12.13
```

Cross-validating can work in parallel because no estimate depends on any other estimate. You can take advantage of the multiple cores present on your computer by setting the parameter n_jobs=-1.

Sampling stratifications for complex data

Cross-validation folds are decided by random sampling. Sometimes it may be necessary to track if and how much of a certain characteristic is present in the training and test folds in order to avoid malformed samples. For instance, the Boston dataset has a binary variable (a feature that has a value of 1 or 0) indicating whether the house bounds the Charles River. This information is important to understand the value of the house and determine whether people would like to spend more for it. You can see the effect of this variable using the following code.

```
import pandas as pd
df = pd.DataFrame(X, columns=boston.feature_names)
df['target'] = y
boxplot = df.boxplot('target', by='CHAS',
    return_type='axes')
```

A boxplot, represented in Figure 18-1, reveals that houses on the river tend to have values higher than other houses. Of course, there are expensive houses all around Boston, but you have to keep an eye about how many river houses you are analyzing because your model has to be general for all of Boston, not just Charles River houses.

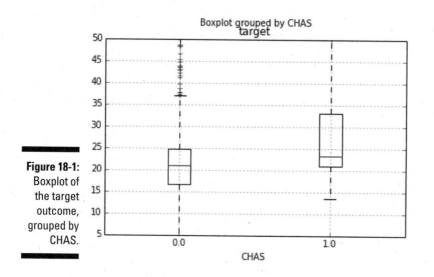

Figure 18-1: Boxplot of the target outcome, grouped by CHAS.

In similar situations, when a characteristic is rare or influential, you can't be sure when it's present in the sample because the folds are created in a random way. Having too many or too few of a particular characteristic in each fold implies that the machine-learning algorithm may derive incorrect rules.

The StratifiedKFold class provides a simple way to control the risk of building malformed samples during cross-validation procedures. It can control the sampling so that certain features, or even certain outcomes (when the target classes are extremely unbalanced), will always be present in your folds in the right proportion. You just need to point out the variable you want to control by using the y parameter, as shown in the following code.

```
from sklearn.cross_validation import StratifiedKFold
stratification = StratifiedKFold(y=X[:,3], n_folds=10,
    shuffle=True, random_state=1)
scores = cross_val_score(regression, X, y,
    scoring='mean_squared_error', cv=stratification,
    n_jobs=1)
print 'Stratified %i folds cross validation mean ' +
    'squared error: %.2f std: %.2f' % (len(
        scores),np.mean(np.abs(scores)),np.std(scores))

Stratified 10 folds cross validation mean squared error:
    23.70 std: 6.10
```

Although the validation error is similar, by controlling the CHAR variable, the standard error of the estimates decreases, making you aware that the variable was influencing the previous cross-validation results.

Selecting Variables Like a Pro

Selecting the right variables can improve the learning process by reducing the amount of noise (useless information) that can influence the learner's estimates. Variable selection, therefore, can effectively reduce the variance of predictions. In order to involve just the useful variables in training and leave out the redundant ones, you can use these techniques:

- **Univariate approach:** Select the variables most related to the target outcome.

- **Greedy or backward approach:** Keep only the variables that you can remove from the learning process without damaging its performance.

Selecting by univariate measures

If you decide to select a variable by its level of association with its target, the class SelectPercentile provides an automatic procedure for keeping only a certain percentage of the best, associated features. The available metrics for association are

- f_regression: Used only for numeric targets and based on linear regression performance.

- f_classif: Used only for categorical targets and based on the Analysis of Variance (ANOVA) statistical test.

✔ chi2: Performs the chi-square statistic for categorical targets, which is less sensible to the nonlinear relationship between the predictive variable and its target.

When evaluating candidates for a classification problem, f_classif and chi2 tend to provide the same set of top variables. It's still a good practice to test the selections from both the association metrics.

Apart from applying a direct selection of the top percentile associations, SelectPercentile can also rank the best variables to make it easier to decide at what percentile to exclude a feature from participating in the learning process. The class SelectKBest is analogous in its functionality, but it selects the top k variables, where k is a number, not a percentile.

```
from sklearn.feature_selection import SelectPercentile
from sklearn.feature_selection import f_regression
Selector_f = SelectPercentile(f_regression, percentile=25)
Selector_f.fit(X,y)
for n,s in zip(boston.feature_names,Selector_f.scores_):

    print 'F-score: %3.2f\t for feature %s ' % (s,n)

F-score: 88.15      for feature CRIM
F-score: 75.26      for feature ZN
F-score: 153.95     for feature INDUS
F-score: 15.97      for feature CHAS
F-score: 112.59     for feature NOX
F-score: 471.85     for feature RM
F-score: 83.48      for feature AGE
F-score: 33.58      for feature DIS
F-score: 85.91      for feature RAD
F-score: 141.76     for feature TAX
F-score: 175.11     for feature PTRATIO
F-score: 63.05      for feature B
F-score: 601.62     for feature LSTAT
```

Using the level of association output helps you to choose the most important variables for your machine-learning model, but you should watch out for these possible problems:

✔ Some variables with high association could also be highly correlated, introducing duplicated information, which acts as noise in the learning process.

✔ Some variables may be penalized, especially binary ones (variables indicating a status or characteristic using the value 1 when it is present, 0 when it is not). For example, notice that the output shows the binary variable CHAS as the least associated with the target variable (but you know from previous examples that it's influential from the cross-validation phase).

The univariate selection process can give you a real advantage when you have a huge number of variables to select from and all other methods turn computationally infeasible. The best procedure is to reduce the value of SelectPercentile by half or more of the available variables, reduce the number of variables to a manageable number, and consequently allow the use of a more sophisticated and more precise method such as a greedy search.

Using a greedy search

When using a univariate selection, you have to decide for yourself how many variables to keep: Greedy selection automatically reduces the number of features involved in a learning model on the basis of their effective contribution to the performance measured by the error measure. The RFECV class, fitting the data, can provide you with information on the number of useful features, point them out to you, and automatically transform the X data, by the method transform, into a reduced variable set, as shown in the following example:

```
from sklearn.feature_selection import RFECV
selector = RFECV(estimator=regression, cv=10,
    scoring='mean_squared_error')
selector.fit(X, y)
print("Optimal number of features: %d"
    % selector.n_features_)

Optimal number of features: 6
```

It's possible to obtain an index to the optimum variable set by calling the attribute support_ from the RFECV class after you fit it.

```
print boston.feature_names[selector.support_]

['CHAS' 'NOX' 'RM' 'DIS' 'PTRATIO' 'LSTAT']
```

Notice that CHAS is now included among the most predictive features, which contrasts with the result from the univariate search in the previous section. The RFECV method can detect whether a variable is important, no matter whether it is binary, categorical, or numeric, because it directly evaluates the role played by the feature in the prediction.

The RFECV method is certainly more efficient, when compared to the univariate approach, because it considers highly correlated features and is tuned to optimize the evaluation measure (which usually is not Chi-square or F-score). Being a greedy process, it's computationally demanding and may only approximate the best set of predictors.

As RFECV learns the best set of variables from data, the selection may overfit, which is what happens with all other machine-learning algorithms. Trying RFECV on different samples of the training data can confirm the best variables to use.

Pumping Up Your Hyperparameters

As a last example for this chapter, you can see the procedures for searching for the optimal hyperparameters of a machine-learning algorithm in order to achieve the best possible predictive performance. Actually, much of the performance of your algorithm has already been decided by

1. **The choice of the algorithm:** Not every machine-learning algorithm is a good fit for every type of data, and choosing the right one for your data can make the difference.

2. **The selection of the right variables:** Predictive performance is increased dramatically by feature creation (new created variables are more predictive than old ones) and feature selection (removing redundancies and noise).

Fine-tuning the correct hyperparameters could provide even better predictive generalizability and pump up your results, especially in the case of complex algorithms that don't work well using the out-of-the-box default settings.

Hyperparameters are parameters that you have to decide by yourself, since an algorithm can't learn them automatically from data. As with all other aspects of the learning process that involve a decision by the data scientist, you have to make your choices carefully after evaluating the cross-validated results.

The Scikit-learn `sklearn.grid_search` module specializes in hyperparameters optimization. It contains a few utilities for automating and simplifying the process of searching for the best values of hyperparameters. The following code provides an illustration of the correct procedures:

```
import numpy as np
from sklearn.datasets import load_iris
iris = load_iris()
X, y = iris.data, iris.target
print X.shape, y.shape

(150L, 4L) (150L,)
```

The example prepares to perform its task by loading the Iris dataset and the NumPy library. At this point, the example can optimize a machine-learning algorithm for predicting Iris species.

Implementing a grid search

The best way to verify the best hyperparameters for an algorithm is to test them all and then pick the best combination. This means, in the case of complex settings of multiple parameters, that you have to run hundreds, if not thousands, of slightly differently tuned models. *Grid searching* is a systematic search method that combines all the possible combinations of the hyperparameters into individual sets. It's a time-consuming technique. However, grid searching provides one of the best ways to optimize a machine-learning application that could have many working combinations, but just a single best one. Hyperparameters that have many acceptable solutions (called *local minima*) may trick you into thinking that you have found the best solution when you could actually improve their performance.

Grid searching is like throwing a net into the sea. It's better to use a large net at first, one that has loose meshes. The large net helps you understand where there are schools of fish in the sea. After you know where the fish are, you can use a smaller net with tight meshes to get the fish that are in the right places. In the same way, when performing grid searching, you start first with a grid search with a few sparse values to test (the loose meshes). After you understand which hyperparameter values to explore (the schools of fish), you can perform a more thorough search. In this way, you also minimize the risk of overfitting by cross-validating too many variables because as a general principle in machine-learning and scientific experimentation, the more things you try, the greater the chances that some fake good result will appear.

Grid searching is easy to perform as a parallel task because the results of a tested combination of hyperparameters are independent from the results of the others. Using a multicore computer at its full power requires that you change n_jobs to –1 when instantiating any of the grid search classes from Scikit-learn.

You have options other than grid searching. Scikit-learn implements a random search algorithm as an alternative to using a grid search. There are other optimization techniques based on Bayesian optimization or on nonlinear optimization techniques such as the Nelder–Mead method, which aren't implemented in the data science packages that you're using in Python now.

In the example for demonstrating how to implement a grid search effectively, you use one of the previously seen simple algorithms, the K-neighbors classifier:

```
from sklearn.neighbors import KNeighborsClassifier
classifier = KNeighborsClassifier(n_neighbors=5,
    weights='uniform', metric= 'minkowski', p=2)
```

The K-neighbors classifier has quite a few hyperparameters that you can set for optimal performance:

- ✔ The number of neighbor points to consider in the estimate
- ✔ How to weight each of them
- ✔ What metric to use for finding the neighbors

Using a range of possible values for all the parameters, you can easily realize that you're going to test a large number of models, exactly 40 in this case:

```
grid = {'n_neighbors': range(1,11), 'weights': ['uniform',
    'distance'], 'p': [1,2]}
print 'Number of tested models: %i' % np.prod(
    [len(grid[element]) for element in grid])
score_metric = 'accuracy'

Number of tested models: 40
```

To set the instructions for the search, you have to build a Python dictionary whose keys are the names of the parameters, and the dictionary's values are lists of the values you want to test. For instance, the example records a range of 1 to 10 for the hyperparameter n_neighbors using the range(1,11) iterator, which produces the sequence of numbers during the grid search.

```
from sklearn.cross_validation import cross_val_score
print 'Baseline with default parameters: %.3f' % np.mean(
    cross_val_score(classifier, X, y, cv=10,
        scoring=score_metric, n_jobs=1))

Baseline with default parameters: 0.967
```

Using the accuracy metric (the percentage of exact answers), the example first tests the baseline, which consists of the algorithm's default parameters (also explicated when instantiating the `classifier` variable with its class). It's difficult to improve an already high accuracy of 0.967 (or 96.7 percent), but the search will locate the answer using a tenfold cross-validation.

```
from sklearn.grid_search import GridSearchCV
search = GridSearchCV(estimator=classifier,
    param_grid=grid, scoring=score_metric, n_jobs=1,
    refit=True, cv=10)
search.fit(X,y)
```

After being instantiated with the learning algorithm, the search dictionary, the scoring metric, and the cross-validation folds, the `GridSearch` class operates with the `fit` method. Optionally, after the grid search ended, it refits the model with the best found parameter combination (`refit=True`), allowing it to immediately start predicting by using the `GridSearch` class itself.

```
print 'Best parameters: %s' % search.best_params_
print 'CV Accuracy of best parameters: %.3f'
    % search.best_score_

Best parameters: {'n_neighbors': 9, 'weights': 'uniform',
    'p': 1}
CV Accuracy of best parameters: 0.973
```

When the search is completed, you can inspect the results using the `best_params_` and `best_score:_` attributes. The best accuracy found was 0.973, an improvement over the initial baseline. You can also inspect the complete sequence of obtained cross-validation scores and their standard deviation:

```
>>> search.grid_scores_
```

By looking through the large number of tested combinations, you notice that more than a few obtained the score of 0.973 when the combinations had nine or ten neighbors. To better understand how the optimization works with respect to the number of neighbors used by your algorithm, you can launch a Scikit-learn class for visualization. The `validation_curve` method provides you with detailed information about how `train` and `validation` behave when used with different `n_neighbors` hyperparameter.

```
from sklearn.learning_curve import validation_curve
train_scores, test_scores = validation_curve(
    KNeighborsClassifier(weights='uniform',
        metric= 'minkowski', p=1), X, y, 'n_neighbors',
        param_range=range(1,11), cv=10, scoring='accuracy',
        n_jobs=1)
```

The `validation_curve` class provides you with two arrays containing the results arranged with the parameters values on the rows and the cross-validation folds on the columns.

```
mean_train  = np.mean(train_scores,axis=1)
mean_test   = np.mean(test_scores,axis=1)
import matplotlib.pyplot as plt
plt.plot(range(1,11),mean_train,'ro--', label='Training')
plt.plot(range(1,11),mean_test,'bD-.',
    label='Cross-validation')
plt.grid()
plt.xlabel('Number of neighbors')
plt.ylabel('accuracy')
plt.legend(loc='upper right', numpoints= 1)
plt.show()
```

Projecting the row means creating a graphic visualization, as shown in Figure 18-2, which helps you understand what is happening with the learning process.

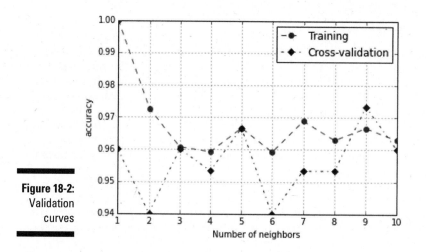

Figure 18-2:
Validation
curves

You can obtain two pieces of information from the visualization:

✔ The peak cross-validation accuracy using nine neighbors is higher than the training score. The training score should always be better than any cross-validation score. The higher score points out that the example overfitted the cross-validation and luck played a role in getting such a good cross-validation score.

✔ The second peak of cross-validation accuracy, at five neighbors, is near the lowest results. Well-scoring areas usually surround optimum values, so this peak is a bit suspect.

Based on the visualization, you should accept the nine- neighbors solution (it is the highest and it is indeed surrounded by other acceptable solutions). As an alternative, given that nine neighbors is a solution on the limit of the search, you could instead launch a new grid search, extending the limit to a higher number of neighbors (above ten) in order to verify whether the accuracy stabilizes, decreases, or even improves.

It is part of the data science process to query, test, and query again. Even though Python and its packages offer you many automated processes in data learning and discovering, it is up to you to ask the right questions and to check whether the answers are the best ones by using statistical tests and visualizations.

Trying a randomized search

Grid searching, though exhaustive, is indeed a time-consuming activity. It's prone to overfitting the cross-validation folds when you have few observations in your dataset and you extensively search for an optimization. Instead, an interesting alternative option is to try a randomized search. In this case, you define a grid search to test only some of the combinations, picked at random.

Even though it may sound like betting on blind luck, a grid search is actually quite useful because it's inefficient — if you pick enough random combinations, you have a high statistical probability of finding an optimum hyperparameter combination, without risking overfitting at all. For instance, in the previous example, the code tested 40 different models using a systematic search. Using a randomized search, you can reduce the number of tests by 75 percent, to just 10 tests, and reach the same level of optimization!

Using a randomized search is straightforward. You import the class from the `grid_search` module and input the same parameters as the `GridSearchCV`, adding a `n_iter` parameter that indicates how many combinations to sample. As a rule of thumb, you choose from a quarter or a third of the total number of hyperparameter combinations:

```
from sklearn.grid_search import RandomizedSearchCV
random_search = RandomizedSearchCV(estimator=classifier,
    param_distributions=grid, n_iter=10,
    scoring=score_metric, n_jobs=1, refit=True, cv=10, )
random_search.fit(X,y)
```

Having completed the search using the same technique as before, you can explore the results by outputting the best scores and parameters:

```
print 'Best parameters: %s' % random_search.best_params_
print 'CV Accuracy of best parameters: %.3f'
    % random_search.best_score_

Best parameters: {'n_neighbors': 9, 'weights': 'distance',
    'p': 2}
CV Accuracy of best parameters: 0.973
```

From the reported results, it appears that a random search can actually obtain results similar to a much more CPU-expensive grid search.

Chapter 19

Increasing Complexity with Linear and Nonlinear Tricks

. . . .

In This Chapter

▶ Expanding your feature using polynomials

▶ Regularizing regression

▶ Learning from big data

▶ Using support vector machines

. . . .

*P*revious chapters introduced you to some of the simplest, yet effective, machine-learning algorithms, such as linear and logistic regression, Naïve Bayes, and K-Nearest Neighbors (KNN). At this point, you can success-fully complete a regression or classification project in data science. This chapter explores even more complex and powerful machine-learning techniques including the following: reasoning on how to enhance your data; controlling the variance of estimates by regularization; and managing to learn from big data by breaking it into manageable chunks.

This chapter also introduces you to the support vector machine (SVM), a powerful family of algorithms for classification and regression. SVMs are able to perform the most difficult data problems and are a perfect substitute for neural networks such as the multilayer perceptron, which isn't currently present in the Scikit-learn package but is a planned addition in the future. Given the complexity of the subject, more than half of the chapter is devoted to SVM, but it's definitely worth the time.

Using Nonlinear Transformations

Linear models, such as linear and logistic regression, are actually linear combinations that sum your features (weighted by learned coefficients) and provide a simple but effective model. In most situations, they offer a good approximation of the complex reality they represent. Even though they're characterized by a high bias, using a large number of observations can improve their coefficients and make them more competitive with complex algorithms.

However, they can perform better when solving certain problems if you pre-analyze the data using the Exploratory Data Analysis (EDA) approach. After performing the analysis, you can transform and enrich the existing features by

✔ Linearizing the relationships between features and the target variable using transformations that increase their correlation and make their cloud of points in the scatterplot more similar to a line

✔ Making variables interact by multiplying them so that you can better represent their conjoint behavior

✔ Expanding the existing variables using the polynomial expansion in order to represent relationships more realistically (such as ideal point curves, when there is a peak in the variable representing a maximum, akin to a parabola).

You don't have to type the source code for the "Using Nonlinear Transformations," "Regularizing Linear Models," and "Fighting with Big Data Chunk by Chunk" sections of this chapter manually. In fact, it's a lot easier if you use the downloadable source (see the Introduction for download instructions). The source code for this chapter appears in the `P4DS4D; 19; Increasing Complexity.ipynb` source code file.

Doing variable transformations

An example is the best way to explain the kind of transformations you can successfully apply to data to improve a linear model. The example in this section, and the "Regularizing Linear Models" and "Fighting with Big Data Chunk by Chunk" sections that follow, relies on the Boston dataset. The problem relies on regression, and the data originally has ten variables to explain the different housing prices in Boston during the 1970s. The dataset also has implicit ordering. Fortunately, order doesn't influence most algorithms because they learn the data as a whole. When an algorithm learns in a progressive manner, ordering can really interfere with effective model building. By using `seed` (to fix a preordinated sequence of random numbers) and `shuffle` from the `random` package (to shuffle the index), you can reindex the dataset.

```
from sklearn.datasets import load_boston
from random import shuffle
boston = load_boston()
seed(0) # Creates a replicable shuffling
new_index = range(boston.data.shape[0])
shuffle(new_index) # shuffling the index
X, y = boston.data[new_index], boston.target[new_index]
print X.shape, y.shape

(506L, 13L) (506L,)
```

Converting the array of predictors and the target variable into a `pandas` `DataFrame` helps support the series of explorations and operations on data. Moreover, although Scikit-learn requires an `ndarray` as input, it will also accept `DataFrame` objects.

```
import pandas as pd
df = pd.DataFrame(X,columns=boston.feature_names)
df['target'] = y
```

The best way to spot possible transformations is by graphical exploration, and using a scatterplot can tell you a lot about two variables. You need to make the relationship between the predictors and the target outcome as linear as possible, so you should try various combinations, such as the following:

```
scatter = df.plot(kind='scatter', x='LSTAT', y='target', c='r')
```

In Figure 19-1, you see a representation of the resulting scatterplot. Notice that you can approximate the cloud of points by using a curved line rather than a straight line. In particular, when LSTAT is around 5, the target seems to vary between values of 20 to 50. As LSTAT increases, the target decreases to 10, reducing the variation.

Logarithmic transformation can help in such conditions. However, your values should range from zero to one, such as percentages, as demonstrated in this example. In other cases, other useful transformations for your x variable could include $x**2$, $x**3$, $1/x$, $1/x**2$, $1/x**3$, and $sqrt(x)$. The key is to try them and test the result. As for testing, you can use the following script as an example:

```
import numpy as np
from sklearn.feature_selection.univariate_selection import f_regression
F, pval = f_regression(df['LSTAT'],y)
print 'F score for the original feature %.1f' % F
F, pval = f_regression(np.log(df['LSTAT']),y)
print 'F score for the transformed feature %.1f' % F

F score for the original feature 601.6
F score for the transformed feature 1000.2
```

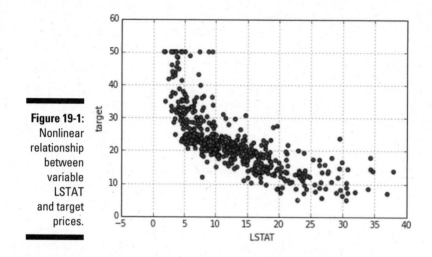

Figure 19-1:
Nonlinear
relationship
between
variable
LSTAT
and target
prices.

The `F score` is useful for variable selection. You can also use it to assess the usefulness of a transformation because both `f_regression` and `f_classif` are themselves based on linear models, and are therefore sensitive to every effective transformation used to make variable relationships more linear.

Creating interactions between variables

In a linear combination, the model reacts to how a variable changes in an independent way with respect to changes in the other variables. In statistics, this kind of model is a *main effects model*.

The Naïve Bayes classifier makes a similar assumption for probabilities, and it also works well with complex text problems.

Even though machine learning works by using approximations and a set of independent variables can make your predictions work well in most situations, sometimes you may miss an important part of the picture. You can easily catch this problem by depicting the variation in your target associated with the conjoint variation of two or more variables in two simple and straightforward ways:

✔ **Existing domain knowledge of the problem:** For instance, in the car market, having a noisy engine is a nuisance in a city car but considered a plus for sports cars (everyone wants to hear that you got an ultra-cool and expensive car). By knowing a consumer preference, you can model a noise level variable and a car type variable together to obtain exact predictions using a predictive analytic model that guesses the car's value based on its features.

✔ **Testing combinations of different variables:** By performing group tests, you can see the effect that certain variables have on your target variable. Therefore, even without knowing about noisy engines and sports cars, you could have caught a different average of preference level when analyzing your dataset split by type of cars and noise level.

The following example shows how to test and detect interactions in the Boston dataset. The first task is to load a few helper classes, as shown here:

```
from sklearn.linear_model import LinearRegression
from sklearn.cross_validation import cross_val_score
from sklearn.cross_validation import KFold
regression = LinearRegression(normalize=True)
crossvalidation = KFold(n=X.shape[0], n_folds=10, shuffle=True, random_state=1)
```

The code reinitializes the pandas DataFrame using only the predictor variables. A for loop matches the different predictors and creates a new variable containing each interaction. The mathematical formulation of an interaction is simply a multiplication.

```
df = pd.DataFrame(X,columns=boston.feature_names)
baseline = np.mean(cross_val_score(regression, df, y, scoring='r2',
                   cv=crossvalidation,
    n_jobs=1))
interactions = list()
for feature_A in boston.feature_names:
   for feature_B in boston.feature_names:
       if feature_A > feature_B:
            df['interaction'] = df[feature_A] * df[feature_B]
            score = np.mean(cross_val_score(regression, df, y, scoring='r2',
               cv=crossvalidation, n_jobs=1))
            if score > baseline:
                interactions.append((feature_A, feature_B, round(score,3)))
print 'Baseline R2: %.3f' % baseline
print 'Top 10 interactions: %s' % sorted(interactions, key=lambda(x):x[2],
   reverse=True)[:10]

Baseline R2: 0.699
Top 10 interactions: [('RM', 'LSTAT', 0.782), ('TAX', 'RM', 0.766), ('RM',
                'RAD', 0.759), ('RM', 'PTRATIO', 0.75), ('RM', 'INDUS', 0.748),
                ('RM', 'NOX', 0.733), ('RM', 'B', 0.731), ('RM', 'AGE', 0.727),
                ('RM', 'DIS', 0.722), ('ZN', 'RM', 0.716)]
```

The code tests the specific addition of each interaction to the model using a 10 folds cross-validation. (The "Cross-validating" section of Chapter 18 tells you more about working with folds.) It records the change in the R2 measure into a stack (a simple list) that an application can order and explore later.

The baseline R2 is 0.699, so a reported improvement of the stack of interactions to 0.782 looks quite impressive! It's important to know how this improvement is made possible. The two variables involved are RM (the average number of rooms) and LSTAT (the percentage of lower-status population).

```
colors = ['k' if v > np.mean(y) else 'w' for v in y]
scatter = df.plot(kind='scatter', x='RM', y='LSTAT', c=colors)
```

The scatterplot in Figure 19-2 clarifies the improvement. In a portion of houses at the center of the plot, it's necessary to know both LSTAT and RM in order to correctly separate the high-value houses from the low-value houses; therefore, an interaction is indispensable in this case.

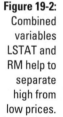

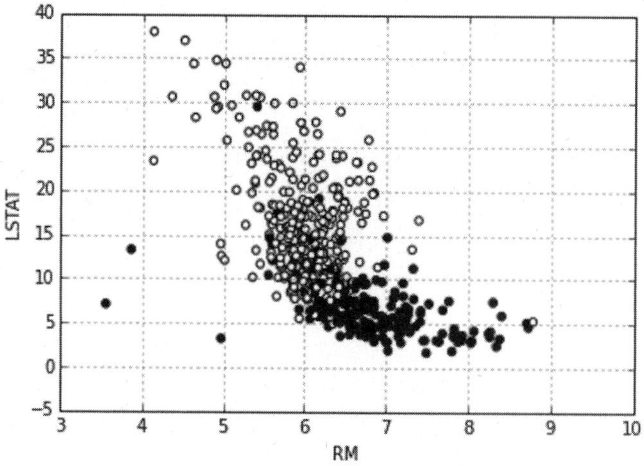

Figure 19-2: Combined variables LSTAT and RM help to separate high from low prices.

Adding interactions and transformed variables leads to an extended linear regression model, a polynomial regression. Data scientists rely on testing and experimenting to validate an approach to solving a problem, so the following code slightly modifies the previous code to redefine the set of predictors using interactions and quadratic terms by squaring the variables:

```
polyX = pd.DataFrame(X,columns=boston.feature_names)
baseline = np.mean(cross_val_score(regression, polyX, y,
              scoring='mean_squared_error',
    cv=crossvalidation, n_jobs=1))
improvements = [baseline]
for feature_A in boston.feature_names:
    polyX[feature_A+'^2'] = polyX[feature_A]**2
    improvements.append(np.mean(cross_val_score(regression, polyX, y,
      scoring='mean_squared_error', cv=crossvalidation, n_jobs=1)))
```

```
for feature_B in boston.feature_names:
    if feature_A > feature_B:
        polyX[feature_A+'*'+feature_B] = polyX[feature_A] * polyX[feature_B]
        improvements.append(np.mean(cross_val_score(regression, polyX, y,
            scoring='mean_squared_error', cv=crossvalidation, n_jobs=1)))
```

To track improvements as the code adds new, complex terms, the example places values in the `improvements` list. Figure 19-3 shows a graph of the results that demonstrates some additions are great because the squared error decreases, and other additions are terrible because they increase the error instead.

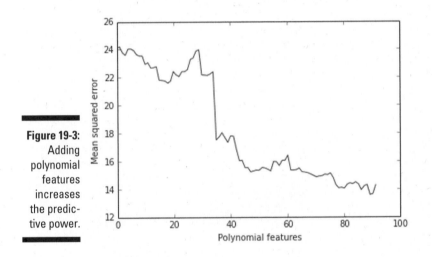

Figure 19-3: Adding polynomial features increases the predictive power.

Of course, you could perform an ongoing test to add a quadratic term or interaction optionally, which is called a univariate and greedy approach. This example is a good foundation for checking other ways of controlling the existing complexity of your datasets or the complexity that you have to induce with transformation and feature creation in the course of data exploration efforts. Before moving on, you check both the shape of the actual dataset and its cross-validated mean squared error.

```
print shape(polyX)
crossvalidation = KFold(n=X.shape[0], n_folds=10, shuffle=True, random_state=1)
print 'Mean squared error %.3f' % abs(np.mean(cross_val_score(regression,
            polyX, y,
    scoring='mean_squared_error', cv=crossvalidation, n_jobs=1)))

(506, 104)
Mean squared error 13.466
```

Even though the mean squared error is good, the ratio between 506 observations and 104 features isn't good at all.

As a rule of thumb, there should be 10–20 observations for every coefficient you want to estimate in linear models. However, experience shows that having at least 30 of them is better.

Regularizing Linear Models

Linear models have a high bias, but as you add more features, more interactions, and more transformations, they start gaining more adaptability to the data characteristics and more memorizing power for data noise, thus increasing the variance of their estimates. Trading high variance for having less bias is not always the best choice, but, as mentioned earlier, sometimes it's the only way to increase the predictive power of linear algorithms.

You can introduce L1 and L2 regularization as a way to control the trade-off between bias and variance in favor of an increased generalization capability of the model. When you introduce one of the regularizations, an additive function that depends on the complexity of the linear model penalizes the optimized cost function. In linear regression, the cost function is the squared error of the predictions, and the cost function is penalized using a summation of the coefficients of the predictor variables.

If the model is complex but the predictive gain is little, the penalization forces the optimization procedure to remove the useless variables, or to reduce their impact on the estimate. The regularization also acts on overcorrelated features — smoothing and combining their contribution, thus stabilizing the results and reducing the consequent variance of the estimates:

- ✔ **L1 (also called Lasso):** Shrinks some coefficients to zero, making your coefficients sparse. It really does variable selection.

- ✔ **L2 (also called Ridge):** Reduces the coefficients of the most problematic features, making them smaller, but never equal to zero. All coefficients keep participating in the estimate, but many become small and irrelevant.

You can control the strength of the regularization using a hyper-parameter, usually a coefficient itself, often called alpha. When alpha approaches 1.0, you have stronger regularization and a greater reduction of the coefficients. In some cases, the coefficients are reduced to zero. Don't confuse alpha with C, a parameter used by `LogisticRegression` and by support vector machines, because C is 1/alpha, so it can be greater than 1. Smaller C numbers actually correspond to more regularization, exactly the opposite of `alpha`.

Regularization works because it is the sum of the coefficients of the predictor variables, therefore it's important that they're on the same scale or the regularization may find it difficult to converge, and variables with larger absolute coefficient values will greatly influence it, generating an infective regularization. It's good practice to standardize the predictor values or bind them to a common min-max, such as the [-1,+1] range. The following sections demonstrate various methods of using both L1 and L2 regularization to achieve various effects.

Relying on Ridge regression (L2)

The first example uses the L2 type regularization, reducing the strength of the coefficients. The Ridge class implements L2 for linear regression. Its usage is simple; it presents just the parameter alpha to fix. Ridge also has another parameter, normalize, that automatically normalizes the inputted predictors to zero mean and unit variance.

```
from sklearn.grid_search import GridSearchCV
from sklearn.linear_model import Ridge
ridge = Ridge(normalize=True)
search = GridSearchCV(estimator=ridge, param_grid={'alpha':np.logspace(-5,2,8)},
                scoring='mean_squared_error', n_jobs=1, refit=True, cv=10)
search.fit(polyX,y)
print 'Best parameters: %s' % search.best_params_
print 'CV MSE of best parameters: %.3f' % abs(search.best_score_)


Best parameters: {'alpha': 0.001}
CV MSE of best parameters: 12.385
```

A good search space for the alpha value is in the range np.logspace (-5,2,8). Of course, if the resulting optimum value is on one of the extremities of the tested range, you need to enlarge the range and retest.

The polyX and y variables used for the examples in this section and the sections that follow are created as part of the example in the "Creating interactions between variables" section, earlier in this chapter. If you haven't worked through that section, the examples in this section will fail to work properly.

Using the Lasso (L1)

The second example uses the L1 regularization, the Lasso class, whose principal characteristic is to reduce the effect of less useful coefficients down toward zero. This action enforces sparsity in the coefficients, with just a few ones having values above zero. The class uses the same parameters of the Ridge class that are demonstrated in the previous section.

```
from sklearn.linear_model import Lasso
lasso = Lasso(normalize=True)
search = GridSearchCV(estimator=lasso, param_grid={'alpha':np.logspace(-5,2,8)},
                scoring='mean_squared_error', n_jobs=1, refit=True, cv=10)
search.fit(polyX,y)
print 'Best parameters: %s' % search.best_params_
print 'CV MSE of best parameters: %.3f' % abs(search.best_score_)

Best parameters: {'alpha': 0.0001}
CV MSE of best parameters: 12.644
```

Leveraging regularization

Because you can indent the sparse coefficients resulting from a L1 regression as a feature selection procedure, you can effectively use the Lasso class for selecting the most important variables. By tuning the alpha parameter, you can select a greater or lesser number of variables. In this case, the code sets the alpha parameter to 0.01, obtaining a much simplified solution as a result.

```
lasso = Lasso(normalize=True, alpha=0.01)
lasso.fit(polyX,y)
print polyX.columns[np.abs(lasso.coef_)>0.0001].values

['CRIM*CHAS' 'ZN*CRIM' 'ZN*CHAS' 'INDUS*DIS' 'CHAS*B' 'NOX^2' 'NOX*DIS'
 'RM^2' 'RM*CRIM' 'RM*NOX' 'RM*PTRATIO' 'RM*B' 'RM*LSTAT' 'RAD*B' 'TAX*DIS'
 'PTRATIO*NOX' 'LSTAT^2']
```

You can apply L1-based variable selection automatically to both regression and classification using the RandomizedLasso and RandomizedLogistic Regression classes. Both classes create a series of randomized L1 regularized models. The code keeps track of the resulting coefficients. At the end of the process, the application keeps any coefficients that the class didn't reduce to zero because they're considered important. You can train the two classes using the fit method, but they don't have a predict method, just a transform method that effectively reduces your dataset, just like most classes in the sklearn.preprocessing module.

Combining L1 & L2: Elasticnet

L2 regularization reduces the impact of correlated features, whereas L1 regularization tends to selects them. A good strategy is to mix them using a weighted sum by using the ElasticNet class. You control both L1 and L2 effects by using the same alpha parameter, but you can decide the L1 effect's share by using the `l1_ratio` parameter. Clearly, if `l1_ratio` is 0, you have a ridge regression; on the other hand, when `l1_ratio` is 1, you have a lasso.

```
from sklearn.linear_model import ElasticNet
elastic = ElasticNet(normalize=True)
search = GridSearchCV(estimator=elastic, param_grid={'alpha':np.logspace(-5,2,8),
    'l1_ratio': [0.25, 0.5, 0.75]},
    scoring='mean_squared_error', n_jobs=1, refit=True, cv=10)
search.fit(polyX,y)
print 'Best parameters: %s' % search.best_params_
print 'CV MSE of best parameters: %.3f' % abs(search.best_score_)

Best parameters: {'alpha': 1.0, 'l1_ratio': 0.5}
CV MSE of best parameters: 12.162
```

Fighting with Big Data Chunk by Chunk

Up to this point, the book has dealt with small example databases. Real data, apart from being messy, can also be quite big — sometimes so big that it can't fit in memory, no matter what the memory specifications of your machine are.

The `polyX` and `y` variables used for the examples in the sections that follow are created as part of the example in the "Creating interactions between variables" section, earlier in this chapter. If you haven't worked through that section, the examples in this section will fail to work properly.

Determining when there is too much data

In a data science project, data can be deemed big when one of these two situations occur:

- It can't fit in the available computer memory.

- Even if the system has enough memory to hold the data, the application can't elaborate the data using machine-learning algorithms in a reasonable amount of time.

Implementing Stochastic Gradient Descent

When you have too much data, you can use the Stochastic Gradient Descent Regressor (SGDRegressor) or Stochastic Gradient Descent Classifier (SGDClassifier) as a linear predictor. The only difference with other methods described earlier in the chapter is that they actually optimize their coefficients using only one observation at a time. It therefore takes more iterations before the code reaches comparable results using a ridge or lasso regression, but it requires much less memory and time.

This is because both predictors rely on Stochastic Gradient Descent (SGD) optimization — a kind of optimization in which the parameter adjustment occurs after the input of every observation, leading to a longer and a bit more erratic journey toward minimizing the error function. Of course, optimizing based on single observations, and not on huge data matrices, can have a tremendous beneficial impact on the algorithm's training time and the amount of memory resources.

When using the SGDs, apart from different cost functions that you have to test for their performance, you can also try using L1, L2, and Elasticnet regularization just by setting the `penalty` parameter and the corresponding controlling `alpha` and `l1_ratio` parameters. Some of the SGDs are more resistant to outliers, such as `modified_huber` for classification or `huber` for regression.

SGD is sensitive to the scale of variables, and that's not just because of regularization, it's because of the way it works internally. Consequently, you must always standardize your features (for instance, by using `StandardScaler`) or you force them in the range `[0,+1]` or `[-1,+1]`. Failing to do so will lead to poor results.

When using SGDs, you'll always have to deal with chunks of data unless you can stretch all the training data into memory. To make the training effective, you should standardize by having the `StandardScaler` infer the mean and standard deviation from the first available data. The mean and standard deviation of the entire dataset is most likely different, but the transformation by an initial estimate will suffice to develop a working learning procedure.

```
from sklearn.linear_model import SGDRegressor
from sklearn.preprocessing import StandardScaler
SGD = SGDRegressor(loss='squared_loss', penalty='l2', alpha=0.0001,
            l1_ratio=0.15,
            n_iter=2000)
scaling = StandardScaler()
scaling.fit(polyX)
scaled_X = scaling.transform(polyX)
print 'CV MSE: %.3f' % abs(np.mean(cross_val_score(SGD, scaled_X, y,
    scoring='mean_squared_error', cv=crossvalidation, n_jobs=1)))

CV MSE: 12.802
```

In the preceding example, you used the `fit` method, which requires that you preload all the training data into memory. You can train the model in successive steps by using the `partial_fit` method instead, which runs a single iteration on the provided data, then keeps it in memory and adjusts it when receiving new data.

```
from sklearn.metrics import mean_squared_error
from sklearn.cross_validation import train_test_split
X_train, X_test, y_train, y_test = train_test_split(scaled_X, y, test_size=0.20,
    random_state=2)
SGD = SGDRegressor(loss='squared_loss', penalty='l2', alpha=0.0001,
            l1_ratio=0.15)
improvements = list()
for z in range(1000):
    SGD.partial_fit(X_train, y_train)
    improvements.append(mean_squared_error(y_test, SGD.predict(X_test)))
```

Having kept track of the algorithm's partial improvements during `1000` iterations over the same data, you can produce a graph and understand how the improvements work as shown in the following code. It's important to note that you could have used different data at each step.

```
import matplotlib.pyplot as plt
plt.subplot(1,2,1)
plt.plot(range(1,11),np.abs(improvements[:10]),'o--')
plt.xlabel('Partial fit initial iterations')
plt.ylabel('Test set mean squared error')
plt.subplot(1,2,2)
plt.plot(range(100,1000,100),np.abs(improvements[100:1000:100]),'o--')
plt.xlabel('Partial fit ending iterations')
plt.show()
```

As visible in the first of the two panes in Figure 19-4, the algorithm initially starts with a high error rate, but it manages to reduce it in just a few iterations, usually 5. After that, the error rate slowly improves by a smaller amount each iteration. After 700 iterations, the error rate reaches a minimum and starts increasing. At that point, you're starting to overfit because data has already caught the rules and you're actually forcing the SGD to learn more when there is nothing left in data other than noise. Consequently, it starts learning noise and erratic rules.

Unless you're working with all the data in memory, grid-searching and cross-validating the best number of iterations will be difficult. A good trick is to keep a chunk of training data to use for validation apart in memory or storage. By checking your performance on that untouched part, you can see when SGD learning performance starts decreasing. At that point, you can interrupt data iteration (a method known as early stopping).

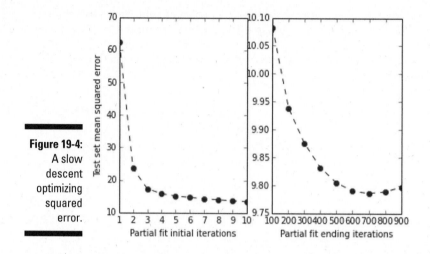

Figure 19-4:
A slow descent optimizing squared error.

Understanding Support Vector Machines

Data scientists deem Support Vector Machines (SVM) to be one of the most complex and powerful machine-learning techniques in their toolbox, so you usually find this topic solely in advanced manuals. However, you shouldn't turn away from this great learning algorithm because the Scikit-learn library offers you a wide and accessible range of SVM-supervised classes for regression and classification. You can even access an unsupervised SVM that appears in the chapters about outliers. When evaluating whether you want to try SVM algorithms as a machine-learning solution, consider these main benefits:

- ✔ Comprehensive family of techniques for binary and multiclass classification, regression, and novelty detection

- ✔ Good prediction generator that provides robust handling of overfitting, noisy data, and outliers

- ✔ Successful handling of situations that involve many variables

- ✔ Effective when you have more variables than examples

- ✔ Fast, even when you're working with up to about 10,000 training examples

- ✔ Detects nonlinearity in your data automatically, so you don't have to apply complex transformations of your variables

Wow, that sounds great. However, you should also consider a few relevant drawbacks before you jump into importing the SVM module:

- ✔ Performs better when applied to binary classification (which was the initial purpose of SVM), so SVM doesn't work as well on other prediction problems

- ✔ Less effective when you have a lot more variables than examples; you have to look for other solutions like SGD

- ✔ Provides you with only a predicted outcome; you can obtain a probability estimate for each response at the cost of more time-consuming computations

- ✔ Works satisfactorily out of the box, but if you want the best results, you have to spend time experimenting in order to tune the many parameters

You don't have to type the source code for this section manually. In fact, it's a lot easier if you use the downloadable source (see the Introduction for download instructions). The source code for this section appears in the `P4DS4D; 19; SVM.ipynb` source code file.

Relying on a computational method

Vladimir Vapnik and his colleagues invented SVM in the 1990s while working at AT&T laboratories. SVM gained success thanks to its high performance in many challenging problems for the machine-learning community of the time, especially when used to help a computer read handwritten input. Today, data scientists frequently apply SVM to an incredible array of problems, from medical diagnosis to image recognition and textual classification. You'll likely find SVM quite useful for your problems, too!

The idea behind the SVM is simple, but the mathematical implementation is quite complex and requires many computations to work. This section helps you understand the technology behind the technique — knowing how a tool works always helps you figure out where and how to employ it best. Start considering the problem of separating two groups of data points — stars and squares scattered on two dimensions. It's a classic binary classification problem in which a learning algorithm has to figure out how to separate one class of instances from the other one using the information provided by the data at hand. Figure 19-5 shows a representation of a similar problem.

If the two groups are separate from one another, you may solve the problem in many different ways just by choosing different separating lines. Of course, you must pay attention to the details and use fine measurements. Even though it may seem like an easy task, you need to consider what happens when the data changes, such as adding more points later. You may not be able to be sure that you chose the right separation line.

Figure 19-6 shows two possible solutions, but even more can exist. Both chosen solutions are too near to the existing observations (as shown by the proximity of the lines to the data points), but there is no reason to think that new observations will behave precisely like those shown in the figure.

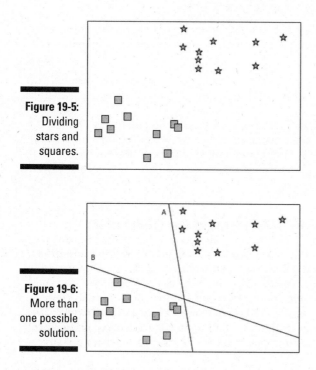

Figure 19-5: Dividing stars and squares.

Figure 19-6: More than one possible solution.

SVM minimizes the risk of choosing the wrong line (as you may have done by selecting solution A or B from Figure 19-6) by choosing the solution characterized by the largest distance from the bordering points of the two groups. Having so much space between groups (the maximum possible) should reduce the chance of picking the wrong solution!

The largest distance between the two groups is the *margin*. When the margin is large enough, you can be quite sure that it'll keep working well, even when you have to classify previously unseen data. The margin is determined by the points that are present on the limit of the margin — the *support vectors* (the support vector machines algorithm takes its name from them).

You can see an SVM solution in Figure 19-7. The figure shows the margin as a dashed line, the separator as the continuous line, and the support vectors as the circled data points.

Figure 19-7:
A viable
SVM
solution for
the problem
of the two
groups.

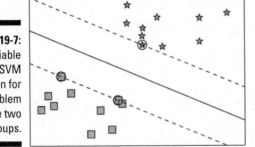

Real-world problems don't always provide neatly separable classes, as in this example. However, a well-tuned SVM can withstand some ambiguity (some misclassified points). An SVM algorithm with the right parameters can really do miracles.

REMEMBER When working with example data, it's easier to look for neat solutions so that the data points can better explain how the algorithm works and you can grasp the core concepts. With real data, though, you need approximations that work. Therefore, you rarely see large and clear margins.

Apart from binary classifications on two dimensions, SVM can also work on complex data. You can consider the data as complex when you have more than two dimensions, or in situations that are similar to the layout depicted in Figure 19-8, when separating the groups by a straight line isn't possible.

Figure 19-8:
A more
complex
group layout
is not a
problem for
SVM.

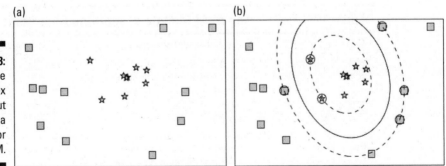

In the presence of many variables, SVM can use a complex separating plane (the *hyperplane*). SVM also works well when you can't separate classes by a straight line or plane because it can explore nonlinear solutions in multidimensional space thanks to a computational technique called the kernel trick.

Fixing many new parameters

Although SVM is complex, it's a great tool. After you find the most suitable SVM version for your problem, you have to apply it to your data and work a little to optimize some of the many parameters available and improve your results. Setting up a working SVM predictive model involves these general steps:

1. Choose the SVM class you'll use.
2. Train your model with the data.
3. Check your validation error and make it your baseline.
4. Try different values for the SVM parameters.
5. Check whether your validation error improves.
6. Train your model again using the data with the best parameters.

As far as choosing the right SVM class goes, you have to think about your problem. For example, you could choose a classification (guess a class) or regression (guess a number). When working with a classification, you must consider whether you need to classify just two groups (binary classification) or more than two (multiclass classification). Another important aspect to consider is the quantity of data you have to process. After taking notes of all your requirements on a list, a quick glance at Table 19-1 will help you to narrow your choices.

Table 19-1	The SVM Module of Learning Algorithms	
Class	**Characteristic usage**	**Key parameters**
sklearn.svm.SVC	Binary and multiclass classification when the number of examples is less than 10,000	C, kernel, degree, gamma
sklearn.svm.NuSVC	Similar to SVC	nu, kernel, degree, gamma
sklearn.svm. LinearSVC	Binary and multiclass classification when the number of examples is more than 10,000; sparse data	Penalty, loss, C

Class	Characteristic usage	Key parameters
`sklearn.svm.SVR`	Regression problems	C, kernel, degree, gamma, epsilon
`sklearn.svm.NuSVR`	Similar to SVR	Nu, C, kernel, degree, gamma
`sklearn.svm.OneClassSVM`	Outliers detection	nu, kernel, degree, gamma

The first step is to check the number of examples in your data. When you have more than 10,000 examples, in order to avoid too slow and cumbersome computations, you can use SVM and still get an acceptable performance only for classification problems by using `sklearn.svm.LinearSVC`. If instead you need to solve a regression problem or the `LinearSVC` isn't fast enough, you need to use a stochastic solution for SVM (as described in the sections that follow).

The Scikit-learn SVM module wraps two powerful libraries written in C, libsvm and liblinear. When fitting a model, there is a flow of data between Python and the two external libraries. A cache smooths the data exchange operations. However, if the cache is too small and you have too many data points, the cache becomes a bottleneck! If you have enough memory, it's a good idea to set a cache size greater than the default 200MB (1000MB, if possible) using the SVM class' `cache_size` parameter. Smaller numbers of examples require only that you decide between classification and regression.

In each case, you'll have two alternative algorithms. For example, for classification, you may use `sklearn.svm.SVC` or `sklearn.svm.NuSVC`. The only difference with the Nu version is the parameters it takes and the use of a slightly different algorithm. In the end, it gets basically the same results, so you normally choose the non-Nu version.

After deciding on which algorithm to use, you find out that you have a bunch of parameters to choose, and the C parameter is always among them. The C parameter indicates how much the algorithm has to adapt to training points. When C is small, the SVM adapts less to the points and tends to take an average direction, just using a few of the points and variables available. Larger C values tend to force the learning process to follow more of the available training points and to get involved with many variables.

The right C is usually a middle value, and you can find it after a bit of experimentation. If your C is too large, you risk overfitting, a situation in which your SVM adapts too much to your data and cannot properly handle new problems. If your C is too small, your prediction will be rougher and imprecise.

You'll experience a situation called underfitting — your model is too simple for the problem you want to solve.

After deciding the C value to use, the important block of parameters to fix is kernel, degree, and gamma. All three interconnect and their value depends on the kernel specification (for instance, the linear kernel doesn't require degree or gamma, so you can use any value). The kernel specification determines whether your SVM model uses a line or a curve in order to guess the class or the point measure. Linear models are simpler and tend to guess well on new data, but sometimes underperform when variables in the data relate to each other in complex ways. Because you can't know in advance whether a linear model works for your problem, it's good practice to start with a linear kernel, fix its C value, and use that model and its performance as a baseline for testing nonlinear solutions afterward.

Classifying with SVC

It's time to build the first SVM model. Because SVM initially performed so well with handwritten classification, starting with a similar problem is a great idea. Using this approach can give you an idea of how powerful this machine-learning technique is. The example uses the digits dataset available from the module datasets in the Scikit-learn package. The digits dataset contains a series of 8-x-8-pixel images of handwritten numbers ranging from 0 to 9.

```
from sklearn import datasets
digits = datasets.load_digits()
X,y = digits.data, digits.target
```

After loading the datasets module, the `load.digits` function imports all the data, from which the example extracts the predictors (`digits.data`) as X and the predicted classes (`digits.target`) as y.

You can look at what's inside this dataset using the `matplotlib` functions `subplot` (for creating an array of drawings arranged in two rows of five columns) and `imshow` (for plotting grayscale pixel values onto an 8-x-8 grid). The code arranges the information inside `digits.images` as a series of matrices, each one containing the pixel data of a number.

```
import matplotlib.pyplot as plt
for k,img in enumerate(range(10)):
    plt.subplot(2, 5, k)
    plt.imshow(digits.images[img],
    cmap='binary',interpolation='none')
plt.show()
```

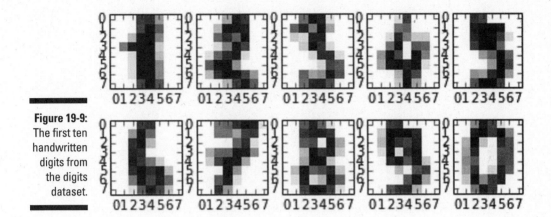

Figure 19-9:
The first ten
handwritten
digits from
the digits
dataset.

The code displays the first ten numbers as an example of the data used in the example. You can see the result in Figure 19-9.

By observing the data, you can also start figuring out that SVM could guess what the number is by associating a probability with the values of specific pixels in the grid. A number 2 could turn on different pixels than a number 1, or maybe different groups of pixels. Data science involves testing many programming approaches and algorithms before reaching a solid result, but it helps to be imaginative and intuitive in order to figure how what you can try first. In fact, if you explore X, you discover that it's made of exactly 64 variables, each one representing the grayscale value of a single pixel, and that you have plentiful examples, exactly 1,797 cases.

```
print X.shape

(1797L, 64L)

X[0]
array([ 0.,   0.,   5.,  13.,   9.,   1.,   0.,   0.,   0.,   0.,  13.,
       15.,  10.,  15.,   5.,   0.,   0.,   3.,  15.,   2.,   0.,  11.,
        8.,   0.,   0.,   4.,  12.,   0.,   0.,   8.,   8.,   0.,   0.,
        5.,   8.,   0.,   0.,   9.,   8.,   0.,   0.,   4.,  11.,   0.,
        1.,  12.,   7.,   0.,   0.,   2.,  14.,   5.,  10.,  12.,   0.,
        0.,   0.,   0.,   6.,  13.,  10.,   0.,   0.,   0.])
```

At this point, you might wonder what to do about labels. You can ask for help from the SciPy package, which provides the itemfreq function:

```
from scipy.stats import itemfreq
print y.shape, itemfreq(y)
```

```
[[   0.   178.]
 [   1.   182.]
 [   2.   177.]
 [   3.   183.]
 [   4.   181.]
 [   5.   182.]
 [   6.   181.]
 [   7.   179.]
 [   8.   174.]
 [   9.   180.]]
```

The output associates the class label (the first number) with its frequency and is worth observing. All the class labels present about the same number of examples. That means that your classes are balanced and that the SVM won't be led to think that one class is more probable than any of the others. If one or more of the classes had a significantly different number of cases, you'd face an unbalanced class problem. An unbalanced class scenario requires you to perform an evaluation:

✔ Keep the unbalanced class and get predictions biased toward the most frequent classes

✔ Establish equality among the classes using weights, which means allowing some observations to count more

✔ Use selection to cut some cases from the classes that have too many cases

An imbalanced class problem requires you to set some additional parameters. `sklearn.svm.SVC` has both a `class_weight` parameter and a `sample_weight` keyword in the `fit` method. The most straightforward and easiest way to solve the problem is to set `class_weight='auto'` when defining your SVC and let the algorithm fix everything by itself.

Now you're ready to test the SVC with the linear kernel. However, don't forget to split your data into training and test sets, or you won't be able to judge the effectiveness of the modeling work. Always use a separate data fraction for performance evaluation or the results will look good now but turn worse when adding fresh data.

```
from sklearn.cross_validation import train_test_split, cross_val_score
from sklearn.preprocessing import MinMaxScaler
# We keep 30% random examples for test
X_train, X_test, y_train, y_test = train_test_split(X, y, test_size=0.3,
         random_state=101)
```

The `train_test_split` function splits X and y into training and test sets, using the `test_size` parameter value of `0.3` as a reference for the split ratio.

```
# We scale the data in the range [-1,1]
scaling = MinMaxScaler(feature_range=(-1, 1)).fit(X_train)
X_train = scaling.transform(X_train)
X_test  = scaling.transform(X_test)
```

As a best practice, after splitting the data into training and test parts, you scale the numeric values, first by getting scaling parameters from the training data and then by applying a transformation on both training and test sets.

Another important action to take before feeding the data into an SVM is scaling. *Scaling* transforms all the values to the range between –1 to 1 (or from 0 to 1, if you prefer). Scaling transformation avoids the problem of having some variables influence the algorithm (they may trick it into thinking they are important because they have big values) and it makes the computations exact, smooth, and fast.

The following code fits the training data to an SVC class with a linear kernel. It also cross-validates and tests the results in terms of accuracy (the percentage of numbers correctly guessed).

```
from sklearn.svm import SVC
# We balance the clasess so you can see how it works
learning_algo = SVC(kernel='linear', class_weight='auto')
```

The code instructs the SVC to use the linear kernel and to reweight the classes automatically. Reweighting the classes ensures that they remain equally sized after the dataset is split into training and test sets.

```
cv_performance = cross_val_score(learning_algo, X_train, y_train, cv=10)
test_performance = learning_algo.fit(X_train, y_train).score(X_test, y_test)
```

The code then assigns two new variables. Cross-validation performance is recorded by the `cross_val_score` function, which returns a list with all ten scores after a ten-fold cross-validation (`cv=10`). The code obtains a test result by using two methods in sequence on the learning algorithm — `fit`, that fits the model, and `score`, which evaluates the result on the test set using mean accuracy (mean percentage of correct results among the classes to predict).

```
print 'Cross-validation accuracy score: %0.3f,
   test accuracy score: %0.3f' % (np.mean(cv_performance),test_performance)
Cross-validation accuracy score: 0.975, test accuracy score: 0.974
```

Finally, the code prints the two variables and evaluates the result. The result is quite good: 97.4 percent correct predictions on the test set!

You might wonder what would happen if you optimize the principal parameter C instead of using the default value of 1.0. The following script provides you with an answer, using gridsearch to look for an optimal value for the C parameter:

```
from sklearn.grid_search import GridSearchCV
learning_algo = SVC(kernel='linear', class_weight='auto', random_state=101)
search_space = {'C': np.logspace(-3, 3, 7)}
gridsearch = GridSearchCV(learning_algo, param_grid=search_space,
              scoring='accuracy',
    refit=True, cv=10)
gridsearch.fit(X_train,y_train)
```

Using GridSearchCV is a little more complex, but it allows you to check many models in sequence. First, you must define a search space variable using a Python dictionary that contains the exploration schedule of the procedure. To define a search space, you create a dictionary (or, if there is more than one dictionary, a dictionary list) for each tested group of parameters. Inside the dictionary, you place the name of the parameters as keys and associate them with a list (or a function generating a list, as in this case) containing the values to test.

The NumPy logspace function creates a list of seven C values, ranging from 10^{-3} to 10^3. This is a computationally expensive number of values to test, but it's also comprehensive, and you can always be safe when you test C and the other SVM parameters using such a range.

You then initialize GridSearchCV, defining the learning algorithm, search space, scoring function, and number of cross-validation folds. The next step is to instruct the procedure, after finding the best solution, to fit the best combination of parameters, so that you can have a ready-to-use predictive model:

```
cv_performance = gridsearch.best_score_
test_performance = gridsearch.score(X_test, y_test)
```

In fact, gridsearch now contains a lot of information about the best score (and best parameters, plus a complete analysis of all the evaluated combinations) and methods, such as score, which are typical of fitted predictive models in Scikit-learn.

```
print 'Cross-validation accuracy score: %0.3f,
   test accuracy score: %0.3f' % (cv_performance,test_performance)
print 'Best C parameter: %0.1f' % gridsearch.best_params_['C']

Cross-validation accuracy score: 0.984, test accuracy score: 0.993
Best C parameter: 100.0
```

The last step prints the results and shows that using a C=100 increases performance quite a bit, both on the cross-validation and the test set.

Going nonlinear is easy

Having defined a simple liner model as a benchmark for the handwritten digit project, you can now test a more complex hypothesis, and SVM offers a range of nonlinear kernels:

- ✔ Polynomial (poly)
- ✔ Radial Basis Function (rbf)
- ✔ Sigmoid (sigmoid)
- ✔ Advanced custom kernels

Even though so many choices exist, you rarely use something different from the radial basis function kernel (rbf for short) because it's faster than other kernels and can approximate almost any nonlinear function.

Here's a basic, practical explanation about how rbf works: It separates the data into many clusters, so it's easy to associate a response to each cluster.

The rbf kernel requires that you set the degree and gamma parameters besides setting C. They're both easy to set (and a good grid search will always find the right value).

The degree parameter has values that begin at 2. It determinates the complexity of the nonlinear function used to separate the points. As a practical suggestion, don't worry too much about degree — test values of 2, 3, and 4 on a grid search. If you notice that the best result has a degree of 4, try shifting the grid range upward and test 3, 4, and 5. Continue proceeding upward as needed, but using a value greater than 5 is rare.

The gamma parameter's role in the algorithm is similar to C (it provides a trade-off between overfit and underfit). It's exclusive of the rbf kernel. High gamma values induce the algorithm to create nonlinear functions that have irregular shapes because they tend to fit the data more closely. Lower values create more regular, spherical functions, ignoring most of the irregularities present in the data.

Now that you know the details of the nonlinear approach, it's time to try rbf on the previous example. Be warned that, given the high number of combinations tested, the computations may take some time to complete, depending on the characteristics of your computer.

```
from sklearn.grid_search import GridSearchCV
learning_algo = SVC(class_weight='auto', random_state=101)
search_space = [{'kernel': ['linear'], 'C': np.logspace(-3, 3, 7)},
                {'kernel': ['rbf'], 'degree':[2,3,4], 'C':np.logspace(-3, 3, 7),
                 'gamma': np.logspace(-3, 2, 6)}]
gridsearch = GridSearchCV(learning_algo, param_grid=search_space,
                scoring='accuracy',
    refit=True, cv=10)
gridsearch.fit(X_train,y_train)
cv_performance = gridsearch.best_score_
test_performance = gridsearch.score(X_test, y_test)
print 'Cross-validation accuracy score: %0.3f,
    test accuracy score: %0.3f' % (cv_performance,test_performance)
print 'Best parameters: %s' % gridsearch.best_params_

Cross-validation accuracy score: 0.988, test accuracy score: 0.987
Best parameters: {'kernel': 'rbf', 'C': 1.0, 'gamma': 0.10000000000000001,
                'degree': 2}
```

Notice that the only difference in this script is that the search space is more sophisticated. By using a list, you enclose two dictionaries — one containing the parameters to test for the linear kernel and another for the rbf kernel. In this way, you can compare the performance of the two approaches at the same time.

The results tell you that rbf performs better. However, it's a small margin of victory over the linear models. In such cases, having more data available could help in determining the better model with greater confidence. Unfortunately, getting more data may be expensive in terms of money and time. When faced with the absence of a clear winning model, the best suggestion is to decide in favor of the simpler model. In this case, the linear kernel is much simpler than rbf.

Performing regression with SVR

Up to now, you have dealt only with classification, but SVM can also handle regression problems. Having seen how a classification works, you don't need to know much more than that the SVM regression class is SVR and there is a new parameter to fix, epsilon. Everything else we discuss for classification works precisely the same with regression.

This example uses a different dataset, a regression dataset. The Boston house price dataset, taken from the StatLib library maintained at Carnegie

Mellon University, appears in many machine-learning and statistical papers that address regression problems. It has 506 cases and 13 numeric variables (one of them is a 1/0 binary variable).

```
from sklearn import datasets
boston = datasets.load_boston()
X,y = boston.data, boston.target
X_train, X_test, y_train, y_test = train_test_split(X, y, test_size=0.3,
    random_state=101)
scaling = MinMaxScaler(feature_range=(-1, 1)).fit(X_train)
X_train = scaling.transform(X_train)
X_test  = scaling.transform(X_test)
```

The target is the median value of houses occupied by an owner, and you'll try to guess it using SVR (epsilon-Support Vector Regression). In addition to C, kernel, degree, and gamma, SVR also has epsilon. *Epsilon* is a measure of how much error the algorithm considers acceptable. A high epsilon implies fewer support points, while a lower epsilon requires a larger number of support points. In other words, epsilon provides another way to trade off underfit against overfit.

As a search space for this parameter, experience tells you that the sequence [0, 0.01, 0.1, 0.5, 1, 2, 4] works quite fine. Starting from a minimum value of 0 (when the algorithm doesn't accept any error) and reaching a maximum of 4, you should enlarge the search space only if you notice that higher epsilon values bring better performance.

Having included epsilon in the search space and assigning SVR as a learning algorithm, you can complete the script. Be warned that, given the high number of combinations evaluated, the computations may take quite some time, depending on the characteristics of your computer.

```
from sklearn.svm import SVR
learning_algo = SVR(random_state=101)
search_space = [{'kernel': ['linear'], 'C': np.logspace(-3, 2, 6), 'epsilon':
            [0, 0.01,
    0.1, 0.5, 1, 2, 4]},{'kernel': ['rbf'], 'degree':[2,3], 'C':np.logspace(-3,
            3, 7),
    'gamma': np.logspace(-3, 2, 6), 'epsilon': [0, 0.01, 0.1, 0.5, 1, 2, 4]}]
gridsearch = GridSearchCV(learning_algo, param_grid=search_space, refit=True,
    scoring= 'r2', cv=10)
gridsearch.fit(X_train,y_train)
cv_performance = gridsearch.best_score_
test_performance = gridsearch.score(X_test, y_test)
print 'Cross-validation R2 score: %0.3f,
    test R2 score: %0.3f' % (cv_performance,test_performance)
print 'Best parameters: %s' % gridsearch.best_params_
```

```
Cross-validation R2 score: 0.833, test R2 score: 0.871
Best parameters: {'epsilon': 2, 'C': 1000.0, 'gamma': 0.10000000000000001,
                  'degree': 2, 'kernel': 'rbf'}
```

Note that on the error measure, as a regression, the error is calculated using R squared, a measure in the range from 0 to 1 that indicates the model's performance (with 1 being the best possible result to achieve).

Creating a stochastic solution with SVM

Now that you're at the end of the overview of the family of SVM machine-learning algorithms, you should see that they're a fantastic tool for a data scientist. Of course, even the best solutions have problems. For example, you might think that the SVM has too many parameters in the SVM. Certainly, the parameters are a nuisance, especially when you have to test so many combinations of them, which can take a lot of CPU time. However, the key problem is the time necessary for training the SVM. You may have noticed that the examples use small datasets with a limited number of variables, and performing some extensive grid searches still takes a lot of time. Real-world datasets are much bigger. Sometimes it may seem to take forever to train and optimize your SVM on your computer.

A possible solution when you have too many cases (a suggested limit is 10,000 examples) is found inside the same SVM module, the LinearSVC class. This algorithm works only with the linear kernel and its focus is to classify (sorry, no regression) large numbers of examples and variables at a higher speed than the standard SVC. Such characteristics make the LinearSVC a good candidate for textual-based classification. LinearSVC has fewer and slightly different parameters to fix than the usual SVM (it's similar to a regression class):

- ✔ C: The penalty parameter. Small values imply more regularization (simpler models with attenuated or set to zero coefficients).

- ✔ loss: A value of l1 (just as in SVM) or l2 (errors weight more, so it strives harder to fit misclassified examples).

- ✔ penalty: A value of l2 (attenuation of less important parameters) or l1 (unimportant parameters are set to zero).

- ✔ dual: A value of true or false. It refers to the type of optimization problem solved and, though it won't change the obtained scoring much, setting the parameter to false results in faster computations than when it is set to true.

The `loss`, `penalty`, and `dual` parameters are also bound by reciprocal constraints, so please refer to Table 19-2 to plan which combination to use in advance.

Table 19-2   The loss, penalty, and dual Constraints

penalty	loss	dual
l1	l2	False
l2	l1	True
l2	l2	True; False

The algorithm doesn't support the combination of `penalty='l1'` and `loss='l1'`. However, the combination of `penalty='l2'` and `loss='l1'` perfectly replicates the SVC optimization approach.

As mentioned previously, `LinearSVC` is quite fast, and a speed test against SVC demonstrates the level of improvement to expect in choosing this algorithm.

```
from sklearn.datasets import make_classification
X,y = make_classification(n_samples=10**4, n_features=15, n_informative=10,
    random_state=101)
X_train, X_test, y_train, y_test = train_test_split(X, y, test_size=0.3,
    random_state=101)
from sklearn.svm import SVC, LinearSVC
slow_SVM = SVC(kernel="linear", random_state=101)
fast_SVM = LinearSVC(random_state=101, penalty='l2', loss='l1')
slow_SVM.fit(X_train, y_train)
fast_SVM.fit(X_train, y_train)
print 'SVC test accuracy score: %0.3f' % slow_SVM.score(X_test, y_test)
print 'LinearSVC test accuracy score: %0.3f' % fast_SVM.score(X_test, y_test)

SVC test accuracy score: 0.808
LinearSVC test accuracy score: 0.808
```

After you create an artificial dataset using `make_classfication`, the code obtains confirmation of how the two algorithms arrive at identical results. At this point, the code tests the speed of the two solutions on the synthetic dataset in order to understand how they scale to using more data.

```
import timeit
X,y = make_classification(n_samples=10**4, n_features=15, n_informative=10,
    random_state=101)
print 'avg secs for SVC, best of 3: %0.1f'
             % np.mean(timeit.timeit("slow_SVM.fit(X, y)",
    "from __main__ import slow_SVM, X, y", number=1))
print 'avg secs for LinearSVC, best of 3: %0.1f' % np.mean(
    timeit.timeit("fast_SVM.fit(X, y)", "from __main__ import fast_SVM,
             X, y", number=1))
```

The example system shows the following result (the output of your system may differ):

```
avg secs for SVC, best of 3: 15.9
avg secs for LinearSVC, best of 3: 0.4
```

Clearly, given the same data quantity, LinearSVC is much faster than SVC. You can calculate its performance ratio as 15.9 / 0.4 = 39.75 times faster than SVC. But what if you grow the sample size from 10**4 to 10**5?

```
avg secs for SVC, best of 3: 3831.6
avg secs for LinearSVC, best of 3: 10.0
```

The results are quite impressive. LinearSVC is 383.16 times faster than SVC. Even if LinearSVC is quite fast at performing tasks, you may need to classify or regress with examples in the range of millions. You need to know whether LinearSVC is still a better choice.

You previously saw how the SGD class, using SGDClassifier and SGDRegressor, helps you implement an SVM-type algorithm in situations with millions of data rows without investing too much computational power. All you have to do is to set their loss to 'hinge' for SGDClassifier and to 'epsilon_insensitive' for SGDRegressor (in which case, you have to tune the epsilon parameter).

Another performance and speed test makes the advantages and limitations of using LinearSVC or SGDClassifier clear:

```
from sklearn.linear_model import SGDClassifier
X,y = make_classification(n_samples=10**6, n_features=15, n_informative=10,
    random_state=101)
X_train, X_test, y_train, y_test = train_test_split(X, y, test_size=0.3,
    random_state=101)
```

The sample is quite big — 1 million cases. If you have enough memory and a lot of time, you may even want to increase the number of trained cases or the number of features and more extensively test how the two algorithms scale with big data.

```
fast_SVM = LinearSVC(random_state=101)
fast_SVM.fit(X_train, y_train)
print 'LinearSVC test accuracy score: %0.3f' % fast_SVM.score(X_test, y_test)
print 'avg secs for LinearSVC, best of 3: %0.1f' % np.mean(
    timeit.timeit("fast_SVM.fit(X_train, y_train)",
        "from __main__ import fast_SVM, X_train, y_train", number=1))

LinearSVC test accuracy score: 0.806
avg secs for LinearSVC, best of 3: 311.2
```

On the test computer, `LinearSVC` completed its computations on 1 million rows in about five minutes. `SGDClassifier` instead took about a second for processing the same data and obtaining an inferior, but comparable, score.

```
stochastic_SVM = SGDClassifier(loss='hinge', n_iter=5, shuffle=True, random_
                state=101)
stochastic_SVM.fit(X_train, y_train)
print 'SGDClassifier test accuracy score: %0.3f' % stochastic_SVM.score(X_test,
                y_test)
print 'avg secs for SGDClassifier, best of 3: %0.1f' % np.mean(
    timeit.timeit("stochastic_SVM.fit(X_train, y_train)",
        "from __main__ import stochastic_SVM, X_train, y_train", number=1))
SGDClassifier test accuracy score: 0.799
avg secs for SGDClassifier, best of 3: 0.8
```

Increasing the `n_iter` parameter can improve the performance, but it proportionally increases the computation time. Increasing the number of iterations up to a certain value (that you have to find out by test) increases the performance. However, after that value, performance starts to decrease because of overfitting.

Chapter 20

Understanding the Power of the Many

In this chapter, you go beyond the single machine-learning models you've seen until now and explore the power of *ensembles*, groups of models that can outperform single models. Ensembles work like the collective intelligence of crowds, using pooled information to make better predictions. The basic idea is that a group of nonperforming algorithms can produce better results than a single well-trained model.

Maybe you've participated in one of those games that ask you to guess the number of sweets in a jar at parties or fairs. Even though a single person has a slim chance of guessing the right number, various experiments have confirmed that if you take the wrong answers of a large number of game participants and average them, you can get close to the right answer! Such incredible shared group knowledge (the wisdom of crowds) is possible because wrong answers tend to distribute around the true one. By taking a mean or median of these wrong answers, you get the direction of the right answer.

You can use this technique to win games by listening carefully to others' answers when participating in such games before providing your informed answer. Of course, you can employ the technique in ways that are more practical. In data science projects involving complex predictions, you can leverage the wisdom of various machine-learning algorithms and become more precise and accurate at predictions than you can when using a single algorithm. This chapter creates a process you can use to leverage the power of many different algorithms to obtain a better single answer.

You don't have to type the source code for this chapter manually. In fact, it's a lot easier if you use the downloadable source (see the Introduction for download instructions). The source code for this chapter appears in the P4DS4D; 20; Understanding the Power of the Many.ipynb source code file.

Starting with a Plain Decision Tree

Decision trees have long been part of data mining tools. The first models date back to the 1970s or even earlier. Decision trees have enjoyed popularity in many fields because of their intuitive algorithm, understandable output, and effectiveness with respect to simple linear models.

With the introduction of better-performing algorithms, decision trees slowly went out of the machine-learning scene for a time, but came back in recent years as an essential building block of ensemble algorithms. Today, tree ensembles such as Random Forest or Gradient Boosting Machines are the core of many data science applications.

Understanding a decision tree

The basis of decision trees is the idea that you can divide your dataset into smaller and smaller parts using specific rules based on the values of the dataset's features. When dividing the dataset in this way, the algorithm must choose splits that increase the chance of guessing the target outcome correctly, either as a class or as an estimate. Therefore, the algorithm must try to maximize the presence of a certain class or a certain average of values in each split.

As an example of an application and execution of a decision tree, you could try to predict the likelihood of passenger survival from the RMS Titanic, the British passenger liner that sank in the North Atlantic Ocean in April 1912 after colliding with an iceberg. Most datasets available about the Titanic tragedy have 1,309 recorded passengers with full stats. The survival rate among passengers was 38.2 percent (of 1,309 passengers, 809 lost their lives). However, based on the passengers' characteristics, you (and the decision tree) can notice that

- ✔ Being male changes the likelihood of survival, lowering it from 38.2 percent to 19.1 percent.

- ✔ Being male, but being younger than 9.5 years of age, raises the chance of survival to 58.1 percent.

- ✔ Being female, regardless of age, implies a survival probability of 72.7 percent.

Using such knowledge, you can easily to build a tree like the one depicted in Figure 20-1. Notice that the tree looks upside down (with the root at the top and all the branches spreading out from there). It starts at the top using the entire sample. Then it splits on the gender feature, creating two *branches*, one that turns into a *leaf*. A leaf is a terminal segmentation. The diagram classifies the leaf cases by using the most frequent class or by calculating the base probability of cases with the same features as the leaf probability. The second branch is further split by age.

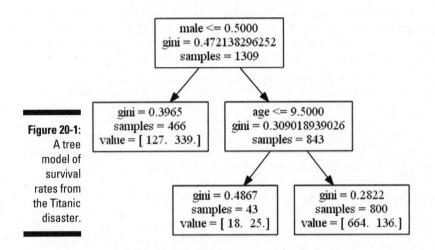

Figure 20-1:
A tree model of survival rates from the Titanic disaster.

To read nodes of the tree, consider that the topmost node begins by reporting the rule used to create the node. The next line is the gini, which is a measure that indicates the quality of the split. The last line reports the number of samples, which is all 1,309 passengers in the root node.

Understanding the rule comes next. The tree takes the left branch when the rule is true and the right one when it is false. So, male <=0.5 rule indicates that the person is a female, since male is encoded as 1 and female is encoded as 0 — the female leaf is on the left. When the decision tree reaches a terminal node, the node lacks a rule. Looking at the female node on the left, you see the results of the rule in brackets. The left number, 127, indicates the number of deaths, whereas the right number, 339, indicates the number of survivors.

After the age split, the tree has another split and then the algorithm stops. The tree has three splits, and the number of times a variable is split is called the *levels*. In this case, the number of males that are less than 9.5 years old is 43 and of those 43, 18 died and 25 lived.

In this case, the split is binary, but multiple splits are also possible, depending on the tree algorithm. In Scikit-learn, the implemented class `DecisionTreeClassifier` and `DecisionTreeRegressor` in the `sklearn.tree` module are all binary trees.

A decision tree can stop splitting the data when

- ✔ There are no more cases to split, so the data appears as part of leaf nodes.

- ✔ The rule used to split a leaf has fewer than a predefined number of cases. This action keeps the algorithm from working with leaves that have little representation in general or are more specific than the data you're analyzing, thus preventing overfitting and variance of estimates.

- ✔ One of the resulting leaves has fewer than a predefined number of cases — another sanity check for avoiding inferring general rules without the confidence provided by a good sample size.

Decision trees tend to overfit the data. By setting the right number for splits and terminal leaves, you can reduce the variance of the estimates. Depending on your starting sample size, a limit of 30 cases is usually a good choice.

Apart from being intuitive and easy to understand and represent (well, it does depend on how many branches and leaves you have in your tree), decision trees offer another strong advantage to the data science practitioner — they don't require any particular data treatment or transformation because they model any nonlinearity using approximations. In fact, they accept any kind of variable, even categorical variables encoded with arbitrary codes for the represented classes. In addition, decision trees handle missing cases. All you need to do is to assign missing cases an unlikely value, such as an extreme or a negative value (depending on your data distribution of nonmissing cases). Finally, decision trees are incredibly resistant to outliers!

Creating classification and regression trees

Data scientists call trees that specialize in guessing classes classification trees; trees that work with estimation instead are known as regression trees. Here's a classification problem, using the Fisher's Iris dataset (you first use this dataset in the "Defining Descriptive Statistics for Numeric Data" section of Chapter 13):

```
from sklearn.datasets import load_iris
iris = load_iris()
X, y = iris.data, iris.target
features = iris.feature_names
```

After loading the data into X, which contains predictors, and y, which holds the classifications, you can define a cross-validation for checking the results using decision trees:

```
from sklearn.cross_validation import cross_val_score
from sklearn.cross_validation import KFold
crossvalidation = KFold(n=X.shape[0], n_folds=5,
   shuffle=True, random_state=1)
```

Using the DecisionTreeClassifier class, you define max_depth inside an iterative loop to experiment with the effect of increasing the complexity of the resulting tree. The expectation is to reach an ideal point quickly and then witness decreasing cross-validation performance because of overfitting:

```
from sklearn import tree
for depth in range(1,10):
    tree_classifier = tree.DecisionTreeClassifier(
        max_depth=depth, random_state=0)
    if tree_classifier.fit(X,y).tree_.max_depth < depth:
     break
    score = np.mean(cross_val_score(tree_classifier, X, y,
        scoring='accuracy', cv=crossvalidation, n_jobs=1))
    print 'Depth: %i Accuracy: %.3f' % (depth,score)

Depth: 1 Accuracy: 0.580
Depth: 2 Accuracy: 0.913
Depth: 3 Accuracy: 0.920
Depth: 4 Accuracy: 0.940
Depth: 5 Accuracy: 0.920
```

The best solution is a tree with four splits. Figure 20-2 shows the complexity of the resulting tree.

To obtain an effective reduction and simplification, you can set min_samples_split to 30 and avoid terminal leaves that are too small. This setting prunes the small terminal leaves in the new resulting tree, diminishing cross-validation accuracy but increasing simplicity and the generalization power of the solution.

```
tree_classifier = tree.DecisionTreeClassifier(
    min_samples_split=30, min_samples_leaf=10,
        random_state=0)
tree_classifier.fit(X,y)
score = np.mean(cross_val_score(tree_classifier, X, y,
    scoring='accuracy', cv=crossvalidation, n_jobs=1))
print 'Accuracy: %.3f' % score

Accuracy: 0.913
```

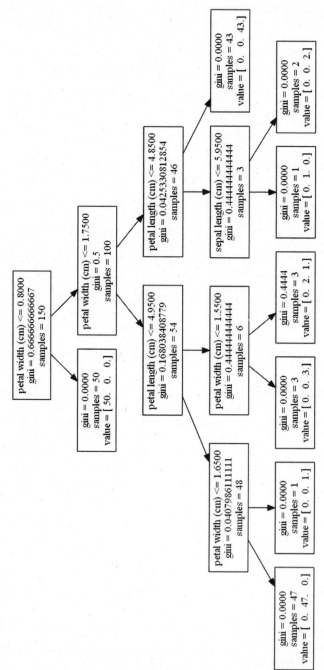

Figure 20-2:
A tree
model of the
Iris dataset
using a
depth of
four splits.

Similarly, using the `DecisionTreeRegressor` class, you can model a regression problem, such as the Boston house price dataset (you first use this dataset in the "Defining applications for data science" section of Chapter 12). When dealing with a regression tree, the terminal leaves offer the average of the cases as the prediction output.

```
from sklearn.datasets import load_boston
boston = load_boston()
X, y = boston.data, boston.target
features = boston.feature_names
```

```
from sklearn.tree import DecisionTreeRegressor
regression_tree = tree.DecisionTreeRegressor(
    min_samples_split=30, min_samples_leaf=10,
        random_state=0)
regression_tree.fit(X,y)
score = np.mean(cross_val_score(regression_tree, X, y,
    scoring='mean_squared_error', cv=crossvalidation,
        n_jobs=1))
print 'Mean squared error: %.3f' % abs(score)

Mean squared error: 22.593
```

Making Machine Learning Accessible

Random Forest is a classification and regression algorithm developed by Leo Breiman and Adele Cutler that uses a large number of decision tree models in order to provide precise predictions by reducing both the bias and variance of the estimates. When you aggregate many models together to produce a single prediction, the result is an *ensemble of models*. Random Forest isn't just an ensemble model, it's also a simple and effective algorithm to use, as intended by its creators, as an out-of-the-box algorithm. It makes machine learning accessible to nonexperts. The Random Forest algorithm uses these steps to perform its predictions:

1. Create a large number of decision trees, each one different from the other, based on different subsets of observations and variables.

2. Bootstrap the dataset of observations for each tree (sampled from the original data with replacement). The same observation can appear multiple times in the same dataset.

3. Randomly select and use only a part of the variables for each tree.

4. Estimate the performance for each tree using the observations excluded by sampling (the Out Of Bag, or OOB, estimate).

5. Obtain the final prediction, which is the average for regression estimates or the most frequent class for prediction, after all the trees have been fitted and used for prediction.

You can reduce bias by using these steps, because the decision trees have a good fit on data and, by their complex splits, can approximate even the most complex relationships between predictors and predicted outcome. Decision trees are known to produce a great variance of estimates, but you reduce this variance by averaging many trees. Noisy predictions, due to variance, tend to distribute evenly above and below the correct value that you want to predict — and when averaged together, they tend to cancel each other, leaving, as a result, a more correct average prediction.

Leo Breiman derived the idea for Random Forest from the bagging technique. Scikit-learn has a bagging class for both regression (`BaggingRegressor`) and classifying (`BaggingClassifier`) that you can be use with any other predictor you prefer to pick from Scikit-learn modules. The `max_samples` and `max_features` parameters let you decide the proportion of cases and variables to sample (not bootsrapped, but sampled, so a case can be used only once) for building each model of the ensemble. The `n_estimators` parameter decides the total number of models in the ensemble. Here's an example that loads the handwritten digit dataset (used for demonstrations later with other ensemble algorithms) and then fits the model by bagging:

```
from sklearn.datasets import load_digits
digit = load_digits()
X, y = digit.data, digit.target
print X.shape, y.shape

(1797L, 64L) (1797L,)
```

```
from sklearn.ensemble import BaggingClassifier
from sklearn import tree
tree_classifier = tree.DecisionTreeClassifier(
    random_state=0)
crossvalidation = KFold(n=X.shape[0], n_folds=5,
    shuffle=True, random_state=1)
bagging = BaggingClassifier(tree_classifier,
    max_samples=0.7, max_features=0.7, n_estimators=300)
scores = np.mean(cross_val_score(bagging, X, y,
    scoring='accuracy', cv=crossvalidation, n_jobs=1))
print 'Accuracy: %.3f' % score

Mean squared error: 0.966
```

In bagging, as in Random Forest, the more models in the ensemble, the better. You run no risk of overfitting because every model is different from the others, and errors tend to spread around the real value. Adding more models just adds stability to the result.

Another characteristic of the algorithm is that it permits estimation of variable importance while taking the presence of all the other predictors into account (a true multivariate approach).

In contrast to single decision trees, you can't easily visualize or understand Random Forest, making it act as a black box (a black box is a transformation that doesn't reveal its inner workings; all you see are its inputs and outputs). Given its opacity, importance estimation is the only way to understand how the algorithm works with respect to the features.

Importance estimation in a Random Forest is obtained in a straightforward way. After building each tree, the code fills each variable with junk data and the example records how much the predictive power decreases. If the variable is important, crowding it with casual data harms the prediction; otherwise, the predictions are left unchanged and the variable is deemed unimportant.

Working with a Random Forest classifier

The example Random Forest classifier keeps using the previously loaded digit dataset:

```
X, y = digit.data, digit.target
from sklearn.ensemble import RandomForestClassifier
from sklearn.cross_validation import cross_val_score
from sklearn.cross_validation import KFold
crossvalidation = KFold(n=X.shape[0], n_folds=3,
    shuffle=True, random_state=1)
RF_cls = RandomForestClassifier(n_estimators=300)
score = np.mean(cross_val_score(RF_cls, X, y,
    scoring='accuracy', cv=crossvalidation, n_jobs=1))
print 'Accuracy: %.3f' % score

Accuracy: 0.977
```

Just setting the number of estimators is sufficient for most problems you encounter, and setting it correctly is a matter of using the highest number possible given the time and resource constraints of the host computer. You can demonstrate this by calculating and drawing a validation curve for the algorithm.

```
from sklearn.learning_curve import validation_curve
train_scores, test_scores = validation_curve(RF_cls, X, y,
    'n_estimators', param_range=[
        10,50,100,200,300,500,800,1000,1500],
    cv=crossvalidation, scoring='accuracy', n_jobs=1)
print 'mean cv accuracy %s' % np.mean(train_scores,axis=1)

mean cv accuracy [ 0.93600445   0.9738453    0.9771842
                   0.97607123   0.9738453    0.97774068
                   0.97885364   0.97774068   0.97885364]
```

Figure 20-3 shows the results provided by the preceding code. The more estimators, the better the results, though at a certain point the gain becomes indeed minimal.

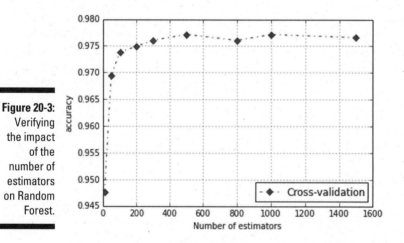

Figure 20-3:
Verifying the impact of the number of estimators on Random Forest.

Working with a Random Forest regressor

`RandomForestRegressor` works in a similar way as the Random Forest for classification, using exactly the same parameters:

```
X, y = boston.data, boston.target
from sklearn.ensemble import RandomForestRegressor
RF_rg = RandomForestRegressor (n_estimators=300,
    random_state=1)
crossvalidation = KFold(n=X.shape[0], n_folds=5,
    shuffle=True, random_state=1)
score = np.mean(cross_val_score(RF_rg, X, y,
    scoring='mean_squared_error', cv=crossvalidation,
        n_jobs=1))
print 'Mean squared error: %.3f' % abs(score)

Mean squared error: 19.436
```

The Random Forest uses decision trees. Decision trees segment the dataset into small partitions, called leaves, when estimating regression values. The Random Forest takes the average of the values in each leaf to create a prediction. Using this procedure causes extreme and high values to disappear from predictions because of the averaging used for each leaf of the forest, producing dumped values instead of much higher or much lower values.

Optimizing a Random Forest

Random Forest models are out-of-box algorithms that can work quite well without optimization or worrying about overfitting. (The more estimators you use, the better the output, depending on your resources.) You can always improve performance by removing redundant and less informative variables, fixing a minimum leaf size, and defining a sampling number that avoids having too many correlated predictors in the sample. The following example shows how to perform these tasks:

```
X, y = digit.data, digit.target
crossvalidation = KFold(n=X.shape[0], n_folds=5,
    shuffle=True, random_state=1)
RF_cls = RandomForestClassifier(n_estimators=300)
scorer = 'accuracy'
```

Using the handwritten digit dataset and a first default classifier, you train a first model to determine the importance of each variable.

```
RF_cls = RandomForestClassifier(n_estimators=300).fit(X,y)
X = RF_cls.transform(X)
print X.shape
```

After you train the model, you can transform the initial X by removing the useless features, thus increasing the algorithm's speed and capability of picking the right branches in its multiple decision trees. At this point, you can optimize both `max_features` and `min_samples_leaf`.

When optimizing `max_features`, you use preconfigured options (`auto` for all features, `sqrt` or `log2` functions applied to the number of features) and integrate them using small feature numbers and a value of 1/3 of the features. Selecting the right number of features to sample tends to reduce the number of times when correlated and similar variables are picked together, thus increasing the predictive performances.

There is a statistical reason to optimize `min_samples_leaf`. Using leaves with few cases often corresponds to overfitting to very specific data combinations. You need to have at least 30 observations to achieve a minimal statistical confidence that data patterns correspond to real and general rules:

```
from sklearn import grid_search
search_grid =  {'max_features': [X.shape[1]/3, 'sqrt',
    'log2', 'auto'], 'min_samples_leaf': [1, 2, 10, 30]}
search_func = grid_search.GridSearchCV(estimator=RF_cls,
    param_grid=search_grid, scoring=scorer, n_jobs=1,
        cv=crossvalidation)
search_func.fit(X,y)
print 'Best parameters: %s' % search_func.best_params_
print 'Best accuracy: %.3f' % search_func.best_score_

Best parameters: {'max_features': 'log2',
                    'min_samples_leaf': 1}
Best accuracy: 0.977
```

Boosting Predictions

Gathering different tree models is not the only ensemble technique possible. In fact, another machine-learning technique, called *boosting,* uses ensembles effectively. In boosting, you grow many trees sequentially. Each tree tries to build a model that successfully predicts what trees that were built before it weren't able to forecast. In the end, the technique pools subsequent models together and uses an average or a majority vote to decide the final prediction.

The following sections present two boosting applications, adaboost and gradient boosting machines. You can use all boosting algorithms for both regression and classification. The examples in these sections start working with classification. The multilabel dataset of handwritten digits is, as it was with Random Forest, a good place to start.

If you have already loaded the data using `load_digits` into the variable `digit`, you just need to reassign the X and y variables as follows:

```
X, y = digit.data, digit.target
```

Knowing that many weak predictors win

`AdaBoostClassifier` fits sequential weak predictors. It is used by default when working with decision trees, but you can choose other algorithms by changing the `base_estimator` parameter. Weak predictors are usually machine-learning predictors that don't perform well because they have too much variance or bias, so they perform slightly better than chance.

The classic example of a weak learner is the decision stump, which is a decision tree grown to only one level. Usually, decision trees are the best-performing option in boosting, so you can safely use the default learner and concentrate on two important parameters to obtain good predictions: `n_estimators` and `learning_rate`.

`learning_rate` determines how each weak predictor contributes to the final result. A high learning rate requires few `n_estimators` before converging to an optimal solution, but it likely won't be the best solution possible. A low learning rate takes longer to train because it requires more predictors before reaching a solution. In addition, it also overfits more slowly.

TIP

Contrary to bagging, boosting can overfit if you use too many estimators. A cross-validation is always helpful in finding the correct number, keeping in mind that lower learning rates take longer to overfit, so picking an almost optimal value by a loose grid-search is easier.

```
from sklearn.ensemble import AdaBoostClassifier
ada = AdaBoostClassifier(n_estimators=1000,
    learning_rate=0.01, random_state=1)
crossvalidation = KFold(n=X.shape[0], n_folds=5,
    shuffle=True, random_state=1)
score = np.mean(cross_val_score(ada, X, y,
    scoring='accuracy', cv=crossvalidation, n_jobs=1))
print 'Accuracy: %.3f' % score

Accuracy: 0.826
```

This example uses the default estimator, which is a full-blown decision tree. If you'd like to try a stump (which needs more estimators), you should instantiate the `AdaBoostClassifier` with `base_estimator=DecisionTreeClassifier(max_depth=1)`.

Creating a gradient boosting classifier

The Gradient Boosting Machine (GBM) is a much better-performing version of the boosting technique seen with Adaboost, the first boosting algorithm ever created. In particular, GBM uses an optimization computation for weighting the subsequent estimators. As with the example in the preceding section, you can try an example with the digit dataset and explore some extra parameters available in GBM.

```
X, y = digit.data, digit.target
crossvalidation = KFold(n=X.shape[0], n_folds=5,
    shuffle=True, random_state=1)
```

Apart from the learning rate and the number of estimators, which are key parameters for optimal learning without overfitting, you must provide values for `subsample` and `max_depth`. `subsample` introduces subsampling into the training (so that the training is done on a different dataset every time), as is done in bagging. `max_depth` defines the maximum level of the built trees. It's usually a good practice to start with three levels, but more levels may be necessary for modeling complex data.

```
from sklearn.ensemble import GradientBoostingClassifier
GBC = GradientBoostingClassifier(n_estimators=300,
    subsample=1.0, max_depth=2, learning_rate=0.1,
    random_state=1)
score = np.mean(cross_val_score(GBC, X, y,
    scoring='accuracy', cv=crossvalidation, n_jobs=1))
print 'Accuracy: %.3f' % score

Accuracy: 0.972
```

An interesting feature of the Scikit-implementation is the `warm_start` parameter. You can't parallelize boosting as you would when using a Random Forest. However, given its sequential nature, you can fetch the data piece-by-piece when dealing with big data. To perform this task, you set the `warm_start` parameter to `True`, so the algorithm always keeps the previous estimators in the sequence.

Creating a gradient boosting regressor

Creating a gradient boosting regressor doesn't present particular differences from creating the classifier. The main difference is the presence of multiple loss functions that you can use (contrast this with `GradientBoostingClassifier`, which has only the deviance loss, analogous to the cost function of a logistic regression).

```
X, y = boston.data, boston.target
from sklearn.ensemble import GradientBoostingRegressor
GBR = GradientBoostingRegressor(n_estimators=1000,
    subsample=1.0, max_depth=3, learning_rate=0.01,
    random_state=1)
crossvalidation = KFold(n=X.shape[0], n_folds=5,
    shuffle=True, random_state=1)
score = np.mean(cross_val_score(GBR, X, y,
    scoring='mean_squared_error', cv=crossvalidation,
    n_jobs=1))
print 'Mean squared error: %.3f' % abs(score)

Mean squared error: 10.105
```

The example trains a `GradientBoostingRegressor` using the default `ls` value for the `loss` parameter, which is analogous to a linear regression. Here are some other choices:

- ✔ `quantile`: This guesses a particular quantile that you specify using the `alpha` parameter (usually it's 0.5, which is the median).

- ✔ `lad` (least absolute deviation): This choice is highly robust to outliers; it tends to ordinally rank correctly the predictions.

- ✔ `huber`: This creates a combination of `ls` and `lad`. It requires that you fix the `alpha` parameter.

Using GBM hyper-parameters

GBM models are quite sensitive to overfitting when you have too many sequential estimators and the model starts fitting the noise in the data. It's important to check the efficiency of the coupled values of the number of estimators and the learning rate. The following example uses the Boston dataset of housing prices:

```
X, y = boston.data, boston.target
crossvalidation = KFold(n=X.shape[0], n_folds=5,
    shuffle=True, random_state=1)
GBR = GradientBoostingRegressor(n_estimators=1000,
    subsample=1.0, max_depth=3, learning_rate=0.01,
    random_state=1)
```

Optimization may take some time because of the computational burden required by the GBM algorithms, especially if you decide to test high values of `max_depth`.

A good strategy is to keep the learning rate fixed and try to optimize `subsample` and `max_depth` with respect to `n_estimators` (keeping in mind that high values of `max_depth` usually imply a lesser number of estimators). After you find the optimum values for `subsample` and `max_depth`, you can start searching for further optimization of `n_estimators` and `learning_rate`.

```
from sklearn import grid_search
search_grid =  {'subsample': [1.0, 0.9], 'max_depth': [2,
    3, 5], 'n_estimators': [500 , 1000, 2000]}
search_func = grid_search.GridSearchCV(estimator=GBR,
    param_grid=search_grid, scoring='mean_squared_error',
    n_jobs=1, cv=crossvalidation)
```

```
search_func.fit(X,y)
print 'Best parameters: %s' % search_func.best_params_
print 'Best mean squared error: %.3f'
  % abs(search_func.best_score_)

Best parameters: {'n_estimators': 2000, 'subsample': 0.9,
    'max_depth': 3}
Best mean squared error: 9.263
```

Part VI
The Part of Tens

Enjoy an additional Part of Tens article about ten ways to make a living as a data scientist at http://www.dummies.com/extras/pythonfordatascience.

In this part . . .

- ✔ Discovering all sorts of amazing resources you can use for data mining and development tasks
- ✔ Getting additional educational materials, many of which are free
- ✔ Finding open source solutions to your data science questions
- ✔ Using leisure time resources to learn more about data science
- ✔ Obtaining more datasets for your data science experiments

Chapter 21

Ten Essential Data Science Resource Collections

*I*n reading this book, you discover quite a lot about data science and Python. Before your head explodes from all the new knowledge you gain, it's important to realize that this book is really just the tip of the iceberg. Yes, there really is more information available out there, and that's what this chapter is all about. The following sections introduce you to a wealth of data science resource collections that you really need to make the best use of your new knowledge.

In this case, a resource collection is simply a listing of really cool links with some text to tell you why they're so great. In some cases, you gain access to articles about data science; in other cases, you're exposed to new tools. In fact, data science is such a huge topic that you could easily find more resources than those discussed here, but the following sections provide a good place to start.

As with anything else on the Internet, links break, sites go out of business, and new sites take their place. If you find that a link is broken, please let me know about it at `John@JohnMuellerBooks.com`.

Gaining Insights with Data Science Weekly

The Data Science Weekly is a free newsletter that you can sign up for to obtain the latest information about changes in data science. However, for this chapter, the most important element is the list of resources you find at http://www.datascienceweekly.org/data-science-resources. The resources cover the following broad range of topics:

- ✔ Data Science Books
- ✔ Data Science Meetups
- ✔ Data Science Massive Open Online Courses (MOOCs)
- ✔ Data Science Datasets
- ✔ Data Science Most Read Articles
- ✔ Data Scientist Talks
- ✔ Data Scientists on Twitter
- ✔ Data Science Blogs

Obtaining a Resource List at U Climb Higher

Even with the right connections online and a good search engine, trying to find just the right resource can be hard. U Climb Higher has published a list of 24 data science resources at http://blog.udacity.com/2014/12/24-data-science-resources-keep-finger-pulse.html that's guaranteed to help keep your finger on the pulse of new strategies and technologies. This resource broaches the following topics: trends and happenings; places to learn more about data science; joining a community; data science news; people who really know data science well; all the latest research

Getting a Good Start with KDnuggets

Learning about data mining and data science is a process. KDnuggets breaks the learning process down into a series of steps at http://www.kdnuggets.com/faq/learning-data-mining-data-science.html. Each step provides you with an overview of what you should be doing and why. You also find links to a variety of resources online to make the learning process considerably easier. Even though the site emphasizes the use of R, Python (clicking the `Getting Started With Python For Data Science` link shows that even Kaggle prefers Python 2.7), and SQL (in that order) to perform data science tasks, the steps will actually work for any of a number of approaches that you might take.

As with any other learning experience, a procedure like the one shown on the KDnuggets site will work for some people and not for others. Everyone learns a little differently. Don't be afraid to improvise. The resources on this site might provide insights into other things that you can do to make your learning process easier.

Accessing the Huge List of Resources on Data Science Central

Many of the resources you find online cover mainstream topics. Data Science Central (`http://www.datasciencecentral.com/`) provides access to a relatively large number of data science experts that will tell you about the most obscure facts of data science. One of the more interesting blog posts appears at `http://www.datasciencecentral.com/profiles/blogs/huge-trello-list-of-great-data-science-resources`.

This resource points you to a Trello list (`https://trello.com/`) of some truly amazing resources. Navigating the huge list can be a bit difficult, but the process is aided by the treelike structure that Trello provides for organizing information. You want to meander through this sort of list when you have time and simply want to see what is available. The categories include the following (with possibly more by the time you read this book):

- Data news
- Data business people track
- Data journalist track
- Data padawan track
- Data scientist track
- Statistics
- R
- Python
- Big data and other tools
- Data
- Others

Obtaining the Facts of Open Source Data Science from Masters

Many organizations now focus on open source for data science solutions. The focus has become so prevalent that you can now get an Open-Source Data Science Masters (OSDSM) education at http://datasciencemasters. org/. The emphasis is on providing you with the materials that are normally lacking from a purely academic education. In other words, the site provides pointers to courses that fill in gaps in your education so that you become more marketable in today's computing environment. The various links provide you with access to online courses, books, and other resources that help you gain a better understanding of just how OSDSM works.

Locating Free Learning Resources with Quora

It's really hard to resist the word *free*, especially when it comes to education, which normally costs many thousands of dollars. The Quora site at http:// www.quora.com/What-are-the-best-free-resources-to-learn-data-science provides a listing of the best nonpaid learning resource for data science.

Most of the links take on a question format, such as, "How do I become a data scientist?" The question-and-answer format is helpful because you might be asking the questions that the site answers. The resulting list of sites, courses, and resources are introductory, for the most part, but they are a good way to get started working in the data science field.

A few of the links are for prestigious institutions such as Harvard. The link provides you with access to course materials such as lecture videos and blackboards. However, you don't get the actual course free of charge. If you want the benefits of the course, you still need to pay for it. Even so, just by viewing the course materials, you can obtain a lot of useful data science knowledge.

Receiving Help with Advanced Topics at Conductrics

The Conductrics site (http://conductrics.com/) as a whole is devoted to selling products that help you perform various data science tasks. However, the site includes a blog that contains a couple of useful blog posts that answer the sorts of advanced questions that you might find it difficult to answer elsewhere. The two posts appear at `http://conductrics.com/data-science-resources/` and `http://conductrics.com/data-science-resources-2`.

The author of the blog posts, Matt Gershoff, makes it clear that the listings are the result of answering people's questions in the past. The list is huge, which is why it appears in two posts rather than one, so Matt must answer many questions. The list focuses mostly on machine learning rather than hardware or specific coding issues. Therefore, you can expect to see entries for topics such as Latent Semantic Indexing (LSI); Single Value Decomposition (SVD); Linear Discriminant Analysis (LDA); non-parametric Bayesian approaches; statistical machine translation; Reinforcement Learning (RL); Temporal Difference (TD) learning; context bandits.

The list goes on and on. Many of these entries won't make much sense to you right now unless you're already heavily involved in data science. However, the authors write many of the articles in a way that helps you pick up the information even if you aren't completely familiar with it. In most cases, your best course of action is to at least scan the article to see whether you can understand it. If the article starts to make sense, read it in detail. Otherwise, hold on to the article reference for later use. You might be surprised to discover that the article you can't completely understand today becomes something you understand with ease tomorrow.

Learning New Tricks from the Aspirational Data Scientist

The Aspirational Data Scientist (`http://newdatascientist.blogspot.com/`) blog site provides you with an amazing array of essays on various data science topics. The author splits the posts into these areas: data science commentary; online course reviews; becoming a data scientist.

Data science attracts practitioners from all sorts of existing fields. The site seems mainly devoted to serving the needs of social scientists moving into the data science field. In fact, the most interesting post that appears at `http://newdatascientist.blogspot.com/p/useful-links.html` provides a listing of resources to help the social scientist move into the data scientist field. The list of resources is organized by author, so you may find names that you already recognize as potential informational resources.

As with any other resource, even if an article is meant for one audience, it often serves the needs of another audience with equal ease. Even if you aren't a social scientist, you might find that the articles contain helpful information as you progress on the road to fully discovering the wonders of data science.

Finding Data Intelligence and Analytics Resources at AnalyticBridge

The AnanlyticBridge site (`http://www.analyticbridge.com/`) contains an amazing array of helpful resources for the data scientist. One of the more helpful resources is the list of data intelligence and analytics resources at `http://www.analyticbridge.com/page/links`. This page contains a wealth of resources you won't find anywhere else that are organized into the following categories: general resources; big data; visualization; best and worst of data science; new analytics startup ideas; rants about healthcare, education, and other topics; career stuff, training, and salary surveys; miscellaneous.

Zeroing In on Developer Resources with Jonathan Bower

More than a few interesting resources appear on GitHub (`https://github.com/`), a site devoted to collaboration, code review, and code management. One of the sites you need to check out is Jonathan Bower's listing of data science resources at `https://github.com/jonathan-bower/DataScienceResources`. The majority of these resources will appeal to the developer, but just about anyone can benefit from them. You find resources categorized into the following topics:

- ✔ Data science, getting started
- ✔ Data pipeline and tools
- ✔ Product
- ✔ Career resources
- ✔ Open source data science resources

The hierarchical formatting of the various topics makes finding just what you need easier. Each major category divides into a list of topics. Within each topic, you find a list of resources that apply to that topic. For example, within Data Pipeline & Tools, you find Python, which includes a link for Anyone Can Code. This is one of the most usable sites in the list.

Chapter 22

Ten Data Challenges
You Should Take

Data science is all about working with data. While working through this book, you have used a number of datasets, including the toy datasets that come with the Scikit-learn library. Of course, these datasets are all great for getting you started, but just as a runner wouldn't stop after conquering the local fun run, so do you need to start training for the marathons of data science by working with larger datasets.

This chapter introduces you to a number of challenging datasets that can help you become a world-class data scientist. By combining what you discover in this book with these new datasets, you can learn how to do amazing things. In fact, some people may view you as a bit of a magician as you pull seemingly impossible data patterns out of your hat. Each of the following datasets provides you with specific skills and helps you achieve different goals.

You can find a wealth of datasets on the Internet. However, not every dataset is created equal, and you need to choose your challenges with care. These ten datasets provide well-known functionality, often provide you with tutorials, and appear in scientific papers. These three features make these datasets stand apart from the competition. Yes, other good datasets are available, but these ten datasets provide skills needed to conquer even bigger challenges, such as that database lurking on your company server.

Meeting the Data Science London + Scikit-learn Challenge

You use Scikit-learn quite a bit while using this book, so you may already understand it a bit. The Kaggle competition at `http://www.kaggle.com/c/data-science-london-Scikit-learn` (the current competition ended in December 2014, but there should be others) provides a practice ground for trying, sharing, and creating examples using the Scikit-learn classification algorithms. All the tools for the previous competition are still in place, and it's still well worth exploring. The goal is to try, create, and share examples of using Scikit-learn's classification capabilities. You can find the data used for the competition at `http://www.kaggle.com/c/data-science-london-scikit-learn/data`. The rules appear at `http://www.kaggle.com/c/data-science-london-scikit-learn/rules`, and you can discover how Kaggle evaluates your submissions at `http://www.kaggle.com/c/data-science-london-scikit-learn/details/evaluation`.

Of course, you might not have any desire to compete. Looking at the leaderboard (`http://www.kaggle.com/c/data-science-london-scikit-learn/leaderboard`) may keep you from seriously considering actual competition because the contest has attracted some serious data scientists. However, you can still enjoy the competition by keeping track of the leaders and also checking out the tutorials at `http://www.kaggle.com/c/data-science-london-scikit-learn/visualization`. Working through the tutorials will help you better understand how data science works, which may be the real prize in going to this site.

Because this site builds on knowledge you already have from the book, it's actually the best place to begin building new skills. That's why this site appears first in the chapter: You can get a good start using other datasets with techniques you already know.

Predicting Survival on the Titanic

You work with the Titanic data to some extent in the book (Chapters 5 and 20) by using `Titanic.csv`. Even if you chose not to compete in the challenge described in the previous section, this challenge is actually much easier because Kaggle designed it for the beginner. You can find it at `http://www.kaggle.com/c/titanic-gettingStarted`. The data model, found at `http://www.kaggle.com/c/titanic-gettingStarted/data`, is different from the one in the book, but the concepts are the same. You can find the rules for this competition at `http://www.kaggle.com/c/titanic-gettingStarted/rules` and the method of evaluation at `http://www.kaggle.com/c/titanic-gettingStarted/details/evaluation`.

You can find the leaderboard for this competition at `http://www.kaggle.com/c/titanic-gettingStarted/leaderboard`. The number of people who have already achieved what amounts to a perfect score should fill you with confidence.

The biggest challenge in this case is that the dataset is quite small and requires that you create new features in order to obtain an accurate score. The competition helps you apply the skills you learn in the "Considering the Art of Feature Creation" section of Chapter 8 and see demonstrated in Chapter 19. You can gain additional insights into the techniques for working through this challenge by viewing the tutorials at `http://www.kaggle.com/c/titanic-gettingStarted/prospector#208`.

Finding a Kaggle Competition that Suits Your Needs

Competitions are great at helping you think through solutions in an environment in which others are doing the same. In the real world, you may find yourself pitted against competition on a regular basis, so competitions provide good experiences in thinking critically and quickly. They also present you with an opportunity to learn from others. The best place to find such competitions is on the Kaggle site at `http://www.kaggle.com/competitions`.

This site will help you locate any past or present Kaggle competition. To find a present competition, click the Active Competitions link. To find a past competition, click the All Competitions link. All the datasets are freely available, so you have a chance to try your skills against any real-world scenario you might want to select. The Kaggle community will provide you with plenty of tutorials, benchmarks, and beat-the-benchmarks posts.

You don't have to select an ongoing competition. For example, you might see a past competition that meets a need and try that instead (benefitting from the published solutions). If you take an active competition you can post your questions on the forum and have some of the most skilled data scientists in the world answer your questions and doubts. Because of the great number of competitions on this site, it's likely that you'll find a competition that will suit your interests!

It's interesting to note that the Kaggle competitions come from companies that don't normally have access to data scientists, so you really are working in a real world environment. Check out the write-up at `http://www.kaggle.com/solutions/competitions` (by clicking the Host link on the main page) to learn more about how Kaggle creates the competitions. You can also use this site to locate a potential job. Just go to `http://www.kaggle.com/jobs` by clicking the Jobs link on the main page.

Honing Your Overfit Strategies

The Madelon Data Set at `https://archive.ics.uci.edu/ml/datasets/Madelon` is an artificial dataset containing a two-class classification problem with continuous input variables. This NIPS 2003 feature selection challenge will seriously test your skills in cross-validating models. The main emphasis of this challenge is to devise strategies for avoiding overfit — an issue that you first confront in the "Finding more things that can go wrong" section of Chapter 16. You find overfit issues mentioned in Chapters 18, 19, and 20 as well. To obtain the dataset, contact Isabelle Guyon at the address found in the Source section of the page at `https://archive.ics.uci.edu/ml/datasets/Madelon`.

This particular dataset attracted the attention of a number of people who created papers about it. The best papers appear in the book *Feature Extraction, Foundations and Applications* at `http://www.springer.com/us/book/9783540354871`. You can also download an associated technical report from `http://clopinet.com/isabelle/Projects/ETH/TM-fextract-class.pdf`. The Advances in Neural Information Processing Systems 17 (NIPS 2004) at `http://papers.nips.cc/book/advances-in-neural-information-processing-systems-17-2004` also contains useful links to papers that will help you with this particular dataset.

Trudging Through the MovieLens Dataset

The MovieLens site (https://movielens.org/) is all about helping you find a movie you might like. After all, with millions of movies out there, finding something new and interesting could take time that you don't want to spend. The setup works by asking you to input ratings for movies you already know about. The MovieLens site then makes recommendations for you based on your ratings. In short, your ratings teach an algorithm what to look for, and then the site applies this algorithm to the entire dataset.

You can obtain the MovieLens dataset at http://grouplens.org/datasets/movielens/. The interesting thing about this site is that you can download all or part of the dataset based on how you want to interact with it. You can find downloads in the following sizes:

- 100,000 ratings from 1,000 users on 1,700 movies

- 1 million ratings from 6,000 users on 4,000 movies

- 10 million ratings and 100,000 tag applications applied to 10,000 movies by 72,000 users

- 20 million ratings and 465,000 tag applications applied to 27,000 movies by 138,000 users

- MovieLens's latest dataset in small or full sizes (the full size contained 21,000,000 ratings and 470,000 tag applications applied to 27,000 movies by 230,000 users as of this writing but will increase in size with time)

This dataset presents you with an opportunity to work with user-generated data using both supervised and unsupervised techniques. The large datasets present special challenges that only big data can provide. You can find some starter information for working with supervised and unsupervised techniques in Chapters 15 and 19.

Getting Rid of Spam Emails

Everyone wants to get rid of spam email — those time wasters that contain everything from invitations to join in a fantastic new venture to pornography. Of course, the best way to accomplish the task is to create an algorithm to do the sorting for you. However, you need to train the algorithm to perform its work, which is where the Spambase Data Set comes into play. You can find the Spambase Data Set at https://archive.ics.uci.edu/ml/datasets/Spambase.

This collection of spam emails came from postmasters and individuals who had filed spam reports. It also includes nonspam email from various sources to allow the creation of filters that let good emails through. This is a complex challenge dealing with textual data and complex, different targets.

You can find a number of papers that cite this particular dataset. The following list provides a quick overview of the pertinent papers and their host sites:

- Los Alamos National Laboratory Stability of Unstable Learning Algorithms (`http://rexa.info/paper/a2734ae038cae739315993 4e860c24a52dc2754d`)

- Modeling for Optimal Probability Prediction (`http://rexa.info/ paper/631197638c7e0317c98e1a8d98e5fce8921aa758`)

- Visualization and Data Mining in an 3D Immersive Environment: Summer Project 2003 (`http://rexa.info/paper/48d6beec2a36a87d9d88b 6de85dd85a75e5ed24d`)

- Online Policy Adaptation for Ensemble Classifiers (`http://rexa. info/paper/3cb3fbd5512e3cd12111b598fece53fcb42c484b`)

Working with Handwritten Information

Pattern recognition, especially working with handwritten information, is an important data science task. The Mixed National Institute of Standards and Technology (MNIST) dataset of handwritten digits at `http://yann.lecun. com/exdb/mnist/` provides a training set of 60,000 examples, and a test set of 10,000 examples. This is a subset of the original National Institute of Standards and Technology (NIST) dataset found at `http://srdata.nist. gov/gateway/gateway?keyword=handwriting+recognition`. It's a good dataset to use to learn how to work with handwritten data without having to perform a lot of preprocessing at the outset.

The dataset appears in four files. The two training and two test files contain images and labels. You need all four files in order to create a complete dataset for working with digits. A potential problem in working with the MNIST dataset is that the image files aren't in a particular format. The format used for storing the images appears at the bottom of the page. Of course, you could always build your own Python application for reading them, but using code that someone else has created is a lot easier. The following list provides places where you can get code to read the MNIST dataset using Python:

- `http://cs.indstate.edu/~jkinne/cs475-f2011/code/ mnistHandwriting.py`

- `http://g.sweyla.com/blog/2012/mnist-numpy/`

✔ http://martin-thoma.com/classify-mnist-with-pybrain/

✔ https://gist.github.com/akesling/5358964

The host page also contains an important listing of methods used to work with the training and test set. The list contains an impressive number of classifiers that should give you some ideas for your own experiments. The point is that this particular dataset is useful for all sorts of different tasks.

You have worked with the digits toy dataset from Scikit-learn in a number of chapters in the book. To use this dataset, you import the digits database using `from sklearn.datasets import load_digits`. This particular dataset appears in Chapters 12, 15, 17, 19, and 20, so you gain a considerable amount of experience in working with a much smaller digits database when you work through the examples in those chapters.

Working with Pictures

The Canadian Institute for Advanced Research (CIFAR) datasets at `http://www.cs.toronto.edu/~kriz/cifar.html` provide you with graphics content to work with in various ways. The CIFAR-10 and CIFAR-100 datasets contain labeled subsets of a dataset with 80 million tiny images (you can read about how the dataset works with the original image dataset in the Learning Multiple Layers of Features from Tiny Images technical report at `http://www.cs.toronto.edu/~kriz/learning-features-2009-TR.pdf`). In the CIFAR-10 dataset, you find 60,000 32 x 32 color images in ten classes (for 6,000 images in each class). Here are the classes you find:

✔ Airplane

✔ Automobile

✔ Bird

✔ Cat

✔ Deer

✔ Dog

✔ Frog

✔ Horse

✔ Ship

✔ Truck

The CIFAR-100 dataset contains more classes. Instead of 10 classes, you get 100 classes containing 600 images each. The size of the dataset is the same, but the number of classes is larger. The classification system is hierarchical in this case. The 100 classes divide into 20 superclasses. For example, in the aquatic mammals superclass, you find the beaver, dolphin, otter, seal, and whale classes.

Both CIFAR datasets come in Python, MATLAB, and binary versions. Make sure that you download the correct version and follow the instructions for using them on the download page. Yes, you could use the other versions with Python, but doing so would require a lot of extra programming, and because you already have access to a Python version, you wouldn't gain anything from the exercise.

This is an excellent challenge to take after you have worked with the digits dataset described in the previous section. Taking this challenge helps you to deal with colorful, complex images. If you worked through the examples in Chapter 14, you already have some experience working with images using the toy Olivetti Faces dataset.

Analyzing Amazon.com Reviews

If you want to work with a really large dataset, try the Amazon.com review dataset at `https://snap.stanford.edu/data/web-Amazon.html`. This dataset consists of reviews from Amazon.com taken over a period of 18 years, including ~35 million reviews up to March 2013. The reviews include product and user information, ratings, and a plain-text review. This is the dataset to tackle after you work through smaller datasets, such as MovieLens. It can help you understand how to work with user-generated data in a business context.

Unlike many of the datasets in this chapter, the Amazon.com dataset comes in a number of forms. Yes, you can download `all.txt.gz` to obtain the entire dataset (11GB of data), but you also have the option to download just portions of the dataset. For example, you can choose to download just the 184,887 reviews associated with baby products by obtaining `Baby.txt.gz` (a 42MB download).

Make sure to check out the bottom of the page. The site owner has thoughtfully provided you with the Python code required to interpret the data. Using this simple function makes working with the immense dataset a lot easier. Even if you choose to create a modified version of the function, you at least have a good starting point.

Interacting with a Huge Graph

Imagine trying to work through the connections between 3.5 billion web pages. You can do just that by downloading the immense dataset at `http://www.bigdatanews.com/profiles/blogs/big-data-set-3-5-billion-web-pages-made-available-for-all-of-us`. The biggest, richest, most complex dataset of all is the Internet itself. Start with a subsample offered by the Common Crawl 2012 web corpus (`http://commoncrawl.org/`) and learn how to extract and elaborate data from web sites. The principle uses for this dataset are:

✔ Search algorithms

✔ Spam detection methods

✔ Graph analysis algorithms

✔ Web science research

Pay particular attention to the Contents section near the middle of the page. Clicking a link takes you to an entry at `http://webdatacommons.org/hyperlinkgraph/` that explains the dataset in more detail. You need the additional information to perform most data science tasks. Near the bottom of the page are links for downloading various levels of the entire graph (fortunately, you don't have to download everything, which would be a 45GB download for the index file and a 331GB download for the arc file).

Don't let the idea of performing an analysis on such a large dataset scare you. If you worked through the examples in Chapter 7, you have worked with simple graph data. This dataset is a similar task but on a significantly larger scale. Yes, size does matter to some extent, but you already know some of the required techniques for getting the job done.

This particular site provides access to a number of other datasets. Links for these datasets are at the bottom of the page. For example, you can find "Great statistical analysis: forecasting meteorite hits" at `http://www.analyticbridge.com/profiles/blogs/great-statistical-analysis-forecasting-meteorite-hits`. In short, if analyzing the entire Internet doesn't appeal to you, try one of the other amazing (and huge) datasets.

Index

About the Authors

Luca Massaron is a data scientist and a marketing research director who specializes in multivariate statistical analysis, machine learning, and customer insight, with over a decade of experience in solving real-world problems and generating value for stakeholders by applying reasoning, statistics, data mining, and algorithms. From being a pioneer of web audience analysis in Italy to achieving the rank of top ten Kaggler on kaggle.com, he has always been passionate about everything regarding data and analysis and about demonstrating the potentiality of data-driven knowledge discovery to both experts and non experts. Favoring simplicity over unnecessary sophistication, he believes that a lot can be achieved in data science by understanding and practicing the essentials of it.

John Mueller is a freelance author and technical editor. He has writing in his blood, having produced 97 books and more than 600 articles to date. The topics range from networking to artificial intelligence and from database management to heads-down programming. Some of his current books include a book on Python for beginners and a book about MATLAB. He has also written a Java e-learning kit, a book on HTML5 development with JavaScript, and another on CSS3. His technical editing skills have helped more than 63 authors refine the content of their manuscripts. John has provided technical editing services to both *Data Based Advisor* and *Coast Compute* magazines. It was during his time with *Data Based Advisor* that John was first exposed to MATLAB, and he has continued to follow the progress in MATLAB development ever since. During his time at Cubic Corporation, John was exposed to reliability engineering and has continued his interest in probability. Be sure to read John's blog at http://blog.johnmuellerbooks.com/.

When John isn't working at the computer, you can find him outside in the garden, cutting wood, or generally enjoying nature. John also likes making wine, baking cookies, and knitting. When not occupied with anything else, he makes glycerin soap and candles, which come in handy for gift baskets. You can reach John on the Internet at John@JohnMuellerBooks.com. John is also setting up a website at http://www.johnmuellerbooks.com/. Feel free to take a look and make suggestions on how he can improve it.

Luca's Dedication

I would like to dedicate this book to my parents, Renzo and Licia, who both love simple and well-explained ideas and who now, by reading the book we wrote, will understand more of my daily work in data science and how this new discipline is going to change the way we understand the world and operate in it.

John's Dedication

This book is dedicated to the scientists, engineers, dreamers, and philosophers of the world — that unheralded group who makes such a large difference in the lives of everyone on the planet.

Luca's Acknowledgments

My greatest thanks to my family, Yukiko and Amelia, for their support and loving patience.

I also thank all my fellow Kagglers for their help and unstoppable exchanging of ideas and opinions. My thanks in particular to Alberto Boschetti, Giuliano Janson, Bastiaan Sjardin, and Zacharias Voulgaris.

John's Acknowledgments

Thanks to my wife, Rebecca. Even though she is gone now, her spirit is in every book I write, in every word that appears on the page. She believed in me when no one else would.

Russ Mullen deserves thanks for his technical edit of this book. He greatly added to the accuracy and depth of the material you see here. Russ worked exceptionally hard helping with the research for this book by locating hard-to-find URLs and also offering a lot of suggestions.

Matt Wagner, my agent, deserves credit for helping me get the contract in the first place and taking care of all the details that most authors don't really consider. I always appreciate his assistance. It's good to know that someone wants to help.

A number of people read all or part of this book to help me refine the approach, test scripts, and generally provide input that all readers wish they could have. These unpaid volunteers helped in ways too numerous to mention here. I especially appreciate the efforts of Eva Beattie, Glenn A. Russell, Osvaldo Téllez Almirall, and Thomas Zinckgraf, who provided general input, read the entire book, and selflessly devoted themselves to this project.

Finally, I would like to thank Kyle Looper, Susan Christophersen, and the rest of the editorial and production staff.

Publisher's Acknowledgments

Acquisitions Editor: Katie Mohr

Project and Copy Editor: Susan Christophersen

Technical Editor: Russ Mullen

Editorial Assistant: Claire Brock

Sr. Editorial Assistant: Cherie Case

Project Coordinator: Vinitha Vikraman

Cover Image: © iStock.com/Magnilion; © iStock.com/nadla